Julian Holler

Hedge Funds and Financial Markets

GABLER RESEARCH

Geld – Banken – Börsen

Herausgegeben von
Prof. Dr. Wolfgang Bessler

Mit der Schriftenreihe Geld – Banken – Börsen wird der zunehmenden Bedeutung der kapitalmarktorientierten Sichtweise innerhalb der Betriebswirtschaftslehre Rechnung getragen. In diese Reihe sollen Dissertationen und Habilitationen aufgenommen werden, die aktuelle Fragestellungen in den Themengebieten Finanzierung und Geldanlage sowie Finanzmärkte und Finanzinstitutionen behandeln und sich durch neue, für Theorie und Praxis relevante Forschungsergebnisse auszeichnen.

Julian Holler

Hedge Funds and Financial Markets

An Asset Management and Corporate Governance Perspective

With a foreword by Prof. Dr. Wolfgang Bessler

GABLER

RESEARCH

Bibliographic information published by the Deutsche Nationalbibliothek
The Deutsche Nationalbibliothek lists this publication in the Deutsche Nationalbibliografie; detailed bibliographic data are available in the Internet at http://dnb.d-nb.de.

Dissertation Justus-Liebig Universität Gießen, 2011

1st Edition 2012

Editorial Office: Marta Grabowski | Sabine Schöller

Gabler Verlag is a brand of Springer Fachmedien.
Springer Fachmedien is part of Springer Science+Business Media.
www.gabler.de

Cover design: KünkelLopka Medienentwicklung, Heidelberg
Printed on acid-free paper

ISBN 978-3-8349-3277-8

Foreword

During the last decade, hedge funds have become one of the most important institutional investors in global financial markets. Although their activities have been viewed critically by regulators, politicians, and the public, this negative perspective is often based more on myth than on thorough economic analysis and empirical facts. Most people lack the necessary information and understanding of the role that hedge funds play in financial markets. Blaming them for the financial crisis or other market turbulences is often based on specific conjectures and not on rigorous research. Interestingly, most of the regulations proposed by German politicians, restricting hedge fund activities have not yet been implemented due to weak support from other countries.

In contrast to public opinion, most academic studies suggest that hedge funds as a new asset class have important implications for professional portfolio managers and for asset allocation decisions in that hedge funds widen the spectrum of new investment opportunities. The most compelling evidence is the relatively high percentage that U.S. university endowments allocate to hedge funds and other alternative asset classes due to their interesting risk-return and correlation properties. Thus, from the perspectives of both the asset management industry and academics, there is evidence that hedge funds may improve asset allocation decisions. From an empirical point of view, this question requires an in-depths analysis with up-to-date and rigorous statistical methods. In the first part of the dissertation, Julian Holler takes on this challenge and provides interesting and convincing empirical results on the contribution of hedge funds in optimal asset allocation decisions. Using Bayesian statistics Julian Holler's empirical findings clearly reveal that the efficient frontier is shifted upwards when hedge funds are included in optimal portfolios. Interestingly, and in contrast to common belief, this is observed particularly for low risk portfolios in downward market periods when risk reduction is most important. Thus, due to their sophisticated investment strategies that may even generate profits in bear markets, hedge funds offer investors protection in declining markets. With these insights, Julian Holler provides an important contribution to the current academic literature on asset management and asset allocation decisions that also has important implications for portfolio managers.

When considering hedge funds and financial markets in a broader context, corporate governance, in addition to asset management, is the other important area in which hedge funds have become intensively involved. In fact, hedge funds have emerged as one of the most active investors in financial markets who use their investments to exercise significant influence on management through different venues. However, whether hedge fund activities result in higher market valuations of companies is an empirical question. Although most research for the U.S. suggests that hedge funds use their influence to increase shareholder value, these conclusions may not hold for other countries or time periods. Therefore, Julian Holler investigates whether hedge funds activities targeting German companies result in an outperformance and whether these results hold in upward and downward market environments. Surprisingly, there is an extremely high level of hedge fund activity in corporate governance in Germany. Julian Holler's analysis reveals that this is due to a control vacuum that resulted from the German banks selling their equity stakes in German companies at the beginning of the last decade. This behavior was particularly related to the provision of tax incentives by the German government which was designed to reduce the power and influence of the German banks in German companies. While this strategy was successful, the consequence is that the hedge funds now fulfill the function that banks had provided before. With his comprehensive empirical analysis Julian Holler offers very interesting new insights and makes a significant contribution to the current literature. As reported in other studies, hedge fund activities result in an outperformance of target companies in bull markets. The novel and exciting insight is that this result reverses during a bear market environment when target companies underperform. One very clear and convincing conclusion from Julian Holler's research is that hedge funds do not create shareholder value in the long run but mostly exploit short-term opportunities in overly optimistic market environments by forcing companies to distribute additional cash to shareholders with dividend increases and share buybacks.

Overall, Julian Holler provides an extensive and excellent review of the literature on hedge funds in asset management and corporate governance that reflects his exceptional understanding of asset management, corporate finance, and the functioning of financial markets. He also provides convincing empirical results and insights by using state-of-the-art statistical methodology and a large data sample. The conclusions are thoughtfully derived and - after having read this dissertation very carefully - the reader may be able to solve the puzzle why hedge funds contribute to optimal asset allocation while at the same time they do not enhance shareholder value with activist strategies. I am convinced that this dissertation is of high value to researchers and practitioners alike. It should be a "must" for regulators and politicians who want to gain a thorough understanding of hedge fund activities and their role in financial markets.

Prof. Dr. Wolfgang Bessler

Preface

The present study has been completed while I was a research assistant at the Center for Banking and Finance at the Justus-Liebig-University Gießen and has been accepted as a dissertation at the Justus-Liebig-University Gießen in July 2011. Completing a dissertation project over a time period of more than five years requires the support of many people. Therefore, I would like to thank those who supported and encouraged my academic work.

First of all, I thank my dissertation supervisor Prof. Dr. Wolfgang Bessler. He constantly provided me with new insights and shaped my thinking on the way financial markets work while I was working on the manuscript of this dissertation and other research projects. He was also very helpful in organizing funding that allowed me to participate in numerous international conferences and several Ph.D. seminars. Special thanks go to Prof. Dr. Volbert Alexander who was the second member of my dissertation committee and reviewed my manuscript.

The quality of my academic work was also greatly improved by the interaction with several other people. In particular, I would like to thank my former colleagues at the Center for Banking and Finance at the Justus-Liebig-University Gießen: Christoph Becker, Dr. Claudia Bittelmeyer, Ute Gartzen, Philipp Kurmann, Dr. Andreas Kurth, Dr. Peter Lückoff, Martin Seim, Dr. Mathias Stanzel, Daniil Wagner and Jan Zimmermann. Our discussions challenged my thinking and provided me with new insights. I also thank Stephanie Wasköniq for editing my manuscript.

Finally, completing a dissertation also requires a lot of time. Therefore, I also want to thank my family and my friends who supported me during this time period. I thank my parents Petra Holler and Dr. Jens-Peter Holler for their continuous support and Dr. Volker Hustedt for many interesting discussions. Finally, I want to thank my wife Dr. Claudia Pötzl who had to dispense with a lot of my time and still provided me with the support needed to complete the present study.

Julian Holler

Short Contents

Contents

List of Figures

List of Tables

Abbreviations

AG	Aktiengesellschaft
AktG	Aktiengesetz
Bafin	Bundesanstalt für Finanzdienstleistungsaufsicht
BHAR	Buy-and-Hold Abnormal Return
BilMoG	Bilanzrechtsmodernisierungsgesetz
bn.	billion
CalTime	Calendar Time
CAR	Cumulative Abnormal Return
CDS	Credit Default Swap
CEO	Chief Executive Officer
CISDM	Center for International Securities and Derivatives Markets
CSFB	Credit Suisse First Boston
CTA	Commodity Trading Advisor
e.g.	for example
ESOP	Employee Stock Ownership Plan
EU	European Union
EUR	Euro
FTSE	Financial Times Stock Exchange
FX	Foreign Exchange
GCT	Generalized Calendar Time
GmbH	Gesellschaft mit beschränkter Haftung

GSCI	Goldman Sachs Commodity Index
HFR	Hedge Fund Research
HML	High Minus Low (Book-to-Market)
i.e.	that is
IAS	International Accounting Standards
IFRS	International Financial Reporting Standards
IMF	International Monetary Fund
IPO	Initial Public Offering
ISE	International Security Exchange
KapAEG	Kapitalaufnahmeerleichterungsgesetz
KonTraG	Gesetz zur Kontrolle und Transparenz im Unternehmensbereich
LBO	Leveraged Buyout
m	million
M&A	Mergers & Acquisitions
MBS	Mortgage Backed Securities
MifiD	Markets in Financial Instruments Directive
MTF	Multilateral Trading Facility
NAREIT	National Association of Real Estate Investment Trusts
NBER	National Bureau of Economic Research
OLS	Ordinary Least Squares
OTC	Over-the-Counter
p	page

p.a.	per annum
PIPE	Private Investment in Public Equity
R&D	Research & Development
Reg NMS	Regulation National Market System
REIT	Real Estate Investment Trust
S&P	Standard & Poors
SE	Societas Europaea
SEC	Securities and Exchange Commission
SEO	Seasoned Equity Offering
SMB	Small-Minus-Big (Market Capitalization)
SOES	Small Order Execution System
TIPS	Treasury Inflation Protected Security
U.S.	United States
UK	United Kingdom
USD	U.S. Dollar
US-GAAP	U.S. Generally Accepted Accounting Principles
VaR	Value at Risk
vs.	versus
WpHG	Wertpapierhandelsgesetz
WpÜG	Wertpapierübernahmegesetz

Introduction

Hedge funds have begun to play an important role in the global financial system. According to data by Hedge Fund Research, hedge funds managed more than 1,800 bn USD in assets in 2007. This is a significant increase compared to 38 bn. USD in 1990. Even after the large withdrawals made by investors and declining market prices during the recent financial crisis, hedge funds managed more than 1,500 bn USD in assets (end of Q3 2009). This implies that the value of assets controlled by hedge funds is approximately equal to 25% of U.S. GDP, which is similar to the amount of capital managed by the major investment banks (Adrian and Brunnermeier, 2007). Analyzing and understanding hedge funds is therefore important because they differ in several important aspects from conventional investment vehicles such as mutual funds and pension funds. In particular, hedge funds are not subject to strong regulatory restrictions and thus can freely use leverage and derivatives for their trading strategies. Moreover, hedge funds offer high-powered incentive contracts allowing them to attract the most talented portfolio managers. As a result, hedge funds can pursue a wide range of sophisticated dynamic trading strategies which enable them to generate returns in nearly all market environments. Thus, hedge funds can offer an attractive combination of risk and return and therefore seem to be an attractive new asset class from an asset management perspective. Additionally, their specific characteristics enable hedge funds to become activist shareholders who actively interfere in the investment and financing policies of portfolio firms. Hence, the growth of hedge funds might also have significant implications for corporate governance. This dissertation will investigate these issues in more detail.

The emergence of hedge funds has implications for asset management as well because it has broadened the investment opportunity set of institutional and retail investors. These investors increasingly search for alternative investments such as private equity, commodities and real estate which might improve the trade-off between risk and return of their portfolios. Initially, hedge funds seemed to offer these portfolio benefits. In particular, several U.S. university endowments allocated up to 40% of their assets into hedge funds and other alternative investments and were able to significantly outperform other institutional investors during the time period prior to the recent financial crisis (Bessler and Drobetz, 2008). However, the performance of these endowments deteriorated substantially during the recent financial crisis because hedge funds and other alternative assets suffered substantial losses during this period of severe market turmoil. Effectively, hedge funds' returns became highly correlated with the returns of other asset classes reducing their diversification benefits during those time periods when diversification is most valuable. This indicates that investments in hedge funds expose investors to a range of additional risks. These might include liquidity risk and exposure to higher-moment risk, which have a limited impact on the returns of conventional asset classes such as stocks and bonds. Given this trade-off between higher returns and additional risk exposures, one important question has emerged: How should investors make their portfolio decisions when they want to invest in hedge funds? Unfortunately, this issue has not been satisfactorily addressed and thus far. In particular, existing empirical research does not provide investors with reliable information on the optimal allocation to hedge funds because it is difficult to capture investor preferences for the higher-order moments and co-moments in hedge fund returns. Moreover, the portfolio implications of hedge funds for long-term investors have not yet been thoroughly investigated, even though most institutional and retail investors have rather long investment horizons. In addition, existing research does not consider differences in the ability of investors to take on the specific risks of hedge fund investments. This is surprising because it is well known that different types of investors differ substantially in terms of their background risk exposures, liability structures, regulations and level of sophistication. Finally, another research question that has not been satisfactorily investigated is whether the asset allocation approach used by endowments, i.e. combining multiple alternative investments into one single portfolio, enables investors to construct superior portfolios. This is an interesting aspect for empirical research given the fact that several U.S. universities generated an impressive outperformance over extended time periods based on this approach. It is important to note that the relevance of these questions has increased significantly over the last couple of years due to profound shifts in the design of the pension systems of many industrialized countries. These shifts increasingly force households to save for their retirement and absorb the associated risks themselves (IMF, 2006). For this reason, designing optimal asset allocations for different types of investors has become a very important and timely issue. Therefore, the potential contribution of hedge funds to investor's portfolios will be investigated in more detail from an asset management perspective in the first part of this dissertation.

The growth of hedge funds also has important implications for companies because hedge funds can exert strong influence on financial policies and business strategies. In particular, some hedge funds engage in shareholder activism and pursue similar objectives as the corporate raiders who operated in the U.S. capital market during the 1980s. For instance, hedge funds have on numerous occassions initiated corporate restructurings, such as bust-ups of diversified firms, and actively interfered in mergers & acquisitions. Moreover, they often also call for financial restructurings in order to increase cash distributions to shareholders. This corporate governance activism might have particularly strong implications in Germany and other Continental European countries where historically capital markets had only very limited influence on corporate decision-making. Recently, a shift towards a more market-oriented system has occurred in the German corporate governance system. This shift became visible in January 2005 when the hedge funds TCI and Atticus tried to influence the management of the Deutsche Börse and suggested a large-scale restructuring of the firm. This had substantial repercussions on Deutsche Börse's role in the subsequent consolidation of the European security exchange industry because the hedge funds became actively involved in the firm's investment and merger & acquisition decisions. Moreover, their intervention also led to significant changes in the financial structure of Deutsche Börse as the hedge funds forced the firm to distribute its liquidity reserves to shareholders. Initially, this engagement was associated with a strong increase in shareholder value during the time period up to the end of 2007 when stock markets were rising. However, over the longer run, the share price of the Deutsche Börse underperformed significantly after stock prices began to plunge during the recent financial crisis. This raises an important question: Should hedge fund activism be interpreted as a corporate governance mechanism that helps to curb managerial moral hazard and enforce more efficient capital market control? Or are activist hedge funds mostly focused on maximizing their own returns to the detriment of other shareholders, debtholders or the company's employees? Existing empirical evidence for the U.S. capital market emphasizes the former interpretation of hedge fund activism and indicates that hedge funds perform a monitoring function in corporate governance. However, it is not clear whether these results also apply in the German corporate governance system, which despite recent reforms still differs substantially from the market-oriented U.S. corporate governance system. This issue will be investigated in more detail in the second part of this dissertation.

Summary of the Structure of this Dissertation

Due to the potential implications of hedge funds for asset management and corporate governance, it is important for investors, companies and regulators to have a complete understanding of the implications of hedge fund activities. Therefore, this dissertation attempts to evaluate hedge funds and their activities from both of these perspectives. The structure of the dissertation is summarized in Figure 1.

Figure 1: Structure of Dissertation

Part I: Hedge Funds and Asset Management

Chapter I – Hedge Funds and their Trading Strategies

Chapter II – Portfolio Benefits of Hedge Funds

Chapter III – Hedge Funds in Portfolio Selection

Chapter IV – Empirical Analysis

Part II: Hedge Funds and Corporate Governance

Chapter I – Hedge Fund Activism and Corporate Governance

Chapter II – Hedge Funds and Corporate Governance Systems

Part III: Empirical Analysis: The Impact of Hedge Funds on German Target Firms

Chapter I – Data Description and Methodology

Chapter II – Hedge Fund Activism in Good Times

Chapter III – Hedge Fund Investments in the Down-Market

Chapter IV – Robustness Checks

The first part of this dissertation investigates hedge funds from the perspective of asset management as they appear to be an interesting investment opportunity for investors.

This interest occurs because hedge funds' sophisticated trading strategies might enable them to offer absolute returns to their investors that are independent of market conditions. This view is supported by the empirical evidence reviewed in the first part of this dissertation, which indicates that hedge funds really can provide these portfolio benefits to investors. However, closer inspection reveals that the outperformance of hedge funds over other asset classes is not only the result of the superior investment skills of their portfolio managers. Instead, their apparent outperformance also reflects their exposures to alternative risk factors which are captured by their dynamic trading strategies. Moreover, the analysis also indicates that hedge funds' exposure to these alternative risk factors creates additional risks in their return distributions. Due to the resulting trade-off between portfolio benefits and additional risks, it is necessary to develop new models for asset allocation and address several important research questions. In particular, what is the size of the optimal allocation to hedge funds? What types of investors would profit most by including hedge funds in their asset allocations? Unfortunately, the analysis in the second part concludes that these issues have not been satisfactorily addressed by academic research so far, which might also help to explain the cautious stance of most institutional and retail investors towards hedge fund investments.

The second part of this dissertation focuses on hedge funds from the perspective of corporate governance. This is also an important research topic given the increasing activities of hedge funds in the corporate governance of publicly traded companies. The crucial question is whether hedge funds' activities help to improve the efficiency of the corporate governance system and, consequently, contribute to a more efficient allocation of capital in the corporate sector. According to the predominant view which is supported by empirical research for the U.S. capital market, hedge funds help to improve corporate governance by reducing agency problems of free cash flows (Brav, Jiang, and Kim, 2009). At the same time, however, the tactics employed by hedge funds can also be used to expropriate other capital providers of the firm. In particular, hedge funds' restructurings might create wealth transfers from debtholders and long-term shareholders. In fact, this explanation is not ruled out by existing research which focuses on the returns to hedge fund activism during quiet economic conditions and investigates share price performance only for short holding periods. Moreover, most research on hedge fund activism is focused on the U.S. corporate governance environment. However, the German corporate governance still differs in some important aspects from the market-based U.S. system in that it used to be dominated by a governing coalition of banks, inside shareholders and the firm's workforce. More recently, several reforms have reduced the influence of this governing coalition creating opportunities for hedge funds to become active in the German capital market. Nevertheless, the German corporate governance system still has not fully adapted the market-based U.S. model (Schmidt, 2004). This might have significant implications on the valuation impact of hedge fund engagements in Germany. Therefore, the second part of this dissertation also contains an extensive empirical study on the short- and long-term valuation effects generated by hedge fund engagements in the German capital market.

This dissertation does not address the implications of hedge funds for all aspects of financial intermediation. In particular, hedge funds might have significant implications on price formation in financial markets because they generate a substantial fraction of trading volume in many markets. For instance, hedge funds pursuing algorithmic-trading strategies generate most order flow on many organized security exchanges and are also among the most important providers of liquidity in many OTC-markets (Financial Times October 30th, 2008). Moreover, hedge funds are often the first investors to begin trading new financial contracts such as structured products, catastrophe bonds or new derivative contracts. Therefore, they facilitate risk transfer, make markets more complete and help to establish markets for these new asset classes. At the same time, however, hedge funds and their dynamic trading strategies can also threaten the stability of the financial system. For instance, this occurred in the fall of 1998 when the hedge fund Long Term Capital Management incurred substantial losses in several large trading positions in Russian government bonds. These losses forced the hedge fund to engage in fire sales which put further downward pressure on asset prices and triggered contagion effects to other financial markets. The source of these systemic risks are special characteristics of hedge funds including the extensive use of leverage, the absence of investment constraints and their ability to accumulate liquidity risks in their portfolios. Interestingly, however, these specific characteristics also explain why hedge funds can also have positive effects providing liquidity to financial markets and speeding up the price discovery process. However, a more detailed analysis of these interactions is difficult because this question raises a range of more general issues. In particular, similar economic risks also characterize the balance sheets of other financial intermediaries who suffer from similar incentive problems as hedge funds. This has become highly visible during the recent financial crisis when several regulated entities incurred high losses on positions in credit default swaps and off-balance sheet positions in structured investment vehicles which, similar to many hedge fund strategies, also earn profits by providing tail risk insurance to other market participants. Therefore, investigating the implications of hedge funds on the level of systemic risk in the financial system requires a very broad perspective. This has to incorporate a detailed analysis of the properties and characteristics of all other major players in the global financial system as well as the interactions among them. This is beyond the scope of this dissertation.

Part I. Hedge Funds from an Asset Management Perspective

The emergence of hedge funds as alternative investments raises important issues from the perspective of investors as hedge funds offer a distinct combination of risk and return. In particular, hedge funds are absolute return investment products that are subject to almost very few investment restrictions. This may attract the most talented investment managers due to their compensation arrangements. Therefore, hedge funds can pursue a wide range of proprietary trading strategies in nearly all financial markets. As a result, hedge funds outperformed most other asset classes and generally exhibit low volatilities. In addition, it is often argued that hedge funds exhibit low correlations with other asset classes and therefore provide their investors with additional diversification opportunities. This suggests that hedge funds offer investors access to a combination of alpha, i.e. positive abnormal returns, and exposures to alternative risk factors that compensate for taking on liquidity and other risks.

From an optimal portfolio perspective this suggests that investors should make allocations to hedge funds. For instance, based on the traditional mean-variance approach (Markowitz, 1952) empirical studies indicate that investors should allocate up to 40% of their capital into hedge funds. However, even among large sophisticated institutional investors only the very successful U.S. university endowment funds hold such large percentages of their portfolios in hedge funds and other alternative assets. In contrast, most other institutional and retail investors are still reluctant to make substantial allocations to hedge funds and other alternative asset classes. The reason is that hedge funds differ in some important aspects from conventional asset classes including their specific risk characteristics such as tail risk exposures, correlation risks and liquidity risks. They also differ in their fee structures which, from the perspective of investors, offset their attractive Sharpe ratios. Therefore, more complex asset allocation models have been developed that attempt to incorporate these specific risk characteristics into optimal asset allocations. However, while these models still find that hedge funds seem to improve the trade-off between risk and return of stock-bond portfolios there remains substantial uncertainty regarding the size and the strategy composition of the optimal portfolio allocation to hedge funds.

In addition to their more complex risk characteristics, two other important issues have not yet received the necessary attention in academic research. First, what are the portfolio implications of hedge funds and other alternative investments for long-term investors such as pension funds or individuals who are saving for retirement? In fact, in the case of conventional asset classes, there is strong evidence that optimal allocations depend on the investors' time horizon due to predictable time-variation in their conditional return distributions (Campbell and Viceira, 2002). This might also apply to investments in hedge funds and other alternative asset classes. There is also evidence for similar time-variations in their expected returns, volatilities and correlations with other asset classes. Second, for many investors optimal asset allocations have to be determined from an asset-liability management perspective that takes into account the investor's various risk exposures. This often includes interest rate and inflation risk in the liabilities of pension funds and insurance companies. Therefore, investors might have to adjust the factors driving the returns of their asset portfolios to the factors driving the value of liabilities.

The most important research questions underlying the analysis in this part are whether hedge funds can improve the risk-return profile of portfolios in general and which type of investors (e.g. retail investors, high net worth individuals, endowments etc.) can achieve the highest portfolio benefits by making optimal allocations to hedge funds. In order to address these questions the following chapters are structured as follows. Chapter I presents the key characteristics of hedge funds from an asset management perspective including their risk-adjusted returns, their risk factor exposures, the implications of higher-order moment risks of hedge fund investments and their correlations with other asset classes. Based on this information, chapter II analyzes their contribution to a well-diversified portfolio of stocks and bonds. It begins with a comparison of the conventional mean-variance approach that is based on the first two moments of the return distribution with more complex asset allocation models that incorporate higher-order moments into the investor's optimization problem. Subsequently, it evaluates hedge fund investments from the perspective of long-term investors such as pension funds or individuals saving for retirement. Finally, it focuses on the interactions between the factor structure of hedge funds and the risk exposures that drive the investment decisions of different types of institutional and retail investors. Chapter III contains the results of an empirical analysis of the portfolio benefits generated by hedge funds, focusing on two issues. First, it attempts to determine whether the portfolio benefits offered by hedge funds are superior to those generated by other alternative investments. Second, it investigates the implications of time-variation in hedge fund returns for optimal portfolio choice.

Chapter I. Hedge Funds and their Trading Strategies

Hedge funds might be an attractive asset class for investors as they pursue a range of sophisticated trading strategies that cannot be duplicated by other institutional investors such as mutual funds and pension funds. These strategies allow them to make profits in both rising as well as falling markets and capitalize on differences in the prices of different securities. This is possible because hedge funds use a specific fund design, which exempts them from most investment regulations and provides large incentives for their managers. Moreover, it reduces the liquidity of investor's hedge fund shares. These issues are investigated in further detail as follows. The first subsection focuses on the legal and contractual structure of hedge funds. Chapter I then proceeds with an analysis of hedge fund trading strategies in the second subsection.

A. The Legal and Contractual Structure of Hedge Funds

Hedge funds have comparative advantages in implementing a wide range of trading strategies and exploiting different asset pricing anomalies due to their special legal structure and the design of their contracts with their investors. This includes four important aspects in that (1) they are subject to only very limited regulation, (2) subject their managers to high-powered incentive mechanisms, (3) impose substantial liquidity restrictions on their investors and (4) use high leverage ratios. These aspects are discussed in more detail in this section because they are important for understanding hedge funds' trading strategies and their potential implications for financial markets.

I. Regulation and Legal Structure

Most institutional investors are subject to a wide range of regulations that impose significant restrictions on their trading strategies. These rules are created because regulators assume that unsophisticated retail investors do not have the knowledge necessary to evaluate more complex investment products. Moreover, they presumably need to be protected from taking on too much risk. Therefore, investment products such as mutual funds and pension funds that are offered to retail investors are not allowed to execute trading strategies that involve short selling or that trade in derivative markets. In addition, these restrictions commonly prohibit fund managers from using leverage or investing in illiquid asset classes.

The legal design of hedge funds takes advantage of loopholes in these regulations to exempt hedge fund managers from these restrictions and to allow them to implement a wider range of trading strategies. For instance, U.S. regulations such as the Investment Company Act of 1940 imposes investment restrictions on all investment companies that offer their services to more than 499 investors (Fung and Hsieh, 1999a). Thus, these restrictions do not apply to hedge funds if they keep the number of investors below this threshold and if they require each of their investors to meet the minimum wealth requirement of USD 5 million stipulated by the Investment Company Act. Similar restrictions apply in Germany where the "Investment Gesetz" regulates investor access to hedge fund products and only allows "qualified" investors who presumably understand and are able to take on the risk of complicated investment products to make direct investments in hedge funds. Retail investors are restricted to funds of hedge funds or certificates when they want to invest in a hedge fund which, nevertheless, exposes them to similar types of risk. Due to these investment restrictions, the investor base of hedge funds is mostly composed of institutional investors such as insurance companies, endowments and pension funds as well as high net worth individuals (Fung and Hsieh, 1999a).

II. Incentive Structure

Most institutional investors do not explicitly link manager compensation to investment performance and only charge fixed management fees that are calculated based on assets under management. Therefore, their compensation is only indirectly linked to realized investment performance because more successful funds tend to attract more capital inflow. In addition, the link between performance and compensation is also weakened by the wide-spread use of fees and kickbacks from different service providers (Stoughton, Wu, and Zechner, 2008).

In contrast, hedge funds directly link manager compensation to investment success and should therefore be able to attract the most talented as well as experienced investment managers. In particular, they implement high-powered incentive structures using a "2/20"-model of fees that consists of management fees of 2% p.a. based on assets under management and performance fees of 20%.[1] It is important to note that

[1] More recently, however, this model has come under intense pressure as many institutional investors attempt to renegotiate the compensation arrangements due to the weak performance of hedge funds during the recent financial crisis (e.g. Financial Times May 2nd, 2010).

performance fees are only paid if the hedge fund outperforms a target return and also beats the previous high watermark which forces the hedge fund to recover previous losses before performance fees can be paid out. The target return is defined as an absolute target such as the risk-free rate plus a fixed risk premium and, therefore, does not create the same problems as compensation arrangements based on relative return targets which are used by other institutional investors. In particular, this enables hedge fund managers to implement trading strategies that profit from both rising and falling markets and also allows them to take on significant idiosyncratic risks because absolute target returns eliminate the incentive to closely track the performance of a given market benchmark (Shleifer, 2000; Scharfstein and Stein, 1990).[2] In addition, this creates strong incentives for hedge fund managers and helps them to attract the most talented investment professionals. Finally, these compensation arrangements are also consistent with their absolute return orientation and accommodate the payoff profile of hedge fund trading strategies (Siegmann and Lucas, 2002).

In general, the introduction of option-like components in managerial compensation appears to be the optimal solution to align the incentives of investment managers and fund investors (Li and Tiwari, 2009). However, the use of hurdle rates and high watermarks also creates new problems because they make the relationship between past performance and compensation asymmetric and create an option-like payoff for hedge fund managers. This may create agency problems between investors and hedge fund managers. In particular, if the implicit options are out of the money then hedge fund managers face significant incentives to take on substantial risk and to engage in "gambling" to push their performance contracts back into the money. This is in contrast to mutual fund managers who are subject to relative performance evaluation, who do not always increase their risk exposure (Basak, Pavlova, and Shapiro, 2007).[3] In particular, "emerging" hedge fund managers face strong incentives for risk taking in order to attract capital and to increase the size of their funds (Aggarwal and Jorion, 2010). To ameliorate these agency problems, hedge fund managers often have to make substantial investments in their own funds (Kouwenberg and Ziemba, 2007). Moreover, these risk-shifting incentives are usually reduced as hedge fund managers have the incentive to maximize the present value of their fee income which will accrue

[2] Moreover, there is evidence that mutual funds do not outperform their benchmarks when their managers deviate from the holdings of their peer group (Gupta-Mukherjee, 2008). Thus, their managers either have no investment skills or these deviations are driven by other motivations.

[3] Whether mutual fund managers are more likely to increase risk depends on their performance relative to their peer group during the course of the performance evaluation period (Kempf, Ruenzi, and Thiele, 2009).

over multiple investment periods in the future so that increasing risk in the current period can have adverse effects on the present value of future fee income (Panageas and Westerfield, 2009; Hodder and Jackwerth, 2007).

Finally, the calculation of performance fees is based on accounting profits and not on realized returns. In the case of hedge funds trading in illiquid markets this can create additional agency conflicts because managers produce portfolio valuations themselves and, therefore, have the ability to distort their reported performance. This is highlighted by recent evidence that many hedge funds tend to report the best performance in the months of November and December, i.e. shortly before they have to provide audited full year performance information (Agarwal, Daniel, and Naik, 2007).

III. Lock-Up Arrangements

Mutual funds and other investment vehicles are open-ended and allow their investors to withdraw their capital at short notice. Therefore, they hold cash reserves to insure against liquidity shocks from unexpected withdrawals by their investors which impose a "cash drag" on their performance and prevent them from trading against longer term mispricings.[4] For instance, Huang (2009) finds evidence that managers of mutual funds shift their portfolios towards more liquid stocks when they expect periods of higher market volatility.

In contrast, hedge fund contracts include long lock-up and redemption-notice periods which force the investor to give advance notice to hedge fund managers and to wait for at least 3 months before they can withdraw their capital from the fund. Moreover, in some cases hedge fund managers have even segregated specific assets from their portfolios and assigned them to "side pockets" which indefinitely restrict the access of investors to these assets. More recently, some hedge funds have also tried to raise permanent capital by making IPOs of their funds or by issuing long-term bonds.[5] As a result, hedge fund managers are often insulated from short-run fluctuations in the sentiment and the liquidity needs of their investors. Thus, the withdrawal risk is reduced and they do not have to unwind positions prematurely. Therefore, hedge funds

[4] More recently, the 'Derivateordnung' governing the use of derivatives by German mutual funds has been changed so that the use of derivatives to synthesize cash and reduce cash drags has been facilitated.

[5] However, it is necessary to distinguish between IPOs of hedge fund shares and IPOs of the management company.

can take advantage of trading opportunities that may only generate profits over longer time periods. Nevertheless, anecdotal evidence from the recent subprime crisis suggests that these provisions cannot completely protect hedge funds from extended periods of market volatility (e.g. Financial Times January 21st, 2009). In addition, this imposes significant liquidity restrictions on the investors which in turn increases the required returns on hedge fund investments (Aragon, 2007).

IV. Prime Brokerage

In contrast to most other institutional investors, hedge funds use leverage to increase the expected returns of their trading strategies. Thus, hedge funds rely on close relationships with investment banks which in their function as prime brokers provide hedge funds with leverage for their trading strategies. In particular, prime broker enable hedge funds to use leverage to finance their portfolios by selling securities on margin and customized over-the-counter derivatives. As a result of these transactions, hedge funds need to post collateral to their prime brokers which is marked-to-market in order to offset the investment bank's counterparty risk. Often, however, hedge funds need to post less collateral than other investors due to the high profitability of hedge funds as customers. This creates substantial competition in the prime brokerage business. Moreover, hedge funds usually use multiple investment banks as prime brokers in order to keep the details of their trading strategies secret and prevent investment banks from front-running or duplicating their trades (Brunnermeier and Pedersen, 2005).

As a result of this relationship, the prospects of hedge funds are intimately tied to the performance of the investment banking industry. In fact, this can create extreme counterparty risks with hedge funds. This became visible during the demise of the U.S. investment bank Lehman Brothers in September 2008. Lehman Brothers had used collateral from hedge funds as collateral in its own refinancing operations ("rehypthecation"). Due to the legal difficulties and the complexity of the liquidation of Lehman's portfolios these hedge funds did not have access to the securities for a long time and, therefore, had to search for other options for raising liquidity (e.g. Financial Times June 21st, 2009).

B. The Trading Strategies of Hedge Funds

Hedge funds can implement a wide range of sophisticated trading strategies which cannot be duplicated by most other institutional investors due to the special fund design of hedge funds. In particular, hedge funds are not constrained to long-only investment approaches that need to identify undervalued securities or asset classes but can also construct portfolios that generate profits in falling markets and that capitalize on pricing differences between related financial instruments. Depending on their systematic risk exposures these strategies are usually classified into the three main categories which are depicted in Figure 2.

Figure 2: Hedge Funds' Trading Strategies

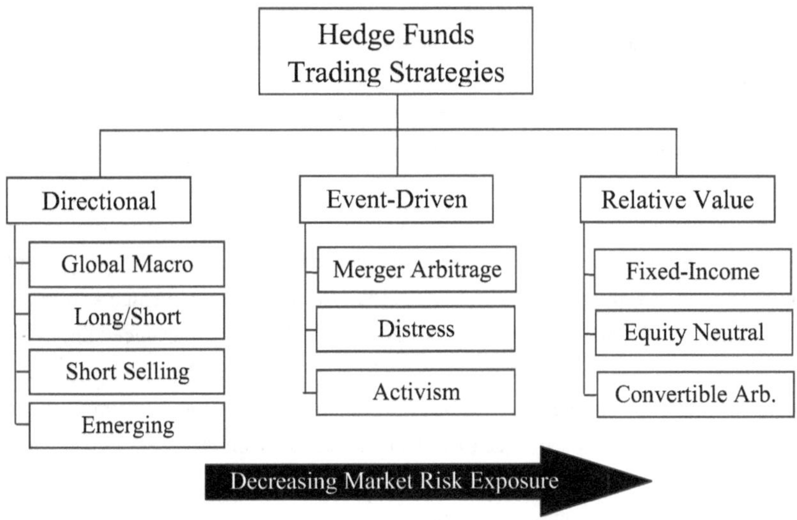

Source: Bessler, Drobetz, and Holler (2007)

I. Directional strategies

Hedge funds pursuing directional strategies attempt to profit from increasing as well as decreasing valuations of asset classes or individual securities. Therefore, they can earn alpha on the long and short side of their portfolios which is not possible for other investment managers who are subject to stringent regulations of their use of derivatives and short-sales. The profitability of these strategies only depends on the investment skills of the hedge fund manager and his ability to make superior forecasts for the direction of asset prices. These directional strategies can be further divided into global macro, long-short equity, short-selling and emerging markets.[6]

Global macro strategies focus on liquid index products and derivatives written on broad equity, bond, commodity and foreign exchange instruments and, thus, are focused on the future behavior of risk premia of these asset classes. These are determined by the level of risk aversion and the magnitude of macro-economic risks (Cochrane, 2005). Therefore, managers implementing global macro strategies need to have superior information regarding future macro-economic developments and risks or superior information on the future dynamics of market sentiment and risk aversion. In particular, many global macro strategies effectively implement "positive feedback trading"-approaches that attempt to ride trends in asset prices that result from time-variation in expected returns and risk premia along the business cycle. The horizon of these strategies usually ranges from one to six months. In the case of longer trends hedge funds often make multiple entries and exits to exploit volatility around the trend (Fung and Hsieh, 2001). In contrast to these fundamental approaches, there are also global macro strategies and managed futures strategies which employ technical analysis of past market trends and trading volumes to generate forecasts for short-term and medium-term trends in different asset classes. These strategies often exploit movements in risk premia and asset prices that are driven by movements in investor sentiment, irrational herding behavior or resolution of higher-order uncertainty during the price formation process (Brunnermeier, 2001). Still other global macro strategies engage in market timing or "negative feedback trading" and attempt to time corrections of imbalances between asset prices and economic fundamentals such as asset price bubbles or misaligned exchange rates. Finally, there are also some global macro strategies that use short-term timing strategies in order to take advantage of the quick adjustment of prices to new fundamental information. This often triggers delayed valuation effects in financial markets such as changes in policy rates by central banks (Bernanke and Kuttner, 2005) and other macro-economic news releases (Hess, Huang, and Niessen, 2008; Boyd, Hu, and Jagannathan, 2005; Ederington and Lee, 1993; Ederington and Ha, 1996). These strategies have a very short investment horizon because price adjustments take place very quickly and last only from 15

[6] Some authors also include a separate category 'managed futures' which contains those directional strategies which execute short-term oriented trading strategies in futures markets.

seconds to 15 minutes depending on the asset class (Frino and Hill, 2001; Zebedee, Bentzen, Hansen, and Lunde, 2008).[7]

The largest amount of capital invested in directional strategies is allocated to long-short equity strategies. These hedge funds trade in individual stocks whose returns are predominantly driven by idiosyncratic cash flow news (Vuolteenaho, 2001). In contrast to other investment managers operating in equity markets, hedge fund managers have two potential sources of alpha. They can place directional bets on increasing and falling valuations of individual stocks. This usually leads to portfolios with net long biases as hedge funds apparently find relatively more undervalued than overvalued stocks. Therefore, this strategy also contains an implicit directional bet on the equity risk premium. Long-short equity hedge fund strategies can be further differentiated into hedge funds pursuing qualitative and quantitative investment approaches. Qualitatively oriented long-short equity strategies are engaged in stock picking and have a short- to medium-term investment horizon. These strategies need superior information on the future development of expected cash-flows and risk of individual companies and target trading opportunities that result from time lags in the incorporation of new information into stocks prices (Eling, 2006). Moreover, these strategies take advantage of the bias in the investment approach of other institutional investors towards finding undervalued assets which might offer unexploited trading opportunities on the short side of their portfolios. Recently, some of these hedge funds have also begun to pursue activist investment approaches in that they engage with the management of target companies in order to push through measures that are well-perceived by capital markets. Quantitative long-short equity strategies create long-short portfolios of stocks in order to generate exposures to factors that capture a range of apparent asset pricing anomalies or behavioral patterns in stock prices (Fama and French, 2006). Finally, some quantitative long-short equity strategies are also engaged in high-frequency trading and attempt to capture very short-term technical patterns in asset prices (Eling, 2006) and earn profits by providing liquidity to equity markets.

Similar to qualitative long-short equity strategies, short-selling strategies also engage in stock picking but only search for stocks that appear to be overvalued according to the hedge funds' valuation model. Based on fundamental analysis, these hedge fund managers try to anticipate or speculate on bad news that will eventually trigger a correction of this overvaluation (L'habitant, 2006). The eventual decline in share

[7] The implementation of these strategies is further complicated by the observation that the impact of each piece of information on market prices depends on the state of the economy (Blanchard, 1981).

prices will often be triggered by specific events such as seasoned equity offerings or dividend cuts (Bessler and Nohel, 1996). Due to their focus on falling valuations these strategies continuously trade against the equity premium which might help to explain their low average performance.

Finally, emerging markets strategies attempt to capitalize on the inefficiency of the emerging financial markets of developing countries. These markets are less liquid and less transparent and, therefore, offer substantial opportunities for stock picking (L'habitant, 2006). However, these strategies have to take on substantial directional risk exposures to the aggregate market because opportunities for short-selling and trading of derivatives to lay off systematic risk exposures are usually limited in these markets. The resulting risks can be substantial as these markets are characterized by time-varying integration into global capital markets and can exhibit pronounced boom-and-bust cycles with large swings in asset prices.

II. Relative Value Strategies

In contrast to most other investment managers, hedge fund managers that pursue relative value strategies focus on the relative and not on the absolute valuation of securities (Cochrane, 2005). They therefore attempt to take advantage of relative mispricings between related financial instruments and implement convergence trades that sell the relatively overpriced security and buy the relatively underpriced security. As a result, these strategies generate profits when the price converges to the equilibrium relationship (Fung and Hsieh, 2002). For instance, assuming a simple n-factor asset-pricing model:

$$r_i = \alpha_i + \beta_i' \cdot f + \varepsilon_i, \tag{1}$$

hedge funds implement positions based on the assumption according to (1) that the relatively undervalued assets will appreciate whereas the relatively overvalued assets will tend to depreciate (Ineichen, 2003). As a result, relative value strategies carry an exposure to changes in the spread between the two assets. Because these spreads are often rather small, relative value strategies operate with leverage ratios. This serves as a "magnifying factor" in order to boost returns. However, these strategies often do not exploit true arbitrage opportunities. There are usually no perfect substitutes for hedging which forces hedge funds to take on the basis risks.

Many hedge funds that pursue relative value strategies operate in fixed-income markets. These markets seem to be well-suited to "quasi-arbitrage"-strategies because fixed-income securities have a relatively short maturity and their future cash-flows are clearly defined in the bond indenture. This facilitates the pricing and hedging of these financial instruments. Moreover, most fixed-income securities are traded in intransparent and rather illiquid over-the-counter markets reducing the speed of price discovery (L'Habitant, 2006). To capitalize on mispricings in these markets, hedge funds use three basic types of strategies. First, many fixed-income arbitrage strategies "trade against the flow" and implement spread positions in order to capitalize on mean reversion in relative prices in fixed income instruments, which are temporarily pushed out of equilibrium by sudden shifts in supply or demand (Ineichen, 2003). For instance, in a "yield curve arbitrage"-strategy, the hedge fund takes positions on temporary deviations between observed market prices and "fundamental values" based on yield curve models (e.g. Vasicek, 1977; Duarte, Longstaff, and Yu, 2007).[8] Second, hedge funds also attempt to capture the positive carry that results from differences between the interest rates on similar fixed-income instruments which appear to be related to structural imbalances in fixed-income markets (Pintar, 2003). For example, "swap spread"-arbitrage strategies capitalize on the statistical observation that the interest rate spread between treasury bonds and constant maturity swaps tends to be positive and exhibit low volatility. Third, hedge funds implement dynamic hedging strategies to capture mispricings of fixed-income instruments and embedded options that result from structural imbalances in fixed-income markets. For example, "volatility arbitrage" strategies attempt to profit from the historical observation that the implied volatility of options tends to be higher than subsequent realized volatility. This premium can be captured over time by selling interest rate options and delta-hedging the resulting directional exposures (Duarte, Longstaff, and Yu, 2007).[9]

A similar approach is used by convertible bond arbitrage strategies which attempt to capture the undervaluation of equity options embedded in convertible bonds, which results from a structural lack of demand in the primary market for convertible bonds

[8] Similarly, "mortgage"-arbitrage uses complicated models of the prepayment option embedded in MBS passthrough securities to identify temporary imbalances in their spread relative to "dollar rolls". In the same way, "capital structure"-arbitrage relies on financial modeling of relative prices between different components of the capital structure of a firm. Hence, there is a difference between structural models which posit an economic relationship between the value of the different components of the capital structure and reduced form models which yield statistical descriptions of the pricing function for credit risk.

[9] However, the difference between implied and realized volatility could actually reflect a risk premium inherent in the option price captured by the hedge fund (Neftci, 1996).

(Eling, 2006; L'habitant, 2006). Effectively, the hedge fund captures this discount over time by "gamma trading", i.e. dynamically hedging the directional equity exposure of the convertible bond.[10] Depending on the moneyness of the embedded equity option, this strategy can be modified to take advantage of mispricings in other valuation factors. For instance, if the option's delta is close to zero then convertible bonds will behave like a straight bond so that hedge funds can attempt to capture imbalances in relative prices between the convertible bond and other bonds or CDS written on the issuer. Moreover, if the delta is close to one then the convertible bond will behave like common stock so that hedge funds can try to take advantage of lead-lag relationships between the convertible bond and the underlying stock (Calamos, 2003). Finally, convertible bonds contain additional embedded options. When these options are over- or undervalued, these mispricings can also be exploited with convertible arbitrage strategies.

In equity markets the scope for arbitrage is limited because the valuation of individual stocks is driven by many valuation factors and is critically dependant on the market perceptions of growth prospects of future cash flows and risk. Hence, most equity market neutral strategies focus on the valuation of portfolios of stocks, which tend to be driven by the same valuation factors, in order to capitalize on temporary deviations in relative prices between subgroups of stocks that reflect different anomalies or differences in liquidity.[11] Thus, these strategies are based on the assumption that the group of relatively undervalued stocks will appreciate, whereas the group of relatively overvalued stocks will tend to depreciate (Ineichen, 2003). Thus, it is expected that over time the valuations of similar stocks tend to revert to the mean valuation of their peer group (Ineichen, 2003). To eliminate systematic risk exposures equity market neutral strategies attempt to create beta-neutral portfolios such that $\sum_i w_i \beta_i = 0$ for all systematic risk factors. As a result, the portfolio return should only be driven by the individual security's alphas. Finally, in a limited number of cases, there are also trading opportunities for equity market neutral strategies in individual equities. These include companies whose shares are traded in multiple markets (Rosenthal and Young, 1990), "pairs trading" which targets mean reversion in the "spread" between two

[10] The partial differential equation in the Black-Scholes-model implies that the net payoff should equal the risk-free rate in perfect frictionless markets (Neftci, 1996). In particular, this strategy is beneficial if the embedded call option is at the money which implies that its gamma is high yielding substantial opportunities for "gamma trading". However, these gains are offset by losses from the decay in the option's time value which occur whenever implied volatility remains higher than realized volatility.

[11] So far, there is no consensus in the literatureas to whether or not these effects indicate that the characteristics or risk factors are determining the cross-section of expected returns (Fama and French, 2007).

stocks with a cointegrated stock price history (Gatev, Goetzmann, and Rouwenhorst, 1999) or negative "stub values" which can arise if the market value of a listed subsidiary is higher than the market value of the parent company (Mitchell, Pulvino, and Stafford, 2002).

Overall, these strategies appear to offer an attractive risk-return trade-off with relatively high Sharpe ratios. This might indicate that relative value strategies successfully take advantage of temporary violations of the law of one price that arise due to either limited liquidity provision, limited arbitrage by other investors or market segmentation. However, exploiting these apparent anomalies can entail substantial risk. For example, Patton (2009) finds evidence that "market neutral"-strategies have significant exposures to directional market movements. Indeed, these strategies are exposed to fluctuations in the spread between both sides of their transactions, which is not arbitrage in the strict sense. These strategies, therefore, have substantial tail risk exposures which are reflected in the skewness and kurtosis of their return distribution and in the phase-locking correlations that increase during periods of market distress. Effectively, most relative value strategies seem to take on liquidity risk because the long leg of their transactions is usually invested in the more illiquid securities so that a substantial fraction of their returns seems to be compensation for taking on liquidity risk.

III. Event-Driven Strategies

Event-driven strategies attempt to generate profits by placing bets on major corporate events such as mergers & acquisitions, distressed restructurings or significant changes in corporate strategies or financial policies that lead to a substantial re-valuation of the firm by investors. These strategies can be further subdivided into merger arbitrage, distressed securities and activist strategies.

Merger arbitrage strategies speculate on the success of takeover offers. They take positions on the takeover spread between the value of a takeover offer and the market price of the target's shares. The profitability of these strategies is composed of two components. First, hedge funds will generate abnormal profits if their managers have superior abilities and are able to anticipate the outcome of merger negotiations. Second, the takeover spread reflects a risk premium for assuming the risk of a failure of the takeover offer which occurs if target management rejects the bid or if a competing bidder emerges (Officer, 2004). In the case of a shortage of arbitrage capital, this takeover spread overcompensates hedge funds for assuming this risk exposure and, therefore, offers hedge funds very attractive trading opportunities (Cornelli and Li, 2002). In addition to this basic merger arbitrage strategy, a number of hedge funds have developed more aggressive strategies that take advantage of provisions in takeover regulations in order to increase returns. In particular, since the acquirer usually needs a certain percentage of shares to close the deal, these hedge funds press for higher prices and compound their returns by holding out, i.e. refusing to tender at the current offer prices (Hsieh and Walkling, 2005; Gomes, 2001; Elsland and Weber, 2004). The risk and return of these strategies depends on the state of the economy which determines the number of potential trading opportunities (Eling, 2006) as well as the probability of takeover success (Mitchell and Pulvino, 2001).

Distressed securities strategies invest in companies that are in financial distress and use different approaches to generate their returns. First, they may earn a liquidity risk premium because the market for distressed securities tends to be illiquid. Thus, the underlying risks are "narrowly held" (Cochrane, 1999) due to limited participation by other investors so that there is incomplete risk sharing leading to an "undervaluation" of these securities. For example, Brophy, Ouimet, and Sialm (2009) show that hedge funds provide equity capital to companies that would otherwise not receive additional financing due to poor fundamentals and high information asymmetries. Second, upon buying into the debt securities of companies undergoing restructurings, hedge funds often try to take advantage of provisions in bankruptcy and reorganization law in order to extract higher returns. These hedge funds attempt to dominate one or more classes of debt securities and tie their acceptance of a reorganization plan to amendments that allocate a larger share of the value of the reorganized company to their class of securities. Consequently, they often extract value from long-term and subordinated debtholders whose value is primarily derived from the future earnings power of the firm and who, therefore, would suffer the most from a failure of the reorganization plan. Finally, on some occassions hedge funds have engaged in the controversial strategies of purchasing default insurance via credit default swaps and blocking the success of the restructuring (e.g. Economist December 13th, 2007).

Recently, event-driven hedge funds have also started to implement more activist trading strategies effectively trying to "generate their own events" by forcing the management of target companies to make decisions that trigger positive valuation effects. These activist campaigns typically involve large-scale asset and financial restructurings such as spin-offs, dividend increases or share repurchases. Usually, it is argued that these strategies earn profits by eliminating valuation discounts emanating from bad corporate governance. At the same time, however, the returns to these strategies might also indicate transfers of value from debtholders or from long-term shareholders to hedge funds and other short-term shareholders.

C. Summary

This section explained that hedge funds differ in some important aspects from other institutional investors, such as mutual funds and pension funds. In particular, their structural design exempts them from most investment regulations and enables them to use short sales, derivatives and leverage to execute their trading strategies. In addition, the structural design also provides high-powered incentives to the managers, due to option-like components in their compensation structures. As a result, hedge funds have substantial investment flexibility and can therefore implement a wide range of trading strategies that cannot be replicated by other institutional investors. In particular, hedge funds are not restricted to long-only investment approaches and can use "directional" strategies to capitalize on both upward and downward movements in asset prices. Moreover, "relative value" strategies allow them to engage in "quasi-arbitrage" trading and exploit relative mispricings between related financial markets. Finally, hedge funds can also use "event-driven" strategies to take advantage of special situations in the corporate sector such as mergers & acquisitions, financial distress and other corporate restructuring activities.

Due to these sophisticated trading strategies, hedge funds might represent an interesting investment opportunity for many investors. Therefore, the subsequent chapters will investigate in detail whether these sophisticated trading strategies allow hedge funds to offer attractive combinations of risk and return that enhance the efficiency of their portfolios.

Chapter II. The Portfolio Benefits of Hedge Funds as an Alternative Asset Class

Hedge funds are among the growing group of alternative asset classes such as real estate, private equity and commodity investments. These investments provide investors with absolute returns that are independent of the returns of conventional asset classes such as stocks and bonds. Hedge funds achieve this objective by implementing a wide range of trading strategies which enable them to achieve an outperformance with low volatilities and limited correlations with other asset classes. This attractive investment performance can be traced back to two different portfolio benefits which are summarized in Figure 3.

Figure 3: Portfolio Benefits of Hedge Funds

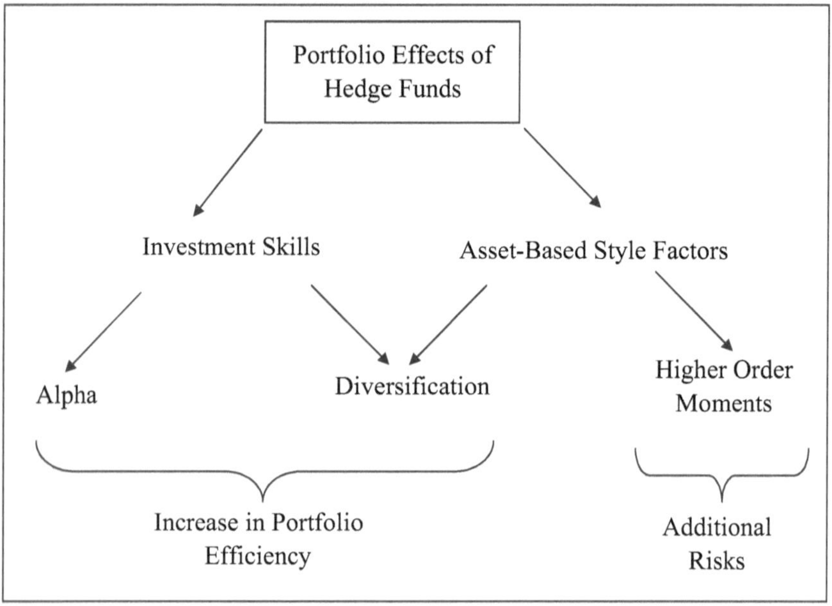

First, hedge fund managers can generate positive risk-adjusted returns if they have superior investment skills which enable them to identify mispriced securities, time major market movements and extract value out of mispriced spreads between related securities. Second, hedge funds offer their investors exposures to alternative risk premia which exhibit low correlations with conventional macro-economic risk factors.

They reflect the systematic liquidity and volatility risk exposures of hedge funds' dynamic trading strategies and create additional diversification opportunities. At the same time, however, they also complicate the evaluation of hedge funds' portfolio benefits because they exhibit a complex non-linear and phase-locking behaviour such that their conditional correlations increase during periods of market distress. Therefore, hedge fund investments expose investors to additional risks including significant skewness and kurtosis in their return distribution, correlation risk and liquidity risks.

The objective of this chapter is to provide further insight into the nature of these portfolio benefits and into the additional risks inherent in hedge fund investments. It begins in section A with a primer on hedge funds from an investor's perspective which is followed by a presentation of the methodological tools designed to analyze hedge fund returns in section B. It then proceeds in section C with an analysis of the risk-adjusted performance and investment skills of hedge fund managers. Section D focuses on the potential diversification benefits inherent in alternative risk factors driving hedge fund returns. In section E recent industry efforts to cheaply replicate hedge fund returns using different statistical models are investigated. Finally, section F compares the portfolio benefits of hedge funds and other alternative investments.

A. The Statistical Properties of Hedge Fund Returns

The returns of hedge funds have several specific characteristics. These include the specific behavior of their return distributions and significant biases in the underlying hedge fund databases. These specific characteristics have to be taken into account when the investment performance of hedge funds is evalulated. Therefore, this section reviews these issues in more detail

I. The Distribution of Hedge Fund Returns

The exposure of hedge funds to alternative risk factors has significant implications for their return distributions compared to the distributions of conventional asset classes. In particular, numerous studies indicate that the univariate distribution of hedge fund returns deviates more strongly from a normal distribution than the returns of stocks and bonds (Kat and Lu, 2002). In particular, all hedge fund strategies are characterized by substantial excess kurtosis, depicted in in Figure 4.

Figure 4: Fat Tails in Hedge Fund Returns

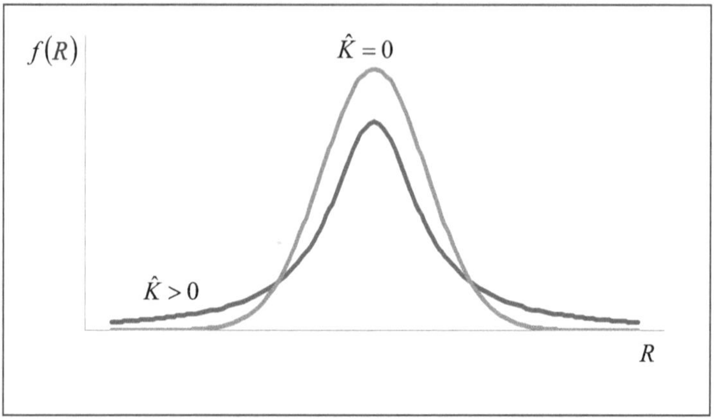

The distribution labeled $\widehat{K} = 0$ represents the density of a normal distribution and the distribution labeled $\widehat{K} > 0$ is characterized by excess kurtosis, i.e. "fat tails" in the return distribution. These tail risks increase the frequency of extremely positive or extremely negative return realizations.

The skewness of return distributions and, consequently, the magnitude of tail risk exposures depends on the particular type of hedge fund strategy. Relative-value strategies are characterized by substantial negative skewness (Gupta and Liang, 2005) indicating that these strategies generate small gains in most states but suffer extremely high losses in some market periods (Chan, Getmansky, Haas, and Lo, 2006). This corresponds to the distribution labeled $\hat{S} < 0$ in Figure 5.

In contrast, directional global macro strategies seem to have a positive skewness so that the shape of their return distribution corresponds to the distribution labeled $\hat{S} > 0$ in Figure 5 (Kat and Lu, 2002). This indicates that these strategies are able to generate extremely high gains with a low probability. Moreover, managers of global macro hedge funds can apparently limit their losses and usually succeed in cutting their losses early so that there is little probability mass in the left tail of the distribution.

Figure 5: Skewness of Hedge Fund Returns

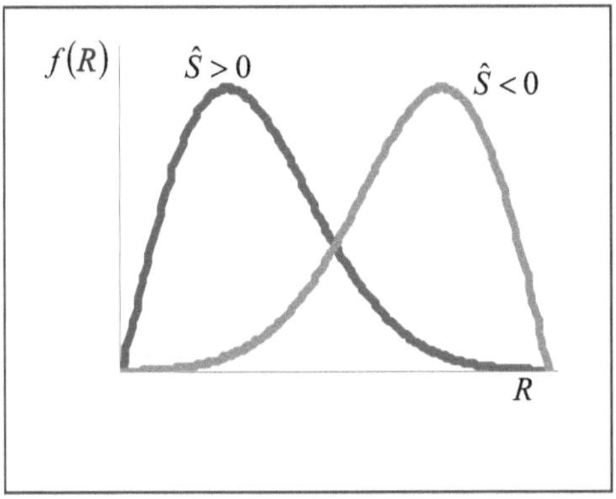

The multivariate characteristics of hedge fund returns differ substantially from other asset classes and also depend on the type of trading strategies. In particular, directional strategies have a relatively high sensitivity to the underlying market in which they execute their trading strategies (Kat and Lu, 2002). In contrast, the returns of relative value strategies have a low correlation during most time periods and event-driven strategies have an intermediate correlation with other asset classes.

The behavior of the univariate and multivariate unconditional moments of hedge fund returns is apparently related to time-variation in the conditional moments of hedge fund returns and in their conditional correlation with other asset classes (Gupta and Liang, 2005). In particular, there is evidence for time-varying volatility in hedge fund returns which can explain the pronounced skewness and kurtosis of hedge funds' unconditional return distributions. In addition, the conditional distribution of many hedge fund strategies exhibits a strong phase-locking behavior. Above all, the returns of most relative-value strategies are independent of the returns of other asset classes during normal time periods. However, they tend to become highly correlated with the returns on other asset classes during periods of market distress (Duarte, Longstaff, and Yu, 2007).

Thus, the distribution of hedge fund returns differs substantially from those of other asset classes in that it is characterized by more pronounced non-normality which has significant implications for investors. In particular, the skewness and kurtosis of hedge fund returns creates high downside risks for investors. In addition, these risks might even be understated due to substantial biases in hedge fund databases. These issues will be analyzed in the next subsection.

II. Biases in Hedge Fund Data

Hedge funds are unregulated investment vehicles and therefore do not have to periodically reveal their realized investment performance and other information as do other fund managers. As a result, estimates of hedge fund risk and return are distorted by several biases because their managers can decide on their own whether or not they wish to report their performance to a database provider. Clearly, they will only choose to do so if it is in their own best interest. Thus, the set of hedge funds reporting their performance data is a biased subset of the aggregate hedge fund universe. Hence, estimates of hedge fund performance will always be distorted by a number of substantial biases.

The survivorship bias results from the fact that reporting hedge funds tend to be more successful funds which have a higher probability of survival leading to an overestimation of average returns. This bias can be approximated by the difference between the average return of sample hedge funds at the end of the evaluation period and the average return of the remaining sample hedge funds at the beginning of the evaluation period.[12] Summarizing sixteen different studies of the survivorship bias in hedge fund returns, Eling (2006) documents that this bias is on average 2.16% p.a. However, estimates vary considerably between different studies, due to different datasets, time periods and measurement methods (Amin and Kat, 2002; Liang, 2000; Lhabitant, 2006). Nevertheless, the survivorship is substantially higher for hedge funds than for mutual funds because their attrition rate is higher (Ackermann, McEnally, and Ravenscraft, 1999) due to their relatively short survival time of only 5.5 years on average (Gregoriou, 2002). This argument is supported by Ackermann, McEnally, and Ravenscraft (1999) who document that the survivorship bias is most pronounced for the subset of hedge funds that stopped reporting their performance data. Moreover, the magnitude of the survivorship bias seems to be related to the trading strategy (Liang, 2000), the legal structure and to the risk-taking behavior of hedge fund managers (Brown, Goetzmann, and Ibbotson, 1999). In addition to the overestimation of average returns the survivorship bias can also distort estimates of the higher moments of the

[12] L'habitant (2006) notes that the more precise method proposed by Malkiel (1995) cannot be employed since the complete sample of hedge funds is not known.

return distribution of the hedge funds (Brown and Goetzmann, 1995; Brown, Goetzmann, and Park, 2001).

The self-selection bias results from hedge fund managers' option to decide whether they want to report their performance data to a database. However, the impact of this bias on average returns is ambiguous because the decision can be driven by different motivations. On the one hand, very successful managers do not need to report their high performance to generate additional publicity or to attract more capital because they have often already reached their optimal fund size or have already reached the legal maximum number of investors. On the other hand, managers with a below-average performance often prefer to hide their dismal track record and choose not to report their data. Thus, the self-selection bias need not become visible in average returns (Fung and Hsieh, 2001). Nevertheless, Ackermann, McEnally, and Ravenscraft (1999) provide evidence that very successful managers generate a self-selection bias which is offset by the survivorship bias and therefore not visible in their aggregate performance data.

The backfilling bias results from the practice of many database providers to add the hedge fund's historical track record ex-post into the database when it starts reporting performance data. This leads to another upward bias in estimates of average returns because hedge fund managers are most likely to start reporting after a period of good performance. Based on the difference between the average performance of hedge funds in the database and the average performance of the same hedge funds since their inception, Fung and Hsieh (2000a) and Capocci and Hübner (2004) estimate that this bias leads to an overstatement of average returns by about 1.5%. Moreover, the magnitude of the backfilling bias is related to the length of the data series inserted into the database which can amount to more than 2 years of past performance data (Barry, 2003). However, there is some research which concludes that the backfilling of performance data need not affect estimates of average performance. For instance, Edwards and Caglayan (2001) find that the backfilling decision is not related to fund performance.

The multi-period sampling bias results from the requirement of empirical studies that hedge funds disclose a minimum number of return observations to the database provider. Since hedge funds that survive for longer time periods tend to be characterized by a superior performance, this introduces an upward bias in estimates of hedge fund performance (Bessler, Drobetz, and Henn, 2005). Empirical evidence is provided by Baquero, ter Horst, and Verbeek (2005) who report a multi-period sampling bias of up to 3.8% p.a.

The problems created by these biases are further compounded by the fact that there is no central database for hedge funds so that hedge fund data is spread across several commercial databases such as TASS, HFR, CISDM and MSCI. This problem is depicted in Figure 6 which indicates that there is a limited overlap even among the most important hedge fund databases. Analyzing past performance of hedge funds is therefore very expensive because a large number of individual databases have to be merged to construct a sample that contains at least all reporting hedge funds.

Figure 6: Hedge Fund Databases and Biases

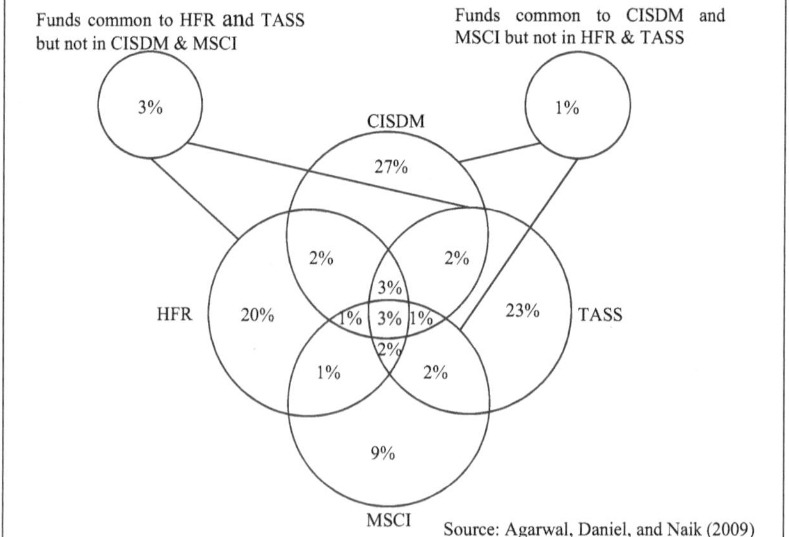

Source: Agarwal, Daniel, and Naik (2009)

In addition to these biases, there is a variety of other problems in analyzing hedge fund performance. These result from measurement errors in the periodic portfolio valuations conducted by hedge fund managers which often create substantial autocorrelations in hedge fund returns. This can be explained by hedge funds' investments in illiquid assets. For instance, Getmansky, Lo, and Makarov (2004) indicate that a substantial part of the outperformance of hedge funds reflects their illiquidity exposure. However, these measurement errors can also occur if hedge fund managers attempt to smooth their reported performance over the course of the year. In particular, Bollen and Pool (2008a) provide evidence that hedge fund managers behave in a similar fashion as corporate executives who smooth reported earnings, in that they find significantly more small gains in monthly returns than small losses. Interestingly, this discontinuity in the distribution of monthly returns is not present in the returns three months prior to an external audit and appears to be a short-term phenomenon that is not discernible in bimonthly returns. Similar evidence is also provided by other empirical studies including Agarwal, Daniel, and Naik (2007), Bollen and Pool (2008b), and Liang (2003). Thus, due to illiquidity exposures and return management the reported returns of many hedge funds do not closely match their true economic returns which can partially explain their low volatility and small correlations with other asset classes. Therefore, many empirical studies correct reported hedge fund returns based on the assumption that this distortion follows an AR(1)-process (Kat and Lu, 2002).

There are substantial data problems for researchers who want to investigate the investment performance of hedge funds. Therefore, Fung and Hsieh (2000) have proposed that fund of hedge funds performance data should be used to approximate the investment performance of hedge funds and benchmark individual hedge funds. Their returns should incorporate the impact of the survivorship, selection and instant history (backfilling) biases. However, researchers using this approach have to assume that the average fund of hedge funds is a good proxy for the aggregate hedge fund universe which may not be accurate since their managers also pursue active allocation strategies.

B. Methods for Analyzing Hedge Funds' Performance

Conventional performance evaluation tools such as Sharpe ratios and Jensen's alphas lead to a very optimistic assessment of hedge fund performance. For instance, early studies on hedge fund performance such as Ackermann, McEnally, and Ravenscraft (1999) and Brown, Goetzmann, and Ibbotson (1999) document that hedge funds offer investors very high Sharpe ratios because hedge funds combine similar average returns as equities with substantially lower standard deviations. Similarly, these early studies also find an outperformance in terms of Jensen's alpha ranging from 6% to 16% p.a.

due to hedge funds' low exposures to systematic market risk. However, these early results are misleading because the performance evaluation tools used in these studies cannot be directly applied to hedge funds. In particular, their returns exhibit substantial skewness and kurtosis which exposes investors to high tail risks and phase-locking correlations with other asset classes. This suggests that investors gain access to the attractive Sharpe ratios and Jensen alphas at the expense of these higher moment risk exposures (Bali, Gokcan, and Liang, 2007).

Due to the higher moment risk exposures, it is necessary to develop special methods for evaluating the performance of hedge funds (Bessler and Lückoff, 2007). Therefore, this section begins with an analysis of investor preferences for higher order moments which are present in hedge fund returns. It then continues with an analysis of multi-factor models designed for the analysis of hedge fund performance that are based on location- and trading-factors.[13] It ends with a review of performance measurement ratios developed for hedge funds that adjust the simple Sharpe ratio for hedge fund exposures to higher moment risks.

I. Investor Preferences for Higher Order Moments

The evaluation of hedge fund performance needs to take into account the higher-order moments as their returns exhibit pronounced non-normalities, and because investor preferences cannot be completely described by the mean and variance of returns.[14] In particular, a large body of theoretical and empirical research demonstrates that valuations of risky assets should be adjusted for the skewness and kurtosis in their return distributions. For instance, assuming that investors want to maximize expected utility $E[U(w)]$, where utility is a function of end-of-period wealth, the Taylor approximation of investor utility of order n is given by (Kraus and Litzenberger, 1976):

[13] In addition to the models presented in this section there are also several other models such as the higher-moment CAPM by Ronaldo and Favre (2005) and the approach by Kat and Palaro (2005) which is focused on matching the moments and co-moments of hedge funds. However, these models have not been widely adapted in the literature and, therefore, are not investigated in more detail.

[14] See Guse (2005) for further evidence on the implications of higher order moments in asset pricing. Most of these empirical results depend on the assumption that the preferences of the representative agent reflecting the pricing kernel are identical to the preferences of individual investors. This is a strong assumption given the strong conditions which are implied by different aggregation theorems for simpler preferences and distributions (Lengwiler, 2006).

$$E[U(w)] = U[E(w)] + \frac{U'[E(w)]}{1!}E[w - E(w)] + \frac{U''[E(w)]}{2!}E[w - E(w)]^2 + \ldots + \frac{U^n[E(w)]}{n!}E[w - E(w)]^n. \tag{2}$$

Similar to familiar two-moment pricing frameworks such as the CAPM, this expression indicates that investors require a positive risk premium to compensate for co-variance risk if marginal utility is decreasing in wealth (Kraus and Litzenberger, 1976). However, according to equation (4), focusing on the first two moments will not be appropriate if the third and fourth term are not zero which indicates that investors require additional risk premia for assuming co-skewness and co-kurtosis risk. High co-skewness boosts an asset's price because it implies that investors have the chance for a very high reward with some non-negative probability. More formally, investors prefer higher skewness if the third derivative is positive which is consistent with increasing relative risk aversion (Arditti, 1967). Moreover, asset prices are lower for assets with higher co-kurtosis which increases the mass in the tails of the distribution, and therefore increasing risk. This is formally the case if the fourth derivative of investors' utility function is negative.

These theoretical predictions are empirically supported in a number of studies that test three- and four-moment CAPMs. A four-moment CAPM can be derived from the approximation of investors' utility equation (4) which can be used to derive the following pricing equation (Fang and Lai, 1997):

$$R_i - R_f = \varphi_1 \cdot Cov(R_m, R_i) + \varphi_2 \cdot Cov(R_m^2, R_i) + \varphi_3 \cdot Cov(R_m^3, R_i). \tag{3}$$

where the terms φ_i are the market prices for systematic variance, skewness and kurtosis risk and the associated covariation terms reflect the loadings of the test assets on these risk factors. Kraus and Litzenberger (1976) find support for a three-moment CAPM using equity market data covering the period from 1926 to 1970. Harvey and Siddique (2000) confirm this finding for the period from 1927 to 1997 and even show that loadings on co-skewness are able to capture book-to-market, size and momentum effects in equity markets. Errunza and Sy (2005) extend this approach to an international equity pricing framework and find that skewness risk can have a larger influence on asset prices than variance risk. Furthermore, Fang and Lai (1997) test a 4-moment CAPM on NYSE stocks for the period between 1969 and 1988 and find a positive risk premium for kurtosis and a negative market price for skewness risk. Christie-David and Choudry (2001) document the importance of higher order moments in a wide range of futures contracts written on equities, interest rates and commodity indices. In all of these different markets the S&P 500 stock market index is used as the benchmark asset, indicating that the same sources of co-skewness and co-kurtosis are priced in all of these markets.

Additional evidence is provided by behavioral finance which investigates the influence of different biases and the implications of heuristics on investment decisions. Based on experimental evidence, the prospect theory developed by Tversky and Kahneman (1991) indicates that the traditional rational expectations model based on the first two moments does not capture all aspects of investor preferences. According to this framework, investors use a value function to evaluate risky gambles which, in contrast to a conventional utility function, is not defined in terms of consumption or terminal wealth but measures losses and gains relative to a reference point. Figure 7 reveals that this function is convex for losses and concave for gains. In addition to the value function, investors also use a weighting function to assess the likelihood of different state-contingent payoffs. This is also depicted in Figure 7. It shows that the function puts higher weights on extreme events in the left tail than the objective probability function.[15]

According to the shape of the value and the weighting function, the prospect theory supports the conclusion from asset-pricing studies that investors have preferences for higher order moments. In particular, the properties of the weighting function suggest that investors are very averse to taking on tail risks which is also consistent with empirical studies on the pricing of deep-out-of-the-money options (Shefrin, 2008). Consequently, performance measures for hedge funds and other alternative asset classes needs to take into account the pronounced skewness and kurtosis in their return distributions.

[15] This is similar to the risk-neutral densities which underlie option-pricing models. However, these risk-neutral densities are characterized by shifts to the left (Neftci, 1996).

Figure 7: Prospect Theory

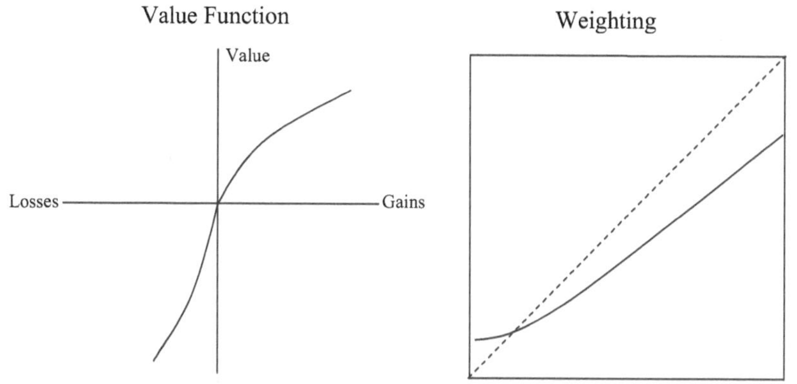

Source: Tversky and Kahnemann (1991)

II. Multi-Factor Models

Most academic research uses multi-factor models to evaluate the performance of hedge funds. These multi-factor models are extensions of the simple Jensen's alpha based on the capital asset pricing model. It estimates portfolio performance from the perspective of investors that hold well-diversified portfolios. Jensen's alpha is defined as the intercept α in a time-series regression of the fund's excess return on the market's excess return:

$$r_{i,t} - r_{f,t} = \alpha + \beta(r_{m,t} - r_{f,t}), \tag{4}$$

where α measures the manager's skill for security selection and market timing and β captures the performance resulting from taking on systematic market risk. However, empirical evidence indicates the existence of additional sources of systematic risk in the cross-section of returns such as the size-, book-to-market- and momentum effects (Bessler, Blake, Lückoff, and Tonks, 2010). Therefore, performance analysis for equity mutual funds is usually based on extensions of the simple Jensen's alpha in that additional risk factors are included in the pricing equation (4).

This approach has also been applied in analyzing hedge fund performance. The additional systematic components in hedge funds' returns are usually differentiated into location factors and exposures to trading-factors:

$$r_{i,t} - r_{f,t} = \alpha + \beta_{Location} r_{Location,t} + \beta_{Trading} r_{Trading,t} \tag{5}$$

Location factors capture the returns of the markets in which hedge funds execute their trading strategies and to which they often have a directional exposure. Since many hedge funds pursue highly dynamic trading strategies, these location factors will often only explain a small fraction of hedge fund returns. Therefore, trading factors are also included in equation (5) to take into account systematic components in hedge fund returns. These trading factors capture the risk exposure of their dynamic trading strategies such as liquidity and volatility risk. It appears that these additional factors effectively capture the higher-moment risk exposures of hedge funds.

This section reviews the relevant literature and begins with an analysis of the specification of trading factors that can capture the systematic components in different hedge fund strategies. It then shows that multi-factor models can also be used to break down the investment skills of hedge fund managers into market and factor timing and security selection skills. Finally, the implications of style drift on the use of multi-factor models are investigated. This is particularly important for hedge fund managers who can quickly adapt their trading strategies to changing market environments.

1. Trading-Factors and Dynamic Trading Strategies

The returns of many hedge fund strategies contain systematic components. They can be replicated by managed portfolios. These managed portfolios change their exposures to different financial markets conditional on observable state variables (Cochrane, 2005). They are usually used as trading factors in the analysis of hedge fund returns for two reasons. First, it is possible to replicate these managed portfolios at a low cost so that hedge fund managers should not be rewarded for portfolio strategies that can be implemented easily based only on publicly observable information. Second, in some cases, these managed portfolios also expose investors to additional risks and, therefore, are not true alpha but reflect compensation for taking on additional systematic risks.

Relative-value strategies try to capitalize on delays in the convergence of relative prices between related financial instruments and continuously realize small gains during normal market conditions but suffer high losses during periods of market distress. The systematic patterns in these strategies can be captured by managed portfolios which have a low market exposure during normal market conditions but high market exposures during crashes. This exposure can be created by different option portfolios (Glosten and Jagannathan, 1994; Merton, 1981, Dybvig and Ross, 1985). In particular, their systematic component can be replicated by continuously selling out-of-the-money put options which indicate that these strategies provide catastrophe insurance to other market participants (Chan, Getmansky, Haas, and Lo, 2006; Agarwal and Naik, 2004). Similarly, this systematic pattern can also be replicated by continuously taking short positions in look-back straddles on spread positions in different markets (Fung and Hsieh, 2002a). These positions also insure other investors against the risk of a substantial widening of spreads during periods of market distress. Because these periods of market distress are also characterized by sudden jumps in volatility, the systematic components in relative value strategies can also be captured by portfolios of volatility swaps (Bondarenko, 2004) indicating that these strategies effectively capitalize on the variance risk premia (Carr and Wu, 2009; Ang, Hodrick, Xing, and Zhang, 2006; Peltomäki, 2007). Similarly, returns on VIX straddles can also be used (Adrian and Brunnermeier, 2009) which reflects the costs of insuring against large absolute shifts in the level of volatility.

In addition to derivative portfolios, trading factors for relative-value strategies can also be constructed based on managed portfolios that directly trade in the underlying financial instruments. For instance, the systematic components of convertible arbitrage strategies can be replicated by trading rules that trade in convertible bonds and take offsetting short positions in the corresponding stocks. These short positions are continuously updated to delta hedge the equity risk of the convertible bonds (Agarwal, Fung, Loon, Cheng, and Naik, 2004). This approach can also be constructed from a portfolio perspective by using an equity index to delta hedge a portfolio of convertible bonds (Agarwal, Fung, Loon, Cheng, and Naik, 2009). Similar trading rules can be designed to capture the systematic components of other relative-value and long-short strategies. For example, Duarte, Longstaff, and Yu (2007) construct trading rules replicating different fixed-income arbitrage strategies and Gatev, Goetzmann, and Rouwenhorst (2006) designed a statistical model to replicate "pairs trading" in equity markets. In addition, Mitchell, Pulvino, and Stafford (2002) replicated "stub trading" between stocks of parent companies and exchange-traded subsidiaries. However, in contrast to the trading factors for convertible arbitrage, these other trading rules have not been used as systematic factors in performance evaluation. The reason is that there are so many trading opportunities in fixed-income and equity markets that it is not possible to find the basis assets for the implementation of the trading rule that correspond to the assets which are actually traded by the hedge funds.

Designing trading factors for directional strategies is more difficult because these strategies largely rely on the managers' investment skills to generate returns. Their managers have substantial discretion to adopt their investment strategies to changing economic environments. Consequently, there is only a limited number of trading factors that model directional strategies. These are generally not driven by additional systematic risk exposures, but reflect returns that can be replicated by trading rules based on publicly observable information. In addition, the returns of trend-following strategies pursued by global macro and managed futures strategies exhibit a similar payoff profile as long look-back straddles which generate large pay-offs when there are large up- or down-movements in asset prices (Fung and Hsieh, 2001). Thus, a managed portfolio that continuously invests into at-the-money look-back straddles generates the same state-contingent market exposure as a trend-following strategy that perfectly times emerging trends. This approach can also capture systematic momentum strategies in other asset classes than stocks (Adrian and Brunnermeier, 2009). Systematic components of these strategies can also be captured by conditional asset-pricing models. They make factor exposures conditional on publicly observable state variables such as the term spread, dividend yield or market volatility. Therefore, they do not reward managers for implementing strategies that only exploit publicly observable information (Ferson and Schadt, 1996). This approach is usually implemented using slow-moving instruments such as dividend yields and term spreads that are related to the business cycle and that are also used to evaluate the performance of conventional asset classes. However, since many hedge funds also seem to exploit more short-term shifts in asset prices employing other instruments such as fund flows, shifts in volatilities etc. might help to detect other easy to replicate trading rules that are also based only on publicly available information. In contrast to strategies focusing on whole asset markets, in most cases it is not feasible to identify systematic components in the returns of directional strategies that trade in individual securities. Only in the case of liquidity-providing strategies, such as quantitative long-short equity strategies that accumulate substantial liquidity risks, it might become feasible to use similar option-based portfolios, as in the case of relative-value strategies. Moreover, Khandani and Lo (2007) constructed a trading rule for long-short equity strategies that takes advantage of market microstructure effects.

Designing trading factors for event-driven strategies is also difficult. In fact, at most it is feasible to exploit the systematic patterns in conventional merger arbitrage strategies that can also be captured by the pay-off of a short-position on the stock market (Mitchell and Pulvino, 2001) because the risk of a failure of mergers increases substantially during periods of declining stock prices. The returns of most other strategies are mostly driven by the investment skills of the hedge fund managers. Hence, the majority of research on the return dynamics of event-driven strategies only considers their directional risk exposures.

2. Market Timing vs. Security Selection Skills

An additional advantage of multi-factor models is that they can differentiate managerial skills further into security selection and market-timing skills. This can be achieved by applying the market-timing models by Treynor and Mazuy (1966) and Henriksson and Merton (1981) to hedge fund returns. For instance, assuming there is only one risk factor, the market-timing model by Henriksson and Merton (1981) is represented by the equation:

$$r_{i,t} - r_{f,t} = \alpha + \beta_m(r_{m,t} - r_{f,t}) + \gamma \cdot I(r_{m,t} - r_{f,t} > 0), \tag{6}$$

where γ measures the manager's timing ability, α reflects his security selection skills and $I(\cdot)$ is an indicator function that is equal to 1 if the market's excess return is positive and zero otherwise. Depending on the market or the strategy pursued by the hedge fund this type of model can easily be extended to measure the ability of hedge fund managers to time other factors.

3. Style Drift

The estimation of the factor models presented in the previous section is based on the assumption that factor loadings are constant over the evaluation period. However, hedge fund managers often quickly change their trading strategies, switching between different markets and adjusting the level of leverage used to finance their portfolios in order to take account of changes in the trading environment. As a result, there are structural breaks in the factor structure of hedge fund returns which can be detected with different statistical tests (Meligkotisidou and Vrontos, 2008).

These structural breaks complicate the analysis of hedge fund factor structures because they induce time-variation in hedge fund factor loadings which can lead to errors in the estimation of risk-adjusted returns (Bollen and Whaley, 2009) and factor exposures (Moix, 2003). This problem can be ameliorated with different approaches. Most simply, the length of the time-series of fund returns used to estimate factor loadings can be reduced so that the weight of "outdated" return information on estimates of contemporaneous risk exposures is reduced. However, this benefit needs to be traded-off against the lower number of observations available for the estimation of the model which will lead to less precise parameter estimates. Nevertheless, to some extent this problem can be better solved by using the Bayesian approach from Pastor and Stambaugh (2002) which uses "seemingly unrelated assets" to estimate alphas for individual mutual funds based on only 12 data points. Time-variation in factor exposures can also be incorporated into the estimation of multi-factor models using more advanced statistical techniques. For instance, Bollen and Whaley (2009) propose employing an optimal changepoint regression or a stochastic beta model that can be estimated with a Kalman filter to take into account hedge funds' time-varying factor loadings.

III. Performance Measurement Ratios

In addition to multi-factor models, the investment performance of hedge funds is often analyzed with performance measurement ratios which are not restricted to only break down hedge fund returns into alpha and different sources of risk premia. Instead these measures allow determining how investors evaluate the package of alpha and risk premia offered by a hedge fund (Siegman and Lucas, 2002). These performance measurement ratios are usually derived from the Sharpe ratio. It is given by:

$$SR = \frac{R_i - R_f}{\sigma_i}. \tag{7}$$

This ratio measures the trade-off between expected return and risk on a stand-alone basis by relating the asset's return R_i above the risk-free rate R_f to the asset's total risk measured by its standard deviation σ_i (Bessler and Lückoff, 2007). Thus, similar to standard portfolio theory, it is based only on the first two moments of the asset's return distribution which does not completely capture substantial skewness and kurtosis in hedge fund returns (Kat and Lu, 2002). In order to address this shortcoming a large number of more complex performance measurement ratios have been developed which try to penalize hedge fund managers for assuming higher moment risks by using other measures of risk in the denominator.

For instance, lower partial moments can be used as a measure of risk that capture the tail risks inherent in hedge fund investments (Bessler and Lückoff, 2007). The most general performance measure based on this idea is the Kappa-measure (Kaplan and Knowles, 2004) which is defined as:

$$K(\tau)_n = \frac{R_i - \tau}{\sqrt[n]{LPM(\tau)_n}}, for\ n > 0, \tag{8}$$

where the lower partial moment of order n (Bessler and Lückoff, 2007) is given by:

$$LPM(\tau)_n = \int_{-\infty}^{\tau} (\tau - r_i)^n f(r_i) dr_i. \tag{9}$$

τ is the investor's target return, r_i is the asset's return and $f(.)$ is the density function describing the distribution of returns. The parameter n describes the order of the lower-partial moment and, therefore, determines the weight that an investor puts on different types of deviations from the target return. For instance, the lower partial moment of order 0 measures the shortfall risk, i.e. the probability of underperforming the target return. The lower partial moment of order 1 measures the expected return conditional on falling below the target return (Bessler and Lückoff, 2007). Using the lower partial moment of order n = 2 the general Kappa-measure collapses to the Sortino ratio which is often used to evaluate the performance of hedge funds:

$$SoR(\tau) = \frac{R_i - \tau}{\sqrt{LPM(\tau)_2}}. \tag{10}$$

Compared to the Sharpe ratio this measure puts more weight on risks in the left tail of the return distribution thereby punishing hedge fund managers who generate high expected returns by constructing portfolios with high loadings on tail risks.

The Kappa-measure can be extended to place more weight on payoffs in the right tail of the return distribution. For instance, the general Omega measure of order n substitutes the higher partial moment of order n for the excess return in the numerator:

$$\Omega(\tau)_n = \frac{HPM(\tau)_n}{LPM(\tau)_n}, for\ n > 0 \tag{11}$$

where the higher-partial moment of order n (Bessler and Lückoff, 2007) is defined by:

$$HPM(\tau)_n = \int_{\tau}^{\infty} (r_i - \tau)^n f(r_i) dr_i. \tag{12}$$

In the case of n=1 this leads to the original Omega measure introduced by Keating and Shadwick (2002) which measures the ratio between the probability of a gain and a loss.

Another set of performance measurement ratios also attempts to capture tail risk exposure in hedge fund investments by using the value-at-risk. For instance, the excess return on value-at-risk (Bessler and Lückoff, 2007) is given by:

$$ERVaR_{i,p} = \frac{r_i - r_f}{VaR_{i,p}}, \tag{13}$$

where the value-at-risk measures the maximum loss which might occur with probability (1-p) and is defined by:

$$VaR(p) = F_{r_i}^{-1}(p). \tag{14}$$

Thus, the value-at-risk is equivalent to the pth-percentile of the return distribution which can be estimated by a variety of methods which capture higher-order moments of the return distribution. This includes estimation methods based on the historical distribution, extreme value theory or other parametric approaches such as the Cornish-Fisher expansion. Thus, by choosing an appropriate method to estimate the value-at-risk, this performance measure can be used to penalize hedge fund managers that only generate higher returns by accumulating tail risks in their portfolios.

The conditional value-at-risk as an extension of the simple value-at-risk has also been used as a measure of tail risk in hedge fund returns leading to the conditional Sharpe ratio:

$$CSR_{i,p} = \frac{r_i - r_f}{CVaR_{i,p}}, \tag{15}$$

where the conditional value-at-risk is defined by:

$$CVaR_{i,p} = E\left(r_i \middle| r_i \leq VaR_p\right). \tag{16}$$

Thus, it measures the expected return in the tail of the return distribution below the value-at-risk. Therefore, this measure puts even more weight on extreme return realizations in the outer left tail of the return distribution than performance measures based on lower-partial moments or based on the simple value-at-risk.

Finally, in the case of hedge funds pursuing trend-following strategies many institutional investors use performance measurement ratios based on the "draw down". For instance, the Calmar ratio is defined as:

$$CR_i = \frac{r_i^d - r_f}{-M_{in}}, \tag{17}$$

where $-M_{in}$ measures the maximum drawdown defined as the minimum return over the observation window. This effectively captures the ability of hedge fund managers to correct time reversals in price trends and measures the regret of not selling at the highest point. Hence, this type of measure is often applied to hedge funds pursuing trend-following strategies (L'bhabitant, 2006).

However, while from a theoretical perspective these performance measurement ratios should lead to improved estimates of hedge funds' risk-adjusted returns, there are several practical problems in the application of these measures. First, since the nature of risks varies substantially between hedge fund strategies a different approach appears to be necessary when selecting the appropriate performance measurement ratio (Bessler and Lückoff, 2007). Second, even though all of these ratios appear to be able to capture tail risks and the non-normality of hedge fund returns they are specified in an ad-hoc manner and are not based on sound economic theory. In particular, in contrast to the Sharpe ratio and Jensen's alpha, these measures are not based on explicit assumptions about investor preferences and, therefore, do not specify which trade-offs between different higher-order moments are most important to investors (Bessler and Lückoff, 2007). Third, these measures can only deliver a superior assessment of the trade-off between risk and return in hedge fund investments if it is possible to make precise estimates of tail risk exposures. This evidently requires a sufficiently large number of return observations in the left tail of hedge fund return distributions. However, this information is often unavailable due to their short return histories and style drift.

IV. Measurement of Performance Persistence

Positive abnormal returns by a hedge fund can indicate that the manager really does possess investment skills or that he was simply lucky. Moreover, hedge funds impose long lock-up periods on their investors thereby forcing them to hold their positions for multiple time periods. Thus, academic research as well as investment professionals also investigate the persistence of hedge funds' performance in order to determine whether positive abnormal returns in one single period carry over into future time periods.

The persistence of hedge fund performance can be analyzed using different statistical approaches. Most of these approaches are based on a two-period framework and attempt to detect whether hedge fund managers that generated an outperformance (underperformance) during an initial formation period continue to deliver an outperformance (underperformance) in the subsequent test period. The simplest parametric test of this hypothesis is based on a cross-sectional regression of hedge fund returns during the formation period on their matched returns in the subsequent test period:

$$r_{i,t} = \alpha + \beta \cdot r_{i,t-1} + \varepsilon_i. \tag{18}$$

If the estimated coefficient β is positive and statistically significant then the hedge fund managers' performance is persistent indicating that the best (worst) performing managers continue to outperform (underperform) in future periods. Non-parametric tests of the same hypothesis can be constructed using rank correlations and include the rank information coefficient and Spearman's rank correlation tests (Eling, 2009).

Furthermore, there is a family of non-parametric tests for performance persistence based on contingency tables (Kat and Menexe, 2002). These tables classify each hedge fund as a winner or loser in both the formation and the test period by comparing their realized performance to the median performance of all funds. Based on this classification a number of different test statistics can be calculated which compare the empirical frequency of hedge funds exhibiting performance persistence, i.e. managers belonging to the same group in both periods, with the theoretical probability under the null hypothesis of no persistence. The simplest test statistic for this hypothesis is the cross-product ratio:

$$CPR = (WW \cdot LL)/(WL \cdot LW), \tag{19}$$

where WW (LL) is the share of hedge funds with a persistent outperformance (underperformance) and WL and LW are the shares of hedge funds that exhibit no persistent performance. Under the null hypothesis of no performance persistence this ratio should be equal to one which can be tested using the Z-statistic.

Finally, tests based on contingency tables can be extended to a multi-period framework (Agarwal and Naik, 2000). Effectively, these multi-period tests compare the empirical frequency with which hedge funds belong to the same group for 2, 3 or more periods to the theoretical probability under the null hypothesis of no performance persistence.

C. Risk-Adjusted Performance of Hedge Funds

Many institutional and retail investors make allocations to hedge funds based on the assumption that hedge fund managers have superior investment skills, and therefore, generate positive risk-adjusted returns. In this section, the relevant empirical evidence is reviewed in order to assess whether this belief is correct and whether hedge fund managers really deliver alpha. Section I begins with a review of empirical studies that investigate whether hedge funds generate alpha and whether the performance of individual hedge fund managers is persistent over time. It then investigates the implications of these effects on portfolios diversified across a large number of hedge funds, such as funds of hedge funds and hedge fund indices which are the preferred investment vehicles for most institutional and retail investors. The following section focuses on the determinants of the cross-section of individual hedge funds' risk-adjusted returns including their legal design, trading strategies and capacity effects.

I. Investment Skills of Hedge Fund Managers compared to Mutual Fund Managers

An important question from an investor's perspective is whether hedge funds are able to generate alpha, and whether they generate higher risk-adjusted returns than other institutional investments such as mutual funds. This question is addressed in the next three subsections by focusing on the investment skills of individual hedge fund managers, performance persistence, and alpha in portfolio products based on hedge funds.

1. Alpha in Individual Hedge Funds

Most empirical research finds that mutual funds do not generate positive risk-adjusted returns indicating that mutual fund managers do not possess valuable investment skills and do not add value to investor portfolios. For instance, Wermers (2000) indicates that after adjusting for fund expenses mutual fund investors realize negative abnormal returns. In contrast, it is often argued that hedge funds should generate alpha because they impose almost no investment restrictions on their managers, and because their attractive compensation arrangements should attract the most talented investment managers.

The empirical evidence generally supports this view and finds that even after adjusting for their specific risk characteristics the average hedge fund generates alpha (Stulz, 2007). Estimating the alpha of hedge funds with different multi-factor models, Boyson (2008) and Agarwal and Naik (2004) document positive investment skills for most managers in their sample. Similarly, using conditional asset pricing models to benchmark hedge fund returns Gupta, Cerrahoglu, and Daglioglu (2003) as well as Kazemi and Schneeweiss (2003) find that hedge funds generate positive risk-adjusted returns. This is in line with the results of Amin and Kat (2003). Similar evidence based on performance measurement ratios is provided by Darolles and Goureroux (2010) who also indicate that hedge funds appear to generate payoffs superior to those of other asset classes.

These results do not change after adjusting for the high management and performance fees of hedge fund investments. Chen and Ibbotson (2006) report that the average hedge fund generates sufficient returns to cover high fees of roughly 3.74% p.a. and still provides the investor with an alpha of 3.04% p.a. From this empirical research it appears that hedge funds generate sufficiently high returns to cover their high costs and, therefore, seem to generate value for investors.

The finding that hedge funds on average generate alpha appears to be robust to several economic and statistical problems inherent in the analysis of hedge fund returns. Vrontos, Vrontos, and Giamouridis (2008) still find positive alpha estimates after using different algorithms to select the set of factors for each individual hedge fund. Moreover, they document that the cross-section of alpha estimates is highly correlated between different factor selection methods. Furthermore, Kosowski, Naik, and Teo (2007) still find positive alpha after adjusting for measurement problems that result from the short return histories available for most hedge funds. Based on the seemingly unrelated assets approach by Pástor and Stambaugh (2002) they find that alpha is on average 0.42% per month, yet it is insignificant, and becomes significant at more than 1% per month for the best performing managers. However, they also document that simple OLS alphas overestimate the true magnitude of hedge fund alpha. Moreover, Kosowski, Naik, and Teo (2007) also find that the cross-sectional average in alpha is not statistically significantly different from zero, indicating that there is a wide dispersion in investment skills among hedge fund managers. These doubts are also supported by Capocci and Hübner (2004) who find that only 25% of individual managers generate positive alpha. Moreover, estimates of alpha for individual hedge funds can be distorted by style drifts. In particular, Bollen and Whaley (2009) find a substantial misclassification of rankings in the case of style drifts.

All in all, this indicates that some individual hedge funds generate positive alpha. However, positive alpha in one period need not necessarily reflect superior investment skills. Instead, it might also be due to luck. Therefore, investors focus on the persistence of the performance of hedge fund managers over multiple time periods. This aspect is investigated in the next section.

2. Performance Persistence - Skill or Luck?

Positive risk-adjusted returns in one single period can be the result of luck or can reflect valuable investment skills. In order to disentangle these two effects it is necessary to investigate investment performance over multiple time periods and determine whether the manager's risk-adjusted performance is persistent over time. In the case of mutual funds there is limited evidence for valuable performance persistence because alpha persists only over short time horizons and performance persistence is concentrated among the worst performing funds (Bollen and Busse, 2005; Bessler, Blake, Lückoff, and Tonks, 2010). This issue seems to be even more important in the case of hedge fund investments because they usually impose long lock-up periods on their investors.

Most empirical research provides evidence that hedge fund managers have investment skills, and that performance persistence is a short-term phenomenon which is detectable for investment horizons of up to one year. Given long lock-up periods of up to two years, this performance persistence cannot be exploited by investors so that hedge funds apparently offer only limited value to investors (Eling, 2009). Additionally, similar to mutual funds, their performance persistence is concentrated among the worst-performing hedge funds which consistently generate negative risk-adjusted returns (Agarwal and Naik, 2000).

This wide variation in empirical results appears to be closely related to differences in the empirical design of the different studies. In particular, while the choice of performance measure does not seem to have a significant impact on empirical results, the specific test statistic seems to have a major impact on results. For instance, Eling (2009) compares the results from applying different test statistics to the same dataset and finds significant differences in empirical results depending on the choice of test statistic. The wide variation in empirical evidence regarding the duration of performance persistence is also difficult to interpret due to the statistical biases of hedge fund data. In fact, early research on performance persistence in hedge fund returns did not adequately adjust for these biases in hedge fund data and detected persistent performance only in short-run returns (Boyson, 2008). For example, Brown, Goetzmann, and Ibbotson (1999) find no evidence for performance persistence at all, and Agarwal and Naik (2000) only find persistent performance for quarterly investment horizons. In contrast, at longer investment horizons such as half-yearly and yearly returns, these early studies find no evidence for performance persistence. More recently, however, several studies find evidence for performance persistence at longer investment horizons after correcting for biases in hedge fund data. Kosowski, Naik and Teo (2007) detect performance persistence for longer investment horizons based on the Bayesian approach by Pastor and Stambaugh (2002). Moreover, Jagannathan, Malakhov, and Novikov (2009) address the problem that hedge fund managers provide audited return data only at yearly intervals so that the monthly or quarterly return data used by most studies exhibit autocorrelation due to illiquidity risk exposure or return smoothing (Agarwal and Naik, 2000; Getmansky, Lo, and Makavor, 2004). They find performance persistence at longer investment horizons after taking this problem into account and provide evidence that 25% of past outperformance carries over into the next three years.

Thus, based on this evidence, it seems fair to conclude that hedge funds offer investors positive alpha, i.e. positive risk-adjusted returns. Moreover, these positive risk-adjusted returns appear to be persistent, at least for some managers. Therefore, hedge funds seem to be an attractive investment for those investors who have the ability to identify truly skilled hedge fund managers.

3. Funds of Hedge Funds and Hedge Fund Indices

Most institutional and retail investors do not directly invest in individual hedge funds. They rather invest in portfolios of hedge funds such as funds of hedge funds or hedge fund indices. Therefore, it is important to investigate whether positive risk-adjusted returns and performance persistence at the level of individual hedge fund managers translates into positive risk-adjusted returns at the level of hedge fund portfolios.

The hypothesis that alpha at the level of individual hedge funds should translate into alpha at the level of hedge fund portfolios is generally supported by empirical studies.

Fung and Hsieh (2004) find that the hedge fund indices from Hedge Fund Research (HFR), which reflect the investment performance of equally weighted hedge fund portfolios, generate positive abnormal returns based on their widely used seven-factor model. Moreover, Capocci and Hübner (2004) also indicate that hedge fund indices generate positive alpha using several factor models that capture hedge funds' location risk exposures. These findings also seem to be robust to the choice of performance measurement model. For instance, Ding and Shawky (2007) find positive alpha in the returns of specific hedge fund strategies approximated by asset weighted averages of hedge funds from the CISDM database based on the three-moment asset pricing model proposed by Harvey and Siddique (2000). Furthermore, Eling (2006) shows that the style indices also generate value for investors based on the extended performance measurement ratios. However, his results also indicate that this finding is sensitive to the estimated level of fees and the magnitude of biases in hedge fund indices.

In contrast, there are some doubts as to whether the average fund of hedge funds is also able to take advantage of the existence of individual hedge funds managers with positive alpha and able to transform this advantage into positive alpha for investors in funds of hedge funds. In particular, Fung, Hsieh, Naik, and Ramadorai (2008) provide evidence that the average manager of funds of hedge funds only delivers positive alpha in specific time periods. Nevertheless, they also find that there is a subset of managers of funds of hedge funds who consistently deliver alpha. Consequently, there are some doubts as to whether managers of funds of hedge funds really add sufficient value by screening and monitoring individual hedge fund managers in order to cover their additional layer of fees.

II. Determinants of the Cross-Section of Hedge Funds Performance

For investors it would be useful to have information to identify ex-ante those hedge funds which are most likely to generate alpha. Therefore, this section investigates the determinants of the cross-section of hedge fund performance and focuses on the impact of trading strategies, fund characteristics, and capital flows.

1. Trading Strategies

There are substantial differences between hedge fund trading strategies so that alpha might depend on and vary between different trading strategies. In particular, the investment skills of hedge fund managers are the only source of superior returns for directional strategies because they have no loadings on alternative risk factors. Therefore, these managers need to have the ability to generate alpha to outperform other passive investments. In contrast, the importance of investment skills should be smaller for most relative value strategies. They also generate returns by constructing exposures to alternative risk factors which help them to outperform other traditional asset classes.

This reasoning is not supported by existing empirical research because it does not find a link between the level of risk-adjusted returns and hedge fund trading strategies. The results of Agarwal and Naik (2004) suggest that hedge funds from all categories seem to deliver positive risk-adjusted returns. They use the equally weighted average of hedge funds from the HFR database and find positive alphas for all strategies except for short-selling. In contrast, Capocci and Hübner (2004) find only positive and significant abnormal returns in the case of event-driven strategies, long-short equity, convertible bond arbitrage, short selling and global macro. Thus, according to their results the differentiation between directional, relative-value and event-driven strategies does not capture differences in the level of alpha. This is also supported by Ding and Shawky (2007) who restrict their analysis to hedge funds executing different strategies in equity markets. According to their results, distressed securities and event-driven multi-strategy are most likely to generate alpha, as more than 60% of these hedge funds have significantly positive alpha. In contrast, among emerging markets and global macro hedge funds less than 30% earn positive alpha. In line with these studies Eling (2006) also finds that at the level of hedge fund indices the distinction between directional, relative-value and event-driven strategies is not related to the magnitude of risk-adjusted returns. Based on the ratio between excess returns and value-at-risk adjusted for skewness and kurtosis, he finds that equity market neutral and global macro strategies appear to be the best performing hedge fund strategies. Overall, this evidence indicates that there is no clear relationship between trading strategies and hedge fund alpha. This result might be related to differences in the samples and models used in different studies.

The finding that there is no direct link between trading strategies and alpha is also reinforced by empirical studies of performance persistence that differentiate their results by trading strategy. For instance, Brown, Goetzmann, and Ibbotson (1999) and Agarwal and Naik (2000) find no evidence that the level of performance persistence depends on the investment style. In contrast, Barès, Gibson, and Gyger (2003) find some evidence that managers in specific style categories, such as relative value and "credit", are more likely to deliver persistent performance for investment horizons of up to one year. Similarly, Brown and Goetzman (2003) and Harri and Brorsen (2004) provide some evidence that performance appears to be related to the hedge fund investment strategy.

All of the studies reviewed so far use the same set of risk factors to measure the performance of hedge funds pursuing different trading strategies. Since there are wide variations in the design of hedge fund trading strategies this approach might not completely capture the risk-return dynamics of each individual strategy. Therefore, some research focuses on specific trading strategies and adopts a more differentiated approach in that the performance measurement model is matched to the hedge fund trading strategies. Chen and Liang (2007) use a market-timing model to benchmark the performance of market-timing hedge funds operating in equity markets. Their empirical results indicate that these managers have investment skills that appear to be particularly valuable in bear markets and in volatile markets. However, applying the same methodology to a wider range of strategies, Chen (2006) finds that only global macro and managed futures strategies in currency and bond markets are able to time their focus markets. In addition, Griffin and Xu (2009) construct characteristics-based benchmarks (Daniel, Grinblatt, Titman, and Wermers, 1997) to measure the performance of long-short equity hedge fund strategies and find that they outperform mutual funds with their long positions by only 1.32% p.a. In addition, hedge funds appear to have only a limited ability to time specific stock sectors. Finally, Eling and Faust (2010) and Bontschev and Eling (2008) focus on emerging markets and distressed securities, respectively, and find that these hedge funds both deliver positive alpha.

In summary, there is conflicting empirical evidence regarding the relationship between trading strategies and abnormal performance. This indicates that other factors, such as the fund design, might be more important determinants for the cross-sectional dispersion in hedge fund alpha.

2. Fund Design

The design and organizational structure of hedge funds seems to be an important determinant of their ability to generate alpha as it creates high incentives for their managers and gives them the discretionary freedom to capitalize on their investment skills. Therefore, differences in risk-adjusted returns across hedge funds might be related to differences in their design.[16]

The strength of the incentives of hedge fund managers is determined by the structure of performance fees and the magnitude of the manager's own capital invested into the fund. Agarwal, Daniel, and Naik (2009) provide evidence that both of these variables have a significant impact on the cross-section of hedge funds' alpha. In particular, they find that hedge funds' alpha is positively related to the delta of managers' implicit call option on future fund performance, which is composed of their contingent claims on future performance fees and the returns on their own investments in the fund. However, the monetary incentives of hedge fund managers can also have adverse implications for investors since they also create strong incentives for risk shifting, which have already been documented in the case of mutual funds. Brown, Goetzmann, and Park (2001) document that if hedge fund managers underperformed during the first half of their evaluation period, then they tend to increase the volatility of their portfolios during the second half of the year. Clearly, this behavior can be detrimental to fund investors. However, more recent evidence suggests that incentives for risk-taking will often be ameliorated because hedge fund managers also need to take account of the implications of today's actions on their compensation in future periods (Hodder and Jackwerth, 2007; Panageas and Westerfield, 2009).

In addition to these direct incentive effects, hedge fund managers are also driven by indirect reputation effects and the need to attract more capital. In particular, younger managers have to outperform their peer group because they still need to attract capital while establishing a reputation among investors by building up a superior track record. This idea is supported by Aggarwal and Jorion (2010) who find that young "emerging" hedge fund managers generate higher alpha, and that their outperformance seems to be persistent for time periods of up to five years after fund inception. Similar evidence is provided by Boyson (2008) who finds that persistence is related to the age of fund managers.

Another important parameter of hedge fund design is the length of lock-up restrictions on investors. These restrictions on investor liquidity increase the investment flexibility of hedge fund managers and allow them to trade in illiquid assets which should in turn help them to generate outperformance. This view is empirically supported by several

[16] There are additional fund characteristics, such as the acceptance of managed accounts, that might have implications on hedge fund performance. However, these are not discussed in this subsection because only one single study (Le Moigne and Savaria, 2006) evaluates their empirical implications.

studies. Agarwal, Daniel, and Naik (2009), Aragon (2007) and Clifford (2008) all find higher risk-adjusted returns for hedge funds with longer lock-up periods. In addition, Agarwal, Daniel, and Naik (2009) also document stronger performance persistence if the hedge fund has longer lock-up periods. While Aragon (2007) attributes these findings to an increased scope for capturing illiquidity discounts and trading in illiquid assets (Getmansky, Lo, and Makarov, 2004), Agarwal, Daniel, and Naik (2009) argue that this result is due to an increase in investment flexibility. Their argument is supported by Eling and Faust (2010) who show that hedge funds pursuing emerging markets strategies outperform mutual funds with a similar investment focus. This indicates that higher investment flexibility allows hedge funds to generate superior returns. However, from an investors' perspective, granting hedge fund managers this investment flexibility involves an important trade-off in that it forces investors to absorb the associated liquidity risk (Aragon, 2007).

Other elements of hedge funds' organizational design also appear to have a significant impact on performance. For instance, Teo (2009) indicates that the local information advantage also applies to hedge funds, as hedge funds that focus on investments in Asia and have managers located in Asia outperform other hedge funds with the same regional focus whose managers are located elsewhere. Moreover, Aggarwal and Jorion (2010) find a superior performance if a new fund is launched with the support of a larger hedge fund group indicating that institutional infrastructure makes a difference.

3. Crowded Trades, Competition and Capacity Effects

Many hedge fund strategies face a limited supply of trading opportunities because they operate in rather illiquid markets or focus on small mispricings related to temporary limits to arbitrage and scarcity of arbitrage capital. As a result, their ability to deliver positive risk-adjusted returns also depends on the level of competition and the amount of capital chasing similar trading opportunities. This idea of a capacity effect has been formalized by Berk and Green (2004) for mutual funds based on two assumptions. First, there are decreasing returns to scale in active management because there are only a limited number of profitable trading ideas. This assumption also applies to many hedge fund strategies because their trades tend to become "crowded" subsequent to additional capital inflows. This leads to higher prices and/or narrower spreads which in turn reduces their expected returns (Goetzmann, Ingersoll, and Ross, 2005). Second, Berk and Green (2004) assume that there is asymmetric information between investors and managers regarding their investment skills so that investors need to rely on past returns to select managers. Again, empirical evidence indicates that this assumption is not only reasonable for mutual funds (Capon, Fitzsimons, and Prince, 1996) but that it also applies to the behavior of investors in hedge funds (Agarwal, Daniel, and Naik 2009; Xiong, Idzorek, Chen, and Ibbotson, 2007). Thus, there might also be a countercyclical relationship between hedge funds' past performance and future performance because hedge funds cannot continue to outperform after periods of good performance due to the high capital inflows. This effect should be particularly strong among those hedge funds that execute their trading strategies in rather illiquid asset markets.

There is indeed empirical evidence that this model does not only apply to the dynamics of mutual fund performance (Bessler, Blake, Lückoff, and Tonks, 2010) but also captures the dynamics between capital flows and expected returns in hedge funds. For instance, using a sample of funds of hedge funds Fung, Hsieh, Naik, and Ramadorai (2008) find that the average level of alpha has decreased over time and that this effect is related to increasing capital inflows. Importantly, this result applies to the average hedge fund because the strategy composition of the average funds of hedge funds should reflect the style composition of the entire hedge fund universe. In addition, Naik, Ramadorai, and Stromqvist (2007) extend this analysis to individual hedge fund strategies and also find a capacity effect. Moreover, this pattern has also been identified in the time-series of expected returns on several individual hedge fund strategies. For instance, Khandani and Lo (2007) provide convincing evidence that the returns to a generic quant strategy deteriorated sharply between 1995 and 2007 due to increasing competition, which might also have forced these hedge funds to increase the use of leverage. Finally, Jylha, Suominnen, and Lyytinen (2008) find that hedge fund returns are related to carry trade returns which, in turn, are negatively correlated with the amount of arbitrage capital.

Additional support for the importance of competition between hedge funds on abnormal returns is provided by studies investigating the supply of trading opportunities for different hedge fund trading strategies. Agarwal, Fung, Loon, and Naik (2009) show that returns to convertible arbitrage are positively related to the availability of trading opportunities, i.e. the issuing activity in the primary market for convertible bonds. Similar effects also seem to be visible in the case of merger arbitrage (Eling, 2006). The outperformance of those hedge funds that survived the initial crash during the recent subprime crisis suggests that the diminished level of competition and the associated wide spreads also helped these hedge funds.

This problem of increased competition putting pressure on expected returns might have increased recently due to several trends in asset management. In particular, investors increasingly distinguish between passive low-fee products and high-fee active products (French, 2008) which is reflected in the growing interest in portable alpha concepts. Moreover, at the same time, a number of investment banks have started to offer passive hedge fund clones to their customers which attempt to replicate the systematic components in hedge fund returns. As a result, investors can now obtain exposures to "alternative beta" more easily at relatively low cost and, therefore, might become willing to pay only for true alpha.[17]

III. Summary

Based on the preceding subsections it seems fair to conclude that hedge funds can indeed generate alpha, i.e. positive risk-adjusted returns for their investors. Moreover, hedge funds' alpha also seems to be persistent, such that it pays to expand resources for manager selection.

However, the magnitude of the portfolio benefits varies significantly between individual hedge fund managers. To some extent, this variation can be explained by observed fund characteristics, such as trading strategies and fund design. Therefore, the average investor needs to rely on an intermediary, such as funds of hedge funds, in order to screen out the best managers and to monitor their performance. Unfortunately, there is some evidence that the managers of these funds of hedge funds do not have the necessary skills and, therefore, often do not generate positive alpha for their investors even though they impose an additional layer of fees on them. This result casts some doubts on the value of hedge fund investments from the perspective of the average investor.

[17] At the same time, the growth of passive investments such as exchange-traded funds might also create more trading opportunities for hedge funds. This might occur due to the decline in the fraction of assets managed by investors who actively process information.

D. Diversification, Correlation Risk and Exposures to Alternative Risk Factors

In addition to earning positive risk-adjusted returns, hedge funds also provide investors with exposures to alternative risk factors that are uncorrelated with conventional macro-economic risk factors and, therefore, can help investors to diversify their portfolios. However, at the same time, their correlations are not stable over time. In particular, for some strategies there is evidence that correlations are phase-locking and increase during market downturns, so that diversification benefits vanish when they are most needed. Since diversification effects can create substantial value for investors this section investigates the sources of these effects for individual strategies, as well as for the whole hedge fund market, in more detail.

I. Analysis for Individual Strategies

Alternative risk factors driving hedge fund returns enable investors to diversify their portfolios because they lead to lower correlations of hedge funds with conventional asset classes such as stocks and bonds. However, the magnitude and stability of the resulting diversification benefits seems to vary significantly between different trading strategies. In particular, the unconditional correlation between directional strategies and the stock market is relatively high. In contrast, the correlation of relative-value strategies with stocks is relatively small indicating that these strategies seem to have limited common factor exposures with other asset classes. In addition, their correlations with other asset classes appear to exhibit a phase-locking behavior that creates substantial correlation risk for investors because diversification benefits evaporate in down-markets when diversification is most valuable (Driessen, Maenhout, and Vilkov, 2009). The strength of this effect also varies between different trading strategies and is most pronounced in the returns of relative value strategies.

These differences in the magnitude and stability of correlations between different trading strategies and other asset classes can be explained by the decomposition of hedge funds' returns into alpha, alternative risk factors and directional factor exposures. The previous section has already shown that hedge funds deliver alpha but also that the level of alpha is not related to the type of trading strategy. Therefore, this section focuses on the contribution of exposures to alternative risk factors to explain correlations of hedge funds with other asset classes.

1. Directional strategies

The returns of directional strategies should be mostly driven by their managers' investment skills, which include their ability to time future movements in broad asset markets and to pick mispriced securities. Therefore, if their managers really possess these skills and quickly adjust their portfolio's factor exposures prior to market declines then they should have low correlations with other asset classes during down-markets and carry only limited correlation risk exposure. For some directional strategies this positive impact of investment skills on diversification benefits might be offset by their use of leverage which can create phase-locking correlations. This correlation risk is created by the decline of market and funding liquidity during adverse market conditions, forcing leveraged investors to prematurely unwind their positions and to realize losses. This risk concerns, in particular, directional strategies such as long-short equity and some emerging markets strategies that take leveraged positions in individual securities which usually offer only limited liquidity. In addition, for these strategies the risks can be compounded by frictions in security lending markets in which hedge funds have to roll-over their positions on a daily basis (Fung and Hsieh, 2006). In contrast, for directional strategies that operate in broad and liquid markets such as global macro and managed futures these risks are rather small.

These arguments are largely supported by empirical evidence on the factor structure of hedge funds pursuing directional strategies which indicates that they deliver high diversification benefits and have only limited correlation risk exposures. In particular, the returns of directional strategies that focus on long-term trends in broad asset classes are empirically captured by portfolios of long look-back straddles which ex-ante have a delta of zero, indicating that they are uncorrelated with other asset classes (Fung and Hsieh, 2001). Similarly, directional strategies focused on short- and medium term movements in asset prices seem to have positive alpha in the form of timing skills. Thus, their directional exposures to other asset classes behave counter-cyclically which in turn implies lower correlations and higher diversification benefits. This behavior is also confirmed by conditional asset-pricing models which make directional exposures to location factors conditional on business cycle variables, such as the term spread or default spread (Ferson and Schadt, 1996). In contrast, directional strategies focused on stock picking, such as long-short equity, usually have a long bias and, therefore, are positively correlated with the aggregate stock market. Additionally, they do not seem to create completely factor neutral portfolios and have additional exposures to conventional risk factors that also describe the cross-section of stock returns such as small-minus-big capitalization (SMB), high-minus-low book-to-market (HML) and momentum.

In addition, there is also empirical evidence confirming the hypothesis that these hedge funds expose their investors to correlation risks. Khandani and Lo (2007) find that the correlations of long-short equity strategies can increase substantially during adverse market conditions because their portfolios contain substantial liquidity risk exposures. However, Meligkotisidou and Vrontos (2008) document structural breaks in factor exposures of hedge funds that cluster around major market events. Similar evidence is provided by Brealey and Kaplanis (2001). Thus, at least some hedge funds quickly adjust their factor exposures in time periods around market shocks which might help to reduce these correlation risks.

Overall, these empirical results indicate that directional strategies provide diversification benefits to investors, but also expose them to the risk of sudden shifts in their correlation structure. In particular, this correlation risk appears to be most pronounced for those directional strategies that trade in individual securities.

2. Relative Value Strategies

Relative value strategies try to exploit spreads between the prices of related securities and, therefore, appear to be unrelated to the price behavior of other asset classes. Indeed, their unconditional correlations with the underlying asset classes are very low indicating that these hedge funds should provide substantial diversification benefits to their investors. However, their long-short portfolios contain substantial liquidity and volatility risk exposures which are often amplified by the large amounts of leverage used to finance these portfolios. As a result, these hedge funds expose their investors to high correlation risks because liquidity decreases and volatility increases during adverse market conditions when most other asset classes suffer strong drops in their valuations. These correlation risk exposures in relative-value strategies are documented by a large body of empirical evidence. For instance, Chan, Getmansky, Haas, and Lo (2006) find that the returns of relative-value strategies exhibit a phase-locking pattern as correlations increase during periods of market crashes.

In line with this phase-locking behavior in correlation coefficients, the properties of trading factors explaining the returns of relative-value strategies also supports the existence of substantial correlation risks. More simply, their short put exposures indicate that relative value strategies insure other market participants against market crashes (Agarwal and Naik, 2004). Moreover, this is also supported by studies which use portfolios of lock-back straddles (Fung and Hsieh, 2002b) or spread portfolios to model the returns of relative-value strategies (Chan, Getmansky, Haas, and Lo 2006; Agarwal and Naik, 2004). The resulting correlation risks seem to reflect their exposures to liquidity risk factors which also exhibit the same phase-locking behavior (Pástor and Stambaugh, 2003). This is also highlighted by the design of trading rules used to replicate some relative value strategies (Agarwal, Fung, Loon, and Naik, 2004; Agarwal, Fung, Loon, and Naik, 2009; Duarte, Longstaff, and Yu, 2006; Gatev, Goetzmann, and Rouwenhorst, 2006; Mitchell, Pulvino, and Stafford, 2002; Lo and Khandani, 2007). These authors consider trading rules for different markets which all have in common that they establish long positions in the relatively less liquid security and short positions in the relatively more liquid security. Thus, these portfolios are exposed to liquidity risks which apparently drive the correlation risks of relative value strategies. The magnitude of these correlation risk exposures are higher in the case of those relative value strategies that operate in less liquid markets. Moreover, these correlation risk exposures increase subsequent to large inflows into the same strategy when trades become "crowded" which makes it more difficult for hedge fund managers to adjust their strategies and shift their asset allocations subsequent to external shocks.Thus, relative value strategies generally provide high diversification benefits to investors, but also expose them to high risks of increasing correlations during time periods of market distress.

3. Event-Driven Strategies

In contrast to directional and relative value strategies it appears difficult to clearly assess the diversification benefits and their correlation risk exposures of event-driven strategies as their design varies substantially between individual hedge funds. Therefore, only the generic merger arbitrage and distressed securities strategies are analyzed in this section.

The simple merger arbitrage strategy is constructed in a fashion similar to relative value strategies and, therefore, exhibits similar diversification benefits and correlation risks. In particular, they are also uncorrelated with other asset classes during most periods but exhibit a strong phase-locking behavior with increasing correlations during periods of market distress (Mitchell and Pulvino, 2001). This pattern is explained by the observation that deal failure probabilities are largely independent during normal market environments. This allows these hedge funds to lock in the merger spread in most of their trades (Jorion, 2008). During periods of market distress, however, deal failure probabilities increase which introduces a systematic component into the returns to merger arbitrage during down-markets (Mitchell and Pulvino, 2001).

Distressed securities strategies can be categorized into two basic forms and their diversification benefits and correlation risk exposures vary substantially. First, some pursue strategies that arbitrage between different components of the capital structure of target firms. Thus, their returns are driven by similar short option portfolios as relative-value strategies (Bontschev and Eling, 2008). Therefore, they are characterized by similar diversification benefits and correlation risk exposures. Second, some pursue buy-and-hold strategies and become actively engaged in corporate restructuring. These hedge funds will usually exhibit exposures to location risk factors such as credit spreads (Bontschev and Eling, 2008). However, these strategies should also create some diversification benefits in that they should contain some alpha.

II. Analysis for the Aggregate Hedge Fund Universe

From the perspective of the average investor an important question is how do the diversification benefits and correlation risks of individual hedge fund strategies affect the properties of the aggregate hedge fund universe. This can have important implications on their portfolios because most investors invest in broad-based hedge fund products, such as funds of hedge funds, which are typically diversified across all the major hedge fund strategies. Therefore, they should have similar investment properties as the aggregate hedge fund universe. For this reason the composition of the aggregate hedge fund universe is highly interesting for investors. It is plotted in Figure 8 based on the Dow Jones Credit Suisse hedge fund index between its inception in January 1994 and October 2009.

According to Figure 8 some significant changes occurred in the composition of the hedge fund universe along with the tremendous growth in assets under management. In particular, at the beginning of the observation period the hedge fund universe was dominated by "global macro" strategies which managed over 60% of all hedge fund assets in 1994. This share has declined steadily over the subsequent time period and since 2000 has stabilized at around 10%. At the same time, "long-short equity" strategies have attracted a large amount of capital so that their assets increased from less than 20% in 1994 to approximately 50% in 2000. Subsequent to the dotcom-bubble these hedge funds suffered substantial outflows and today manage more than 20% of total hedge fund assets. Moreover, another trading strategy which has increased in popularity is "event-driven" which has grown from less than 10% in 1994 to almost 30% at the end of 2009. Furthermore, starting around 2002 "multi-strategy" hedge funds have emerged and today manage about 20% of total hedge fund assets. Finally, another interesting observation in Figure 8 is that relative-value strategies have always managed only a very small fraction of total hedge fund assets during the entire period.

Figure 8: Composition of the Dow Jones Credit Suisse Hedge Fund Index

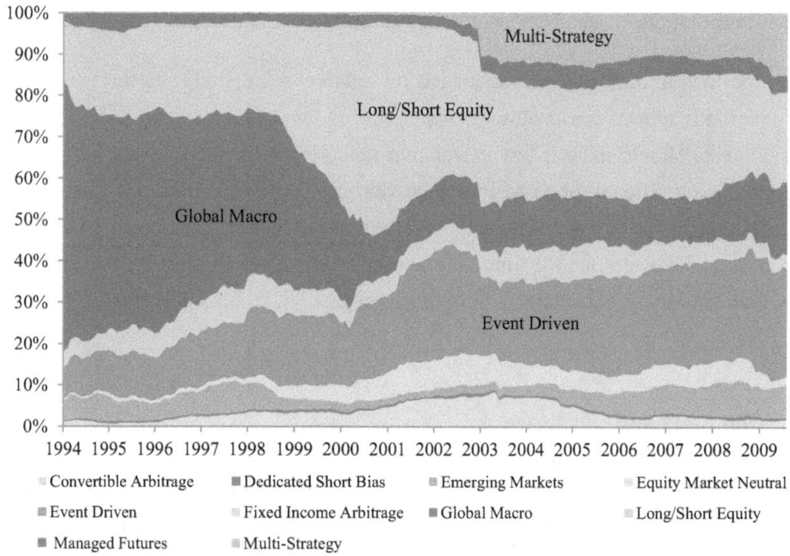

This figure shows the relative shares of different hedge fund strategies in the CSFB index over the time period from December 1993 to October 2009.

These shifts have important implications for investors because they affect the diversification benefits and correlation risks of the typical hedge fund portfolio product. In particular, at the beginning of the time period summarized in Figure 8 "global macro" strategies dominated the aggregate hedge fund universe. These hedge funds have substantial opportunities to shift their assets between different capital markets and can capitalize on up- and downward trends in asset prices. Therefore, they can smooth out shocks in specific markets leading to low correlations with other asset classes. This is reflected in the empirical results by Bessler and Holler (2009) who indicate that the aggregate hedge fund universe was characterized by a low dependence on stock markets at the early stages of its development. However, for subsequent time periods Bessler and Holler (2009) find that the relationship between stock markets and the aggregate hedge fund universe has increased. As a result, the diversification benefits of hedge funds have declined over time. This observation can be explained by the shifts in Figure 8. In particular, there is a strong growth in equity-linked trading strategies, such as long-short equity and event-driven strategies, that often execute their trading strategies in equity markets and trade financial instruments, such as corporate debt securities, that have similar factor exposures as stocks.

Given the low amount of assets managed by relative value strategies throughout the entire period it appears reasonable to assume that an investment in the aggregate hedge fund universe should exhibit low correlation risk. However, the average hedge fund generated a significant underperformance during the recent financial crisis. This indicates that its returns were characterized by a phase-locking relationship with other asset classes. Thus, despite the limited importance of relative-value strategies there is a fairly high amount of correlation risk in the aggregate hedge fund universe.

III. Summary and Conclusion

Hedge funds can provide investors with substantial diversification benefits in the form of low correlations with other asset classes. At the same time, however, these diversification benefits often come with substantial correlation risks in that there is a phase-locking pattern in correlations which increase during periods of market distress. Thus, the diversification benefits of hedge funds often decline during time periods when they are most valuable. Therefore, investors have to take into account this trade-off between diversification benefits and correlation risk.

Similar to the future level of risk-adjusted returns, the correlation structure of hedge funds might also change over time. Most importantly, this occurs because there is an increasing trend towards a stronger institutionalization of the hedge fund industry which has been reinforced due to hedge funds' losses during the recent financial crisis. In particular, many institutional investors, as the main providers of capital to hedge funds, will become increasingly unwilling to invest in hedge funds without any "strings attached". Thus, the discretionary freedom of many hedge fund managers will be curtailed, which in turn prevents them from quickly shifting their assets between different financial markets. Additional pressure on hedge funds to adapt to a changing economic environment is also created by ongoing efforts to step up the regulation of hedge funds. These two factors might have significant implications on the properties of their returns in general and of their correlations in particular.

E. Summary and Conclusion

This chapter has summarized empirical evidence indicating that hedge funds can provide investors with portfolio benefits in the form of positive risk-adjusted returns, alternative risk premia and additional diversification benefits. However, at the same time they also expose investors to additional risks which are less pronounced in conventional asset classes such as stocks and bonds. In particular, their exposures to alternative risk factors also generate substantial skewness and kurtosis in their return distributions and can also create correlation risks in the form of phase-locking correlations that increase during periods of distress in financial markets. Consequently, investors need to take these effects into account when they want to take advantage of the portfolio benefits of hedge funds. In particular, this might force investors to employ more sophisticated asset allocation models which will be reviewed in the next chapter.

In addition to these aspects, which have already been the subject of intensive academic research, there are still some important research questions that have not yet received sufficient attention. In particular, there is only limited research that investigates the implications of lock-up restrictions from an asset management perspective. Moreover, the recent financial crisis has indicated that the behavior of "co-investors" is also a substantial source of risk. These risks materialize during periods of market distress when the funds' investors do not have the same investment horizons or levels of risk aversion. In such a case early withdrawals by short-term or more risk averse investors can also force other investors to absorb a fraction of the liquidation losses generated by distressed valuations. In fact, this has led some large investors such as the sovereign wealth fund "Temasek" to rethink their engagements in hedge funds (Financial Times

April 9th, 2010). All in all, while substantial progress has been made in understanding the risk and return of hedge fund investments there are still some important research questions that need to be answered.

Chapter III. Hedge Funds and other Alternative Investments in Portfolio Choice
Under pressure to generate returns, many institutional and retail investors consider increasing their allocations to hedge funds and other alternative investments to capture alpha and exposures to uncorrelated risk factors offered by these new investment opportunities. According to standard methods for portfolio construction, such as mean-variance analysis, investors should have significant allocations to hedge funds and other alternative investments to capture these portfolio benefits. For instance, Bessler, Drobetz, and Henn (2005) indicate that up to 30% of a portfolio consisting of stocks and bonds should be reallocated to hedge funds and other studies propose even higher allocations. However, constructing asset allocation models for portfolios that include hedge funds is more complicated because an additional range of issues has to be taken into account. These issues are depicted in Figure 9.

Figure 9: Aspects in Portfolio Construction with Hedge Funds

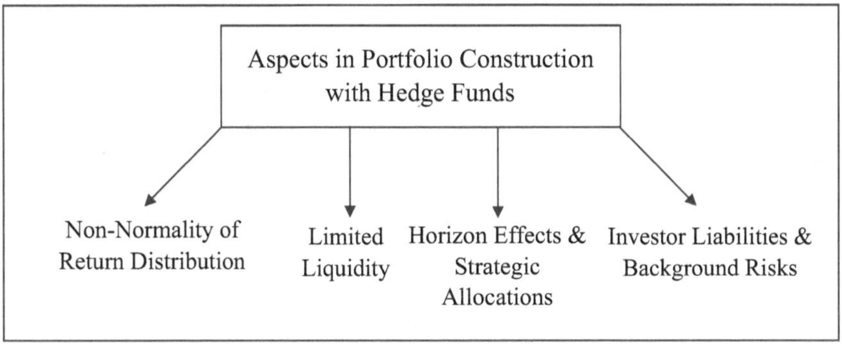

In particular, hedge funds expose investors to additional risks including pronounced skewness and kurtosis of their return distributions which is not reflected in standard mean-variance analysis. Therefore, it is not clear whether hedge funds and other alternative investments really add value to investors' portfolios and whether investors should make these high allocations to alternative investments. Therefore, academic researchers and practioners have developed new methods for portfolio construction that adjust asset allocations for these specific risks. Even though these models still imply substantial allocations to hedge funds, most large institutional investors such as pension funds and insurance companies actually hold only small allocations in hedge funds in their portfolios. This suggests that there are still some issues which have not been adequately addressed by academic research and which create uncertainty regarding the true benefits of hedge fund investments. In particular, as presented in Figure 9, hedge fund investments offer investors only limited liquidity. Moreover, optimal allocations usually depend on the investor's time horizon in that "intertemporal hedging" effects make the trade-off between risk and return conditional on the investment horizon. This can create significant differences in optimal myopic asset allocations and optimal strategic asset allocations for most asset classes. However, there is only limited research on the potential magnitude of "intertemporal hedging" benefits in hedge fund investments. Therefore, it is not clear whether hedge funds really add value to the portfolios of long-term investors. A final aspect of Figure 9, which has so far been neglected in empirical studies, is the structure of investors' liabilities and background risks which define the explicit and implicit risk exposures that an investor needs to incorporate into his portfolio decisions. In fact, depending on the sign and magnitude of potential interaction effects between these risk exposures and hedge fund returns, there might be substantial differences in investors' willingness to invest in hedge funds.

The objective of this chapter is to analyze those problems inherent in the asset allocation of hedge fund investments in more detail and to point out the most important issues that need to be addressed from an investor's perspective. Sections A and B begin with an overview of existing research on optimal asset allocation, including hedge funds. Section A presents a review of the design of asset allocation models and section B summarizes the empirical results of studies that use these models to optimize asset allocations. The next two sections highlight important gaps that still exist in the literature and try to draw some preliminary conclusions from related empirical research. Section C focuses on the value of hedge fund investments from the perspective of long-term investors and section D evaluates the implications of hedge funds for different types of investors.

A. Alternative Methods for Portfolio Construction

Most investors rely on asset allocation models that are based on the traditional mean-variance approach which appears to reasonably capture the risk-return profile of conventional asset classes such as stocks and bonds. However, this approach cannot completely capture the risk-return profile of hedge funds and other alternative investments because they often follow highly non-normal return distributions.

Therefore, investors might have to abandon simple mean-variance analysis and implement more complex asset allocation models. These models are presented in this section, which starts with a review of the traditional mean-variance framework. It then proceeds with the major approaches designed to incorporate investor preferences for higher order moments into the asset allocation process. These approaches will then be used in the next section to determine optimal allocations to hedge funds and other alternative investments and to assess their portfolio benefits.

I. Mean Variance Analysis

The mean variance approach was pioneered by Markowitz (1952) and was the first rigorous analytical model of portfolio choice. The model shows how portfolio efficiency is improved when different assets are combined in a portfolio. This model is based on the assumption that each asset is completely characterized by its expected return, variance and covariances with all other assets. Therefore, investors want to minimize portfolio variance for each given level of expected return. The optimization problem is given by (Markowitz, 1952):

$$\min_{w_t} w_t' \cdot \Sigma_{t+1} \cdot w_t = \sigma_{P,t}^2 \tag{20}$$

$$\text{subject to} \quad R_{P,t+1} = w_t' \cdot R_{i,t+1} \tag{21}$$

$$\imath' \cdot w_t = 1, \tag{22}$$

where w_t is a vector of portfolio weights, $R_{i,t+1}$ is a vector of expected asset returns, $R_{P,t+1}$ is the portfolio's expected return, Σ_{t+1} is the covariance-matrix of asset returns, $\sigma_{P,t}^2$ is the portfolio's variance and $\imath$ is a column vector of ones. This optimization problem states that each rational investor should choose those portfolio weights w_t that minimize the portfolio variance for a given level of expected return.[18] The solution to this problem is often represented graphically as the mean-variance efficient frontier (see Figure 10) that contains the set of all optimal portfolios in terms of expected return relative to risk measured in terms of variance or standard deviation.

[18] Adding a risk-free rate leads to Tobin's (1958) mutual fund theorem, i.e. all investors should hold the same two portfolios and differ only in the proportions invested in each asset which depends on their coefficient of risk aversion.

Figure 10: Mean-Variance Efficient Frontier

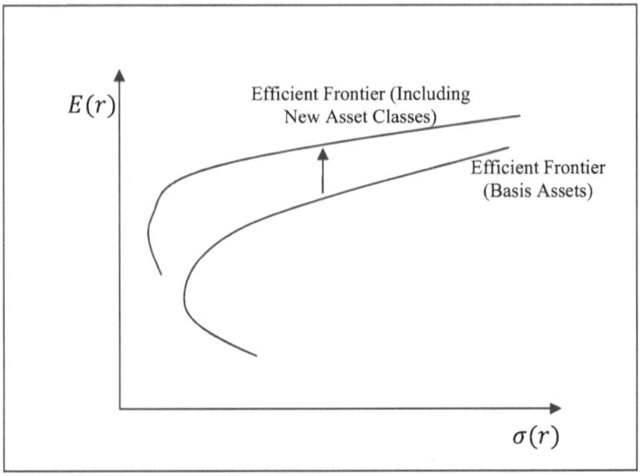

Figure 10 shows that the attractiveness of the available investment opportunity set depends on the level of the mean-variance frontier which, in turn, depends on the expected returns of available assets and their correlation structure. Investors can therefore improve the trade-off between risk and return of their portfolios if they find assets with positive abnormal returns or that have lower correlations with the other assets in the portfolio. Therefore, the mean-variance frontier can be shifted upwards by adding new asset classes which either offer true risk-less alpha or that contain exposures to new risk factors which are not spanned by the factor structure of the existing assets in the investor's portfolio (Grinblatt and Titmann, 1987). Thus, if the investment opportunity set is constrained to conventional asset classes, such as stocks and bonds, it is difficult to shift the efficient frontier upwards because the returns on any additional asset are likely to be spanned by the existing set of assets in the portfolio. This is due to the fact that most conventional assets are driven by the same set of fundamental macro-economic risk factors (Fama and French, 1993).

Mean-variance analysis can also be reconciled with standard micro-economic theory because the optimization problem in equations (20-22) is equivalent to an expected utility maximization problem based on a second-order Taylor expansion of the investor's utility function (Lengwiler, 2006). If this approximation reasonably captures investor preferences then the covariance between asset returns and consumption (end of period wealth) will be the only source of aggregate risk (Cochrane, 2005) and only the first two moments of portfolio returns affect portfolio choice. Therefore, mean-variance analysis is only an appropriate tool if asset returns are normally distributed, if investors have quadratic utility functions or if the investor has a very short investment horizon because it is only in these cases that a second-order Taylor expansion yields an accurate approximation. However, this generally implies that asset returns should be normally distributed because the assumption of quadratic utility implies increasing absolute risk aversion.

The mean-variance approach can also address other important issues in portfolio choice. In particular, most investors are subject to binding short-sale constraints which can be incorporated into mean-variance analysis by adding the following constraint:

$$w \geq 0, \tag{23}$$

into the optimization problem in (20-22). This leads to a less attractive efficient frontier since adding another constraint rules out the global optimum and forces the investor to settle on a corner solution for some levels of expected return (Kuhn-Tucker conditions). In particular, this constraint hurts investors that strive for high returns because it prevents them from levering their portfolios by shorting those assets with a low Sharpe ratio and investing the proceeds in assets with a higher Sharpe ratio (Elton and Gruber, 1995).

Moreover, in contrast to other asset allocation approaches, the mean-variance approach also enables investors to test whether measured portfolio benefits of additional assets are statistically significant and, therefore, whether hedge funds should be considered as a distinct asset class (Petrella, 2005) or whether they are due to random sampling errors. These issues can be differentiated with different spanning tests that check whether an observed shift in the efficient frontier is statistically significant. For instance, the spanning test by Huberman and Kandel (1987) tests if the returns on an additional asset are already included in the factor structure of the existing assets in the portfolio by running a simple linear regression:

$$r_{i,t} = \alpha + \beta_1 r_{1,t} + \cdots + \beta_K r_{K,t}. \tag{24}$$

Based on the results from this estimation Huberman and Kandel (1987) construct a test statistic that checks the following null hypothesis:

$$H_0: \alpha = 0 \vee \sum_{i=1}^{K} \beta_i - 1 = 0. \tag{25}$$

Thus, there is only little reliable evidence that adding another asset really provides additional portfolio benefits if the null hypothesis is rejected. Based on this idea a range of more complex spanning tests have been developed. These incorporate additional restrictions such as short-sale constraints and conditioning information (De Roon, Nijman, and Werker, 2001; Bekaert and Urias, 1996).

II. Higher-Moment Asset Allocation Models

The return distributions of many asset classes do not conform to a normal distribution and therefore are not completely described by the first two moments of their return distribution. Consequently, the mean-variance framework might lead to substantial errors in asset allocations because investors do not have quadratic utility functions and have preferences for specific higher order moments and co-moments.[19] This problem is particularly severe in the case of hedge funds and other alternative investments whose returns are characterized by substantial skewness and kurtosis. Thus, in order to address these problems, academic researchers and investment professionals have developed different asset allocation models that incorporate preferences for higher-order moments.

Many of these approaches are based on measures of downside risk. These take into account the fact that investors are averse to taking on the tail risks that come along with skewness and kurtosis. These risks are often present in the returns of hedge funds and other alternative investments.[20] For instance, the value-at-risk can be used as a measure of downside risk in the objective function to determine optimal portfolio weights (Alexander and Baptista, 2002):

$$max_w \frac{R_P - R_f}{VAR_P}. \tag{26}$$

This approach can incorporate the non-normality of asset returns into portfolio optimization if the value-at-risk is estimated with a method that captures tail risks of the return distribution. Suitable methods include estimation of percentiles from the empirical distribution, extreme value theory or the Cornish-Fisher expansion (Favre

[19] Samuelson (1967) extends the Markowitz approach to account for skewed and leptokurtic distributions for the special case of pareto-levy distributions.

[20] While the economic intuition of this approach appears to be rather simple, finding the mathematical solution to the resulting optimization problem is in most cases tedious as no closed-form solutions are available. Thus, sophisticated numerical algorithms are required. There are some problems with respect to multiple optima when optimizing with respect to higher moments. Moreover, there is the problem that an even larger number of parameters has to be estimated. For instance, while the covariance matrix in case of n assets is characterized by n*n elements, the 'co-skewness tensor' has n*n*n elements (Althayde and Flôres, 2004).

and Galeano, 2002). However, if the simple estimate of value-at-risk based on the assumption of a normal distribution is used, then this approach will be equivalent to the mean-variance approach (Alexander and Baptista, 2002) and will not adjust asset allocations for higher-order risk exposures.

Another measure of downside risk which can be used to incorporate higher order moments and co-moments into optimal asset allocations is the conditional value-at-risk (Yamai and Yoshiba, 2005). This leads to the following objective function:

$$max_w \frac{R_P - R_f}{CVAR_P} \tag{27}$$

$$\text{where } CVAR_P = -E[R_P | R_P \leq -VAR_P], \tag{28}$$

which determines optimal portfolio weights by maximizing the ratio between the portfolio's excess return and the conditional value-at-risk (Agarwal and Naik, 2004; Giamouridis and Vrontos, 2007). In contrast to the value-at-risk extended for higher-order moments this measure puts an even larger weight on tail risks in that it only focuses on the size of catastrophic losses in the left tail of the distribution.

A final measure of downside risk used to optimize portfolios with non-normally distributed assets is the shortfall variance (Füss, Rehkugler, and Disch, 2005):

$$max_w \frac{R_P - R_f}{LPM(\tau)_2} \tag{29}$$

This objective function is based on the lower partial moment of order n=2 as a measure of risk which also overweights the risk of large losses in the tail of the distribution relative to small losses.

In addition to downside risk measures, it is also possible to take into account investor preferences for higher order moments using the expected utility maximization framework (Morton, Popova, and Popova, 2006). In general, this approach is based on the solution of the following optimization problem:

$$\max E(U(c)) = \int f(c) \cdot U(c) dc, \tag{30}$$

where $f(c)$ is the density describing the distribution of future states of the economy and $U(c)$ is a utility function that specifies investor preferences for state-contingent payoffs (consumption). This framework can take into account preferences for higher order moments if an appropriate utility function is selected.

Moreover, some authors propose using "prospect theory"- preferences which put more weight on downside risk which is defined as returns below the investor's minimum required return ρ (Lengwiler, 2006; Barberis, Huang, and Santos, 2001):

$$v(s,r,z) = \begin{cases} s \cdot (R-\rho)\ if\ R > \rho \\ \lambda(z) \cdot s \cdot (R-\rho)\ if\ R < \rho \end{cases} \tag{31}$$

This specification of investor preferences not only emphasizes investor's aversion to tail risks, but also captures the loss aversion which is contained in the value function governing investor preferences in prospect theory.

The skewness and kurtosis of the return distribution can be incorporated into the expected utility framework using different approaches. More simply, the historical distribution can be used in a full-scale optimization approach which can create computational problems if a large number of asset classes is considered. Furthermore, a range of parametric approaches such as regime-switching models, jump-diffusion processes (Cvitannic, Polimenis, and Zapatero, 2007) or copula models can be used to capture higher moments and correlation risk in the distributions of asset returns (Guse, 2005).

Finally, polynomial goal programming also allows for incorporating investor preferences for higher order moments into asset allocation decisions. This approach is based on the observations of Kraus and Litzenberger (1976) and Scott and Horvath (1980) that investors prefer odd moments that tilt the return distribution towards positive outcomes and dislike even moments which increase the dispersion of returns therefore creating additional uncertainty (Althayde and Flôres, 2004; Davies, Kat, and Lu, 2005). Based on these assumptions polynomial goal programming specifies the following maximization problem in which the investor takes into account the mean, variance, skewness and kurtosis of asset returns in his portfolio selection problem (Hafner and Wallmeier, 2007):

$$max\ z = (1+d_{SR})^{\alpha} + (1+d_{SK})^{\beta} + (1+d_{KT})^{\gamma} \tag{32}$$

with $$d_{SR} = \frac{SR^{MAX}-SR}{SR^{MAX}} \tag{33}$$

$$d_{SK} = \frac{SK^{MAX}-SK}{SK^{MAX}} \tag{34}$$

$$d_{KT} = \frac{KT-KT^{MIN}}{KT^{MIN}}, \tag{35}$$

where d_{SR}, d_{SK} and d_{KT} denote the deviations between the portfolio's Sharpe ratio, skewness and kurtosis relative to the optimal levels that can be attained by optimizing for a global optimum level of each parameter separately. The parameter α, β and γ measure the investors' preferences for variance, skewness and kurtosis. However, there are substantial problems inherent in the empirical implementation of this approach. In particular, Hafner and Wallmeier (2007) document large jumps in asset weights if specific thresholds for preference parameters are crossed which seems to be intimately related to the nonlinear nature of the objective function.

B. Optimal Allocations to Hedge Funds and other Alternative Investments

The asset allocation models reviewed in the previous section enable investors to assess whether additional asset classes improve portfolio efficiency and lead to a better trade-off between risk and return. This is important because within the set of conventional asset classes, such as stocks and bonds, there are only limited opportunities for increasing portfolio efficiency. Therefore, many institutional and retail investors consider allocations to hedge funds and other alternative investments to improve their trade-off between risk and return. This subsection evaluates whether hedge funds really deliver these benefits in a portfolio context. It first presents the results of empirical studies which use the mean-variance approach and in general suggest very large allocations to alternative investments. Next empirical studies are presented that estimate optimal allocations to hedge funds and other alternative investments based on more complex asset allocation models that incorporate preferences for higher order moments. The following subsection reviews the results of comparable empirical studies for other alternative investments. The last subsection concludes with a discussion of these results, which compares the portfolio benefits of hedge funds and other alternative investments.

I. Optimal Allocations to Hedge Funds based on Mean-Variance Analysis

According to the mean-variance approach, hedge funds should lead to substantial improvements in portfolio efficiency because their returns contain alpha and are driven by new alternative risk factors (Fung and Hsieh, 1999b; Füss, Rehkugler, and Disch, 2005). This reasoning is supported by several studies that document upward shifts of the efficient frontier if hedge funds are added to diversified portfolios of stocks and bonds. In addition, optimal allocations to hedge funds are high in that all all studies prescribe high allocations of more than 20%, even though they are based on different benchmark allocations, different hedge fund proxies and different time periods (For an extensive overview see Signer 2003). Bessler, Drobetz, and Henn (2005) document a significant upward shift in the efficient frontier for the period from 1994 to 2004 if hedge funds approximated with the Dow Jones Credit Suisse index are added to a stock-bond portfolio. Moreover, they show that by increasing the size of the allocation to hedge funds the portfolio's expected return and the standard deviation increase, shifting the efficient frontier upwards. At the same time, however, this increase in the portfolio's Sharpe ratio comes with a higher non-normality of portfolio returns. Similarly, Bessler, Holler, and Kurmann (2010) also document better trade-offs between expected return and standard deviation for portfolios, including hedge funds, even when short-sale constraints are added to the investor's optimization problem. This result also supports the idea that hedge funds alleviate the impact of short-sale constraints and allow investors to implement more efficient portfolios. In addition, based on a Bayesian model to forecast expected alpha, they find that the size of the hedge fund allocation depends on the investor's expectation regarding the investment skills of the hedge fund manager.

In line with this evidence, Amenc and Martellini (2002) report that mean-variance efficient portfolios outperform in out-of-sample tests if hedge funds are included. In particular, their analysis focuses on the performance of the minimum-variance portfolio so that their results are not distorted by estimation errors in expected returns, which usually bias asset allocation decisions towards the asset class with the best past performance. In addition, Edwards and Caglayan (2001b) consider the contribution of individual hedge fund strategies to a portfolio that is diversified across a range of standard asset classes including stocks and bonds. They also indicate that the inclusion of hedge funds leads to substantial improvements in portfolio efficiency in terms of higher Sharpe ratios. However, the portfolio weights of some strategies exceed 90% of the total portfolio value in some time periods. This appears too high to be consistent with general equilibrium, in which there is only limited scope for hedge funds' active trading strategies. In addition, for such high allocations to hedge funds, the skewness and kurtosis of individual strategy returns will probably translate into significant skewness and kurtosis at the portfolio level even though this problem might be ameliorated by a focus on specific market environments, as in the study by Edwards and Caglayan (2001b). Finally, Conner (2003) emphasizes that mean-variance allocations need to be adjusted downwards if the hedge fund is characterized by illiquidity risk exposures because this leads to an overestimation of past returns and an underestimation of volatility and correlation.

These shifts in the efficient frontier appear to be statistically significant, such that hedge funds can be considered as an alternative asset class. For instance, Kooli (2006) implements spanning tests to infer whether hedge funds add value to a portfolio consisting of conventional asset classes such as stocks, government bonds, corporate bonds and commodities. Similar to existing evidence for other alternative asset classes, he shows that hedge funds are not spanned by the risk factors driving conventional asset classes and, therefore, lead to an improvement of the efficient frontier. However, this improvement seems to be primarily the result of an improvement of the position of the global minimum-variance portfolio and not an improvement of the position of the tangency portfolio. Thus, the value of hedge funds' portfolio benefits appears to be most significant at low levels of risk.

II. Optimal Allocations to Hedge Funds and Higher Order Moments

The returns of hedge funds are characterized by significant higher-order moment risks. Therefore, several empirical studies investigate whether investors should make large allocations to hedge funds after adjusting the optimal allocations for the pronounced skewness and kurtosis in hedge fund returns.[21]

The empirical evidence indicates that even after adjusting for higher-moment risks, investors should make substantial allocations to hedge funds. For instance, Favre and Galeano (2002) and Signer (2003) optimize allocations to hedge funds based on an extended value-at-risk which incorporates higher-order moments using the Cornish-Fisher expansion. In line with the common practice of many institutional investors, they set a maximum investment restriction for the allocation into hedge funds at 10% of total assets. All three studies find that investors will fully exploit this constraint and invest the maximum permissible amount of 10% into hedge funds. Nevertheless, comparing results based on the extended value-at-risk with a simple value-at-risk optimization suggests that the simple optimization might lead investors to overestimate the increase in portfolio efficiency. In particular, the results in Signer (2003) show that for some hedge fund strategies the increase in efficiency appears to be larger if a simple value-at-risk is used, rather than the adjusted value-at-risk. Thus, in line with

[21] There are also some papers who use these approaches to optimize funds of hedge fund portfolios. This includes Morton, Popova, and Popova (2006) and Agarwal and Naik (2004).

Fung and Hsieh (1999b) the simple mean-variance approach will not necessarily lead to wrong allocations but will lead to wrong assessments of portfolio risk.

Large allocations to hedge funds are also documented by Füss, Rehkugler, and Disch (2005) who determine optimal portfolio weights by maximizing the return to shortfall variance. They approximate a hedge fund investment with the returns of the Dow Jones Credit Suisse Hedge Fund index and find large portfolio weights in hedge funds that exceed 30% of total portfolio value. This is similar to their results for optimal weights based on a mean-variance optimization. However, they also show that optimal portfolio weights differ substantially between their approach and the mean-variance approach if they consider allocations to individual hedge fund strategies. This highlights that higher moment risk exposures of hedge funds can be largely eliminated if investors choose to invest in a portfolio consisting of a sufficient number of hedge funds from different style categories (L'habitant, 2006).

Studies based on the expected utility framework also suggest large allocations to hedge funds. They indicate that, in particular, more risk averse investors are likely to prefer higher allocations to hedge funds. For instance, Hood and Nofsinger (2007) find higher hedge fund allocations for more risk-averse investors if they use power utility and optimize allocations to hedge funds and other traditional asset classes. Similar results are reported by Chen, Feldman, and Goda (2002) using "prospect theory"-preferences. They also find higher allocations to hedge funds if risk and loss aversion are higher.

Studies using polynomial goal programming also indicate that allocations to hedge funds increase portfolio efficiency. For instance, Davies, Kat, and Lu (2005) use this model to optimize allocations to different asset classes including stocks and bonds as well as different hedge fund style indices. Overall, they find that optimal portfolios exhibit large weights in bonds and only small weights in stocks.[22] They explain this result by the fact that the co-skewness between bonds and hedge funds is higher whereas the co-kurtosis between bonds and hedge funds is lower.[23] Similarly, Proelss and Schweizer (2009) apply this approach to infer investor preferences for taking on hedge fund risk.

Overall, the results of these different studies suggest that hedge funds improve the risk-return trade-off of investors' portfolios even after taking higher order risk

[22] Actually, the weight is negative as they impose no short-sale constraints.
[23] This is consistent with results by Amin and Kat (2003b) and Davies, Kat, and Lu (2003).

exposures into account. However, depending on the research design which varies substantially in terms of assumptions regarding investor preferences for higher order moments, there are apparently significant differences in the optimal size of the allocation to hedge funds.

III. Comparison of Optimal Allocations with other Alternative Investments

Investors also have the opportunity to invest in a range of other alternative investments such as private equity, venture capital, real estate etc. This might lead to similar improvements in portfolio efficiency. Therefore, investors might prefer to invest in other alternative investments that often come with significantly lower transaction costs and fees. Consequently, in order to evaluate the attractiveness of hedge funds it seems necessary to compare their portfolio benefits with the portfolio benefits offered by other alternative investments.

Considering each alternative investment by itself it seems that they all substantially increase the efficiency of stock and bond portfolios. For instance, Winkelmann (2004) finds significant portfolio benefits for private equity allocations. Moreover, real estate also seems to be an interesting asset class because empirical evidence based on mean-variance analysis suggests that investors should allocate up to 50% of their capital to real estate investments if they initially hold only bonds and stocks in their portfolios (Craft, 2005). This finding applies to both public and private real estate investments. However, Chiang and Lee (2007) note that the results of spanning tests depend on the benchmark assets in the case of public real estate. In contrast, private real estate investments are never spanned by conventional risk factors in the tests by Chiang and Lee (2007). In addition, commodity investments also seem to boost portfolio efficiency. In particular, Scherer and Li (2008) note that commodity investments are not spanned by other asset classes indicating that they improve the risk-return trade-offs of portfolios in a mean-variance framework.

These results suggest that all alternative investments improve the efficiency of stock-bond portfolios and that investors should allocate part of their capital to real estate, commodities etc. However, most investors can choose between different types of alternative investments or decide to invest in multiple alternative asset classes at the same time. Therefore, empirical research has also analyzed the relationship between these alternative investments in a portfolio context. For example, Kooli (2006) implements spanning tests to infer whether hedge funds add value to a portfolio consisting of stocks, government bonds, corporate bonds and commodities. He finds that hedge funds are not spanned by the factors driving these other asset classes and, therefore, contribute to generating better risk-return trade-offs. Moreover, Hagelin, Pramborg, and Stenberg (2006) indicate that hedge funds lead to larger increases in portfolio efficiency than international diversification using the empirical distribution combined with log utility. Finally, Edwards and Caglayan (2001b) find that commodity investments appear to be superior investments to most hedge fund strategies because they offer better downside protection. These results indicate that it is necessary to further differentiate between different hedge fund styles.

However, most of these studies only compare two alternative asset classes at the same time. In fact, there seem to be only two academic studies (Bessler, Holler, and Kurmann, 2010; Schweizer 2008) that consider the asset allocation problem of an investor who is considering investing in multiple alternative asset classes. These results indicate that hedge funds still increase portfolio efficiency and will be presented in more detail later on in chapter IV.

IV. Summary and Conclusion

Mean-variance analysis and the asset allocation models incorporating higher-order moments generate optimal portfolios that are characterized by substantial allocations to hedge funds and other alternative investments. This suggests that investors should not quickly discard the more simple, but also more robust, mean-variance approach for a variety of reasons.

First, it seems that the objective function based by an asset allocation model does not have a material impact on optimized allocations. This is emphasized by the results of Levy and Levy (2004) and Fung and Hsieh (1999) who indicate that allocations based on mean-variance analysis are very robust to misspecifications of the portfolio return distribution and investor preferences.

Second, most investors do not directly invest in individual hedge funds, but consider investments in hedge fund portfolios such as funds of hedge funds and products based on hedge fund indices that are diversified across different trading strategies and different managers. The returns of these hedge fund portfolios are characterized by significantly smaller deviations from normality than single hedge fund returns. For instance, there is empirical evidence indicating that excess skewness and excess kurtosis decline with an increasing number of randomly drawn hedge funds (L'habitant and Learned, 2005). As a result, the differences between the values of the objective functions used by mean-variance analysis and more complex asset allocation models tend to be quite small. In fact, the distribution of mean-variance efficient portfolios including hedge funds only deviates significantly from a normal distribution for very high allocations to hedge funds. These are not consistent with general equilibrium due to the limited supply of trading opportunities for hedge funds (Bessler and Holler, 2009). Moreover, similar to other asset classes, the non-normality in the unconditional distribution of hedge fund returns also appears to be driven by time-variation in their conditional distribution. Thus, an investor with a one-period horizon who needs an estimate of conditional moments for the next period does not need to resort to more complex asset allocation models.

Third, estimation risks and tests for statistical significance are difficult to implement based on more complex higher-order moment asset allocation models. In particular, it is not clear whether differences in asset allocations derived from different models are really significantly different from each other. In the case of mean-variance analysis there is already substantial evidence that errors in the estimation of the first two moments and co-moments of asset returns can translate into substantial errors in portfolio weights.[24] This estimation risk is magnified if more complex asset allocation models are used which require investors to estimate a larger number of input parameters. In addition, estimation risk is substantially higher for higher-order moments because there are usually only a limited number of return observations in the tail of the distribution. This suggests that simple mean-variance analysis should lead to more robust results.

In conclusion, investors should not quickly discard the mean-variance approach so long as they only consider small investments in hedge fund portfolios because otherwise the additional problems that accompany more complex approaches are most likely to outweigh any benefits. However, even within the simple mean-variance approach there are still some important questions regarding the portfolio implications of hedge fund investments. In particular, there is no research on the implications of liquidity risk and related correlation risk in alternative investments. Therefore, only indirect conclusions based on research for other asset classes is available which helps

[24] There is a range of practical problems in implementing this approach such as generating forecasts of expected returns, the high sensitivity of portfolio weights to estimation errors, and the incorporation of investor expectations into the model.

to draw some conclusions for portfolio decisions involving hedge funds and other alternative investments (Das and Uppal, 2004). In general, this research suggests that correlation risks in the form of jumps in volatility or jumps in asset prices make it optimal for investors to behave as though a part of their portfolios is illiquid (Liu, Longstaff, and Pan, 2003). Thus, they should restrain their portfolio weights to the interval (0,1) to avoid the risk of being unable to trade quickly out of illiquid positions. This suggests that investors should only invest into asset classes subject to correlation risk if they can absorb liquidity risk exposures. [25] Thus, there are still a number of interesting research questions regarding the portfolio implications of hedge funds and other alternative investments.

However, one important issue is still not resolved. This concerns the precise size of the allocation to hedge funds which differs substantially between different models and different studies. This can be explained by the fact that there is still no consensus on the best asset allocation model and on the definition of the optimal hedge fund investment.

C. Strategic Asset Allocations for Long-Term Investors and Hedge Funds

Determining optimal allocations to hedge funds and other alternative investments becomes even more difficult when investors, such as pension funds or retail investors saving for retirement, want to allocate capital for long time periods covering multiple business cycles. In this case evidence from conventional asset classes, such as stocks and bonds, indicates that asset allocations can differ substantially from optimal allocations determined by mean-variance analysis or other models that are based on a one-period horizon and/or iid-returns. The difference in optimal portfolio weights can be explained by "intertemporal hedging"-effects that result from time-variation in expected asset returns, variances and covariances. These patterns have also been documented in the returns of hedge funds and other alternative investments so that long-term investors might have to take account of similar effects when they consider allocations to hedge funds and other alternative investments.

This issue is important because most investors have a fairly long investment horizon. Therefore, the objective of this section is to infer the implications for a portfolio's trade-off between risk and return in the long run. It begins with an analysis of the

[25] Thus, investors need to have deep pockets and ready access to other sources of liquidity for ongoing spending needs if they want to make substantial allocations to hedge funds.

economic drivers of "intertemporal hedging"-benefits. Based on these insights, this section investigates whether similar effects are observable in the dynamics of the conditional distribution of hedge funds and other alternative investments and discusses the implications for optimal long-run allocations in these alternative investments.

I. Strategic vs. Tactical Asset Allocation

The optimal asset allocation differs substantially depending on the investment horizon when asset returns are not independently and identically distributed over time, which can induce predictable components into asset returns (Samuelson, 1969). These predictable components create "intertemporal hedging"-benefits, such that optimal asset allocations for long-term investors consist of two components. The first component reflects "myopic" demand which is equivalent to the optimal allocation of short-term investors. The second component reflects "intertemporal hedging demand" (Campbell and Viceira, 2002) which increases the optimal allocation to an asset if:

$$Cov_t\left[r_{t+1}, -(E_{t+1} - E_t)\sum_j^{\infty} \rho^j \cdot r_{IO,t+j}\right] > 0 \tag{36}$$

According to equation (36), long-term investors will hold higher allocations in assets whose expected returns are going to be high when the value of their investment opportunity set has been declining over the previous period. This implies that an asset offers "intertemporal hedging"-benefits if its expected returns contain some predictable components. For instance, this is the case for stocks and bonds whose expected returns and risk premia exhibit a countercyclical behavior along the business cycle and are highest (lowest) at the bottom (top) of the business cycle (Fama and French, 1989; Ilmanen, 1995; Cochrane, 2005).[26] Therefore, intertemporal hedging demand for stock investments is positive supporting the argument that stocks are a good investment for long-term investors (Siegel, 1994).

In addition to this term structure of risk-return trade-offs (Campbell and Viceira, 2005), return predictability can also affect the correlation structure of assets over different time horizons if there are common factors in the return-generating process of different assets (Baur and Lucey, 2009; Krishnan, Petkova, and Ritchken, 2009).[27] This also has repercussions on optimal allocations for long-term investors. For

[26] These patterns can be driven by market frictions and inefficiencies (Ferson and Harvey, 1991).

[27] There is also some literature looking at stock-bond correlations at very short-term intervals using daily returns (e.g. Gebhardt, Hviskjaer, and Swaminathan, 2005).

instance, correlations between stocks and bonds appear to increase over longer periods as both are driven by similar macro-economic risks.

Finally, there is also time variation in volatility such as the well-documented ARCH- and GARCH-effects in asset returns which could also have implications on optimal asset allocations. However, these fluctuations in conditional volatilities appear to be rather short-lived and, therefore, only have a second-order effect on optimal long-run asset allocations (Campbell and Viceira, 2002). Overall, this brief discussion indicates that the optimal asset allocation for long-term investors depends on the investors' investment horizon due to time-variation in expected returns, volatilities and correlation.

II. Strategic Allocations of Hedge Funds

Hedge fund investments will generate "intertemporal hedging"-benefits if there is predictable time-variation in their expected returns, which can result from two sources. First, return predictability might result from time-variation in alpha of hedge fund investments.[28] For instance, the expected alpha of many hedge fund strategies seems to be related to past capital flows due to capacity effects (Naik, Ramadorai, and Stromqvist, 2007; Fung, Hsieh, Naik, and Ramadorai, 2008; Khandani and Lo, 2007). In addition, some hedge fund strategies find more trading opportunities in specific market environments making it easier to deliver alpha. This applies, for example, to relative-value strategies such as convertible arbitrage that perform better if markets are more volatile or if there is more issuing activity in primary markets. Based on this reasoning, Avramov, Barras, and Kosowski (2008) indeed identify predicable variation in hedge funds' alpha over time using lagged fund flows and market volatility as instruments in their predictive regressions. Similar results are reported by Amenc, El Bied, and Martellini (2003) who also use volatility as an instrument. Second, return predictability might also reflect time-variation in the factor risk premia earned by hedge funds. For instance, capacity effects might also reduce the level of risk premia earned by hedge funds' trading strategies subsequent to periods of high capital inflows. However, according to the results of Avramov, Barras, and Kosowski (2008) this channel has no impact on the predictability of hedge fund returns so that time-variation in hedge funds' expected returns is completely captured by time-variation in alpha.

[28] There is also evidence for time-varying alpha in mutual funds (e.g. Avramov and Wermers, 2006).

So far there is only one study that explicitly considers the impact of observed time-variation in expected returns on optimal long-term allocations to hedge funds. Specifically, Hoevenaars, Molenaar, Schotman, and Steenkamp (2008) estimate the implied covariance matrix between hedge funds and other asset classes for different investment horizons. Their results indicate that hedge funds appear to be good inflation hedges in the long run but are nevertheless highly correlated with stocks. However, the vector-autoregressive regression approach used to model expected returns is linear in the state-variables driving expected returns. Therefore, this framework cannot completely accommodate hedge fund returns which are often non-linearly related to other asset classes. Thus, there are many open research questions regarding the portfolio implications of hedge funds for long-term investors.

The lack of empirical research appears to be closely related to the limited amount of data, as the longest time-series of hedge fund data goes back only as far as 1992. Some authors have attempted to ameliorate this problem by reconstructing the hypothetical performance of some hedge fund strategies using asset-based style factors. For instance, Agarwal and Naik (2004) reconstructed the presumed performance of hedge funds back to 1927 using their exposure to different asset-based style factors, finding that hedge funds earned lower average returns and incurred higher risks than other asset classes over this long time period. However, this type of analysis cannot take into account the influence of the skills of hedge fund managers which can yield additional risk-adjusted returns and allows them to quickly change their factor exposures if market conditions change.

Investment opportunities in other alternative investments also exhibit a pronounced time-variation which suggests that they might provide investors with additional "intertemporal hedging"-benefits. For instance, there appears to be a cyclical relationship between capital inflows, the state of the economy and expected returns in venture capital and private equity markets which might also create these "intertemporal hedging"-effects from a portfolio perspective (Gompers, Kovner, Lerner, and Scharfstein, 2008). Moreover, expected returns on real estate investments are also predictable leading to horizon effects in optimal allocations to this alternative asset class. For instance, Li and Wang (1995) document similar patterns of return predictability in REIT returns as in the stock market. Moreover, Fugazza, Guidolin, and Nicodano (2007) provide evidence that the trade-off between risk and return on real estate investments improves for longer investment horizons. However, Clayton and MacKinnon (2001) show that the relationship of real estate returns to other asset classes underwent some significant changes. Similar to hedge funds, commodity investments appear to be uncorrelated with stocks and bonds in most market environments. However, these correlations appear to increase substantially in specific market environments (Kat and Oomen, 2006). And finally, similar time-variation in conditional moments is also observable in investments in emerging markets. For instance, Goetzmann, Li, and Rouwenhorst (2005) find that correlations of world equity markets are time-varying so that their diversification benefits fluctuate with the business cycle. In addition, their correlations seem to depend on the synchronicity of the business cycles of different countries as measured correlations are highest when both countries enter simultaneously into a recession (Erb, Harvey, and Viskanta, 1994).

Thus, other alternative investments that are less expensive and offer more liquidity also seem to offer intertemporal-hedging benefits. Therefore, it seems necessary to directly compare these alternative asset classes from a long-run perspective. This analysis is conducted by Hoevenaars, Molenaar, Schotman, and Steenkamp (2008) who conclude that commodities appear to be the best alternative investment because they are good inflation hedges in both the short and the long run. In addition, they are rather uncorrelated with the stock market. In contrast, other alternative asset classes, such as listed real estate, appear to yield no portfolio benefits since they are spanned by stock and bond returns in both the short and the long run.

Nevertheless, there are still many open questions regarding the value of hedge funds for long-term investors. This has become visible during the most recent financial crisis when long-term investors effectively suffered from their hedge fund investments as hedge funds had to fulfill redemption requests by their less patient and more loss averse investors (Financial Times April 9th, 2010).

III. Tactical Asset Allocation with Hedge Funds

Tactical asset allocation programs quickly reallocate their portfolios between different asset classes in order to exploit trading signals and predictable time-variation in their expected returns and risk. More simply, this is based on predictive regressions in which the expected returns of the different asset classes under consideration are regressed on a set of lagged state variables that model shifts in the investment opportunity set.

This approach might also be applicable to hedge funds because there is empirical evidence that there is also return predictability in hedge fund returns. For instance, Avramov, Kosowski, Naik, and Teo (2007) show that hedge fund returns can be predicted using lagged state variables including fund flows and volatility as well as conventional business cycle instruments. This return predictability can be exploited to implement successful tactical asset allocation programs. For instance, Amenc, El Bied, and Martellini (2003) document that tactical asset allocation increases returns of pure equity and pure debt portfolios if conventional macro factors and volatility are used to predict returns. Similarly, Avramov, Kosowski, Naik, and Teo (2008) document that this approach can also be used by funds of hedge fund managers to generate additional value by reallocating capital between different hedge fund strategies. However, the approach used in all of these papers only takes into account shifts in the mean of returns. Therefore, extending the regime-switching approach by Ang and Bekaert (2002) to tactial asset allocation involving hedge funds might lead to further improvements in portfolio efficiency.

Tactical asset allocation might also generate benefits if other alternative asset classes are considered. For instance, Brocato and Stead (1998) investigate optimal asset allocation in different market environments when the investor invests into several asset classes (but no hedge funds). They show that taking into account the state of economy leads to significant improvements in the realized risk-return trade-off because the correlations between most asset classes seem to increase during recessions. Similarly, Jensen and Mercer (2003) analyze the same asset allocation problem using the monetary cycle to generate trading signals. This allows them to conduct out-of-sample tests. They also find that tying asset allocation to the state of the economy leads to significant improvements in the realized risk return trade-off which are robust to sensible approximations of transaction costs.

Again, there are many open questions regarding the value of hedge funds as instruments for tactical asset allocation. In particular, due to lock-up restrictions it is nearly impossible to use direct hedge fund investments for tactical asset allocation programs even though the empirical evidence suggests that most time-variation in hedge fund returns is due to predictable time-variation in alpha. Therefore, it seems more plausible that investors should use passive hedge fund replication products in order to trade on time-variation of risk premia on alternative risk factors.

IV. Summary and Conclusion

There is reason to believe that optimal asset allocations in hedge funds also depend on the investment horizon of the investors due to "intertemporal hedging"-effects that can result from correlations between expected returns on hedge funds and changes in the value of the investor's investment opportunity set. In particular, these correlations might arise as a result of a cyclical relationship between hedge funds' alpha and hedge fund capital over longer time periods which have been identified by different empirical studies. However, so far the implications of these effects have not been thoroughly investigated from an asset management perspective. In fact, this is difficult to accomplish since hedge funds are a relatively young asset class creating two problems. First, the available time-series of data are relatively short which makes it difficult to estimate the models and forces researchers to resort to indirect approaches such as hedge fund replication. Second, the hedge fund industry is still in a constant state of change which makes it difficult to infer how the hedge funds and their investment properties will evolve over long time periods.

D. Hedge Fund Investments from the Perspective of Different Investor Types

This last section focuses on the question of which groups of investors will most likely benefit from hedge fund investments. This is an important issue because the ability to assume the tail risks, liquidity risks and correlation risks of hedge fund investments might differ among various groups of investors such as endowments, pension funds, life insurance companies and retail investors. This section first investigates the suitability of hedge fund investments for different types of institutional investors and then discusses their suitability for retail investors.

I. Suitability for different Types of Institutional Investors

There are significant differences between the portfolios of different types of institutional investors, such as insurance companies and endowments, regarding the share of their capital invested in hedge funds and other alternative investments. In fact, the portfolios of university endowments usually exhibit the largest allocations to hedge funds and other alternative investments which apparently helped them to generate an outperformance over longer time periods. More recently, however, the performance of these endowments has deteriorated during the recent financial crisis. While the prolonged periods of outperformance by endowments should have attracted other institutional investors, most pension funds and insurance companies still have only very small allocations in hedge funds and other alternative investments. Therefore, the question emerges, what factors are driving these substantial differences in asset allocations between endowments and other institutional investors? These differences might be related to asset-liability management considerations of different types of investors. These are already well researched for other types of risk, such as interest-rate risk (Bessler, 1989). However, so far hedge funds have not been investigated in more detail from the perspective of asset-liability management. Thus, this question is addressed in the following subsections.

1. Asset Allocations for Institutional Investors

Asset allocation for institutional investors differs from portfolio choice for other investors for several reasons. This includes asset-liability considerations and regulations and differences in investment skills which have substantial effects on portfolio holdings and investment strategies.

Most institutional investors cannot restrict their portfolio choice decisions to the investment characteristics of their asset portfolios. Instead they also have to take into account interactions between their asset portfolios with their explicit or implicit liabilities which reflect the value of the claims against them by their investors or policyholders. Since the value of these liabilities also fluctuates due to changes in interest and inflation rates and other parameters asset allocation models need to optimize portfolios with respect to the distribution of the returns on the investor's net worth which is given by (Elton and Gruber, 1992):

$$R_{Net\,Worth} = \frac{A}{A-L} \cdot (1 + R_A) - \frac{L}{A-L} \cdot (1 + R_L) - 1. \quad (37)$$

This distribution not only depends on the returns of their asset portfolio but it is also affected by the interaction between asset returns R_A and changes in the value of their liabilities R_L. Therefore, institutional investors should only make allocations to specific investments if the structure of their liabilities provides them with a superior ability to take on the underlying risks so that the associated risk premium overcompensates them for their risk exposure (Cochrane, 1999).

Hence, the factor structure of asset returns has important consequences and determines whether a given investor should invest in specific assets. In particular, the existence of multiple priced sources of risk in asset returns implies that investors should hedge against changes in the relative prices of several factors (Fama, 1996). Based on the assumption that asset returns are driven by m factors, this implies that the following constraint has to be added to the investor's optimization program defined by conventional mean-variance analysis (22-24):

$$\beta' \cdot w = \beta_P \tag{38}$$

β is an m x n matrix containing the exposures of all n assets to the m factors, w is the vector of portfolio weights and β_P is the vector containing the target exposures of the investor to the m factors. Adding this constraint implies that investors simultaneously choose their desired risk-return profile and their desired exposure to different sources of systematic risk which can differ substantially between different types of institutional investors. This occurs because there are pronounced differences between different institutional investors regarding their ability to hold exposures against specific sources of risk, which ultimately depends on the structure of their liabilities. As a result, optimal allocations in hedge funds and other alternative investments vary dramatically between different types of institutional investors even if they want to achieve the same trade-off between risk and return and have the same level of risk aversion.

In addition to determining the desired factor exposures the structure of the liabilities also determines whether institutional investors have to beat their minimum target returns in each individual period, or whether they have more discretionary freedom to shift payouts to their investors or policyholders over time. In particular, it can be shown that institutional investors whose portfolio value must at any cost exceed a minimum value in each period will have a preference for convex payoffs if they can accept more risk above the minimum level (Leland, 1980). As a result, there can be significant differences in the ability to assume the risks inherent in different asset classes between insurance companies, endowments and other alternative investments.

Asset-liability considerations asset allocation for institutional investors is also affected by two other factors. First, the investment policy of most institutional investors is constrained by government regulations that specify the set of permissible asset classes, and imposes position limits and minimum diversification requirements. Second, there are substantial differences regarding the level of sophistication between different institutional investors which affects their ability to screen out different investment opportunities, perform due diligence of asset managers and monitor their ongoing investment performance. The relevance of these aspects differs between various types of institutional investors. Therefore, the next two subsections investigate these issues in detail for endowments and pension funds, respectively.

2. University Endowment Funds

Endowments have been among the first institutional investors that made substantial allocations to alternative investments and hedge funds. For instance, Schoar, Wang, and Lerner (2007) report that that Ivy league universities were among the first investors to increase their allocations to alternative investments. This led to a significant outperformance of these funds compared to other institutional investors for a long time. But this also imposed some significant losses on these funds during the recent financial crisis.

Endowments might have been able to achieve this outperformance with alternative investments because they have comparative advantages in assuming their specific risks (Cochrane, 1999). In particular, the major objective of every endowment is to provide a perpetual stream of real income to fund the stated purpose of its sponsor. Its asset allocation therefore needs to preserve its real wealth in the long run and at the same time generate sufficient income to cover current spending needs (Merton, 1993). Endowments generally strive to achieve this objective based on an absolute return target. Thus, hedge funds and other alternative investments following a total return approach seem to be a natural match for endowments. In addition, the timing and amounts of their spending needs are not absolutely fixed so that they tend to have limited short-term liquidity needs and can have a long-term perspective for their investments. As a result, they can tolerate medium term deviations from their target returns and volatility as long as accumulated profits over longer time periods are sufficient to cover inflation and spending needs. Therefore, they have comparative advantages in assuming the tail risks and liquidity risks inherent in illiquid alternative investments and hedge funds (Brown, Garlappi, and Tiu, 2007).

However, the ability to take on the risks of alternative investments differs substantially between individual endowment funds due to differences in their background risks which affect the level and volatility of the spending needs that have to be financed from their asset portfolios. Dimmock (2010) documents that endowments with a higher volatility of non-financial income prefer to construct less risky and more liquid asset portfolios.

Besides comparative advantages in taking on the risk of alternative investments their superior performance might also reflect the superior investment skills of their managers. This argument is supported by the finding that there is a huge variability between different universities. In particular, only the endowments of specific U.S. universities delivered a persistent outperformance over long time periods (Lerner, Schoar, and Wang, 2007; Lerner, Schoar, and Wongsunsai, 2007). In line with this argument there is also considerable cross-sectional variation in the performance of U.S. endowments. Regarding their private equity allocations this also appears to be related to differences in their investment skills (Lerner, Schoar, and Wongsunsai, 2007). Overall, it seems fair to conclude that hedge funds are attractive investments from the perspective of endowment funds who have already allocated large amounts of capital to this new asset class.

3. Pension Funds and Life Insurance Companies

In contrast to endowments, the majority of pension funds and insurance companies only hesitantly started to make larger allocations to hedge funds and other alternative investments. For instance, Dobler, Häring, Kolberg, and Müller (2002) report that only one third of German insurance companies are invested in hedge funds.[29] As a result of these differences in asset allocations, pension funds and life insurance companies were not able to match the stellar outperformance delivered by several U.S. university endowments. Thus, the question emerges why did they not attempt to duplicate the asset allocations of these endowment funds in order to achieve a similar investment performance?

At first glance, this might be related to differences in the structure of their liabilities which reflect the value of their policyholder's claims on future pension payments (Elton and Gruber, 1992).[30] In contrast to the implicit liabilities of endowments, these obligations are fixed so that pension funds have very limited opportunities to defer payments or shift them over time. To ensure that they are able to honor their future liabilities they pursue the objective of maximizing the risk-adjusted return on their surplus or net worth (Chun, Ciochetti, and Shilling, 2000; Elton and Gruber, 1992)

[29] However, Eling (2006) also reports that insurance companies generally had low weights in risky assets between 1994 and 2003. This can be interpreted as evidence that German insurance companies are generally highly risk averse.

[30] This analysis is based on the assumption that the pension fund is operating as a defined benefit plan. In the case of defined contribution plans, which transfer all risks to end investors, the analysis in the preceding section on retail investors applies.

which helps corporate sponsors of pension funds maximize firm value (Jin, Merton, and Bodie, 2006) and enables life insurance companies to offer more attractive conditions to their clients. Their objective function can therefore be approximated as:

$$U = E(SR) - \frac{1}{2} \cdot \frac{\sigma(SR)^2}{\lambda} \text{ with } SR = \sum_{i=1}^{n} R_i \cdot x_i - R_L \cdot x_L, \quad (39)$$

where λ is a coefficient of risk aversion, R_i is the expected return on asset i, R_L is the required return on their liabilities and x_i and x_L are the respective weights (Chun, Ciochetti, and Shilling, 2000).

Optimal asset allocations based on (41) differ substantially from optimal asset-only portfolios and can be broken down into two components (Elton and Gruber, 1992; Plantinga and van der Meer, 1999). The first component is designed to hedge the institutional investor against the risks inherent in his liabilities and is therefore composed of assets that have a high correlation with the value of liabilities and replicate their factor structure. In the case of pension funds and life insurance companies it implies that this component is composed of assets whose value is driven by the dynamics of interest rates and inflation rates which are the predominant drivers of future pension payments. Thus, these institutional investors will usually make substantial allocations to bonds which are the risk-less assets for them as long as the bonds' duration corresponds to the duration of their liabilities (Leibowitz and Henriksson, 1988). In addition, they often use allocations to stocks to hedge their inflation risk exposure which results from future increases in wages for their policyholders (Bookstaber and Gold, 1988).

If this hedging component makes up the largest fraction of their portfolios, then this might explain the limited demand for hedge funds and other alternative investments by these institutional investors. For instance, Hoevenaars, Molenaar, Schotman, and Sternkamp (2008) show that even though hedge funds appear to be good inflation hedges in the long run, their correlations with stocks are high for longer investment horizons reducing the potential portfolio benefits. Consequently, their results indicate that commodities appear to be the most attractive asset class for these institutional investors. Thus, hedge funds do not appear to be the most attractive asset class to hedge their liabilities. However, they might still be a more attractive investment opportunity than real estate. For instance, Craft (2005) finds evidence for a reduction in optimal real estate allocation from close to 50% to 6-13% because real estate is not highly correlated with pension liabilities.

The second component is the surplus portfolio which reflects the difference between the current values of assets and liabilities (Elton and Gruber, 1992). Many pension funds and life insurance companies segregate the assets dedicated to this surplus portfolio from the liability-matching portfolio and manage them with the objective of generating additional portfolio returns. For this surplus portfolio, hedge funds and other alternative investments might be an interesting investment.

It seems that differences in liability structures can explain a substantial part of the smaller allocations to hedge funds and other alternative investments by insurance companies and pension funds as compared to endowments. In addition, their opportunities for making large allocations to new asset classes are constrained by two additional factors. First, the investment policies of pension funds and life insurance companies are governed by stringent regulatory restrictions. Eling (2006) analyzes the implications of these restrictions on optimal portfolio choice for insurance companies and finds that hedge funds still push up the efficient frontier so that insurance companies should increase their allocations to hedge funds. However, his analysis is based on a simple mean-variance setting that does not incorporate the interest- and inflation risks inherent in the liabilities of insurance companies. Thus, further analysis is needed in order to confirm this initial result. Second, limited allocations to alternative investments might also reflect lower investment skills of the managers of pension funds and insurance companies compared to managers of endowments. In particular, investment skills appear to be highly relevant when making allocations to alternative investments due to high information asymmetries regarding managers' skills. This requires specialized knowledge for due diligence. Moreover, risk management for hedge funds and other alternative investments is more complicated than for conventional asset classes (Kassberger and Kiesel, 2007).

Based on the existing evidence it seems that hedge funds are only a suitable investment for the surplus portfolios of pension funds and life insurance companies. It might also be possible to use hedge funds for investments in their liability-matching portfolios which are significantly larger. However, current research has not generated sufficient insights into their long-term risk-return profile and their ability to hedge the liabilities of these institutional investors in the long-term. Given this uncertainty regarding important properties of hedge fund investments, the cautious adoption of hedge fund investments by this group of institutional investors appears to be rational. This approach is further supported by the fact that most investors have to rely on investments in funds of hedge funds because they do not have the necessary skills to select and monitor hedge fund managers, creating an additional layer of fees.

II. Suitability for Retail Investors

Retail investors cannot invest directly into hedge funds due to strict regulations in most countries. Instead they have to rely on funds of hedge funds or hedge fund certificates in order to invest into this new asset class. According to U.S. regulations only high net worth individuals are allowed to invest directly into single hedge funds. These restrictions are commonly justified with the argument that private investors lack the necessary knowledge to evaluate hedge fund investments and cannot bear the risks. However, since hedge funds can provide investors with substantial portfolio benefits it is interesting to review these arguments.

There are indeed some economic reasons which indicate that most retail investors have only limited abilities to assume the tail risks and liquidity risks of hedge funds and other alternative investments. First of all, asset allocation for retail investors needs to take into account that the present value of future labor income is a substantial component of total wealth. Therefore, retail investors should only make substantial allocations to risky assets such as hedge funds and other alternative investments if their future labor income is rather constant over time and, therefore, can be interpreted as a substitute for bond allocations (Bodie, Merton, and Samuelson, 1992). However, this will only apply to a very limited number of retail investors, including tenured university professors and civil servants. For most other retail investors future labor income is risky which diminishes their ability to take on the risks inherent in hedge fund investments. For instance, Cocco, Gomes, and Maenhout (2005) show that even the small risk of a disastrous labor income shock should make investors adopt safer investment policies. Finally, these effects on the optimal asset allocation of an investor also depend on his stage in the lifecycle (Koijen, Nijman, and Werker, 2010).

In addition to the preference for less risky assets in general there are also arguments that only concern hedge fund investments. First, most retail investors have already tied up a significant fraction of their net worth in their non-tradable labor income and real estate. Thus, they have limited ability to absorb the liquidity risks which are imposed on them by hedge funds' lock-up constraints. Second, investing in hedge funds requires substantial investment skills because hedge funds pursue sophisticated trading strategies and offer only limited information on their investment style to their own investors. Risk management for hedge fund investments is also more complicated than for most conventional asset classes. Thus, as most retail investors typically lack the necessary skills, they should not invest in hedge funds.

All in all, it seems appropriate to impose restrictions on direct investments into hedge funds and permit only high net worth individuals, who have the ability to assume the tail risks and liquidity risks, to invest directly into single hedge funds (Cochrane, 1999). However, the arguments that retail investors lack the necessary investments skills and cannot assume the associated risks also apply to many other financial products.

E. Conclusion

Overall, hedge funds appear to be an interesting new asset class because they provide investors with portfolio benefits in the form of positive risk-adjusted returns, exposures to alternative risk premia and generate positive diversification effects. At the same time, however, they expose investors to additional risks including pronounced higher-moments in their return distributions which are related to tail risks, liquidity risks and correlation risks. Therefore, the crucial question has emerged of how this trade-off between portfolio benefits and additional risks should be handled, and which approach should be used to incorporate hedge funds into investors' portfolios. So far, the current research in this area is not satisfactory and still leaves several important research questions. First, what is the optimal size of the allocation to hedge funds? Regarding this question, the existing research can only be interpreted as evidence that investors should make a meaningful alloction to hedge funds. However, the precise magnitude recommended by different studies varies considerably. Second, what are the portfolio implications for long-term investors? Existing research is almost exclusively focused on single period models and does not address this issue which is important for the majority of institutional and retail investors. Third, which group of investors is likely to achieve the highest gains by investing in hedge funds? Again, existing research neglects this important aspect of portfolio choice and implicitly assumes that endowments, insurance companies, pension funds and retail investors are one homogenous group. Thus, it neglects differences in their characteristics such as their explicit and implicit liabilities, regulations and their levels of sophistication which could affect their ability to assume the risks inherent in hedge fund investments. Given the lack of answers to these questions it is not surprising that many institutional and retail investors still adopt a cautious approach to hedge fund investments.

Chapter IV. Hedge Funds in Different Financial Market Environments

Hedge funds can generate attractive portfolio benefits for investors. In particular, the analysis in the preceding two chapters has shown that hedge funds offer investors access to alpha, i.e. positive risk-adjusted returns and exposures to alternative risk factors. These are not correlated with the macro-economic risk factors driving the returns of conventional asset classes. Therefore, hedge funds can often help investors to create more efficient portfolios. This is reflected in upward shifts in the efficient frontier which have been documented in several empirical studies.

However, existing empirical research neglects some important issues. First of all, investors might also be able to achieve similar portfolio benefits using other alternative asset classes such as private equity, real estate and commodities. For instance, U.S. university endowments achieved a significant outperformance over traditional asset classes by making large allocations to hedge funds as well as other alternative asset classes (Bessler and Drobetz, 2008; Lerner, Schoar, and Wang, 2008). Second, during the recent financial crisis, the investment performance of hedge funds has deteriorated substantially as they suffered significant losses in their portfolios. Moreover, recent studies indicate that diversification benefits of hedge funds have declined over the last ten years due to a slow but persistent upward trend in the co-movement of hedge fund returns with conventional asset classes (Bessler and Holler, 2009). This indicates that there is also time variation in hedge funds' expected returns, volatilities and correlations. Hence, the proportion of investor's wealth allocated to hedge funds should also depend on the current state of the economy, reflecting time-varying investment opportunities. These important issues have already been thoroughly investigated for conventional asset classes such as stocks and bonds (Campbell and Viceira, 2002)[31] However, even though these effects might have important implications for investors' portfolios, this issue has not been directly addressed by existing empirical research.

To investigate the potential for hedge funds to create more efficient asset allocations this chapter addresses the following issues. First, it analyzes optimal asset allocation decisions when investors take into account time-variation in investment opportunities by constructing optimal portfolios, including traditional and alternative asset classes in

[31] Moreover, similar to stock and bond investments, this indicates that the well-documented non-normality in the unconditional distribution of hedge fund returns might be driven by time-variation in their conditional moments. The problem of non-normal returns is actually similar in magnitude than in conventional asset classes which also exhibit significant skewness and kurtosis in their unconditional return distribution.

different financial market environments. A major insight is that the portfolio benefits of hedge fund investments crucially depend on the market environment because their risk-return trade-off and their correlation with other asset classes exhibit substantial time-variation. This result has important implications for investors because hedge funds have lock-up periods of up to two years, which might prevent investors from capitalizing on these shifts in investment opportunities. Second, it considers the importance of investors' expectations regarding the ability of hedge funds to provide positive risk-adjusted returns (alpha) by implementing a Bayesian asset allocation framework. To estimate a hedge funds' alpha a multiple regression benchmark is employed. This benchmark includes traditional and alternative asset classes such as stocks, bonds, real estate and commodities. In line with previous research that uses similar Bayesian approaches for the time period before the recent financial crisis (Cvitanic, Lazrak, Martellini, and Zapatero, 2003; Bessler and Holler, 2009) it provides evidence that the mean-variance optimal allocation to hedge funds increases for more optimistic investors. In fact, these investors replace equity investments with hedge funds and take advantage of the higher Sharpe ratios that accompany a similar level of correlation with bond investments.[32] Finally, the broad set of traditional and alternative asset classes allows determining whether statistically similar mean-variance efficient frontiers can be achieved with other asset classes. These often impose lower fees and smaller liquidity restrictions on investors and are more transparent. This particular question is addressed by conducting mean-variance spanning tests as proposed by Huberman and Kandel (1987) and Kan and Zhou (2008). Their empirical evidence suggests that hedge funds contribute to a statistically significant improvement of the efficient frontier primarily during times of rising stock markets.

The chapter proceeds as follows. The empirical methodology including the Bayesian approach to asset allocation and mean-variance spanning tests is discussed in Section A. Section B presents the data sample and an overview of competing alternative asset classes. Sections C and D contain the empirical evidence of the portfolio benefits of hedge funds from the perspective of a mean-variance optimizing investor. Finally, Section E concludes with a discussion of the major results.

[32] Effectively, these significant shifts of asset allocations into hedge fund investments entails two related bets. First, these reallocations are based on the belief that hedge funds will continue to outperform other asset classes. Therefore, investors make a bet on the premia of the alternative risk factors driving the systematic component in hedge fund returns. Second, they bet on the ability of hedge fund managers to deliver additional alpha (Lo, 2009; Eling, 2009).

A. Methodology

I. Bayesian Asset Allocation Framework

One objective of this empirical analysis is to model the impact of return expectations on optimal asset allocations. For this purpose, an asset allocation framework is required which allows incorporating information on investors' prior beliefs into portfolio construction (Baks, Metrick, and Wachter, 2001; Pástor, 2000; Pástor and Stambaugh, 2000). Therefore, an approach closely related to Cvitannic, Lazrak, Martellini, and Zapatero (2003) is implemented in the empirical analysis. In particular, a Bayesian asset allocation framework is employed that is based on Bayes' rule:

$$p(\theta \mid y) = \frac{p(y \mid \theta) \times p(\theta)}{p(y)}, \tag{40}$$

where $p(y \mid \theta)$ is the likelihood function which corresponds to the information set used in frequentist econometrics, $p(y)$ is the unconditional distribution of the dependent variable and $p(\theta)$ is the prior probability containing all prior information on the distribution of the unknown parameters. By merging investor's prior expectations of hedge funds' ability to deliver an outperformance with the empirical evidence contained in the likelihood function Bayesian statistics allows one to calculate the posterior probability of generating an outperformance.

This approach is applied to an investor's asset allocation problem by specifying a Bayesian regression framework with informative prior beliefs on alpha. More precisely, it is assumed that hedge fund returns r_{it} are linearly related to a set of benchmark asset returns F_t:

$$r_{it} = \alpha_i + \beta_i \cdot F_t + \varepsilon_{it}, \tag{41}$$

where β_i denotes the factor loadings and ε_{it} is the white-noise error term. The term α_i measures alpha, i.e. hedge fund's outperformance over the set of benchmark assets. Thus, in contrast to Cvitannic, Lazrak, Martellini, and Zapatero (2003) the approach allows one to consider multiple benchmark assets at the same time. To capture the degree of investor's confidence in the ability of hedge funds to deliver alpha, an informative prior on α_i is chosen:

$$\alpha \mid \Sigma \sim No\left(0, \sigma_\alpha^2 \cdot \frac{1}{s^2} \Sigma\right), \tag{42}$$

where s^2 is the sampling variance, Σ is the variance-covariance matrix of the residuals and σ_{α}^2 is the prior variance which reflects the investor's confidence in hedge funds' alpha. It is important to note that it is assumed that investors have no prior knowledge on factor loadings by setting their priors equal to the respective OLS estimates. Applying Bayes' theorem to combine the likelihood function and the prior density yields the posterior density which can then be used to estimate expected returns conditional on investor's beliefs in alpha:

$$\tilde{r}_{HF,t} = \tilde{\alpha} + \beta_1 \cdot \tilde{r}_{1,t} + \ldots + \beta_n \cdot \tilde{r}_{n,t}. \tag{43}$$

These expectations on asset returns $\tilde{r}$ combined with the historical variance-covariance matrix can then be used to obtain optimal portfolio weights for a mean-variance optimizing investor by solving the following optimization problem:

$$\min_{w_t} w_t' \cdot \Sigma_{t+1} \cdot w_t = \sigma_{P,t}^2, \tag{44}$$

$$\text{subject to} \quad R_{P,t+1} = w_t' \cdot R_{i,t+1}, \tag{45}$$

$$\imath' \cdot w_t = 1, \tag{46}$$

$$w_t \geq 0, \tag{47}$$

where w_t is a vector of portfolio weights for time period t, $\sigma_{P,t}^2$ is the portfolio variance, Σ_{t+1} is the expected covariance matrix which is approximated by the historical variances and covariances of asset returns, $R_{i,t+1}$ is a vector of expected returns for all assets, $R_{P,t+1}$ is the portfolio's expected return, and $\imath$ is a vector of ones.

II. Mean-Variance Spanning Tests

Finally, we conduct statistical tests for whether the improvement in portfolio efficiency is statistically significant. Huberman and Kandel (1987) were the first to propose a simple regression-based test for mean-variance spanning. Let $[R_{Kt}', R_{Nt}']'$ denote the vectors of returns on risky assets where subscript K (N) denotes the returns on the benchmark assets (test assets). They suggest projecting R_{Nt} on R_{Kt} in the form of a simple linear regression:

$$R_{Nt} = \alpha + \beta R_{Kt} + \varepsilon_t, \tag{48}$$

with $E(\varepsilon_t) = 0_N$ and $E(\varepsilon_t R'_{Kt}) = O_{NxK}$, where 0_N is an N-vector of zeros and O_{NxK} is an N x K matrix of zeros. Under the null hypothesis "no spanning", the conditions $\alpha = 0$ and $\delta = 1_N - \beta 1_K = 0$ hold, where 1_N is an N-vector of ones and 1_K is an K-vector of ones. Kan and Zhou (2008) show that the first condition is a test of whether the tangency portfolio has zero weights in the test assets and that the second condition is a test of whether the global minimum-variance portfolio has zero weights in the test assets. To analyze this combined null hypothesis, Huberman and Kandel (1987) employ a likelihood ratio test statistic that follows a chi-square distribution with $2n$ degrees of freedom where n represents the number of test assets.[33]

Kan and Zhou (2008) point out that this simple spanning test places relatively more weight on the distance between the standard deviations of the two global minimum-variance portfolios. Hence, the difference in the respective tangency portfolios is less important even though it might have a higher economic relevance for mean-variance optimizing investors. Therefore, Kan and Zhou (2008) suggest a step-down procedure by first testing $\alpha = 0$ and then testing $\delta = 0$ conditional on the constraint $\alpha = 0$. Under this procedure the hypothesis of mean-variance spanning is rejected if both tests are rejected at conventional significance levels.[34] If the rejection is driven by the first test, it can be infered that this is due to the fact that the two tangency portfolios are statistically different. If the rejection is related to the second test, this is because the two global minimum variance portfolios are statistically different.

B. Data

I. Asset Classes

The empirical analysis covers the time period from December 1993 to July 2010. This corresponds to 200 monthly observations. The asset classes considered for portfolio construction are developed market equities, emerging market equities, government and corporate bonds, real estate, commodities, and hedge funds. All asset classes are represented by indices that ensure sufficient transparency and liquidity. Hedge fund investments are approximated by the Dow Jones Credit Suisse aggregate hedge fund index, which is a value-weighted average across a large number of individual hedge

[33] The hypothesis of spanning can also be tested by a Wald or LM test, respectively. Since these test statistics yield identical results to the likelihood ratio test, they are not reported.

[34] The first test statistic follows an F-distribution with N and T-K-N degrees of freedom while the second test statistic follows an F-distribution with N and T-K-N+1 degrees of freedom.

funds reflecting the composition of total assets under management in the hedge fund industry. This allows one to analyze the interaction of a diversified hedge fund investment with other asset classes in a portfolio context.

For developed and emerging stock markets we use the S&P 500 total return and the MSCI Emerging Markets total return indices, respectively. Bond market investments are represented by the performance of a total return index replicating an investment in constant 10-year maturity U.S. government bonds. The performance of corporate bonds is proxied by the Bank of America/Merril Lynch U.S. BBB-A total return index. To compare the investment performance of hedge funds to other alternative asset classes the S&P GSCI total return index is used to reflect the returns on a diversified portfolio of commodities, the FTSE/NAREIT total return index is used to represent real estate investments and the S&P GSCI Gold Spot Index measures the returns of an investment in gold. All relevant data is denominated in U.S. Dollars and is provided by Thomson Reuters Datastream.

With commodities, real estate, and emerging market equities a broad set of competing alternative asset classes is considered that might provide similar portfolio benefits to investments in hedge funds. Diversified commodity investments provide investors with exposures to developments in a wide range of commodity markets. Their returns can be broken down further into different components (Gorton and Rouwenhorst, 2006).[35] Their spot returns reflects changes in commodity prices which are often closely related to the returns of other asset classes. Most importantly, the spot return on commodity investments seem to be positively correlated with future inflation so that commodities may be used to hedge inflation risks in investor portfolios (Gorton and Rouwenhorst, 2006).[36] Commodity investments can also generate roll returns when they are constructed based on commodity futures contracts. These roll returns reflect the term structure of commodity prices and are generated when positions in expiring futures are rolled over into the next contract. From a portfolio perspective, commodity investments seem to substantially enhance the performance of traditional stock-bond portfolios (Jensen, Johnson, and Mercer, 2002).[37] Moreover, Cheung and

[35] Moreover, depending on the construction of the underlying commodity index, there often emerge diversification returns that result from a rebalancing of the underlying index (Fama and Booth, 1992).

[36] Commodities can act as an inflation and equity hedge because corporate profits are driven by relative prices. While output prices are rather sticky, input prices (e.g. commodity prices) are rather volatile. The resulting earnings volatility leads to volatile equity prices (Froot, 1995).

[37] By considering a broad set of traditional and alternative asset classes, Hoevenaars, Molenaar, Schotman, and Steenkamp (2008) provide further evidence for commodities' attractiveness from an inflation hedging perspective.

Miu (2010) provide evidence that commodity futures investments exhibit infrequent but impressive periods of significant outperformance. However, their results also indicate that commodities offer only regime-dependent diversification benefits.

Real estate as an alternative asset class provides investors with several portfolio benefits. First, it can be considered as an effective inflation hedge because the value and rents of real estate holdings increase in line with inflation. Second, real estate investments are often relatively illiquid allowing, in particular, long-term investors to capture the resulting liquidity risk premia (Amihud and Mendelson, 1986). Third, early research indicates that real estate seems to be driven by distinct risk factors (Ibbotson and Siegel, 1984). This suggests that returns on real estate investments are not completely spanned by the set of macro-economic risk factors pricing stocks and bonds (Chiang and Lee, 2007). Considering the potential role of real estate for constructing optimal portfolios, empirical research by Craft (2005) suggests that mean-variance optimizing investors should allocate up to 50 percent of their portfolio holdings in real estate.

Emerging market equity investments are also often considered as an alternative asset class. They usually have high expected returns which appear to be related to additional risk factors such as liquidity risk as well as political and institutional instability (Iqbal, Brooks, and Galagedera, 2010).[38] Emerging market equities exhibit relatively low correlations with conventional asset classes which reflect the segmentation of these markets from international equity markets. However, their co-movements experience strong time-varying patterns and increase substantially during periods of market distress (Erb, Harvey, and Viskanta, 1994; Longin and Solnik, 1995, 2001; Ang and Bekaert, 2002). From a portfolio perspective, Chiou, Lee, and Chang (2009) demonstrate that emerging market equities allow investors to improve their portfolios' risk-adjusted returns. Moreover, they emphasize the importance of particular investment constraints, such as short-selling restrictions, when taking into account the feasibility of emerging market equity investments.

[38] In addition, a number of authors note that emerging markets are only partially integrated with world capital markets (De Jong and De Roon, 2005; Bekaert and Harvey, 1995), thereby offering international investors valuable diversification benefits.

II. Definition of Different Market Environments

To assess the portfolio benefits of hedge funds and other alternative investments in different market environments, the total time period between 1993 and 2010 is separated into four sub-periods. These periods are delineated by the performance of stock markets approximated by the S&P 500 index and follow the peaks and troughs faced by a typical buy-and-hold stock market investor (Figure 11). This approach is adopted for several reasons. First, stock prices incorporate expectations on future business prospects so that this approach utilizes this valuable information inherent in stock prices. Second, analysts and investment advisors in general undertake substantial research efforts on the performance of stock markets. Thus, their investment recommendations and portfolio allocation decisions are highly dependent on stock market performance and expectations, respectively, underlining the practical perspective of this approach. Third, the stock market and its distinct cyclical movements provide an ideal setting for studying the diversification benefits of hedge funds in the context of traditional, as well as alternative asset classes, over time.

The approach used in this study differs from the cut-offs implemented by similar studies. For instance, Brocato and Steed (1998) use NBER turning points to delineate sub-periods. However, these turning points are only available ex-post and the time lags until the required information becomes public differ between individual business cycles. Jensen and Mercer (2003) use the monetary cycle defined as the first change in short-term interest rate by the central bank that runs counter to the previous trend. However, by relying on signals generated by monetary policy, the resulting sub-periods might become relatively short. This reduces the statistical power of the regression and spanning analyses employed in the empirical analysis. As a robustness check it is tested in the following empirical analysis whether the sub-periods are structurally different with respect to their mean returns and return variances. Indeed, the relevant test statistics for differences in means and variances indicate that the null hypotheses of no differences between the estimates are predominantly rejected.

The first sub-period ranges from December 1993 to August 2000 and covers a number of important events such as the Asian crisis, the Russian default, and the collapse of LTCM as well as the build-up of the technology bubble. The end of the new economy bubble that was accompanied by a tremendous decline in worldwide stock markets is covered within the second sub-period running from August 2000 to September 2002. Moreover, this period includes the terrorist attacks on the World-Trade Center of September 2001 which led to a substantial rise in risk aversion among market participants. Subsequently, stock markets recovered between September 2002 and October 2007 which constitutes the third sub-period analyzed in the empirical section. While this period comprises the unprecedented losses of quantitative long-short equity hedge funds it is not expected that this event biases the empirical results since these funds rebounded significantly within the same month (Khandani and Lo, 2010). The final sub-period from October 2007 to July 2010 incorporates the recent financial crisis that led to significant declines in values of equities, hedge funds and other alternative asset classes.

Figure 11: Definition of Sub-Periods conditional on Stock-Market Performance

C. Optimal Allocation in Hedge Funds – Full Period

The existing empirical evidence suggests that hedge fund investments help investors to construct more efficient portfolios. However, these efficiency gains are generally associated with substantial costs as hedge fund investments come with high management and performance fees and impose significant liquidity constraints on investors. Therefore, it is interesting to analyze whether similar portfolio benefits can be achieved by considering other alternative investments in addition to hedge funds in a portfolio context. In particular, some of these alternative investments are traded in financial markets in the form of exchange-traded products offering investors more transparency, higher liquidity and lower transaction costs.

I. Risk and Return over the Full Sample Period

In this section we focus on the return characteristics and correlations of all asset classes over the full sample period. These results might provide insights into the attractiveness of the different asset classes and may indicate potential substitution effects between them. The univariate characteristics of the monthly return time-series are provided in Table 1.

Table 1: Descriptive Statistics of Asset Classes

Asset Class	Mean	SD	Skew	Kurt	Sharpe	JB
HFI	0.76%***	2.24%	-0.20	5.37	0.23	48.32***
S&P 500	0.69%**	4.52%	-0.74	3.98	0.10	25.81***
MSCI EM	0.77%	7.11%	-0.77	4.84	0.07	47.61***
US Gov10	0.51%***	2.19%	0.09	4.73	0.12	25.17***
US BBB-A	0.55%***	1.71%	-1.18	9.35	0.18	380.39***
NAREIT	0.93%**	5.79%	-0.95	10.32	0.12	473.70***
GSCI	0.57%	6.54%	-0.39	4.48	0.05	23.19***
Gold	0.66%**	4.47%	0.26	5.03	0.09	36.55***

This table provides sample moments, Sharpe ratios and Jarque-Bera statistics of the eight asset classes considered in the empirical analysis. The time period covers the months from December 1993 to July 2010. Mean denotes time-series mean of monthly returns while SD denotes the associated standard deviation. Skew and Kurt represent the third and fourth moment of the return distribution. Sharpe shows the the Sharpe ratios of the respective asset classes assuming a risk-free interest rate of 3% per year and JB is the Jarque-Bera statistic for testing normality of returns. ***, **, * indicate statistical significance at the 1%, 5%, and 10% level respectively. Source: Bessler, Holler and Kurmann (2010).

On a stand-alone basis, hedge funds seem to be an attractive investment offering investors the highest Sharpe ratio (0.23) among all asset classes. Moreover, with respect to their skewness and kurtosis, hedge fund returns appear to be rather similar to the returns of other asset classes. Since the Dow Jones Credit Suisse aggregate hedge fund index comprises a large number of individual funds, this is consistent with L'habitant and Learned (2005). They document that the levels of excess skewness and excess kurtosis decline rapidly with an increasing number of individual hedge funds in the portfolio. Thus, as most investors take positions in funds of hedge funds and other products that diversify across many individual hedge fund managers and strategies, the problem of non-normal returns seems to be similar in magnitude to portfolios consisting of conventional asset classes.

For the other asset classes, the Sharpe ratios range from 0.05 for the GSCI to 0.18 for U.S. corporate bonds. The relatively small ratio for the diversified commodity index is mainly driven by its high standard deviation of 6.54 percent which is only exceeded by the volatility of emerging market equities with 7.11 percent. While the latter is not surprising, the variation in monthly commodity returns might be primarily driven by the tremendous increase and subsequent decline of oil prices during the period between 2007 and 2008.[39] Therefore, we might expect that the GSCI provided rather limited diversification benefits for mean-variance optimizing investors over the full sample period. For the fixed income instruments, Table 1 indicates similar monthly mean returns for government and corporate bonds while corporate bonds experienced a slightly lower volatility underlining its attractive risk-return relationship.

Turning to the interaction between the different asset classes, Table 2 provides evidence for the potential diversification benefits and substitution effects in terms of Pearson pair-wise correlation coefficients. Over the entire sample period from 1993 to 2010, there are significant doubts as to whether hedge funds also generated diversification benefits for investors holding conventional stock-bond portfolios. In fact, the correlations between the aggregate hedge fund market and developed market equities were highly significant at 0.55 and between hedge funds and corporate bonds at 0.37. In contrast, there seem to have been diversification opportunities for investors predominantly holding government bonds because the correlation coefficient between hedge funds and government bonds was slightly negative, although insignificant. Overall, except for the highly significant co-movement between developed and emerging equity markets, the evidence in Table 2 reveals that no coefficient exceeds 0.63 in absolute terms. Consequently, remarkable diversification benefits can be expected when a broad set of alternative asset classes is added to an investor's portfolio.

[39] In fact, the GSCI is heavily tilted towards energy-related commodities. As of 30th April 2010, energy-related commodities account for 71.8 percent of the total index (Standard and Poor's, 2010). It is important to note that crude oil has a weight of 37.5 percent, thereby representing the dominant index constituent.

Table 2: Correlation Matrix of Asset Classes

	HFI	S&P500	MSCI EM	US Gov10	US BBB-A	NAREIT	GSCI	GOLD
HFI	1							
S&P500	0.55***	1						
MSCI EM	0.61***	0.73***	1					
US Gov10	-0.03	-0.12*	-0.21***	1				
US BBB-A	0.37***	0.31***	0.27***	0.63***	1			
NAREIT	0.32***	0.55***	0.48***	-0.04	0.34***	1		
GSCI	0.34***	0.20**	0.32***	-0.04	0.20***	0.17**	1	
GOLD	0.15**	-0.02	0.21***	0.20***	0.25***	0.11	0.24***	1

This table provides the correlation matrix for the asset classes considered in the analysis over the time period December 1993 to July 2010. ***, **, * indicate statistical significance at the 1%, 5%, and 10% level respectively. Source: Bessler, Holler, and Kurmann (2010).

II. Efficient Frontiers and Optimal Asset Allocations

To analyze the diversification benefits of hedge funds in more detail, efficient portfolio allocations including hedge funds are compared with an optimal base investment ("BaseCase") which invests in all asset classes except for hedge funds. In order to capture the role of investors' beliefs regarding a hedge funds' ability to deliver positive risk-adjusted returns, the prior for alpha is varied. In particular, results are reported for i) a pessimistic investor who predicts that hedge funds are not able to provide alpha at all ("Alpha0"), ii) an optimistic investor who is confident that hedge funds provide the same level of abnormal returns as in the past ("Alpha1") and iii) a highly optimistic investor who expects that hedge funds provide risk-adjusted returns twice the magnitude of the optimistic investors' beliefs ("Alpha2").

Figure 12 provides evidence that investors' expectations for a hedge funds' ability to deliver positive risk-adjusted returns has a visible effect on optimal portfolio allocations and efficient frontiers. Compared to the benchmark portfolio, hedge funds' share in efficient portfolios increases substantially with investors' optimism. In the case that the investor expects hedge funds to deliver zero alpha, the diversification benefits are present only for in the low-risk portfolios and, therefore, only marginally improve the efficient frontier. At moderate levels of volatility, the optimal portfolios include significant shares of gold, real estate, and developed market equities. When portfolio risk is further increased, gold and equities are substituted for real estate investments. This underlines the dominant performance of real estate compared to the other asset classes over the full sample period. As investors expect hedge funds to generate positive risk-adjusted returns their portfolio share rises substantially leading to a higher allocations to other asset classes, except for real estate. In turn, the portfolios of highly optimistic investors consist primarily of hedge funds that are augmented by government and corporate bond investments. Therefore, the respective efficient frontier shifts upwards with a tremendous reduction in risk that is primarily driven by the portfolio's concentration in relatively low-volatility assets. However, due to major allocations to hedge funds, these portfolios might impose considerable transaction costs and liquidity restrictions on investors.

Figure 12: Efficient Frontiers and Asset Allocation for the Full Sample Period

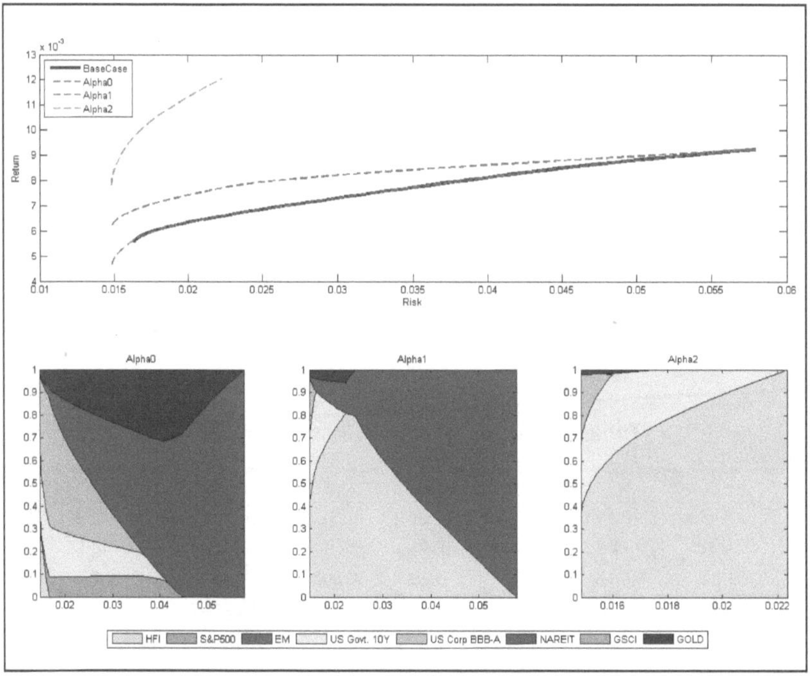

The figure shows efficient frontiers and portfolio compositions for the full sample period respectively. Source: Bessler, Holler, and Kurmann (2010).

III. Spanning Tests

Table 3 reports the results for spanning test for the full sample period. Based on the highly significant alpha estimate of 45 basis points per month, hedge fund returns outperformed the benchmark assets during the period from 1993 to 2010. However, the coefficient of determination is only 45.8 percent. This indicates that relevant risk factors driving hedge fund returns have been neglected. While the regression coefficients on equities, corporate bonds, and commodities are statistically significant, their magnitudes are rather small. As the sum of beta coefficients equals 0.49, the benchmark assets apparently do not capture all significant return characteristics of hedge funds. The LR test statistic supports the first indication that hedge funds provide diversification benefits to mean-variance optimizing investors. Therefore, the null hypothesis of no spanning can be rejected at high levels of significance. Thus, the efficient frontier comprising of hedge funds seems to provide more attractive investment opportunities than a portfolio that is restricted to the benchmark assets. To make sure that the rejection of the spanning hypothesis is not primarily driven by the difference between the tangency portfolios or the difference between the global minimum variance portfolios, the step-down procedure suggested by Kan and Zhou (2008) is implemented. In Panel B, both F-test statistics are highly significant and clearly reject the respective null hypotheses. However, closer inspection of the corresponding p-values reveals that the expansion of the mean-variance efficient frontier mainly comes from the change in the global minimum variance portfolios. Overall, these results suggest that irrespective of investor's optimism, hedge funds provided substantial diversification benefits to mean-variance optimizing investors for the entire sample period from December 1990 to July 2010.

Table 3: Tests for Mean-Variance Spanning

Panel A									
	Alpha	S&P 500	MSCI EM	US Gov10	US BBB-A	NAREIT	GSCI	Gold	R^2
Coeff.	0.0045***	0.11**	0.11***	-0.11	0.36***	-0.04	0.05**	0.01	45.8%
P-Value	0.004	0.009	0.002	0.200	0.002	0.159	0.018	0.831	

Panel B			
	LR	F_1	F_2
Statistic	46.58***	12.89***	35.29***
P-Value	0.000	0.000	0.000

This table provides regression results for mean-variance spanning tests over the full sample period (December 1993-July 2010). In Panel A, we report multi-factor regression coefficients and p-values for a model including a constant term in addition to the benchmark assets. As dependent variable we use monthly returns for the Dow Jones Credit Suisse aggregate hedge fund index. The column denoted R^2 represents the coefficient of determination. In Panel B, we report spanning test-statistics. LR stands for the likelihood ratio test, F_1 and F_2 denote the test statistics and respective p-values for the step-down procedure suggested by Kan and Zhou (2008). ***, **, * indicate statistical significance at the 1%, 5%, and 10% level respectively. Source: Bessler, Holler, and Kurmann (2010).

D. Hedge Fund Investments in Different Market Environments

So far, the analysis has taken the perspective of a representative investor that optimizes his asset allocations over a long time period of almost 17 years. As mentioned before, the sample period contains several important political and economic events and was characterized by different market environments. Therefore, it should be expected that a rational investor adjusted his portfolio weights over time. In order to investigate this important issue, the focus is now on the diversification benefits of hedge funds during the different market environments as defined in Section IV.2. This analysis provides additional insights regarding the contribution of hedge funds to portfolio efficiency when time-varying investment opportunities and inter-asset correlation structures are taken into account.

I. Risk and Return over Time - Time-Varying Investment Opportunities

Table 4 provides univariate descriptive statistics for each of the four sub-periods. The relatively low volatility of hedge funds that has already been observed for the full sample period becomes immediately evident. Only during the first sub-period when the hedge fund universe was dominated by global macro strategies (Bessler and Holler, 2009), was the standard deviation of government and corporate bond investments lower than the volatility of hedge fund returns. For the other time periods, hedge funds constituted the asset class with the lowest volatility. As expected, emerging market equities, real estate, and commodities are the riskiest asset classes in all four sub-periods. Jarque-Bera test statistics indicate deviations from normality primarily during times of rising stock markets. Surprisingly, hedge fund returns (funds of hedge funds) seem to follow a non-normal distribution only during the recent financial crisis when their portfolios suffered unprecedented losses. In terms of performance, hedge funds, fixed income instruments, and real estate exhibited positive mean returns during both sub-periods between 1993 and 2002. However, only fixed income instruments were able to generate mean returns that were significantly different from zero in both sub-periods. Regarding the respective Sharpe ratios, corporate bonds were the most attractive asset class with returns per unit of risk of 0.20 and 0.46. After the technology bubble, emerging market equities and real estate provided the highest mean returns while their reward-to-risk profiles of 0.58 and 0.30, respectively, were inferior to the Sharpe ratio of the aggregate hedge fund index of 0.66. Eventually, the recent financial crisis generated substantial inflows to government and corporate bond instruments. This can often be observed in times of market distress (Baur and Lucey, 2009). In addition, there were high inflows in gold investments, primarily driven by increasing doubts about the general stability of financial markets and concerns of rising inflation. Not surprisingly, these asset classes were the only ones that exhibited positive Sharpe ratios during this period of severe market turbulence.

Table 4: Univariate Descriptive Statistics – Subperiods

Period	Statistic	HFI	S&P500	MSCI EM	US Gov10	US BBB-A	NAREIT	GSCI	Gold
1	Mean	0.0110***	0.0173***	0.0011	0.0045**	0.0052***	0.0074*	0.0093	-0.0036
	SD	0.0291	0.0405	0.0689	0.0192	0.0137	0.0353	0.0540	0.0333
	Skew	-0.10	-0.84	-0.98	0.04	0.09	0.17	0.28	1.74
	Kurt	3.48	4.65	6.05	3.27	3.31	3.85	3.47	9.80
	Sharpe	0.29	0.37	-0.02	0.10	0.20	0.14	0.13	-0.18
	JB	0.90	18.41***	43.72***	0.27	0.43	2.76	1.80	194.26***
2	Mean	0.0020	-0.0222**	-0.0138	0.0100**	0.0080***	0.0107	-0.0019	0.0062
	SD	0.0095	0.0511	0.0741	0.0212	0.0120	0.0333	0.0541	0.0309
	Skew	0.17	0.22	0.12	-0.65	-0.08	-0.21	0.51	0.00
	Kurt	3.20	2.23	2.21	2.86	2.66	2.29	3.29	2.15
	Sharpe	-0.06	-0.48	-0.22	0.35	0.46	0.25	-0.08	0.12
	JB	0.16	0.81	0.72	1.81	0.14	0.72	1.16	0.76
3	Mean	0.0097***	0.0125***	0.0303***	0.0025	0.0045**	0.0161***	0.0137	0.0157***
	SD	0.0109	0.0278	0.0483	0.0206	0.0143	0.0451	0.0646	0.0450
	Skew	-0.23	0.22	-0.55	-0.68	-0.54	-1.35	-0.31	0.16
	Kurt	2.74	3.44	2.99	4.68	4.16	5.23	2.59	2.59
	Sharpe	0.66	0.36	0.58	0.00	0.14	0.30	0.17	0.29
	JB	0.71	0.99	3.08	11.87**	6.42**	31.19***	1.40	0.68
4	Mean	-0.0005	-0.0064	-0.0021	0.0074	0.0064	-0.0001	-0.0119	0.0144
	SD	0.0242	0.0632	0.0976	0.0297	0.0290	0.1133	0.0933	0.0680
	Skew	-1.06	-0.45	-0.41	0.66	-1.46	-0.44	-0.55	-0.55
	Kurt	4.01	2.64	3.36	4.43	6.32	3.96	3.83	3.79
	Sharpe	-0.13	-0.14	-0.05	0.17	0.13	-0.02	-0.15	0.18
	JB	7.53**	1.30	1.12	5.23**	26.85***	2.32	2.60	2.50

This table provides sample moments, Sharpe ratios and Jarque-Bera statistics of the eight asset classes during the four sub-periods considered in the empirical analysis. Mean denotes time-series mean of monthly returns while SD denotes the associated standard deviation. Skew and Kurt represent the third and fourth moment of the return distribution respectively. Sharpe denotes the the Sharpe ratio of the respective asset classes assuming a risk-free interest rate of 3% p.a. and JB is the Jarque-Bera statistic for testing normality of returns. ***, **, * indicate statistical significance at the 1%, 5%, and 10% level respectively. Source: Bessler, Holler, and Kurmann (2010).

Turning to the correlation coefficients, Table 5 suggests a highly significant co-movement of hedge fund returns with developed and emerging market equities over all individual sub-periods. Importantly, the correlation with emerging market equities steadily increased for these time periods. Therefore, the diversification opportunities offered by hedge funds might have diminished within a developed-emerging market equity portfolio. During the transition from the third to the fourth sub-period, hedge funds' correlation coefficients with corporate bonds and commodities increased substantially to 0.68 and 0.76, respectively, while government bond returns exhibited a significantly negative relationship with hedge fund returns. Most of the time, gold as an asset class exhibited no statistically significant co-movement with hedge fund returns. Overall, the evidence in Table 5 suggests that inter-asset correlation structures are time-varying which should have considerable effects on the efficient portfolios of mean-variance optimizing investors.

Table 5: Correlation between Hedge Funds and other Asset Classes

Sub-Period	12/1993 - 08/2000	08/2000 - 09/2002	09/2002 - 10/2007	10/2007 - 07/2010
S&P500	0.52***	0.54***	0.46***	0.73***
MSCI EM	0.55***	0.68***	0.75***	0.83***
US Gov10	0.19*	-0.23	-0.01	-0.35**
US BBB-A	0.37***	0.19	0.14	0.68***
NAREIT	0.23**	0.59***	0.29**	0.54***
GSCI	0.20*	-0.13	0.27**	0.76***
GOLD	0.08	0.16	0.48***	0.24

This table shows the correlation coefficients between the aggregate hedge fund index and the benchmark assets for each sub-period. ***, **, * indicate statistical significance at the 1%, 5%, and 10% level respectively. Source: Bessler, Holler, and Kurmann (2010).

To examine the relative importance of the benchmark assets in describing hedge fund returns, a sequential variance decomposition procedure is employed with a rolling window estimation of 24 months (Bessler and Opfer, 2005; Bessler and Holler, 2009). In fact, Figure 13 reveals that a growing fraction of the variance of hedge fund returns is explained by equity market fluctuations over the full sample period. While their share decreases during the time period encompassing the technology bubble, the following years are characterized by an increasing influence of equity market movements. With the exception of corporate bonds, the remaining asset classes drive only minor shares of hedge funds' return variance between 1993 and 2010. However, this observation might be partly explained by the orthogonalization sequence chosen to break down hedge funds' return variance. Nevertheless, it becomes visible that the explanatory power of the benchmark assets is increasing over time. Therefore, in addition to the time-varying inter-asset correlations between hedge funds and the benchmark assets observed in Table 5, there are further indications for expecting time-dependent diversification benefits of hedge funds due to their increasing dependence on the benchmark assets.

Figure 13: Democratic Variance Decomposition of Hedge Fund Returns

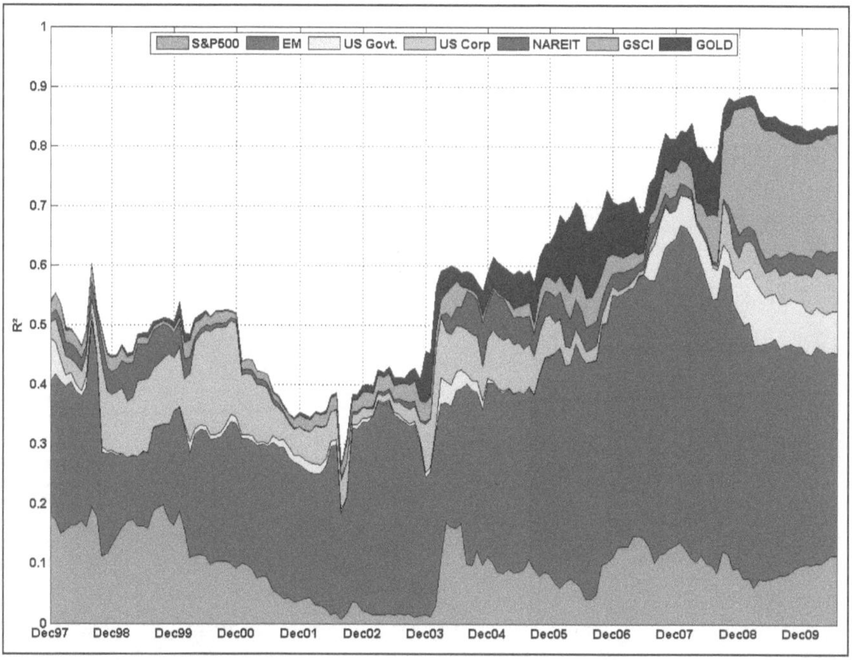

The figure shows the relative importance of different asset classes for the total return variance of hedge funds. Source: Bessler, Holler, and Kurmann (2010).

II. Efficient Frontiers and Optimal Allocations in Up- and Down-Markets

1. The First Sub-Period: 1993-2000

Figure 14 indicates that only highly optimistic investors achieved a remarkable shift of their efficient frontier during the first sub-period. With increasing investor optimism, the primary trade-off seems to exist between developed market equities and hedge funds as well as between commodities and hedge funds. Commodities experienced positive but highly volatile returns over the time period from 1993 to 2000. This explains their declining attractiveness for investors expecting hedge funds to generate positive alpha. The relatively robust allocations to corporate bonds make intuitive sense. Their mean return of 0.52 percent per month is highly significant and comes with the lowest volatility level of 1.37 percent for all asset classes during this time period. This underlines their remarkable risk-return relationship in combination with an attractive covariance structure of returns. Overall, an investor who believes in a hedge funds' ability to generate alpha makes significant allocations to hedge funds. These shrink with his risk appetite. Once a certain volatility level is exceeded, portfolio weights in developed market equities dominate due to their relatively high Sharpe ratios.

Figure 14: Efficient Frontiers and Asset Allocation for the First Sub-Period

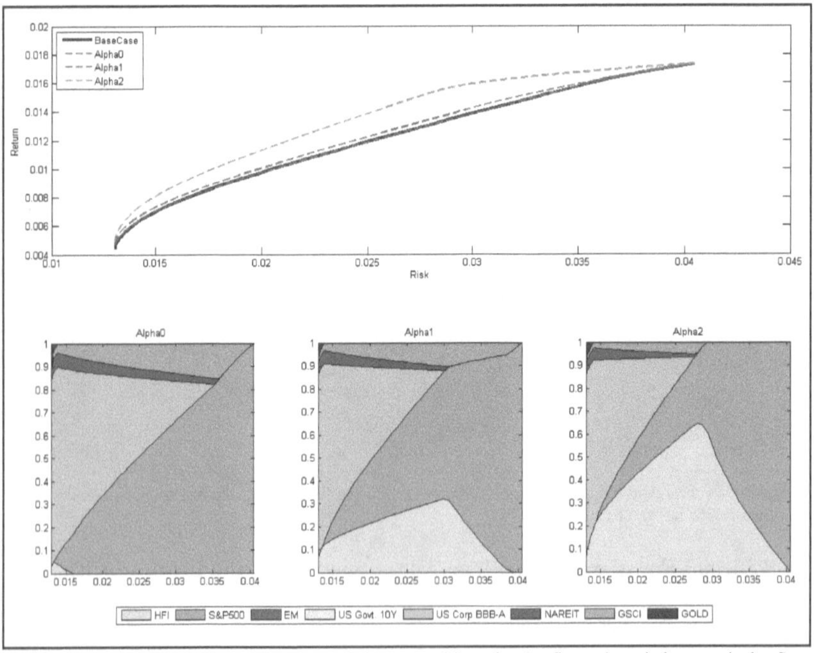

The figure shows efficient frontiers and portfolio compositions for the first sub-period respectively. Source: Bessler, Holler, and Kurmann (2010).

2. The Second Sub-Period: 2000-2002

With the end of the technology bubble stock markets declined rapidly leading to negative mean returns accompanied by remarkable levels of volatility (Figure 11, Table 4). Therefore, it is not surprising that equity-related investments are not included in optimal portfolios between August 2000 and December 2003 (Figure 15). The contribution of hedge funds to optimal portfolios is reflected in an expansion of efficient frontiers at low levels of risk, i.e. up to a monthly standard deviation of 1 percent. This diversification benefit does not depend on an investors' optimism regarding hedge funds' ability to generate positive risk-adjusted returns because the alpha estimate in the multi-factor regression is close to zero. This result is potentially related to the shift from highly volatile opportunistic strategies to relative value strategies which led to a sharp decline in the volatility of the aggregate hedge fund market (Bessler and Holler, 2009). However, the most important asset classes contributing to the construction of efficient portfolios in this market environment include corporate bonds, government bonds, and real estate investments. These assets exhibit Sharpe ratios of 0.46, 0.35 and 0.25, respectively, underlining their attractive risk-return profile.

Figure 15: Efficient Frontiers and Asset Allocation for the Second Sub-Period

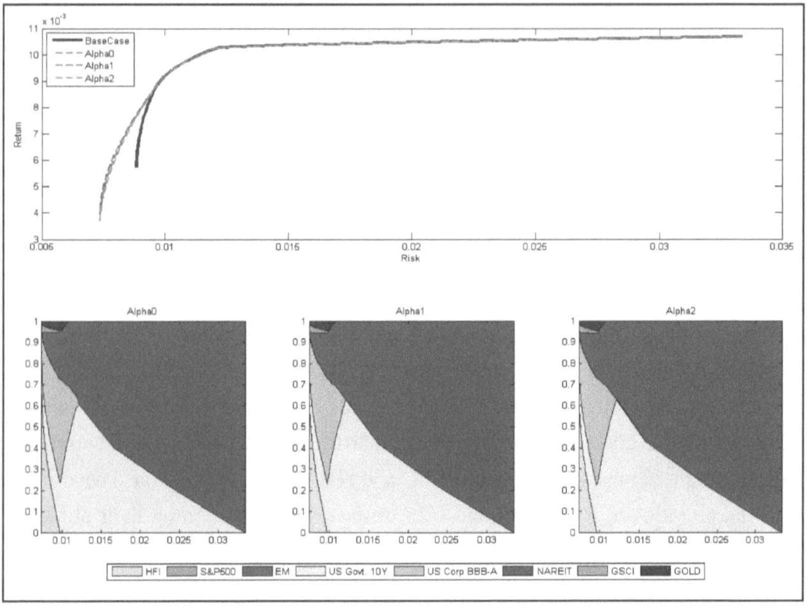

The figure shows efficient frontiers and portfolio compositions for the second sub-period respectively. Source: Bessler, Holler, and Kurmann (2010).

3. The Third Sub-Period: 2002-2007

Turning to the time period following the technology bubble, it becomes evident that hedge funds provide additional diversification benefits irrespective of investors' optimism regarding hedge fund alphas. In Figure 16, even a pessimistic investor allocates a significant share of his wealth to hedge funds which leads to an increase in expected returns at low levels of risk. With increasing optimism, investors make even higher allocations to hedge funds. However, hedge fund portfolio weights decline as portfolio volatility increases due to the higher Sharpe ratio offered by emerging market investments between 2002 and 2007. In fact, by moving from pessimistic to optimistic investors, corporate bonds and developed market equities are substituted for hedge funds while highly optimistic investors further reduce the share of real estate and commodities in their optimal asset allocation.

Figure 16: Efficient Frontiers and Asset Allocation for the Third Sub-Period

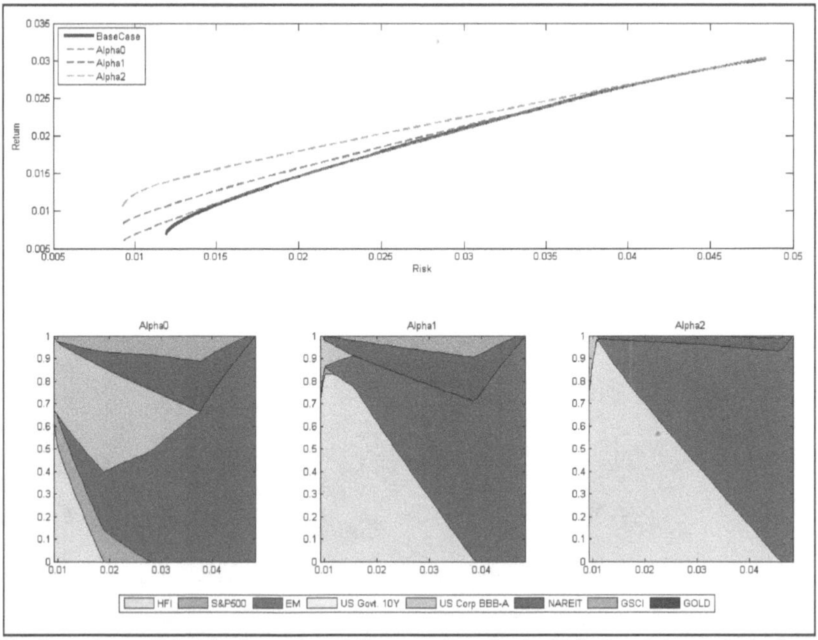

The figure shows efficient frontiers and portfolio compositions for the third sub-period respectively. Source: Bessler, Holler, and Kurmann (2010).

4. The Fourth Sub-Period: 2007-2010

During the final period of the empirical analysis, i.e. the financial crisis that came along with a tremendous decline of equity, real estate and commodity markets, hedge funds suffered unprecedented losses. To a large extent, these losses were driven by a substantial increase in the number of hedge fund investors liquidating their positions. Consistent with the optimization results for the second sub-period, Figure 17 reveals that hedge funds primarily improve portfolio diversification at low levels of risk, i.e. up to a volatility level of about 2.5 percent per month. However, although an outward shift of efficient frontiers is observable with increasing investor optimism they differ only marginally due to alpha estimates close to zero. Therefore, in periods of market distress hedge funds seem to be valuable for investors that prefer portfolios exhibiting relatively low volatilities when other asset classes show substantial return volatility.

Figure 17: Efficient Frontiers and Asset Allocation for the Fourth Sub-Period

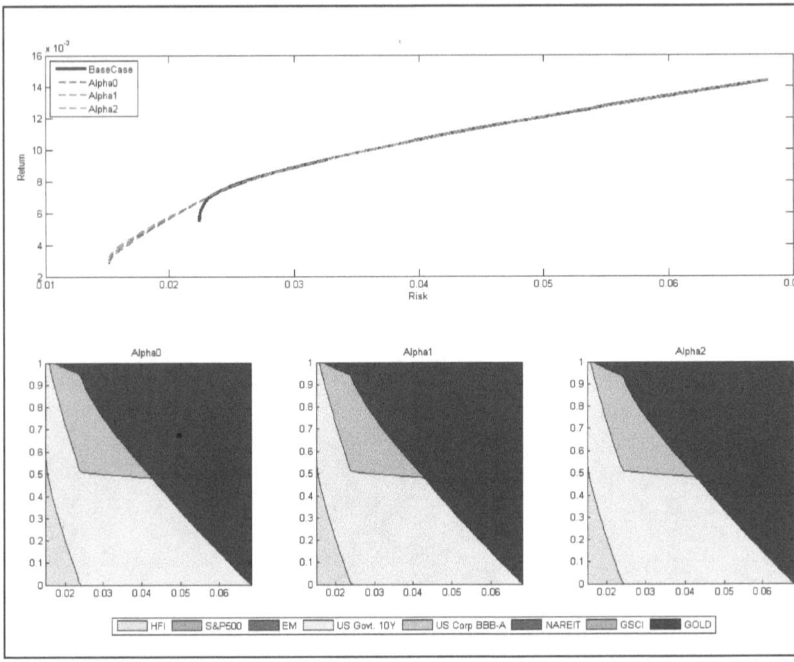

The figure shows efficient frontiers and portfolio compositions for the fourth sub-period respectively. Source: Bessler, Holler, and Kurmann (2010).

III. Spanning Tests for different Market Environments

Table 6 reports mean-variance spanning test results for the individual sub-periods. Although there are substantial diversification benefits for the entire sample period, the results for various sub-periods differ. In particular, hedge funds do not significantly improve the efficient investment opportunity set during the months between December 1993 and August 2000 (Panel A). While regression coefficients on three benchmark assets are significant, the explanatory power of the overall model remains relatively small at 45.3 percent. The likelihood ratio test as well as the F-tests encompassing the step-down procedure support the null hypothesis of no spanning. As a result, in this period hedge funds do not improve the mean-variance efficient frontier and do not significantly change the tangency and the global minimum-variance portfolios.

Turning to the second sub-period in Panel B, the likelihood ratio test indicates a rejection of the null hypothesis which is due to the significant shift of the global minimum variance portfolio. The respective F_2 test statistic is highly significant while the F_1 statistic shows that hedge funds do not significantly improve the efficiency of the tangency portfolio. This result is consistent with the shift of the efficient frontier in Figure 15 because the inclusion of hedge funds enlarges the efficient investment opportunity set exclusively at low levels of volatility. Regarding the overall performance of the benchmark model, coefficients estimates are only significant for two factors, but the model explains almost 71 percent of hedge funds' total return variance.

In Panel C, it becomes clear that the efficient frontier incorporating hedge funds dominates the respective benchmark frontier during the period from September 2002 to October 2007. Both step-down test statistics reject the null hypothesis at conventional significance levels. Therefore, hedge funds exhibit significant shares in the tangency portfolio as well as in the global minimum variance portfolio. However, the test statistic for differences in the global minimum variance portfolios is marginally more significant. This seems to be the primary driver of the expansion of the efficient frontier. During this time period, hedge funds were able to provide investors risk-adjusted returns of 35 basis points per month that underline their substantial portfolio benefits.

In the final sub-period encompassing the recent financial crisis, hedge funds exhibit statistically significant factor exposures against U.S. government bonds, corporate bonds, and commodities (Panel D). As discussed in section VI.1, these asset classes also exhibited substantial increases in their correlations with the aggregate hedge fund index between the third and fourth sub period. In terms of mean-variance spanning, the likelihood ratio test rejects the null hypothesis at conventional significance levels. However, the rejection is solely driven by the difference of the global minimum variance portfolios as indicated by the highly significant F_2 test statistic. In contrast, the tangency portfolios do not materially differ in their composition because the F_1 test statistic is not statistically significant. This evidence is consistent with the expansion of the efficient frontier for low volatility levels up to 2.5 percent per month in Figure 17. Given the spanning test results for sub-period 2 and sub-period 4, hedge funds' contribution in times of falling stock markets seem to be limited to an improvement in portfolio efficiency at low risk levels and, therefore, provide investors a relatively safe asset class in times of equity market turbulence.

IV. Summary

Hedge funds provide diversification benefits for mean-variance optimizing investors in different market environments. In this context, the level of investors' optimism regarding hedge funds' ability to provide positive risk-adjusted returns plays a central role. Especially in times of rising stock markets, highly optimistic mean-variance optimizing investors allocate a large share of their wealth to hedge funds. Therefore, with increasing optimism, portfolios become effectively less diversified which might imply considerable costs in terms of low portfolio liquidity during periods of market distress. Moreover, the benefits of hedge funds for portfolio construction measured by the shift in the efficient frontier are state dependent. While the inclusion of hedge funds leads to an upward shift of the efficient frontier during rising stock markets, their primary contribution in times of falling stock markets seems to be an expansion of the efficient frontier at low risk levels. Furthermore, spanning tests suggest that hedge funds primarily contribute to portfolio efficiency due to their significant share in global minimum variance portfolios.

Table 6: Tests for Mean-Variance Spanning

				Panel A 12/1993-08/2000					
	Alpha	S&P 500	MSCI EM	US Gov10	US BBB-A	NAREIT	GSCI	Gold	R^2
Coefficient	0.0038	0.09	0.14**	-0.89**	1.76***	-0.04	0.06	-0.04	45.3%
P-Value	0.228	0.396	0.019	0.027	0.003	0.597	0.205	0.594	
		LR			F_1			F_2	
Statistic		2.30			1.48			0.62	
P-Value		0.317			0.228			0.435	
				Panel B 08/2000-09/2002					
	Alpha	S&P 500	MSCI EM	US Gov10	US BBB-A	NAREIT	GSCI	Gold	R^2
Coefficient	-0.0004	0.04	0.06*	0.17	0.06	0.14**	-0.03	0.06	70.8%
P-Value	0.846	0.400	0.084	0.230	0.763	0.011	0.192	0.179	
		LR			F_1			F_2	
Statistic		16.13***			0.04			16.23***	
P-Value		0.000			0.846			0.001	
				Panel C 09/2002-10/2007					
	Alpha	S&P 500	MSCI EM	US Gov10	US BBB-A	NAREIT	GSCI	Gold	R^2
Coefficient	0.0035***	0.02	0.13***	-0.19	0.32*	0.01	0.03*	0.03	64.2%
P-Value	0.003	0.732	0.000	0.119	0.068	0.696	0.094	0.236	
		LR			F_1			F_2	
Statistic		48.11***			9.51***			46.75***	
P-Value		0.000			0.003			0.000	
				Panel D 10/2007-07/2010					
	Alpha	S&P 500	MSCI EM	US Gov10	US BBB-A	NAREIT	GSCI	Gold	R^2
Coefficient	0.0003	0.09	0.05	-0.28***	0.36***	-0.03	0.06**	-0.03	87.2%
P-Value	0.854	0.277	0.330	0.001	0.001	0.302	0.030	0.365	
		LR			F_1			F_2	
Statistic		45.36***			0.35			76.65***	
P-Value		0.000			0.85			0.000	

This table provides regression results for mean-variance spanning tests over individual sample periods. In the upper part of each Panel, we report multi-factor regression coefficients and p-values for a model including a constant term in addition to the benchmark assets. As dependent variable we use monthly returns for the Dow Jones Credit Suisse aggregate hedge fund index. The column denoted R^2 represents the coefficient of determination. In the lower part of each Panel, we report spanning test-statistics. LR stands for the likelihood ratio test while F_1 and F_2 denote the test statistics and respective p-values for the step-down procedure suggested by Kan and Zhou (2008). ***, **, * indicate statistical significance at the 1%, 5%, and 10% level respectively. Source: Bessler, Holler, and Kurmann (2010).

E. Conclusion

This chapter analyzed the additional diversification benefits of hedge funds when they are combined with traditional and other alternative asset classes into one portfolio. By investigating the contribution of hedge funds for mean-variance optimizing investors over the time period from 1993 to 2010 the analysis explicitly controls for the empirical observation of increasing return co-movements of hedge funds with other asset classes. Moreover, a Bayesian framework is implemented that allows incorporating investors' prior beliefs regarding hedge funds' ability to provide positive risk-adjusted returns into the portfolio construction process. The empirical results indicate that the portfolio benefits of hedge fund investments crucially depend on the market environment because the risk-return trade-off offered by hedge funds exhibits substantial time-variation. While the analysis over the full sample period suggests a visible shift of the efficient frontier irrespective of investors' level of optimism, the results for different sub-periods indicate that outward shifts of the efficient frontier seem to be limited to time-periods of rising stock markets. By employing regression-based mean-variance spanning tests the results indicate that hedge funds primarily contribute to portfolio efficiency through their significant shares in global minimum variance portfolios. Based on this evidence, hedge funds seem to be an attractive asset class at lower volatility levels. However, with increasing allocations to hedge funds, investors might impose considerable illiquidity risk on their portfolios due to their lock-up restrictions. In addition, the overall increasing correlations of hedge funds with global equity markets and other asset classes cast some doubts on their future contribution to portfolio efficiency.

Part II. The Impact of Hedge Funds on Corporate Governance System

Hedge funds do not often remain passive arm's length investors and try to make substantial changes to firms' business strategies and financial policies. For instance, in January 2005 the Anglo-Saxon hedge funds TCI and Atticus attacked the German security exchange firm Deutsche Börse arguing that management was not putting sufficient effort into creating shareholder value. As a result of this interference, the Deutsche Börse made important changes to its corporate governance as well as to its financing and investment policies. This example suggests that the increased activism by hedge funds can change the balance of power between managers and shareholders and therefore has significant implications for corporate governance.[40] This growing influence of hedge funds in corporate governance raises some interesting questions. Most importantly, does this new form of shareholder activism make corporate governance more efficient? From an economic point of view, this is the case if hedge funds promote more efficient investment and financing decisions leading to a more efficient allocation of capital. For instance, the campaign by TCI and Atticus against the Deutsche Börse led to a substantial outperformance of its share price between the beginning of the activist campaign and the end of 2007. However, over the longer run the Deutsche Börse's performance deteriorated when its share price suffered substantial losses during the recent subprime crisis. This raises the question of whether hedge funds really increase shareholder value or whether short-term increases in share prices reflect other effects. For instance, short-term increases in share prices might also be the result of wealth transfers from debtholders or from long-term shareholders.

This part investigates these issues in more detail and is structured as follows. Chapter I focuses on the approaches of activist hedge funds. It analyzes their restructuring demands in order to determine whether they ameliorate agency problems or whether they create new agency problems. Chapter II investigates the potential impact of hedge funds on the German corporate governance system. This is also an important research question since the implications of hedge fund activism might depend on the overall corporate governance and capital market environment.

[40] Hedge funds can also have other implications for firms because their dynamic trading strategies affect market liquidity and might create additional opportunities for raising financing and sharing risk.

Chapter I. Hedge Fund Activism and Corporate Governance

Some hedge funds have specialized in shareholder activism. These hedge funds acquire small stakes in target companies and use them to call for substantial changes in business strategies, financial policies and governance arrangements. These attacks are typically associated with significant increases in share prices. Thus, it is often argued that hedge funds perform a monitoring function in corporate governance and that they focus on firms that do not maximize firm value. In particular, hedge funds seem to improve corporate financial policies and help to reduce agency problems of free cash flows by forcing managers to disgorge excess cash flows to shareholders. Moreover, they seem to force managers to dismantle inefficient corporate empires and push them into value-creating mergers & acquisitions. Consequently, hedge funds help to constrain managerial moral hazard and reduce agency problems of free cash flows. However, their measures also often increase the risk of the operations and financial policies of target firms and lead to a front-loading of payouts to shareholders. This suggests that hedge fund activism might also create new agency problems and destroy firm value in the long run.

This chapter investigates how activist hedge funds exert control over target firms and evaluates the potential impact of their demands on firm value. It begins with a brief overview of the most important corporate governance mechanisms in section A. Subsequently, the focus of section B is on the tactics employed by activist hedge funds. This highlights how they can exert control over target firms even though they hold only small stakes in target firms. In section C the hypothesis that activist hedge funds perform a monitoring function in corporate governance is analyzed. Specifically, it investigates under what conditions the proposed changes to firm-level corporate governance, business strategies and financial policies can help to increase the value of target firms. Section D investigates the alternative hypothesis that activist hedge funds generate returns by expropriating long-term shareholders and debtholders. The final Section E concludes this chapter.

A. An Overview of Corporate Governance Mechanisms

The separation of ownership and control between shareholders and managers creates agency problems which can destroy firm value. These agency problems arise because shareholders have to delegate control of the firm's daily operations and many important decisions to the firm's management. As a result, managers have substantial informational advantages and have the discretionary freedom to pursue their own personal goals. According to Jensen's free cash flow hypothesis this will often lead to a loss in shareholder value (Jensen, 1986). This occurs because managers often prefer to direct free cash flows towards unproductive investments and build "corporate empires". In order to contain these agency problems the economies of all developed countries have created elaborate corporate governance systems. These consist of different governance mechanisms which help to ensure that all participants in the firm receive fair compensation for their investment in the firm (Shleifer and Vishny, 1997a).[41] These mechanisms can be differentiated into internal and external governance mechanisms.

Internal corporate governance mechanisms include the board of directors and executive compensation.[42] The board of directors acts as a delegated monitor on behalf of shareholders. Its task is to supervise senior management and ensure that managers act in the best interest of shareholders. In order to fullfil this monitoring function supervisory boards have far-reaching legal rights in most corporate governance systems. In particular, the board is responsible for hiring and firing senior managers and designing executive compensation arrangements. Moreover, boards of directors have to be consulted on key decisions that can have a significant impact on the firm's value. This includes large-scale investment projects, mergers & acquisitions and financing decisions (Tirole, 2006). Executive compensation is the other internal governance mechanism that can also be used to mitigate agency problems. In particular, it can help to align the interests of managers with the objectives of outside shareholders. Therefore, the renumeration of senior management typically consists predominantly of stock options. These stock options make executive compensation highly sensitive to changes in shareholder wealth.

External corporate governance mechanisms include the ownership structure of the firm and the market for corporate control. The ownership structure determines the intensity of the monitoring of managers' behavior by the owners of the firm. This occurs because only owners with a sufficiently large stake are willing to expand the necessary resources to monitor the firm's performance. Large stakes effectively provide owners with a sufficiently large share of the value created by their monitoring efforts (Grossman and Hart, 1980). For instance, this is often the case for institutional

[41] There are also conflicts of interests between shareholders and debtholders. However, debtholders periodically re-contract with the firm. This occurs when their loans have to be rolled over and, therefore, have substantial opportunities for exerting influence on firms.

[42] The distinction between internal and external governance mechanisms is important for the design of corporate governance systems and for comparing the U.S. and the German system.

investors such as the U.S. pension funds Calpers and TIIA Craft. These only have a financial interst in their portfolio firms and are therefore focused on maximizing shareholder value. However, some large owners can also create an additional set of agency problems from the perspective of small minority shareholders. In particular, many blockholders also obtain private benefits of control from their controlling position. For instance, this is likely when the large owner is a bank or industrial firm that also has other business relationships with the firm. The market for corporate control is the other external governance mechanism that can also help to mitigate managerial moral hazard. In particular, a lack of value creation will be reflected in low share prices increasing the probability of a hostile takeover. This threat puts pressure on managers because this will typically lead to a change in senior management and a restructuring of the firm.

Overall, there are different governance mechanisms which can constrain managerial moral hazard. However, the design of these governance mechanisms also creates different problems allowing managers to entrench their position. For instance, boards of directors are usually unable to eliminate managerial moral hazard because their design has substantial weaknesses in many countries (Jensen, 1993). In particular, boards of both U.S. and German firms are often not completely independent. This occurs because managers can influence the nomination process for board members and they often have personal relationships with senior management. Moreover, managers can often exert influence on the design of executive compensation and reduce the sensitity of pay-to-performance. Moreover, the effectiveness of the market for corporate control is often reduced when managers implement different takeover defences which increase the costs of hostile takeovers. As a result, hedge fund activism might perform the function of an additional governance mechanism that curbs managerial moral hazard when other governance mechanisms fail.

B. Hedge Fund Approach to Corporate Control

Activist hedge funds "try to change the status quo through voice without a change in control" (Gillan and Starks, 1998). Thus, they exert significant influence on major corporate decisions even though they only hold a limited fraction of voting rights. This is possible for at least two reasons. First, activist hedge funds employ specific tactics which allow them to coordinate coalitions of other shareholders, including other hedge funds or other institutional investors. Second, their organizational design provides them with comparative advantages in holding concentrated positions in target firms which are necessary to implement these tactics. In particular, it enables them to overcome free-rider problems which prevent other shareholders from actively monitoring managerial behavior. These economic mechanisms underlying hedge fund activism are investigated in more detail in this section. The first subsection investigates why hedge funds have comparative advantages in holding concentrated and illiquid blocks in target companies and can therefore become actively involved in corporate governance. The second subsection analyzes how activist hedge funds use these blocks to exert pressure on incumbent management.

I. Comparative Advantages in Activism and Monitoring

Monitoring by capital markets is usually limited due to the free-rider problem. This occurs because small investors holding neglible stakes have no incentive to monitor managerial performance (Grossman and Hart, 1980). A solution for this "rational apathy" in the case of fully dispersed ownership structures is ownership concentration (Stiglitz, 1985; Shleifer and Vishny, 1986). Therefore, institutional investors with significant positions in the firm can play an important role in corporate governance and monitor managerial performance (Del Guerico and Hawkins, 1999; Gillan and Starks, 2000). For instance, large pension funds such as Calpers and TIIA CREF and corporate raiders such as Carl Icahn used to play this role in the U.S. capital market in the 1980s and 1990s (Holderness and Sheehan, 1985). More recently hedge funds have started to acquire concentrated positions in target firms in order to play this role. They are in a unique position to do so for several reasons.

First of all, hedge funds can accumulate concentrated positions in target companies because their performance is evaluated against a total return benchmark and because there are no regulatory limits on their portfolio holdings (Fung and Hsieh, 1999a). As a result, they have strong incentives to actively monitor portfolio firms and are not subject to the free-rider problem. Moreover, they can hold large idiosyncratic risk exposures which are created by concentrated positions in target firms (Admati, Pfleiderer, and Zechner, 1994). In contrast, most other institutional investors, such as mutual funds, are evaluated against a relative performance benchmark. This forces them to mimic the composition of the benchmark that is followed by their peer group (Scharfstein and Stein, 1990). In addition, their managers benefit only indirectly from superior performance. Their compensation increases only if good performance triggers inflows into their funds increasing assets under management (Del Guercio and Tkac,

2008). However, the compensation arrangements of hedge funds also have some drawbacks in that they can create conflicts of interest with debtholders. This occurs because their option-like characteristics create high incentives for hedge funds to increase the risk of target companies (John and John, 2006).

Second, hedge funds impose lock-up periods and redemption notice periods on their investors. These typically restrict investors from accessing their funds for time periods ranging from one to two years. This insures hedge funds against the risk of early withdrawals. Consequently, this ameliorates the agency problem between fund managers and investors which arises when hedge fund managers have an informational advantage regarding the profitability of their trading opportunities (Shleifer and Vishny, 1997b). Therefore, this allows them to take a long-term perspective and to participate in the restructuring of firms over extended periods of time. This is in contrast to mutual funds which are open-ended investment vehicles. Therefore, they cannot assume the liquidity risks created by holding concentrated positions in target firms and cannot absorb the risk of large fluctuations in share prices that can occur during the course of prolonged activist campaigns (Chen, Harford, and Li, 2007).

Finally, hedge funds have comparative advantages in acquiring concentrated positions because they can employ sophisticated trading tactics. In particular, hedge funds can use derivatives to conceal their trading activities because disclosure regulations in many countries do not fully take account of derivative contracts and stock lending operations. Therefore, many hedge funds seem to actively use these instruments to build up and sell-off their positions without making regulatory position disclosures (Hu and Black, 2007). As a result, their economic exposure can substantially exceed disclosure thresholds before they decide to disclose their presence.[43] This enables them to hide their trades and acquire blocks at a limited price impact.[44] Otherwise, the hedge fund would only capture a limited fraction of the value enhancement due to the free-rider problem and, therefore, would not have the incentive to initiate an attack in the first place. This appears to be highly valuable when capital markets do not offer

[43] Derivative trading by activist hedge funds can also cause several other problems when they also hold positions in competing companies, push firms into mergers & acquisitions, or even profit from declining share prices (Christoffersen, Geczy, Musto, and Reed, 2007; Brav and Matthews, 2011; Bethel, Hu, and Wang, 2009; Hu and Black, 2007).

[44] A crucial legal question with far-reaching economic consequences is whether hedge funds have the legal right to profit from an event-driven stock price reaction, when this event is the result of a hedge fund's strategy which is due to its private information. In fact, this problem is similar to insider trading which might help to compound information more quickly into asset prices (Manne, 1966) but also crowds out small shareholders and ultimately makes markets less liquid and less efficient (Fishman and Hagerty, 1992).

sufficient liquidity to hide their order flow (Bolton and von Thadden, 1998; Kyle and Villa, 1991). However, a hedge funds' use of derivatives creates conflicts of interest with other shareholders. In particular, old shareholders sell out at the depressed pre-attack share price and do not participate in the value created by the restructuring. Moreover, hedge funds also use these tactics to quietly sell off their stakes. This allows them to abandon their campaigns without notifying other investors. Consequently, the ability to trade in derivatives weakens the lock-in effect which usually creates strong incentives for monitoring and influencing portfolio firms (Brav, Jiang, Partnoy, and Thomas, 2008). This creates severe conflicts of interest in the case of hedge funds which are apparently more interested in generating media attention and "snowball"-effects. These hedge funds can try to generate temporary boosts in share prices (Barber and Odean, 2008; Fang and Press, 2009; Tetlock, 2007) and do not focus on increasing firm value (Bessler, Drobetz, and Holler, 2010a). Apparently, these hedge funds try to sell out at temporarily inflated share prices without engaging with target management in order to increase firm value.

II. Hedge Fund Approach to exert Control

Activist hedge funds usually follow a two-stepped approach when they want to control target companies. In the first step, they privately approach the management of target firms in order to present their restructuring demands. If management does not give in to their demands they resort to more confrontational public attacks on incumbent managers. These include campaigns in the financial media, the publication of open letters to senior managers and board members and the filing of lawsuits (DAI and McKinsey, 2009). This approach allows hedge funds to exert substantial influence on important corporate decisions even though they only own a limited fraction of voting rights. This is possible because this approach enables them to form coalitions with two different groups of investors.

First, hedge funds can form coalitions with dispersed minority shareholders by communicating their restructuring plans to them. Therefore, the public campaigns used by activist hedge funds can be effectively interpreted as a communication mechanism that is used to rally the support of other minority shareholders. However, this tactic can only be successful if hedge funds convince a sufficient fraction of minority shareholders of their proposals (Bradley, Brav, Goldstein, and Jiang, 2010). This requires them to effectively communicate their intentions to other shareholders.

Whether this is possible depends on the legal environment which defines how shareholders can interact and how they can put their proposals on the agenda of the shareholder's meeting (Bradley, Brav, Goldstein, and Jiang, 2010). Moreover, their interventions need to be credible so that other investors can be confident that the hedge fund genuinely has the intention and will be able to execute the plan. For example, this can be achieved by accumulating a sufficiently large stake that allows them to make a legal filing of their position. This sends a costly signal to the market that they have acquired a large position in the target firm. Moreover, interventions will be more credible if the hedge fund has already acquired a reputation among other market participants for being able to identify undervalued targets and to restructure mismanaged firms. This can entail some problems because activist hedge funds can also send false signals to exploit the tendency of investors to buy attention-grabbing stocks (Barber and Odean, 2008; Dyck, Volchkova, and Zingales, 2008). This might enable them to capitalize on short-term boosts in share prices without incurring the costs for restructuring the target firm.

Second, activist hedge funds can form coalitions with other hedge funds. In this case they form an implicit alliance of hedge funds "acting in concert" that controls a sufficiently large number of voting rights. However, this approach can sometimes create conflicts of interest with other shareholders. In particular, by formally acting as independent investors they circumvent disclosure requirements. This enables them to hide their stake-building efforts and acquire their positions without generating a price impact. In addition, this can enable them to circumvent the legal requirement to make a mandatory bid for all outstanding shares (§30 WpÜG). Therefore, these implicit alliances also deprive minority shareholders of the opportunity to tender their shares to the hedge funds.

Managers often try to protect their controlling position against this outside interference. Therefore, they frequently employ different tactics which are quite similar to the takeover defences employed by managers against hostile takeovers. For instance, on several occasions managers have tried to attract new "anchor investors" who perform a similar role as "white knights" whose interests are usually more aligned with managers' objectives. Moreover, similar to the use of "green mail" and standstill agreements to silence hostile acquierors managers have also tried on some occasions to buy out hedge funds. For instance, the management of the Japanese utility company J-Power agreed to a share repurchase at above market prices that only included the stake of the activist hedge fund TCI. However, some of the defence strategies used by managers to fend off hostile takeovers cannot be used to deter activist hedge funds. For example, this applies to open-market share repurchases which can be used to deter hostile acquirers (Billett and Xue, 2007). In contrast, they do not deter activist hedge funds which rely on minority positions to implement their strategies (Falaye, 2004). Therefore, managers need to resort to other approaches in order to destabilize and eventually break up the coalitions led by activist hedge funds.[45]

Overall, their approach seems to enable hedge funds to exert substantial influence on corporate governance. For instance, Boyson and Mooradian (2008) indicate that most hedge funds do not publicly spell out their objectives. This suggests that the simple threat of escalating their campaigns to an open confrontation seems to be sufficient to make managers listen. In particular, firms will become most vulnerable to hedge funds if two conditions hold: (1) the ownership structure is sufficiently dispersed; (2) there are no non-financial blockholders with private benefits.

C. Monitoring of Managerial Moral Hazard

Activist hedge funds force managers to restructure the operations and financial policies of their firms. Moreover, they also actively interfere in the corporate governance of target firms. Their attacks typically lead to substantial payouts of cash flows to shareholders and frequently refocus the business model of target firms. Moreover, these attacks often trigger increases in the share prices of target companies. Therefore, it is usually argued that hedge funds target firms suffering from agency problems of free cash flows and weak corporate governance. According to this view, hedge fund activism is the response of capital markets to the failure of other governance mechanisms to effectively monitor corporate managers. This suggests that hedge funds increase the efficiency of the corporate governance system and promote a more efficient allocation of capital. This hypothesis is investigated in more detail in this section. Subsection I focuses on hedge funds' demands regarding the gorporate governance of target firms. Subsection II evaluates under what conditions the financial restructurings proposed by activist hedge funds can create value. Subsection III

[45] In addition, some managers have also tried to implement measures that put downward pressure on their own firm's share prices and therefore also exert pressure on the often leveraged portfolios of activist hedge funds. For instance, this apparently occurred during the confrontation between 'Cewe Colar' and the hedge funds 'Marcap' and 'K Capital' when the management presumably tried to manipulate its share price (Börsenzeitung April 24th, 2007). In such a case, hedge funds have to respond with lawsuits against incumbent managers or try to accelerate shareholder votes on their proposals.

investigates the implications of hedge funds on a firm's business strategies and corporate structures.

I. Adjustments of Firm-level Corporate Governance

Often a hedge fund's restructuring plan also addresses important elements of the corporate governance of target firms. In particular, they frequently focus on specific firm-level governance arrangements which are used by managers to protect their position against outside influence by shareholders. For instance, they can implement staggered boards which prolong the time period before activists can take full control of the firm's board of directors. Many empirical studies document that this behavior can have a negative impact on firm value (Aggarwal, Erel, Stulz, and Williamson, 2009; Gompers, Ishii, and Metrick, 2003; Drobetz, Schillhofer, and Zimmermann, 2004; Beiner, Drobetz, Schmid, and Zimmermann, 2006; Ammann, Oesch, and Schmid, 2009).

Consequently, activist hedge funds can raise firm value if they force managers to adapt firm-level corporate governance arrangements to increase the influence of outside shareholders. For instance, hedge funds can achieve this objective when they call for the resignation of senior management or board members who suffer from conflicts of interest and therefore do not represent the best interest of shareholders. Moreover, this also helps hedge funds to ensure that their other demands relating to the business strategies and financial policies of target firms will be implemented. This occurs because shareholders are usually not permitted by corporate law to directly interfere in the management of the firm.[46] Moreover, this can also raise value when activist hedge funds force boards to adapt executive compensation arrangements in order to make executive compensation more sensitive to shareholder returns. Furthermore, this also applies when activist hedge funds try to reduce the discretionary freedom enjoyed by incumbent managers and facilitate outside interference in major corporate decisions. For instance, on several occasions hedge funds have pushed for the elimination of takeover defences such as staggered boards which were implemented by incumbent management in the firm's charter. Similarly, they often try to ensure that important decisions have to be approved directly by shareholders. For example, in Germany they regularly vote against "Vorratsbeschlüsse" in the general assembly. Otherwise, this

[46] This is similar to the approach of private equity funds and corporate raiders that make full takeovers of target companies (Cornelli and Karakas, 2008).

would give managers far-reaching mandates for raising new equity capital with no shareholder control over the exact use of funds.

Another set of corporate governance problems emerges when the firm has a dominant shareholder who obtains private benefits of control from his controlling position in the firm. On several occasions, activist hedge funds apparently have also helped to ameliorate these agency problems. For instance, this occurs when dominant shareholders want to buy out the remaining minority shareholders and try to dilute their stakes by taking advantage of specific provisions in takeover laws (Wenger and Hecker, 1994). Moreover, this also occurs when hedge funds interfere in specific transactions such as the unification of dual-class share structures, which can be abused by controlling inside shareholders to expropriate outside shareholders (Bigelli, Mehrotra, and Rau, 2008).

Overall, this indicates that this type of hedge fund activism can raise value by interfering in firm-level corporate governance arrangements in order to reduce managers' discretionary freedom. Therefore, it can be interpreted as a corporate governance mechanism that helps to curb managerial moral hazard.

II. Financial Restructurings

Hedge fund's restructuring plans frequently focus on the financial policies of target firms. In particular, in most cases the proposals of activist hedge funds contain substantial changes to the firm's financial policies such as raising dividends, paying out special dividends and repurchasing its own shares. Thus, hedge fund activism is typically associated with an increase in leverage and a reduction in financial slack. Managers often do not implement these measures themselves due to agency problems and corporate governance malfunctions. This suggests that hedge funds force target firms to implement more efficient financial policies and raise value. This is supported by the observation that their interferences are typically associated with significantly positive share price reactions. This section investigates the conditions under which this hypothesis applies. The first subsection delineates the determinants of optimal financial policies and relates them to firm characteristics. The second subsection discusses whether hedge fund activism really helps to create value and to make corporate governance more efficient.

1. Corporate Financial Policies and Firm Value

According to the seminal work by Modigliani and Miller (1958, 1961) financial policies, such as capital structure decisions and dividend policy, have no impact on firm value in perfect capital markets. In real world capital markets, however, there are different market imperfections including agency problems, information asymmetries and taxes.[47] These market imperfections can lead to an optimal capital structure that balances the benefits and costs of debt financing in order to minimize the firm's cost of capital.[48]

Higher leverage can increase firm value for two reasons. First, higher leverage reduces agency problems of free cash flow. Paying out free cash flows to shareholders reduces inefficiencies in the firm's investment policy because managers would otherwise waste free cash flows on value-destroying investments that increase the size and diversification of the firm (Jensen, 1986; Fama, 1980). Therefore, increasing leverage can increase firm value. Furthermore, this positive effect is reinforced because higher leverage exposes the firm more frequently to monitoring in primary capital markets (Easterbrook, 1984).[49] Second, higher leverage can also increase firm value due to the tax benefits of debt financing. In contrast to dividend payments, interest payments reduce the firm's taxable earnings. This reduces tax payments to the government which in turn increases the total amount of cash flows available to debt and equityholders.[50]

At the same time, however, higher leverage can also reduce firm value. In particular, it increases the expected costs of financial distress (Titman, 1984; Barclay and Smith, 2005).[51] The direct costs of financial distress consist of the legal and administrative fees for lawyers, accountants and bankers that are incurred during financial distress. Even more important are the indirect costs of financial distress (Almeida and

[47] There is also a large body of literature starting with Ross (1977) interpreting financing choices as costly signals. However hedge funds are not insiders and therefore should not have private inside information. Thus, it is unlikely that share price reactions reflect inside information. There are also other factors that might affect optimal capital structure including the firm's competitive position (Myers, 2003; Harris and Raviv, 1991), operating leverage (MacKay and Philipps, 2005) and the firm's ownership structure (Harris and Raviv, 1988; Stulz, 1988; Harris and Raviv, 1991).

[48] The following discussion is focused on the debt-equity choice. However, it also applies to other financial choices. For instance, dividend payouts are equivalent to a reduction of the firm's equity base.

[49] This argument is based on the assumption that collective action problems are smaller in primary capital markets (Grossman and Hart, 1980; Allen and Michaely, 2003).

[50] The tax advantage of debt financing can be offset if the investor can defer the realization of taxes on capital gains on their equity holdings (Myers, 2003).

[51] The emergence of hedge funds can also have an impact on the costs of financial distress, i.e. on the recovery rate.

Philippon, 2007; Weiss and Wruck, 1998; Andrade and Kaplan, 1998) which result from different effects. First, financial distress reduces the commitment of suppliers, costumers and the company's workforce to the firm. Second, more debt increases the risk of asset substitution leading to an increase in the cost of debt capital.[52] Third, debt financing can also create debt overhang problems which lead to underinvestment at high levels of leverage. Effectively, shareholders are not willing to provide additional funding to the firm for new investment during periods of financial distress because most of the value generated would be captured by debtholders (Myers, 1977).

In addition to this trade-off between the costs and benefits of debt financing, optimal financial policies are also affected by information asymmetries. In particular, firms should follow a pecking-order of financing choices and issue the least information-sensitive securities first in order to minimize adverse-selection costs (Myers and Majluf, 1984).

These factors suggest that the optimal financial policy of a firm is closely related to the firm's investment opportunity set. In particular, mature firms with steady cash flows operating in stable industries should implement more aggressive financial policies, i.e. use higher leverage ratios, hold smaller cash reserves and make larger payouts to shareholders. This occurs because these firms have limited valuable growth options creating high agency problems of free cash flow. In contrast, growth firms need more cash flows to exploit valuable growth options.[53] In addition, the income streams of mature firms are more stable. This increases the probability that they will be able to realize the tax benefits of debt financing (Myers, 2003).[54] Furthermore, the costs of financial distress are lower for mature firms because most of their value is composed of "assets-in-place". In contrast to firm-specific growth options, these assets suffer only small declines in value during financial distress (Benmelech and Bergman, 2009; Shleifer and Vishny, 1992) and provide shareholders with only limited investment flexibility. Finally, the financing of mature firms is usually less constrained by information asymmetries. Therefore, they face smaller adverse selection discounts when they tap capital markets because outside investors can easily assess the value of

---

[52] At moderate levels of leverage, these agency problem only have a second-order effect on the cost of capital (Eisdorfer, 2008; Parrino and Weisbach, 1999).

[53] The development of growth options requires investments in both financial and human capital. Thus, in order to induce managers and employees to accumulate highly firm-specific human capital, firms might have to prefer more conservative financial policies (Myers, 2000; Zingales, 2000).

[54] However, this tax advantage for mature firms is reduced if they operate in asset-intensive industries and therefore also generate large depreciation tax shields (Barclay and Smith, 2005).

"assets-in-place". In contrast, evaluating the value of growth options requires more private information (Myers and Majluf, 1984; Myers 1983; John 1993; Chay and Suh, 2009; Riddick and Whited, 2009).

This reasoning is supported by different empirical studies. These studies provide evidence that the relationship between firm value and financial structure depends on the nature of the firms' investment opportunity sets. For instance, Ahn, Denis, and Denis (2006) and McConnell and Servaes (1995) find that the relationship between firm value and leverage is positive for mature low-growth firms and negative for high growth firms. Similarly, there is empirical evidence that higher cash holdings lead to larger valuation discounts for mature value firms (Dittmar and Mahrt-Smith, 2007). These findings should be reflected in the characteristics of hedge funds' targets.

2. Hedge Fund Interference and Agency Problems of Free Cash Flows

Hedge funds typically force managers to adopt financing measures that lead to more leverage and that reduce cash flows available for investment for managers. Therefore, hedge fund activism plays a positive role in corporate governance if they focus on mature firms. These firms are often characterized by high free cash flows and limited growth opportunities and should therefore implement more aggressive financial structures with higher leverage, higher payout ratios and lower cash reserves (DeAngelo, DeAngelo, and Stulz, 2006; DeAngelo and DeAngelo, 2006; Denis and Osobov, 2008). In contrast, hedge funds should not impose these measures on growth firms. These firms should adopt conservative financial policies with low leverage and low payout ratios because their value is mostly comprised of growth options. These can only be realized if firms have sufficient financial slack (Gamba and Triantis, 2008; Smith and Watts, 1992). Indeed, several empirical studies indicate that hedge funds seem to apply this reasoning. In particular, these studies provide evidence that hedge funds attack "value firms" which operate in mature industries and are more likely to suffer from agency problems of free cash flows. Moreover, these studies also document that these interventions are generally associated with short- and long-term increases in share prices (see Brav, Jiang, and Kim (2009) for a review of these studies).

These results suggest that hedge fund activism should be interpreted as an important governance mechanism that helps to discipline managers. This is important because there is also empirical evidence that other governance mechanisms do not often force managers to implement optimal financial policies. For instance, Berger, Ofek, and Yermack (1997) find that entrenched managers who are not subject to monitoring by concentrated ownership or other active monitors and who are not incentiviced by high-powered stock-based compensation seek to avoid the disciplining effect created by debt financing. Similarly, Garvey and Hanka (1999) report that increases in the protection of managers against the market for corporate control after changes in corporate law are associated with declines in leverage. In line with this evidence, Jung, Kim, and Stulz (1996) document that most seasoned equity offerings are conducted by firms with poor investment opportunities and entrenched managers, i.e. firms that should rather increase leverage in order to maximize value. Furthermore, entrenched managers do not optimally rebalance leverage ratios immediately when the marginal costs of inefficient capital structures begin to exceed the transaction costs of refinancing (Frank and Goyal, 2008; Kayhan and Titman, 2007; Morellec, Nikolov, and Schürhoff, 2008; Morrellec, 2004). Finally, there is also evidence that entrenched managers reduce firm value by holding excessive cash reserves. For instance, in both the U.S. and Europe the results by Dittmar and Mahrt-Smith (2007) and Schauten, van Dijk, and van der Waal (2008) indicate that cash reserves of weakly governed firms are valued at higher discounts by capital markets. Moreover, these firms also tend to spend their cash holdings more quickly, leading to a negative operating performance. This explains the finding by Harford, Mansi, and Maxwell (2008) that cash reserves of poorly governed firms tend to be smaller compared to cash reserves of well-governed firms.[55]

However, hedge funds' demands can also create conflicts of interests with other minority shareholders. For instance, in 2008 the hedge fund TCI privately negotiated a targeted share repurchase with the management of J-Power that allowed TCI to exit at a 30% premium to the current share price in secondary market trading.[56] In a nutshell, this indicates that hedge funds can allow managers to protect their private benefits of control. They allow managers to use corporate resources to pay off hostile shareholders who in exchange stop their hostile campaigns (Peyer and Vermaelen,

[55] Jiraporn and Gleason (2007) provide some contradictory evidence. However, their findings are based on the Gompers, Ishii, and Metrick (2003) measure of shareholder rights which effectively measures only the effectiveness of the market for corporate control and therefore is restricted to one single dimension of corporate governance.

[56] There can also be conflicts of interest between different types of minority shareholders when they differ in their preferences for the form of payouts (Becker, Cronqvist, and Fahlenbrach, 2010), the structure of their liabilities etc. (Brennan, 2003). While these agency problems can also imply transfers of value the potential magnitude of distortions appears to be small.

2005; Dann and DeAngelo, 1983; Chang and Hertzel, 2004; Harris and Glegg, 2009).[57] However, there is no empirical evidence for a wide-spread use of these tactics.

Overall, hedge funds interfering in corporate financial policies seem to fullfil a similar function to that of private equity firms implementing leveraged buyouts in that they "motivate managers to disgorge cash rather than invest it below the cost of capital or ... wasting it on organizational inefficiencies" (Jensen, 1986). However, while the demands by activist hedge funds always force firms to disgorge cash flows, and apparently help to reduce agency problems of free cash flow, some important research questions remain unanswered. In particular, this concerns the wide variation in the details of the measures proposed by hedge funds. For example, payouts to shareholders have been made in the form of large special dividends or share repurchases. This variation has not been completely addressed by existing empirical and theoretical research. For instance, Jensen (1986) makes a strong case in favor of debt-financed share repurchases. This is in line with Jagannathan, Stephens, and Weisbach (2000) who argue that share repurchases provide high flexibility to extract temporary cash windfalls. However, at the same time, increasing dividends might also be interpreted as a stronger device to control free cash flow problems because dividends contain a costly commitment to continue disgorging cash flows in the future. Thus, there are arguments in favor of dividends, special dividends and share repurchases. Consequently, this issue cannot be resolved using conventional models based on agency theory. It seems that this variation might also be related to provisions of corporate law and capital market regulation. In particular, different forms of payouts trigger different tax effects and are constrained by the composition of the firm's capital reserves. Finally, in the case of share repurchases another unresolved issue is the trading behavior of hedge funds, i.e. do they also tender their shares at the premium offered by the firm or do they wait in order to capitalize on subsequent increases in share prices?

---

[57] See Bebchuk (1994) and Dann and DeAngelo (1983) for legal problems inherent in these transactions. However, several authors have proposed that targeted repurchases should be interpreted as the final event in a sequence of events defining the whole control contest. Therefore, the cumulative stock return over the entire engagement of the activist should be used to evaluate whether managers and the activist really colluded to the detriment of other minority shareholders (Denis, 1990; Mikkelson and Ruback, 1991).

III. Corporate Restructurings

Hedge funds' restructuring plans often include substantial changes to the business strategy and the structure of target firms. On many occassions, they have forced firms to refocus their operations by divesting whole business units and non-core assets. Moreover, they also frequently play an active role in shaping the outcome of merger & acquisition strategies. Since these decisions are also often distorted by agency problems and corporate governance malfunctions, it is usually argued that hedge funds play a positive role in corporate governance and force managers to create value for shareholders. This section investigates this argument in more detail. The first subsection reviews the relationship between the boundaries of the firm, synergies and firm value. The second subsection investigates corporate restructurings which lead to a break-up of target firms. The third subsection analyzes the implications of hedge funds for the efficiency of M&A decisions.

1. Boundaries of the Firm, Synergies and Firm Value

Managers should only combine multiple business segments and different assets into one firm if there are synergies between the individual components. In this case, the value of the firm as a whole will be higher than the sum of the values of the stand-alone assets (Rubinstein, 1973). This is related to the fundamental problem of the optimal boundaries of the firm which is addressed in a large body of literature on the "theory of the firm". In particular, this literature emphasizes that integration is beneficial if there are complementarities between the individual business units (Rhodes-Kropf and Robinson, 2008).

In the case of conglomerate firms operating in several unrelated lines of business there are usually no operating synergies. Due to the limited overlap of the operations of individual business units, it is hardly possible to create synergies by increasing revenues via cross-selling. In addition, there are few opportunities for reducing operating costs and realizing scope economies in conglomerates because there are usually few common inputs or cost complementarities between the different segments (Pepall, Richards, and Norman, 2004). However, conglomerates can create financial synergies. In particular, conglomerate firms can enjoy financing advantages in debt markets due to a co-insurance effect between their individual business units. This lowers the volatility of their operating cash flows, boosting their debt capacity and increasing the value of their tax shields (Lewellen, 1971; Devos, Kadapakkom, and Krishnamurthy 2009).[58]

At the same time, conglomerate firms will often suffer from more severe coordination and agency problems that emerge when firms increase in size and become more complex. These problems reflect imperfections in the internal capital markets of conglomerate firms where managers of individual business units compete for capital. For instance, due to their informational advantages relative to top management the managers of individual business units are able to misrepresent the prospects of their units. This often leads to inefficient cross-subsidization of underperforming units (Scharfstein and Stein, 2000). Moreover, managers can use the free cash flow of profitable segments to expand into new, more promising industries in order to increase the size of their empires (Colak, 2010). In particular, this applies if there are some business units that have a high share of assets-in-place, operate in mature industries and generate high current cash flows (Prezas, 2009). Furthermore, internal capital markets create additional bureaucratic rigidities (Shin and Stulz, 1998) and bargaining problems between top management and business unit managers (Rajan, Servaes, and Zingales, 2000). Moreover, incentive contracts for business unit managers cannot be conditioned on market information and therefore need to use accounting information which creates additional distortions.[59] In addition to these incentive problems, the internal capital markets of conglomerates make the firm less transparent from the perspective of outside shareholders. This increases adverse selection risks which in turn increase the firm's cost of capital relative to "pure plays" into which investors can invest at lower information risk (Hund, Monk, and Tice, 2008).

These agency and coordination problems are typically less pronounced in horizontally and vertically integrated firms. In addition, these firms also have more opportunities for realizing operating synergies. For instance, horizontal integration can create value because it combines firms operating at the same stage of the industry's value chain. Especially in industries with high fixed costs this allows the firm to exploit scale economies and to reduce operating costs. Moreover, horizontal integration can

[58] See Leland (2007) for short comings in this argument and under which conditions this does not hold when differences in tax rates, default spreads, etc. are taken into account.

[59] In contrast, in technology-intensive industries corporate diversification might create value because there are large information asymmetries between managers and outside capital markets. Hence, corporate managers might have valuable inside information and possess the specialized knowledge needed to evaluate technology-driven investment projects giving them comparative advantages in screening and monitoring relative to outside capital markets (Williamson, 1970; Hubbard and Palia, 1999; Schipper and Thompson, 1983; Matsusaka, 1993; Shleifer and Vishny, 1991).

generate synergies by giving the firm more market power in product markets leading to an increase in revenues (Mathews and Robinson, 2008).[60] Vertical integration of adjacent stages in the value chain can also create synergies under specific conditions. In particular, in asset-intensive industries these mergers can help to smooth out capacity utilization over time by internalizing transactions with down-stream suppliers or up-stream customers. This can create value because it reduces the risk of future hold-ups and/or allows both business units to collude or engage in foreclosure (Shenoy, 2008; Mathews and Robinson, 2008). These operating synergies can be offset to some extent by the additional costs of vertical integration, such as higher coordination costs, less flexibility in conjunction with more complex operations, and higher fixed costs.

Thus, conglomerate integration is less likely to create firm value than horizontal or vertical integration. This reasoning is generally supported by many empirical studies. In particular, there is a "conglomerate discount" at which diversified firms are valued in capital markets compared to portfolios of "pure plays" operating in the same industries. Starting with the research by Lang and Stulz (1994) and Berger and Ofek (1995) this valuation discount has been detected by a large number of empirical studies. Importantly, Ammann, Hoechle, and Schmid (2009) indicate that this finding is robust to a number of measurement problems identified in earlier studies including a selection bias (Villalonga, 2004a/b; Graham, Lemmon, and Wolf, 2002; Campa and Kedia, 2002), inaccurate measurement of debt values (Mansi and Reeb, 2002) and the definition of business segments in financial statements (Villalonga, 2004a). Moreover, this hypothesis is also supported by several studies on the investment efficiency of conglomerates. For instance, the conglomerate discount seems to become larger if the business units of a conglomerate face specialized competition (Santalo and Becerra, 2008) suggesting that internal capital markets do not make as efficient investment decisions as focused firms. Similarly, there is evidence that investment projects initiated by conglomerate firms exhibit lower operating performance than similar project initiated by focused firms (Natividad, 2008). However, the magnitude of these investment distortions also depends on the industries in which the conglomerate is operating. In particular, Aggarwal and Zhao (2009) provide empirical evidence that for conglomerates operating in newly emerging industries, where transaction costs tend to be relatively high for stand-alone firms, there is no conglomerate discount. Finally,

[60] However, the size of this effect is likely to be small due to the objective of antitrust authorities of preventing firms from dominating markets (Devos, Kadapakkam, and Krishnamurthy, 2009).

this reasoning is supported by empirical evidence that firm value increases if firms refocus their business models and dismantle internal capital markets. For instance, asset sales, spin-offs and carve-outs create value if they reduce information asymmetries, eliminate the bargaining problems inherent in internal capital markets, (Vijh, 2002; Schipper and Smith, 1986; Vijh, 1999), and refocus the business model of the firm (John and Ofek, 1995; Desai and Jain, 1999; Lang, Poulsen, and Stulz, 1995).

2. Break-Ups and Corporate Refocusing

Hedge funds often force firms into large-scale restructurings such as spin-offs, carve-outs and asset sales. These restructurings can create value if they target firms that are trading at a conglomerate discount due to excessive corporate diversification. This empire building is often related to agency problems of free cash flow, which are typically most pronounced in mature firms. This suggests that hedge fund activism can play an important role in corporate governance when the hedge funds target this specific type of firm. However, even though this reasoning is intuitive and consistent with observing positive share price reactions, the existing empirical research does not directly confirm that target firms really have inefficient corporate structures prior to the hedge fund engagement. Instead, most studies only provide indirect evidence for such agency problems in that they compare accounting ratios and valuation measures between hedge fund targets and their peer groups.[61]

Nevertheless, there is some indirect evidence that activist hedge funds might play an important monitoring role. In particular, there is substantial evidence that other governance mechanisms often fail to prevent managers from building empires and diversifying their firm's operations. For instance, Denis, Denis, and Sarin (1997) find evidence that the propensity to diversify is decreasing in managerial ownership and in the size of outside blockholdings. Moreover, they also document that corporate diversification decreases subsequent to external control threats, which provides further support for the hypothesis that corporate diversification is the result of agency problems of free cash flow. Moreover, there is also evidence that the magnitude of the conglomerate discount depends on the composition of managerial compensation packages (Martynova, 2006). Furthermore, the market for corporate control also has a significant impact on corporate diversification and investment policy. For instance,

[61] In order to provide direct evidence for inefficient corporate structures it would be necessary to estimate the difference between target firm's market value and the valuation of the sum of their parts (see Ammann, Hoechle, and Schmid, 2009)

Jiraporn, Kim, Davidson, and Singh (2006) find that weak shareholder rights measured by the Gompers, Ishii, and Metrick (2003) approach lead to more diversification across different industries. Similarly, Jiraporn, Kim, and Davidson (2008) document that weaker monitoring by boards of directors leads to a higher diversification discount if outside directors are "busy" and hold multiple board seats at other companies. Finally, Hyland and Diltz (2002) find that managerial moral hazard explains managers' decisions to diversify their operations even though this will impose a conglomerate discount on the firm's valuation in capital markets.[62] In addition, valuation effects triggered by restructuring transactions are stronger if transactions are governance-related, supporting the view that hedge funds pushing firms into these transactions should be interpreted as active monitors. In particular, valuation effects are particularly pronounced if the firm is characterized by weak corporate governance prior to the transaction. For instance, Allen and McConnell (1998) and Elsas and Löffler (2008) both find that announcement period returns are higher if management is more entrenched. This empirical evidence suggests that there is often a need for activist shareholders such as hedge funds in order to address the shortcomings of other governance mechanisms.

The structure of the transactions proposed by hedge funds provides additional support for the hypothesis that activist hedge funds focus on firms suffering from agency problems and corporate governance malfunctions. In particular, activist hedge funds often combine the restructuring of firms' asset portfolios with leveraged recapitalizations. This eliminates future agency problems because entrenched managers also seem to be more likely to retain the proceeds from asset sales which can generate agency problems of free cash flow in the future (Ataullah, Davidson, and Le, 2010). Effectively, activist shareholders such as hedge funds anticipate agency problems of free cash flows that would otherwise emerge after the transaction (Allen and McConnell, 1998).[63] In addition, recapitalizations commit managers to fully executing the restructuring plan by putting large amounts of leverage on their balance sheets (Myers, 2003). This creates a binding commitment for managers to restructure the firm's operations and to sell off non-core assets in order to be able to pay back the debt.

---

[62] However, there are also some studies arguing that corporate diversification is not strongly related to the firm's corporate governance (Anderson, Bates, Bizjak, and Lemmon, 2000; Singh, Mathur, and Gleason, 2004).

[63] There is also empirical evidence that asset sales combined with increases in leverage and payouts are associated with higher valuation effects (Bates, 2005).

Overall, hedge funds interfering in corporate structures can play an important role in corporate governance. Nevertheless, there are still some open research questions. In particular, there is currently no research investigating the design of the transactions demanded by hedge funds to break up firms. For instance, if hedge funds really tried to reduce agency problems of free cash flow then they should be more likely to push managers into spin-offs or asset sales than into carve-outs because these transactions lead to a complete separation of these assets from the firm. Moreover, in the case of a spin-off there is no evidence of what hedge funds do with their shares of the subsidiary (Patro, 2008).[64]

3. Mergers & Acquisitions

Activist hedge funds also frequently interfere in mergers & acquisitions which are among the most important corporate investment decisions. Therefore, mergers & acquisitions can trigger substantial valuation effects in capital markets. However, these investment decisions are often not only driven by the objective of realizing synergies and creating value. Instead, managerial investment decisions are often biased by agency problems of free cash flow or managerial hubris (Berkovitch and Narayanan, 1993). This suggests that activist hedge funds might also play a valuable monitoring function and improve the efficiency of merger decisions. This section investigates this hypothesis in more detail. The first subsection focuses on cases of hedge fund activism that attempt to derail mergers & acquisitions. The second subsection investigates under what conditions hedge funds can create value by actively supporting mergers & acquisitions.

a. Prevention of Mergers & Acquisitions

On numerous occasions hedge funds have actively opposed mergers & acquisitions. These interventions are usually based on the argument that the mergers proposed by managers destroy value. This argument is supported by the observation that these hedge fund interventions usually trigger strongly positive share price reactions. This suggests that the management is willing to overpay for the completion of the deal, i.e. the price offered is too high compared to the expected merger gain:

---

[64] In addition, the method of payment in asset sales might be interesting in that there is research suggesting that valuation effects are stronger for both firms if the payment not only consists of cash but also contains an equity component (Hege, Lovo, Slovin, and Sushka, 2009; Slovin, Sushka, and Polonchek, 2005).

$$\Delta\Pi = \left(\Delta V_{Target} + \Delta V_{Acquirer}\right) - P < 0 \qquad (49)$$

In this case the synergies $\left(\Delta V_{Target} + \Delta V_{Acquirer}\right)$ created by the merger are smaller than the takeover premium P. Consequently, the merger is a negative net present value investment from the perspective of acquiring shareholders. This implies an irreversible loss in value for acquiring shareholders due to the transfer of value to target shareholders (Denis, Denis, and Sarin, 1997). This occurs in a large number of corporate acquisitions (Andrade, Mitchell, and Stafford, 2001). In particular, diversifying mergers made by growth companies and mergers by bidders with a past underperformance tend to be associated with negative short-term stock price reactions (Morck, Shleifer, and Vishny, 1990). Moreover, managers apparently often fail to realize forecasted synergies leading to negative long-run stock returns (Ben-David and Roulstone, 2008).[65]

These value-destroying mergers are often the result of agency problems of free cash flow (Harford, 1999; Lang, Stulz, and Walkling, 1991) or overoptimistic managers (Roll, 1986; Malmendier and Tate, 2008).[66] This suggests that activist hedge funds can play an important role in corporate governance because other corporate governance mechanisms often fail to prevent these mergers & acquisitions. For instance, there is empirical evidence that low managerial ownership leads to less value creation for the shareholders of the bidder (Lewellen, Loderer, and Rosenfeld, 1985). Furthermore, if executive compensation is only weakly aligned with shareholder preferences then managers are more likely to make value-reducing M&A's (Datta, Iskandar-Datta, and Raman, 2001) Additionally, there is evidence that boards are often ineffective monitors and do not punish senior management for bad acquisitions by reducing executive compensation (Harford and Li, 2007; Fich, Starks, and Yore, 2008). Finally, there is also often insufficient monitoring by other shareholders. In particular, there is empirical evidence that short-term investors appear to facilitate value-reducing mergers and appear to be less effective monitors (Gaspar, Massa, and Matos, 2005).

Overall, the positive share price reactions around these interferences suggest that activist hedge funds really create value when they interfere in takeover attempts. They

[65] However, negative share price reactions can also be explained by other factors including the release of negative information on the prospects of the firm or its industry (Shahrur and Venkateswaran, 2009) and overvaluation of the bidder (Loughran and Vijh, 1997).

[66] Mergers by these firms can also be the result of other effects including rational herding behavior by corporate managers (Brunnermeier, 2001; Rhodes-Kropf and Viswanathan, 2004; Bowman, Fuller, and Nain, 2009) or a winner's curse resulting from competition for the takeover target between multiple bidders (Boone and Mulherin, 2008a).

monitor managers whose investment decisions are not effectively controlled by other governance mechanisms. In addition, by preventing mergers & acquisitions, hedge funds might also help to create value for acquiring shareholders by forcing managers to adjust the method of payment (Bessler, Drobetz, and Zimmermann, 2010). However, there is no empirical research that directly investigates under what conditions activist hedge funds try to prevent mergers & acquisitions.

b. Support of Mergers & Acquisitions

Managers are often reluctant to surrender control and sell their firms to an acquirer. Therefore, activist hedge funds can also play another important role in corporate governance when they push firms into mergers & acquisitions. For instance, Greenwood and Schoar (2009) report that a large fraction of the long-term increase of the market value of target firms is the result of subsequent takeovers of target firms. This suggests that hedge funds can create value by facilitating mergers & acquisitions that help firms to quickly adjust their business models against exogenous shocks (Mitchell and Mulherin, 1996).[67]

This role appears to be particularly important in consolidating or contracting industries where mergers can create value by cutting excess capacity (Andrade and Stafford, 2002) and eliminating marginal facilities (Jensen, 1993). However, due to corporate governance malfunctions managers do not often initiate these mergers themselves as they curb their private benefits. Moreover, other parts of the organization such as the company's workforce also resist these mergers because they would destroy the value of their firm-specific investments which cannot be quickly redeployed to other firms (Holmström and Kaplan, 2001; Jensen, 1993). This resistance is illustrated by DeAngelo and DeAngelo (1991) who investigate the resistance of unions and the labor force to down-sizing and the closure of marginal facilities in the U.S. steel industry in the 1980s. As a result of these frictions, firms are at a comparative disadvantage compared to capital markets in reallocating capital from declining to growing industries (Holmström and Kaplan, 2001).

Activist hedge funds might help to overcome these problems and push through consolidating mergers. Similar to LBOs, hedge funds are not constrained by the

[67] These exogenous shocks might be the result of technological innovation, deregulation, supply shocks, demand reductions, overinvestment in new technologies or information technolgy (Andrade, Mitchell, and Stafford, 2001; Jensen, 1993; Brown, Mulherin, and Weidenmier, 2008; Brown, Dittmar, and Servaes, 2005).

collective action problems that prevent small shareholders from exercising their property rights to force firms in distressed industries to consolidate (Lambrecht and Myers, 2007). Moreover, similar to an LBO, activist hedge funds often impose additional debt on the newly merged firm which is necessary to preserve managers's incentives to complete the consolidation and restructuring (Lambrechts and Myers, 2007). In addition, the hedge funds' approach appears to be superior to the traditional leveraged buyouts approach because they can also capitalize on the synergies between both firms (Lambrecht and Myers, 2007). For instance, they enable both firms to match their most efficient facility when firms from the same or adjacent stages of the industry's value chain are combined (Dutz, 1989).[68] Thus, activist hedge funds promoting mergers & acquisitions might assume the function of capital markets in reallocating capital across industries, and especially from declining to growing industries (Holmström and Kaplan, 2001).

Activist hedge funds pushing for mergers might also fullfil a similar role in expanding industries where mergers can create value by combining complementary resources and technology (Akdogu, 2009). In these mergers managers and the company's workforce bear a smaller risk that their firm-specific investments are devalued. Thus, the hedge funds' interference seems to be less important in order to overcome the organizations' resistance to change (Holmström and Kaplan, 2001). However, hedge funds' involvement can be an important mechanism for overcoming bargaining problems between shareholders of the bidding and target firms, regarding the distribution of the merger gain. This occurs because, similar to other large institutional investors (Matvos and Ostrovsky, 2008), hedge funds often hold simultaneous positions in both companies making them indifferent to the allocation of merger gains between the target and the bidder. This can create conflicts of interest with shareholders of either firm. In addition, hedge funds can also create further agency problems because they can use derivatives to create synthetic voting rights. On several occasions, these have been used by hedge funds to capitalize on overpriced takeover offers without participating in the declining share price of the acquiring firm (Hu and Black, 2007).

The ability of activist hedge funds to promote value-increasing mergers & acquisitions depends on more than their ability to coordinate other shareholders of the bidding company to support the transaction. The recent growth of hedge funds pursuing merger arbitrage strategies adds further complexity to the creation of value in mergers

[68] See Dutz (1989) and Ghemawat and Nelebuff (1990) for an industrial organization perspective on these issues which yields further interesting insights.

& acquisitions. This occurs because they pursue several dynamic trading strategies that can significantly affect the negotiation process.[69] The conventional merger arbitrage strategy should reduce the level of takeover premia needed to complete deals and thereby increasing the probability of takeover success. These strategies are only interested in the success of the takeover offer because they hold an exposure to the takeover spread.[70] This arbitrage spread often overcompensates hedge funds for the risk of deal failure due to a shortage of arbitrage capital and "limits to arbitrage" (Baker and Savasoglu, 2002). Thus, they can make substantial returns by tendering their accumulated shares to the bidding company (Cornelli and Li, 2002). As a result, the free-rider problem is reduced and the bidder can more easily complete takeover bids. In addition, merger arbitrageurs have private information regarding the size of their holdings which affect the bid's probability of success so that their returns are not only driven by their superior ability to forecast the success rate of takeover attempts (Larcker and Lys, 1987). Rather, merger arbitrageurs also seem to play a more active role in that they increase their stakes when they know that the probability of success is already high, leading to a further increase in the success rate of the deal (Cornelli and Li, 2002).[71] At the same time, these strategies usually short sell the acquirers' shares which can increase the cost of the deal because it creates downward pressure on its own share price. This reduces the value of the stock component of the takeover offer and can therefore force the acquirer to increase his offer (Mitchell, Pulvino, and Stafford, 2004). Nevertheless, it seems fair to conclude that overall the presence of hedge funds pursuing this merger arbitrage strategy should help to reduce bid premia and allow the bidder to capture a larger fraction of the merger gain. This should help firms to execute value-increasing mergers & acquisitions.

At the same time, other trading strategies by hedge funds engaged in merger arbitrage can frustrate mergers & acquisitions and transfer a larger share of the merger gain to target shareholders. Effectively, these hedge funds "hold out" and refuse to tender their shares in the target firm at the current offer price. This increases the risk of a failure of

[69] For further information on the takeover process and the division of takeover gains between the acquirer and the target see Andrade, Mitchell, and Stafford (2001), Kau, Linck, and Rubin (2008), Eckbo (2009), Stulz (1988), Shleifer and Vishny (1986), Stulz, Walkling, and Song (1990), Bauguess, Moeller, Schlingemann, and Zutter (2009), Gaspar, Massa, and Matos (2005), Morellec and Zhadanov (2005) and Bethel, Hu, and Wang (2009).

[70] The precise structure of the hedge depends on several factors. For instance, it depends on the structure of the takeover offer (Officer, 2004; Macias 2009), the bidding strategy of the acquirer, the level of bidding competition (Boone and Mulherin, 2008b) and the implementation of takeover defences (Betton, Eckbo, and Thorburn, 2008).

[71] At a given point this will reduce their expected profits in that the price for each additional share increases too much.

the deal due to specific provisions in corporate and takeover law. These stipulate that an acquirer needs to accumulate a defined percentage of shares in order to obtain effective control of the target.[72] Hence, as the acquirer approaches this threshold his valuation of each additional share of the target increases. Therefore, these "hold outs" force the acquirer to increase the takeover premium offered to target shareholders because hedge funds holding substantial blocks in the target are pivotal to the success of the takeover offer. Similar strategies can be observed during freeze-outs when a successful acquirer attempts to push out remaining minority shareholders to save listing and regulatory costs (Gomes, 2001; Bates, Lemmon, and Linck, 2006).

There is empirical evidence that hedge funds pursuing all of these different strategies during mergers & acquisitions can have a significant impact on the outcome of takeover attempts (Hsieh and Walkling, 2005). However, the objectives of the individual strategies are diametrically opposed to each other so that it is more relevant to assess their aggregate impact on the market for corporate control. So far, this question has not been addressed by empirical research.

IV. Conclusion

Hedge fund activism can create value when hedge funds focus on mature firms which often suffer from agency problems of free cash flows. These agency problems often lead to inefficient financial policies and suboptimal business strategies and corporate structures. Since other corporate governance mechanisms often fail to address these problems, activist hedge funds can create value when they force firms to recapitalize their balance sheets or to make substantial changes to their asset portfolios.[73] This is documented by several empirical studies. These studies provide evidence that hedge funds attack mature "value firms" and that their interventions are associated with short- and long-term increases in shareholder value (see Brav, Jiang, and Kim (2009) for a review). In addition, there is empirical evidence that the frequency of hedge fund

[72] While a simple majority of 50% plus one share is sufficient to control most corporate decisions in Germany, more important decisions require a qualified majority of 75% plus one share. Moreover, if the acquirer wants to make a full takeover, he has to purchase at least 95% of outstanding shares before he can proceed to a squeeze-out. The German government is currently considering whether this threshold should be reduced to 90%.

[73] A common characteristic of all of these interventions is that resolution of uncertainty in the market is quick because these transactions are highly visible. This might explain why activist hedge funds rarely make direct interferences into normal investment decisions such as capital expenditures and R&D which do not often immediately trigger large valuation effects (Chan, Martin and Kensinger, 1990; McConnell and Muscarella, 1985).

attacks is positively correlated with financial market conditions. For instance, Bessler, Drobetz, and Holler (2010b) report a sharp drop in the number of stake-building events in the German capital market subsequent to the beginning of the recent financial crisis. This finding is also consistent with the hypothesis that hedge funds perform a monitoring function in corporate governance. In fact, hedge fund activism seems to work as a state-contingent governance mechanism which puts pressure on managers during those time periods when agency problems of free cash flows are most pronounced. For instance, many studies document a procyclical relationship between cash flows and investments (Blanchard, Lopez-de-Silanes, and Shleifer, 1994).[74] This is usually interpreted as evidence that managers waste free cash flows on negative net present value investments when they have access to large amounts of cash and face limited financing constraints during economic upturns (Moeller, Schlingemann, and Stulz, 2005; Jensen, 2005). Moreover, managers seem to become overly optimistic and are more likely to herd during bull market periods (Rhodes-Kropf and Viswanathan, 2004; Bowman, Fuller, and Nain, 2009). In addition, most restructuring measures proposed by hedge funds can only be executed at favorable valuations during up-markets. For instance, this applies to asset sales, spin-offs (Schlingemann, Stulz, and Walkling, 2002) and large scale refinancing, such as leveraged recapitalizations (Betton, Eckbo, and Thorburn, 2008). Consequently, the value of hedge funds as a governance mechanism appears to be most pronounced during boom periods when product markets, as the ultimate driver of economic efficiency, put only limited pressure on managers (Shleifer and Vishny, 1997a).

D. Wealth Transfers and Conflicts of Interests with other Stakeholders

The predominant view among academics and market participants is that hedge fund activism improves corporate governance. According to this view the restructuring measures implemented by hedge funds help to reduce agency problems of free cash flows and therefore increase firm value. This reasoning seems to be empirically supported by strong positive share price reactions subsequent to hedge fund engagements. However, these share price reactions can also be reconciled using two other explanations. On the one hand, they might reflect transfers of value from debtholders to shareholder because the initiated restructuring often also increases the business and financial risk of target firms. On the other hand, these share price

[74] However, there are also other interpretations of this sensitivity of investments to free cash flows. These usually emphasize the role of financing constraints in external capital markets (Tirole, 2006).

reactions might indicate transfers of value from long-term shareholders to hedge funds if capital markets behave myopically.[75] Consequently, hedge fund activism might create new agency problems and can reduce total firm value in the long run. These agency problems are addressed in this section. The first subsection focuses on the potential agency problems between hedge funds and the firm's debtholders. The second subsection analyzes the agency problems that can exist between hedge funds and long-term shareholders.

I. Risk Shifting and Wealth Transfers from Debtholders

The restructuring measures proposed by activist hedge funds sometimes also increase the business and financial risk of target firms. Therefore, it is possible that the objective of their interventions is not only to improve corporate governance. Instead, they might also be interested in increasing risk in order to increase shareholder value to the detriment of debtholders. These risk-shifting effects can occur because equity is a call option on the firm's assets with an exercise price equal to the face value of outstanding debt written by the firm's debtholders (Black and Scholes, 1973). As a result, any increase in the value of the firm's equity due to an increase in asset volatility or due to a reduction of the option's exercise price will trigger an offsetting decline in the value of the firm's debt.[76] This suggests that activist hedge funds can make gains to the detriment of the target's debtholders if they increase the systematic risk β_j of its stock.[77] Compared to other shareholders, these risk-shifting incentives for hedge funds are compounded by the option-like structure of their managers' compensation which amplifies incentives for increasing operating and financial risk (John and John, 2006; Galai and Masulis, 1976). The systematic risk can broken down into (Mandelker and Rhee, 1984):

$$\beta_j = DFL \cdot DOL \cdot \beta_j^0 \tag{50}$$

[75] From a theoretical point of view there are also other reasons for why conflicts of interests can also arise between different shareholders. For instance, they can differ in their valuation of stocks due to differences in their evaluation of different financing alternatives as a result of information asymmetries, taxes and transaction costs and due to differences in their portfolio structures and investment horizons (Bagwell, 1991).

[76] However, one could also argue that in perfect markets, there is no wealth transfer due to risk shifting. In particular, debtholders should demand a compensation for bearing these agency risks at the investment stage so that the resulted losses are absorbed ex-ante by current shareholders due to higher costs of debt financing (Parrino and Weisbach, 1999).

[77] If idiosyncratic risk is also priced, then hedge funds could also gain by increasing the idiosyncratic risk of a target's stock.

Thus, activist hedge funds can transfer value to themselves by increasing the firm's financial risk defined by its degree of financial leverage DFL or by increasing its business risk. This depends on its degree of operating leverage DOL and the fundamental business risk β_j^0 of the firm's industry and operations.

Activist hedge funds can increase financial risk when they press for higher payouts to shareholders and force targets to take on more leverage. This increases the financial leverage DFL of the firm because it depletes the retained earnings and other equity reserves of the firm. This reduces the exercise price of the shareholder's call option, leading to an increase in the value of equity to the detriment of the firm's debt (Bott, 2002; Drukarczyk, 1993). In addition, the increase in financial risk is often compounded because these transactions also reduce the firm's financial slack thus lowering the firm's ability to withstand intermediate liquidity shocks (Morris, 1976). Moreover, the decline in debt value due to higher financial risk will not usually be offset by improvements in investment efficiency generated by the reduction of free cash-flow problems. This occurs because debtholders own a fixed claim on the firm's cash flows. Therefore, they will only share in this increase in firm value if prior to the hedge fund intervention managers wasted free cash-flows on a very large scale leading to a very high probability of default (Cremers, Nair, and Wei, 2007). Overall, financial restructurings initiated by hedge funds can therefore be associated with falling debt values because debtholders are forced to absorb a larger share of the risk of the firm's operating cash flows.

Similar effects might occur if activist hedge funds interfere in business strategies leading to substantial changes in the asset portfolios of target firms. In particular, they can also create "risk shifting"-effects when they demand firms to break-up conglomerate corporate structures and refocus their business models. These transactions not only increase value due to lower information asymmetries but also increase value due to the dismantling of inefficient internal capital markets. They also have substantial implications on the firm's business risk. In particular, these restructurings can increase the volatility of the firm's asset values and operating cash flows leading to an increase in equity valuations. At the same time, however, this reduces the value of debtholders' fixed claim which bears the higher downside risk and does not share in the upside potential of the restructuring (Renneboog and Szilagyi, 2008). This negative effect for debtholders is likely to be particularly strong when hedge funds' interventions eliminate the co-insurance effect leading to a substantial increase in idiosyncratic risk.[78] Therefore, wealth transfers can become large when hedge funds break up conglomerate firms whose individual business units operated in completely independent industries. In addition, this effect is stronger when break-ups lead to increases in the systematic risk of the firm's asset portfolio. This can occur when the risk profile of the individual business units differed significantly prior to the restructuring (Shastri, 1990). Therefore, wealth transfers become larger in those cases in which the remaining operations of the firm exhibit high operating leverage and therefore have higher systematic risk than the assets sold. For instance, this can be the case if hedge funds force firms to spin-off non-core assets that have low asset risk.

Activist hedge funds might also create risk-shifting effects to the detriment of debtholders when they force firms into mergers & acquitions. These often entail significant shifts in the firms' operations and financial structures and can therefore trigger substantial shifts in business and financial risk.[79] In particular, whether the bondholders of the target and of the bidding firm will suffer a decline in value depends on the pre-merger risk profile of both companies. Hence, risk shifting is most likely to occur if the levels of asset risk of both companies differed substantially prior to the merger and if the asset risk of both companies is highly correlated (Shastri, 1990). In addition, the pre-merger capital structure of both firms also determines the potential magnitude of risk-shifting effects. In particular, the relatively less risky bonds are more susceptible to incur losses whereas the relatively risky bonds are set to gain in value (Shastri, 1990; Billett, King, and Mauer, 2004).

Whether hedge funds can really utilize these risk-shifting effects to exploit debtholders depends on the structure of the firm's debt contracts. These often contain covenants that restrict borrowing firms from implementing measures that devalue debtholder's claims (Brockman and Unlu, 2009; Roberts and Sufi, 2009). For instance, these covenants force the firm to keep a minimum level of net worth and prohibit them from issuing additional senior debt and engaging in asset sales (Jensen and Meckling, 1976; Black and Scholes, 1973; Myers, 2003; Smith and Warner, 1979).[80] In addition, in response to the emergence of hostile takeovers, debt contracts often contain poison put covenants. These enable debtholders to resell the debt to the firm at a specified price in

[78] Idiosyncratic risk is relevant for debtholders who are usually not perfectly diversified.

[79] This is also reflected in empirical evidence that higher vulnerability to the market for corporate control is associated with a higher cost of debt (Cremers, Nair, and Wei, 2007; Qiu and Yu, 2009).

[80] However, restricting firms only from issuing more senior debt will not perfectly protect senior debtholders because there are frequent violations of the absolute priority rule in bankruptcy proceedings.

the case of a hostile takeover. Moreover, debtholders protect the value of their claims by adjusting other provisions of debt contracts including maturities and embedded options. For instance, this includes conversion rights (Mayers, 1998) and put options which increase debtholders bargaining power against shareholders (Dunn and Spatt, 1999; David, 2001). As a result, it is unlikely that hedge funds can exploit debtholders. This occurs because sufficiently large payouts to shareholders or large-scale asset restructuring would lead to a covenant violation placing the firm into a technical default.

II. Myopia and Wealth Transfers from Long-Term Shareholders

Hedge funds might also have a negative impact on corporate governance if they try to make short-term profits at the expense of long-term shareholders. For instance, it is often argued that activist hedge funds interfere in investment decisions in order to increase short-term cash flows and earnings. This can be achieved, for example, by reducing capital expenditures, cutting R&D budgets or canceling mergers & acquisitions (Bange and De Bondt, 1998). Likewise, activist hedge funds might also achieve similar objectives with financial restructurings which typically allow firms to increase current-period payouts to shareholders by borrowing against future expected income.[81] This front-loading of future cash flows and earnings to the current period enables hedge funds to boost current period share prices when capital markets are not perfectly efficient.[82] In particular, the associated increases in current period profitability send out positive signals to other market participants so that the resulting increase in share prices allows hedge funds to make a quick exit.[83] At the same time, however, this strategy of generating temporary boosts in share prices imposes substantial costs on long-term shareholders. In the long run, this "false signaling" will

[81] For instance, hedge funds can push managers to execute refinancing transactions to arbitrage mispricings between the company's debt and equity securities (O'Brien, Schmid Klein, and Hilliard, 2007; Shefrin, 2005). In the case of undervalued credit risk, this allows them to generate quick profits by forcing firms into leveraged recapitalizations. The recent drive by hedge funds to force companies to increase their leverage went along with very favorable conditions in debt markets. Thus, similar to the LBO-wave during the 1980s, the imposition of higher leverage ratios on target companies allowed hedge funds to take advantage of very favorable rates in debt markets during the last couple of years. Similar to the time period investigated by Kaplan and Stein (1993) this might be related to an increased willingness of banks and debt markets to provide leveraged finance to companies.

[82] See Stein (1996) on how to make correct capital budgeting decisions when capital markets are myopic and inefficient. There is also evidence that managers face strong incentives to behave myopically and to herd in their investment decision making (Hall and Weinstein, 1996; Stein, 1989; Holden and Lundstrum, 2009).

[83] This behavior is similar to the behavior of corporate managers who often try to send out positive signals in order to generate or sustain an overvaluation of their company's shares (Jensen, 2005).

lead to declining share prices when firms are not able to meet higher growth expectations in future periods. Moreover, these measures can reduce long-term shareholder value in that they force firms to cancel positive net present value projects to preserve cash for payouts to shareholders. Also, managers might need to favor investment projects generating high cash flows in the short run and reject growth-enhancing projects with long lead times in order to cover higher interest payments created by leveraged recapitalizations (Peyer and Shivdasani, 2001). These problems should be most severe when hedge funds target firms in "growth" industries. These firms need to invest in growth options and innovations that have long lead times before they eventually generate profits.

Whether hedge fund activism really causes this kind of wealth transfers depends on the efficiency of capital markets. In the case of efficient capital markets these strategies will not work. The market is able to "look through" these tactics so that share prices always reflect the present value of future cash flows discounted at the risk-adjusted cost of capital. In contrast, if capital markets are inefficient and behave myopically then stock prices will not sufficiently discount the associated sacrifices in long-run growth. However, the issue of market efficiency is still unresolved in academic research. In fact, most support for the hypothesis that capital markets are inefficient and myopic is derived from theoretical models (see Brunnermeier, 2001; Stein, 1998; Lakonishok, Shleifer, and Vishny, 1994; Shleifer, 2000; Shleifer and Vishny, 1990; Froot, Scharfstein, and Stein, 1992). However, empirical research has not led to a consensus on this important research question. For instance, on the one hand Lakonishok, Shleifer, and Vishny (1994) argue that the existence of a "value effect" indicates that investors make biased forecasts and extrapolate past earnings too far into the future. Similarly, some researchers argue that their empirical results indicate that investors overvalue temporary boosts in short-term cash flows and do not completely discount the negative implications for long-run growth (Jacobson and Aaker, 1993; Edmans, 2009). On the other hand, Fama and French (2007) forcefully argue that the documented effects provide no evidence for inefficient markets (Zhang, 2005). This is supported by others such as Chou, Liu, and Zantout (2009) who find that the market is not fooled by large one-time payoffs, such as special dividends and other forms of "false signaling" (Chan, Ikenberry, Lee, and Wang, 2010).[84] Consequently, empirical

[84] In addition to myopia, share prices in inefficient capital markets can also be characterized by 'catering'-effects in that investors have preferences for specific stock characteristics that need not be related to the determinants of long-run value. Again, if there is 'limited arbitrage' in capital markets, these preferences affect share prices (Baker and Wurgler, 2004a; Baker and Wurgler, 2004b). Similar

research has not yet led to a consensus regarding the level of efficiency of capital markets.

In addition, long-term shareholders should oppose hedge funds which try to use these tactics. In particular, there is evidence that long-term blockholders who have sufficient incentives to collect information and engage in monitoring will be able to look through such attempts to boost short-term value. Thus, they use their superior information to actively trade against less informed traders and attenuate their impact on share prices which in turn reduces hedge funds' ability to distort share prices (Edmans, 2009; Wahal and McConnell, 2000; Bushee, 1998). Therefore, the ability of hedge funds to generate these wealth transfers from long-term to short-term shareholders should depend on the fraction of long-term shareholders in the target's ownership structure. However, this reasoning does not apply if most institutional investors investing in the firm's stock pursue momentum strategies (Bushee, 1998). Moreover, it might become easier for hedge funds to implement their strategies if the fraction of sophisticated institutional investors in the target's ownership structure is small. This implies that the higher fraction of unsophisticated retail investors, who are often more likely to purchase attention-grabbing stocks (Barber and Odean, 2008), is higher. The resulting "snowball" or momentum effects can be exploited by hedge funds.

Finally for two reasons, it is unclear whether hedge funds really create these distortions. First, hedge funds are not necessarily short-term investors. On the one hand, it seems plausible to assume that hedge funds have a relatively short investment horizon because many activist hedge funds use leverage to finance their positions. This exposes hedge funds to the risk of an early run by their creditors which in turn limits their ability to trade on long-term information (Brunnermeier, 2001). But on the other hand, given the relatively large size of their stakes, they can become locked into their positions and encounter problems when they try to completely hedge their exposures. Second, whether capital markets are really perfectly efficient still appears to be an open research question.

E. Empirical Evidence

The returns to hedge fund activism can be theoretically explained by three different hypotheses including improvements in corporate governance, wealth transfers from

effects might also induce firms and hedge funds to mimick the repurchasing decisions of other firms (Massa, Rehman, and Vermaelen, 2007) debtholders and expropriation of long-term shareholders. Consequently, in order to differentiate between these hypotheses, a growing number of empirical studies investigate the valuation effects surrounding hedge fund interventions.

Empirical studies for the U.S. market conclude that hedge fund activism helps to reduce agency problems of free cash flows and therefore improves the efficiency of the corporate governance system (Brav, Jiang, and Kim, 2009). For instance, based on a sample of 404 U.S. events between 2003 and 2005, Klein and Zur (2009) document short- and long-term increases in share prices subsequent to the publication of the intitial 13D-Filings and provide evidence that these valuation effects appear to be driven by the extraction of free cash flows. In fact, based on the self-professed objectives of hedge funds stated in their 13D-Filings, most of them appear to be pushing for major changes in the company's strategy and corporate governance. Similarly, Brav, Jiang, Partnoy, and Thomas (2008) confirm these findings using an even larger sample of 888 U.S. events between 2004 and 2005. According to their results, positive valuation effects are driven by changes in operating strategies. This is also consistent with the notion that hedge funds help to improve corporate governance. Similar results are reported by Boyson and Mooradian (2008) who use a dataset covering the long time period from 1994 to 2005. Interestingly, they provide evidence that short-run valuation effects and changes in operating performance are positively related to the aggressiveness of the hedge funds measured by the investment purpose stated in their 13D filings. All of these results are supported by Clifford (2008) who also highlights the importance of a hedge funds' organizational design and demonstrates that activist funds impose longer lock-up and withdrawal-notice periods on their investors than other hedge funds. Finally, consistent with the hypothesis that hedge funds improve corporate governance, Greenwood and Schoar (2009) find that short-run and long-run valuation effects are driven by subsequent takeovers in which hedge funds force underperforming managers to put their companies up for sale.

For other countries, there is only limited empirical evidence. For the German market, Bessler, Drobetz, and Holler (2010a) and Achleitner, Betzer, and Gider (2008) confirm that the characteristics of hedge fund targets are consistent with agency problems of free cash flow. For the United Kingdom Becht, Franks, Mayer, and Rossi (2009) analyze shareholder activism in a clinical study of the investments of the Hermes Focus Fund. Based on proprietary data, they indicate that in contrast to most other activist shareholders this fund privately engages with target management to implement significant changes to the company's operating and financing strategies.[85] Finally, focusing on several European countries Croci (2007) provides evidence for a small group of activist shareholders.

While all of these studies are consistent with the hypothesis that hedge funds improve corporate governance they cannot rule out the possibility that the observed returns might also be driven by other factors. In particular, they cannot rule out that observed increases in share prices are associated with wealth transfers from debtholders. Moreover, most studies are based on a relatively short time interval located in the middle of the most recent up-market which was characterized by increasing valuations and positive investor sentiment. Hence, most existing studies cannot consider whether there is a time-variation in the returns to hedge fund activism which might indicate that activist hedge funds also generate returns by market timing and/or by exploiting other behavioral effects. In fact, there is anecdotal evidence that many activist hedge funds suffered substantial losses during the most recent subprime crisis. This might indicate that their previous high returns were the result of excessive optimism by other market participants in the hedge funds' ability to improve target companies.

F. Conclusion

Activist hedge funds often use their stakes in target firms in order to exert substantial influence on important corporate decisions. In particular, they frequently force managers to make large payouts to shareholders in the form of dividend increases and share repurchases. Moreover, they also often interfere in corporate investment policy and ask managers to restructure their firm's asset portfolios, abandon large-scale investment projects and also push firms into mergers & acquisitions. This hedge fund activism can create value if target firms are at an advanced stage of their lifecycle and operate in mature industries. These firms tend to generate high profits and free cash flows but do not have valuable investment opportunities.[86] In the case of weak corporate governance, managers of these firms often waste these free cash flows on unprofitable investment projects and on underperforming business units. Consequently, hedge fund interference can increase firm value by constraining the discretionary freedom of managers and preventing them from recycling cash flows

[85] There are several other related papers which do not directly focus on hedge fund activism. These include Dai (2007), Renneboog, Simons, and Wright (2007), Andres, Betzer, and Weir (2007), Achleitner, Andres, Betzer, and Weir (2010).
[86] See Maksimovic and Philipps (2008) for a review of the literature on industry life cycles.

into the firm. However, hedge fund activism might also destroy firm value. This can occur, for instance, when their restructuring measures lead to a substantial increase in the risk of target firms reducing the value of the firm's debt. Moreover, hedge fund activism might also reduce the long-run growth potential of firms. This occurs because paying out cash flows to shareholders reduces the firm's ability to realize the value of their growth option. Nevertheless, most empirical research comes to the conclusion that hedge fund activism helps to reduce agency problems and creates value (Brav, Jiang, and Kim, 2009). Consequently, activist hedge funds seem to play a similar role in corporate governance as that played by corporate raiders and leveraged buyouts which targeted firms suffering from agency problems of free cash flows during the 1980s.

However, hedge fund activism can only address problems in the design of business strategies and financial policies that can be ameliorated by large-scale restructuring measures such as recapitalizations, asset sales and mergers & acquisitions. This occurs for two reasons. First, activist hedge funds have limited operational skills and therefore cannot help to ameliorate inefficiencies in the details of the firm's operations (Achleitner, Betzer, and Gider, 2008; Greenwood and Schoar, 2009). Second, the share price reactions to less visible measures are more uncertain and it takes a longer time period before they will be fully reflected in the firm's share price. Instead, the highly visible restructuring measures proposed by hedge funds are usually quickly incorporated in the firm's share price.

Chapter II. Corporate Governance Systems and the Influence of Hedge Funds

Hedge funds and other activist investors have only recently started to become more active in German corporate governance. In particular, while hedge funds have been active in the U.S. capital market for a long time (Boyson and Mooradian, 2008), the first high-profile case of shareholder activism in Germany occurred as late as 2005. This involved the two hedge funds TCI and Atticus who forced the management of the Deutsche Börse to implement several restructuring measures which are typically also used by hedge funds in the U.S. capital market. This delayed emergence of hedge fund activism appears to be related to differences between the German and the U.S. corporate governance systems.[87] Most importantly, the German corporate governance system used to be dominated by a governing coalition consisting of inside shareholders, banks and the company's workforce (Schmidt, 2004). This prevented capital market investors from influencing German firms. More recently, the influence of this governing coalition was eroded by substantial changes in the German legal system and capital market environment. Apparently, this created a control vacuum in the corporate governance of many German firms and enabled activist hedge funds to target German firms. These issues are further investigated in this chapter. Section A focuses on the balance of power in the traditional German corporate governance system that was characterized by an absence of shareholder activism. Section B highlights recent changes and investigates how hedge funds can apply their activist strategies in the German capital market. Section C summarizes the most important issues and concludes this chapter.

A. The Traditional German Insider-based Corporate Governance System

There are substantial differences between the design of the traditional German and U.S. corporate governance systems. Most importantly, the German system used to be dominated by a governing coalition of insiders and put only limited emphasis on the interests of capital market investors. Therefore, the traditional German corporate governance system is often considered as the archetype of an insider-based corporate governance system. This did not leave many opportunities for activist shareholders, such as hedge funds, to exert influence on important strategic and financial decisions. Consequently, analyzing the traditional German corporate governance system helps to understand why shareholder activism by hedge funds and other shareholders only

[87] These are generally assumed to be the dominant drivers of the design of national corporate governance systems (La Porta, Lopez-de-Silanes, Shleifer, and Vishny, 1998).

began to emerge with a significant time lag. Therefore, this issue is investigated in this section. The first subsection explains how the old governing coalition used to control German firms. The second subsection analyzes why capital markets had only limited opportunities for opposing this governing coalition. The third subsection concludes.

I. The Old Governing Coalition in the German Corporate Governance System

The traditional German corporate governance system used to be dominated by a governing coalition which controlled the supervisory boards of most German firms. This governing coalition was composed of three groups whose interests often collided with the objectives of capital market investors (Schmidt, 2004).[88]

The first influential member of the governing coalition was the banks. In particular, the large German banking groups such as Deutsche Bank, Commerzbank and Dresdner Bank exerted substantial influence on the large German firms. This is documented by Baums and von Randow (1995) who report that banks held 12% of all available board seats and excercised 84% of the voting rights at the shareholder meetings of the average German blue chip company in 1992. Similar results are reported by Dittmann, Maug, and Schneider (2010) who also find evidence for a high representation of banks on the boards of German firms in the traditional German corporate governance system. Banks had these controlling positions in the governance of large German firms for several reasons. First, banks were the major providers of external financing to firms who often had close relationships with individual banks (Rieckers and Spindler, 2004). Combined with the strong legal protection of creditors in Germany (Bae and Goyal, 2009) banks had significant bargaining power over firms who needed to maintain these valuable relationships and had difficulties in assessing other financing sources (Bessler, Sherman, and Kaen, 1998). Second, the strong influence of banks was accommodated by German corporate law which classified bank's claims in bankruptcy proceedings as debt, even if the bank held seats on supervisory boards or owned equity stakes and was therefore also responsible for the firm's financial difficulties (Dittmann, Maug, and Schneider, 2010; Kroszner and Strahan, 2001). Third, banks were able to exercise a large share of voting rights in many firms. On the one hand, they used to be major shareholders in the big firms holding direct equity stakes and

[88] This coalition controlled the agenda and decision-making of German boards. Therefore, due to the large scale of the resulting agency problems other defects in the design of German boards such as the absence of performance-based pay and the practice of former CEOs becoming chairman of the board are only of secondary importance (Mann, 2003).

indirect stakes via their mutual funds business. On the other hand, banks were also able to exercise their customer's voting rights because most clients did not direct the voting behavior of banks acting as custodians for them (Baums and von Randow, 1995; Dittmann, Maug, and Schneider, 2010). This led to a violation of the principle of "one-share-one-vote" so that banks had more voting power than warranted by their own equity investments. Thus, even though most large German firms formally appeared to have a dispersed ownership structure, they were not subject to effective control by capital markets (Faccio and Lang, 2002).

At first sight, one could conclude that this high representation of banks should help to control managerial moral hazard and boost firm performance. In particular, German banks have long-term relationships with firms and should therefore encourage them to assume a long-term perspective. In addition, concentrated debt positions in the hand of banks can also help to monitor managerial moral hazard since banks have high incentives to monitor and can refuse to roll over debt (Tirole, 2006; Diamond, 1984). At the same time, however, this influence of banks created substantial conflicts of interest regarding the level of risk-taking. In particular, banks' debt exposures used to be significantly larger than their equity investments. Therefore, the resulting conflicts of interest were apparently larger than their monitoring benefits such that bank ownership tended to reduce firm value (Böhmer, 2000). These agency problems were further reinforced by the German universal banking system in which banks were involved in both commercial and investment banking. This created incentives for banks to generate additional investment banking revenues by aligning themselves with corporate managers (Böhmer, 2001; Stanzel, 2007).[89] As a result of these agency problems, banks were more inclined to use their controlling influence to favor investment and financing strategies which reduce business and financial risk (Emmons and Schmid, 1998). This might include diversifying takeovers, restricting payouts to shareholders and adopting conservative capital structures. In addition, banks had high incentives to interfere in corporate mergers & acquisitions and to protect incumbent insiders from the market for corporate control because shareholder-driven restructurings might reduce the value of their debt claims (Qiu and Yu, 2009; Klock, Mansi, and Maxwell, 2005).

[89] Banks themselves were not subject to stringent control by outside capital markets in that they were embedded in a network of cross-holdings and proxy voting with each other and with large industrial firms. Therefore, bank managers were effectively insulated from interference by outside capital markets (Kaserer and Wenger, 1998). Moreover, in the case of small and medium-sized firms these problems were often reinforced because they had lending relationships with the regional banks which are effectively controlled by state- and municipal-level governments and, therefore, might pursue goals other than generating profits (Allen and Gale, 1995).

The second important member of the governing coalition used to be inside shareholders. These had controlling positions in most small- and medium-sized firms in Germany (Faccio and Lang, 2002; Franks and Mayer, 2001, Adams, 1999; Schmidt, 2004). For instance, Barca and Becht (2001) report that 82.5% (64.2%) of all listed German companies had one blockholder with a stake exceeding 25% (50%). Due to the large size of their stakes, the benefits of taking board seats and monitoring management overcompensated these investors for the associated information costs. Therefore, they were not subject to the free-rider problem (Grossman and Hart, 1980) suggesting that they should help to boost firm value. At the same time, however, the strong influence of these blockholders also created new agency problems with outside minority shareholders because their objectives often diverged from another. As a result, depending on their identity and their ability to capture private benefits of control, these controlling shareholders had adverse implications on firm value.[90] In the case of families or management, inside ownership is likely to reduce firm value due to an "entrenchment effect". This occurs because higher inside ownership protects managers and family investors from outside interference by the market for corporate control (Bhagat and Jefferis, 2002; Stulz, 1988; Cheng, Najar, and Rajan, 2004). Therefore, these insiders can use their controlling position to extract private benefits of control (Roe, 1996). For example, this can be achieved by using intercorporate asset sales and transfer pricing arrangements between different family-affiliated firms in order to expropriate minority shareholders (Bigelli, Mehrotra, and Rau, 2008; Barclay and Holderness, 1989; Dyck and Zingales, 2004a/b). Moreover, they can adjust payout policies, capital structure and corporate strategies to reduce risk, consume perks or exploit minority shareholders.[91] Corporations as inside shareholders are likely to have a negative impact on firm value because they often have substantial conflicts of interest with other shareholders. For instance, corporations have incentives to use crossholdings to deepen supplier-costumer relationships (Fee, Hadlock, and Thomas, 2006) or to stabilize strategic alliances. Moreover, they have high incentives to use their influence to obtain favorable terms in transfer pricing arrangements or in inter-corporate asset sales (Meoli, Paleari, and Urga, 2006). Furthermore, they can use their equity stakes to obtain access to and abuse inside information. Moreover, managers

[90] This is in sharp contrast to the intial proposition by Demsetz (1983) and Demsetz and Lehn (1985) that the ownership structure has no impact on firm value because it is the endogenous result of a value-maximizing process.

[91] At low levels of inside ownership, these negative effects on firm value might be overcompensated by an 'incentive alignment effect'. This can occur when inside ownership aligns the payoffs of controlling insiders and outside investors (Jensen and Meckling, 1976).

can use cross-holdings to entrench their position by engineering networks of cross-holdings with friendly managers of other firms which protects them against monitoring and interference by outside shareholders (Woidtke, 2002).[92] This suggests that corporations are not only interested in the value of the company as a stand-alone entity but also pursue other objectives with their investments and try to extract private benefits of control (Barclay, Holderness, and Sheehan, 2009).[93]

The final member of the governing coalition in the traditional German corporate governance is the company's workforce. This group has the right to nominate one third (half) of the board members if the firm has more than 500 (2000) employees (MitBestG). This allows the firm's workforce to exert a significant influence on corporate decision-making and to protect their firm-specific human capital which used to be necessary to accommodate the inflexibility of German labor markets (Schmidt, 2004). At the same time, however, this created substantial conflicts of interests with outside shareholders. In fact, similar to controlling insiders and banks, workers have a preference for low-risk business strategies and financing policies. Therefore, Hellwig (2001) argues that the company's workforce is the "natural ally" of underperforming managers.[94] These agency problems are compounded in many German firms because the function of labor representation within the board is often assumed by leading union members. In contrast to regular members of the firm's workforce, these board members cannot contribute hands-on information to the board's decision-making process. Instead they have high incentives to use these highly visible positions to promote their broader public policy objectives that need not always be related to the company's affairs (Fauver and Fürst, 2006). In addition, these union members also have high incentives to entrench weak managers (Atennassov and Kim, 2009).

---

[92] Nevertheless, under some conditions these inter-corporate investments can also be value-enhancing, e.g. if they allow both firms to establish joint ventures that provide both of them with additional cash flows (Holderness, 2003). This appears to be most likely if potential synergies from cooperation are high or if both firms operate in unrelated lines of business so that there are no 'anxilliary interests' that could create conflicts of interest (Moldenhauer, 2007).

[93] In many German firms these agency problems used to be amplified in that the proportion of voting rights controlled by family or corporate insiders exceeded their share of cash flow rights. Many German firms issued multiple share classes, including preference shares without voting rights, leading to a violation of the principle of one-share-one-vote which in turn facilitates expropriation of minority shareholders (Masulis, Wang, and Xie, 2009; Ehrhardt, Kuklinski, and Nowak, 2004). Moreover, pyramids can also be used to decouple cash flow and voting rights (Almeida and Wolfenzon, 2006a; Franks and Mayer, 2001).

[94] Related evidence for the U.S. is provided by Hanka (1998), Cronqvist, Heyman, Nilsson, Svaleryd, and Vlachos (2009), Faleye, Mehrotra, and Morck (2006) and Gordon and Pound (1990).

Overall, the above arguments suggest that the German corporate governance system used to be dominated by a governing coalition of inside shareholders, banks and the company's workforce. Proponents of this system argue that it fostered stability and enabled managers to adopt a long-term perspective (Rajan and Zingales, 2003). However, these groups are not only interested in the market value of the firm but derive private benefits from their controlling position. This creates substantial conflicts of interests with outside shareholders who have limited opportunities for influencing corporate decision-making.

II. Limited Influence of Capital Markets on German Corporate Governance

The traditional German corporate governance system placed only a very limited emphasis on the perspective of capital markets. For instance, hostile takeovers and shareholder activism hardly played a relevant role in controlling managerial behavior. This was reflected in the low level of activity in the market for corporate control in Germany where only four truly hostile takeovers have ever taken place (Schmidt, 2004). Moreover, there was also a very limited incidence of shareholder activism in Germany. Croci (2007) reports only 13 cases of shareholder activism in Germany between 1990 and 2001.[95] This limited influence of capital markets on German corporate governance can be explained by a number of factors (Schmidt, Drukarczyk, Honold, Schüler, Tetens, and Prigge, 1997).

Most importantly, the dominating position of the governing coalition of inside blockholders, banks and the company's workforce was entrenched. It controlled the majority of voting rights so that potential raiders or shareholder activists were not able to acquire meaningful blocks to exert control. Therefore, capital market participants were effectively locked out of the control of the firm and could not influence key decisions without the prior consent of the members of the old governing coalition (Allen and Gale, 1995). Moreover, mergers & acquisitions were not driven by capital markets. Instead, it seemed that banks were often using their influence to arrange takeovers that suited their own interests (Böhmer, 2000). For instance, in a clinical study Jenkinsson and Ljungqvist (2001) indicate that banks helped firms to acquire blocks in other firms. This is supported by Köke (2004) who documents that poor

[95] Given the large size of the German economy, this number is low, even in comparison to other Continental European countries included in this study such as Italy, France and Switzerland. However, the study is only focused on the activities of 14 well-known activist shareholders so that it might not reflect the true levels of activitiy.

performance makes a change in control via block trades more likely in Germany.[96] However, German banks' debt exposures usually substantially exceeded their direct equity exposures. This creates significant incentives for banks to favor risk-reducing mergers & acquisitions that need not create shareholder value. In addition, there is some evidence that they helped firms and controlling inside shareholders to expropriate minority shareholders in corporate transactions (Wenger and Hecker, 1994; Faccio and Stolin, 2006).

In addition, the influence of capital markets was limited by the high bargaining power of the company's workforce. This had substantial effects on the outcome of hostile takeovers and control contests for several reasons. First, labor representatives on the board could derail takeover bids because the board can issue recommendations to shareholders and monitors management`s use of takeover defenses. In fact, even though most of the takeover defenses often used in the U.S. capital market were not available in Germany, executives were able to use a large number of other takeover defenses (Höpner and Jackson, 2001; Franks and Mayer, 1998; Jenkinsson and Ljungqvist, 2001). As a result, labor representatives could exert substantial influence on the outcome of takeover attempts. Second, mandatory co-determination and board representation created many opportunities for the company's workforce to complicate post-merger integration and restructuring programs (Pagano and Volpi, 2005).

Furthermore, the influence of capital markets was constrained by provisions in German corporate law which created problems for hostile acquirers and corporate raiders when they wanted to quickly control target companies. For instance, there are substantial time lags between acquiring a voting majority and obtaining full control because an immediate dismissal of board members and senior managements is not in accordance with German corporate law. Furthermore, it was difficult to engage in shareholder activism because German laws and regulations did not offer sufficient legal protection of minority shareholders' rights. In particular, potential shareholder activists did not have access to the necessary legal mechanisms to put pressure on target management. This includes oppressed minorities mechanisms, pre-emptive rights against dilution and the ability to sue directors and managers (Dyck and Zingales, 2004a/b). As a result, the regulation of German capital markets effectively reinforced the entrenchment of the governing coalition. The development of a market for corporate control was also constrained by the intransparency of German firms

[96] This behavior of banks seems to be similar to the role of U.S. banks which also act as intermediaries in mergers & acquisitions in the U.S. market for corporate control (Ivashina, Nair, Saunders, Massoud, and Stover, 2009; Kolasinski and Kothari, 2008).

which created additional information risks for raiders and shareholder activists. In particular, this concerns intransparent financial statements, ownership structures and limited prohibitions on insider trading (Schmidt, 2004).

Finally, the influence of market-based governance mechanisms, such as hostile takeovers and shareholder activism, was low due to the limited liquidity of German capital markets. This limited the ability of activist shareholders to accumulate and to sell the shares of target companies at a limited price impact. Moreover, liquid capital markets quickly reflect the value enhancements generated by activist shareholders and therefore facilitate "active monitoring" (Tirole, 2006). Furthermore, limited liquidity also constrained the effectiveness of internal governance mechanisms such as executive compensation (Holmström and Tirole, 1993). In fact, executive compensation was not even related to share prices in Germany. Instead, Elston and Goldberg (2003) document that the compensation of German executives was closely related to accounting performance measures such as return on equity and sales growth. As a result, executive compensation exhibited only a limited sensitivity to firms' share price performance. Clearly, the structure of executive compensation directly corresponds to the limited importance of outside capital markets in the German corporate governance and was consistent with the interests of the governing coalition of corporate insiders.[97]

Overall, this limited influence of capital markets is in sharp contrast to the U.S. corporate governance system where for a long time hostile takeovers and activist shareholders have played a crucial role in disciplining managers.

III. Conclusion

The preceding discussion emphasizes that the German corporate governance used to be dominated by inside shareholders, banks and the company's workforce. This governing coalition was often able to capture high private benefits from its controlling position leading to substantial conflicts of interest with capital market investors. As a result, shareholder activists, such as hedge funds, effectively had limited influence on

[97] Similarly, this reasoning applies to the renumeration and incentive structure of board members. In addition, this practice was reinforced by several legal obstacles in implementing stock option programs. For instance, German corporate law (AktG) did not allow companies to issue naked options. Therefore, companies had to issue convertible bonds in order to tie manager's remuneration to the company's share price. Furthermore, German corporate law also used to prohibit share repurchases which are commonly used to implement stock option programs by U.S. firms.

the business strategies and financial policies of German firms. This limited influence of capital markets had important economic implications. In particular, it constrained the development of capital markets and reinforced the reliance of firms on bank financing.[98] The resulting underdevelopment of German capital markets might have put firms at a competitive disadvantage relative to firms from other countries because capital markets are better suited than banks to finance innovation and other high risk projects (Allen and Gale, 1999). These factors appear to be the predominant sources of economic growth in most modern economies (Bittelmeyer, 2007; Bessler and Bittelmeyer, 2008).

B. Activist Hedge Funds in the German Corporate Governance System

Starting in the late 1990s, the traditional German corporate governance system began to change and to adopt elements of a more market-oriented system. In particular, changing patterns in corporate financing and reforms of capital market regulations eroded the influence of the old governing coalition that used to dominate corporate governance. This created a control vacuum in the corporate governance of many firms. As a result, activist hedge funds also began to target firms traded in the capital market. These might have been attractive targets for activist hedge funds because presumably their business strategies and financial policies were still implemented by the old governing coalition. Therefore, this section investigates the impact of hedge funds on the corporate governance of German firms. Subsection I investigates the impact of recent changes in the corporate governance system that enabled hedge funds to target German firms. Subsection II evaluates how activist hedge funds can implement their restructuring measures in German target firms. In particular, it highlights the implications of corporate law and the development of capital markets on the feasibility of hedge fund activism. Subsection III highlights specific agency problems that can occur between hedge funds and other shareholders due to specific aspects of capital market regulation. Subsection IV concludes.

[98] In addition, the low level of liquidity and valuations in German capital markets did not offer controlling blockholders attractive opportunities to sell off their stakes and therefore entrenched the structure of the German corporate governance system (Pagano, 1993; Boot, Gopalan, and Thakor, 2006).

I. Reforms of the German Corporate Governance and the Emergence of Hedge Funds Activism

Recently, the German corporate governance experienced a substantial shift towards a more market-based system. In particular, banks and corporate investors began to reduce their involvement in the corporate governance of German firms. Moreover, shareholder rights were improved by several legal reforms and the importance of capital markets for corporate financing increased substantially.[99] As a result, a control vaccum emerged in corporate governance which enabled activist hedge funds to target many German firms.

1. Dissolution of the Old Governing Coalition

In the traditional German corporate governance system, hedge funds were not able to exert influence on business strategies and financial policies because the corporate governance of most firms was dominated by members of the old governing coalition. Therefore, several developments in corporate governance which reduced the influence of banks and inside shareholders might have created opportunities for activist hedge funds to target German firms.

First of all, the influence of inside shareholders declined substantially because banks and many industrial firms sold off their portfolios of cross-holdings. This process was facilitated by the reform of the German tax code in 2002. This reform eliminated the "tax lock-in" of corporate blockholders (Dai, Maydew, Shackelford, and Zhang, 2008) and abolished the taxation of capital gains on inter-corporate investments. Moreover, the large German banks also sold off their stakes because they refocused their business models towards capital markets. Therefore, banks' benefits of playing a pivotal role in the corporate governance of German firms were reduced (Schmidt, 2004). As a result, the ownership structures of many firms became more dispersed and the network of the former "Germany Inc." began to dissolve. This created a control vacuum in the ownership structures of many firms. In many cases, this gap was filled by institutional investors acting as financial blockholders who are mostly interested in maximizing firm value (Hackethal, Schmidt, and Tyrell, 2004). In particular, foreign institutional investors started to increase their allocations to the German capital market. This increase in foreign ownership was also accommodated by changes in the taxation of

[99] Relevant legal reforms also include the introduction of investor-oriented IFRS accounting standards and other disclosure regulations (KonTraG).

dividends paid to foreign shareholders. German mutual funds and pension funds also gained importance in the German financial system subsequent to shifts in the German pension system (Bundesbank, 2001). Thus, the ownership structures of many firms became more dispersed. However, it is important to note that this process did not affect all firms to the same extent. In particular, the gap in the ownership structure of some firms was filled by other non-financial blockholders such as foreign firms and family investors (Weber, 2008). Moreover, this process mostly affected the larger firms that did not have controlling family shareholders. These inside blockholders continued to exert substantial control over their mostly small- and medium-sized firms (Weber, 2008).

The reduction in the influence of the old governing coalition was reinforced by changes in corporate law. For instance, the influence of banks was curtailed by the KonTraG. This law introduced the requirement for custodian banks to ask for their client's permission when they want to exercise their voting rights. Moreover, the treatment of "equity-replacing" loans during bankruptcy proceedings underwent significant changes. In particular, the rules governing the treatment of loans by owners of privately held GmbH's now also applied to loans by shareholders of publicly-listed AG's (Rieckers and Spindler, 2004). Therefore, loans by banks that also hold an equity stake in a firm are currently classified as equity in bankruptcy proceedings. Finally, the involvement of banks in corporate governance was also made more transparent as banks now need to disclose the names of bank employees holding seats on supervisory boards (Third Act on the Promotion of Financial Markets). In addition, the legal position of other members of the old governing coalition was also curtailed. This includes the prohibition or phasing-out of preference shares and shares with multiple voting rights (Third Act on the Promotion of Financial Markets, 1998). Moreover, oppressed minority rights were introduced giving minority shareholders the right to call for an extraordinary shareholder's meeting under specific conditions.

However, the company's workforce as the third group of the old governing coalition remained largely intact. In fact, it was only the creation of the "SE" which reduced to some extent the influence of German unions in that labor representatives on supervisory boards are not only elected by the firm's German employees but also by its foreign workforce.

2. Opportunities for Activist Hedge Funds

The reduced influence of banks and corporate shareholders created opportunities for capital market participants to exert more influence on corporate governance and other important corporate decisions. In many cases, activist hedge funds took advantage of these opportunities because other capital market participants did not use their increased bargaining power in corporate governance.

In particular, there was no visible increase in the frequency of hostile takeovers (Schmidt, 2004). This seems surprising given that several reforms were implemented that should have facilitated hostile takeovers (Goergen, Martynova, and Renneboog, 2005; Martynova, 2006; Berglöf and Burkart, 2003). These include the development of a legal framework for a market for corporate control (e.g. the introduction of the takeover codes in 1995 and and 2002).[100] Moreover, the costs of takeovers were also reduced by the tax reform in 2000 which abolished capital gains taxes on write-ups on acquired assets. In addition, the increasing liquidity of German equity markets should also have facilitated the acquisition of hostile stakes (Kyle and Villa, 1991; Maug, 1998). Furthermore, institutional ownership also increased significantly. This should also help potential acquirers to complete hostile takeovers because institutional investors do not need to be compensated for their loss in private benefits subsequent to a hostile takeover (Holmström and Kaplan, 2001).

However, the absence of hostile takeovers can be explained by several factors. In particular, the strong bargaining position of the company's workforce as the third element of the old governing coalition was not affected by the reforms. In fact, the old system of co-determination was not revised meaning that labor and union representatives on the boards of German firms still have the power to frustrate hostile takeover attempts. In addition, there are still some non-financial blockholders with private benefits of control in the ownership structure of many German firms. These insiders tend to increase the costs of takeovers due to the design of the new German takeover framework (Martynova, 2006).[101]

---

[100] See Berglöf and Burkart (2003) and Jenkinsson and Ljungqvist (2001) for a detailed discussion of the economics of German takeover regulations and Martynova (2006) for a comparison of reforms in takeover regulation in other EU countries.

[101] In particular, the mandatory bid rule in combination with the equal treatment rule forces potential acquirers not only to compensate old blockholders for their loss of private benefits but requires acquirers to extend this additional payment to all other shareholders. This increases the cost of takeovers and therefore reduces the interests of raiders in those German targets that have not yet restructured their ownership.

Moreover, there was also no increase in the involvement of German mutual funds and pension funds in the corporate governance of German firms. Unlike institutional investors such as CalPers and TIIA CREF in the U.S. capital market, German institutional investors continued to assume a rather passive role in corporate governance and did not take advantage of the withdrawal of banks and other industrial investors. In fact, this passive behavior is highlighted by their behavior during the first high profile hedge fund attack in Germany when the German institutional investors quickly sold their stakes in the Deutsche Börse subsequent to the emergence of the hedge funds TCI and Atticus. These shares were immediately picked up by foreign institutional investors who ultimately were crucial to the success of the hedge funds intervention.[102]

The preceding discussion indicates that capital market investors did not take advantage of the control vacuum created by the dissolution of the old governing coalition. Consequently, agency problems between management and capital market investors were not addressed, increasing opportunities for managers to expropriate shareholders. For example, managers entrenched their position by increasing the fraction of inside directors (Höpner, 2001). Moreover, the value of managerial compensation arrangements including stock options, which were first introduced in Germany by the Deutsche Bank and Daimler in 1996, increased substantially (Dietz, 2004; Schmidt and Schwalbach, 2007). In addition, the value of these compensation programs was often not closely linked to share price performance (Tuschke and Sanders, 2003; Schmidt, 2004). Therefore, they did not align the interests of managers and outside shareholders. Instead, they allowed managers to boost their compensation at the expense of shareholders. In addition, these agency problems were amplified by the ongoing influence of the firm's labor force (Schmidt, 2004). This suggests that the virtual absence of monitoring created a systemic crisis in German corporate governance leaving high discretionary freedom for managers to pursue their own objectives (Schmidt, 2004; Schmidt and Spindler, 2004). Therefore, the emergence of activist hedge funds can be interpreted as a response by the capital market system to this control vacuum in the German corporate governance system.

[102] This passive behavior might also suggest that these institutional investors were still subject to conflicts because they were affiliated with the large German banks (Bundesbank, 2001; Woidtke, 2002). As a result of this passive behavior, the growing dispersion of the ownership structures of German firms was associated with declining attendance rates at company's general assemblies.

II. Ability of Hedge Funds to Restructure German Firms

The dissolution of the old governing coalition generated trading opportunities for activist hedge funds in Germany because it created a control vacuum in the ownership structure of many German firms. However, this is not a sufficient condition for the successful implementation of an activist campaign. Instead, the success of hedge fund activism also depends on other factors including specific provisions in corporate law, firm characteristics and the development of capital markets. Therefore, these issues are investigated in this section in order to evaluate what type of restructuring programs can be successfully imposed on German target firms by activist hedge funds.

1. Controlling German Target Firms

The control vacuum in the ownership structure of many German firms should facilitate hedge fund activism. Nevertheless, the ability of hedge funds to control target firms is still constrained by specific provisions in German corporate law. In particular, they need to gain control of the target firm's board of directors because shareholders are not allowed to directly interfere in corporate decision-making (§ 120 II AktG).[103] Instead, this task is assigned to the firm's senior management which is monitored by the supervisory board. Moreover, the supervisory board also selects senior management and has to approve important corporate decisions such as spin-offs, asset sales and other major restructuring transactions (§111 IV S. 2 AktG). Importantly, however, shareholders also cannot exert direct influence on the decisions of supervisory board members. As a result, hedge funds can only directly interfere in a limited set of decisions which have to be put to a shareholder vote in the firm's general assembly. This includes specific types of takeovers, equity-related financing transactions and the election of board members. Therefore, activist hedge funds often try to elect their representatives onto the supervisory board in order to ensure the complete implementation of their restructuring programs. In general, this requires that they assemble coalitions representing at least 50% of outstanding shares that are present at the firm's generally assembly.

However, hedge funds face several obstacles when they want to control the board of directors of German firms. In particular, the composition of German boards often puts constraints on activist hedge funds. On the one hand, there are labor representatives

[103] The general assembly only needs to be consulted when managers want to change the fundamental characteristics of the firm's business (§ 119 I AktG and 'Holzmüller-Grundsätze').

holding one half of seats on the supervisory board of firms with more than 2000 employees. On the other hand, many bankers still sit on the supervisory boards of a large number of firms even though most banks have sold off their portfolios of cross-holdings (Dittmann, Maug, and Schneider, 2010). These board members often represent interests that do not coincide with the objectives of hedge funds. Replacing these board members is often difficult because a qualified majority of 75% is needed in order to oust board members prior to the expiration of their terms.

Moreover, activist hedge funds are also constrained by other provisions of German corporate law when they try to enforce decisions at the general assembly. In order to push through their proposals or block specific plans by management they need to assemble coalitions representing between 25% and 75% depending on the type of decision. Moreover, they need to acquire more than 5% of voting shares when they want to call for an extraordinary shareholder's meeting prior to the ordinary general assembly. Finally, German corporate law also determines how activist hedge funds can counter the defensive measures implemented by managers. For instance, on some occasions managers have implemented measures that depress the company's share price creating substantial problems for activist hedge funds whose positions are frequently leveraged. Therefore, hedge funds have to try to call for an extraordinary shareholder meeting in order to replace board members and senior management prior to the regular annual shareholder's meeting. Moreover, on some occasions hedge funds have also filed lawsuits against managers or board members responsible for these decisions.

2. Implementation of Hedge Funds' Restructuring Plans

The type of restructuring measures that hedge funds can successfully apply to German target firms is also often constrained by several factors. In particular, most of their restructuring measures can only be profitably implemented when the target firm has access to liquid capital markets. Moreover, German corporate law also puts constraints on specific types of restructuring measures that are frequently used by activist hedge funds.

a. Financial Restructuring

Activist hedge funds often try to push target firms into financial restructurings that force them to make large payouts to shareholders in the form of higher dividends or share repurchases. This usually requires that the target firms raise additional debt capital. However, banks are typically unwilling to support these measures because they increase the financial risk of the firm. Therefore, these restructurings can only be implemented if target firms have access to debt capital markets at attractive conditions. This suggests that recent developments in the structure of German capital markets should have facilitated financial restructurings of German target firms. Most importantly, the volume of public debt markets has grown substantially subsequent to the introduction of the Euro (Pagano and von Thadden, 2004). Similarly, other forms of debt such as leveraged loans have become available to a growing fraction of German firms. In addition to the growth of debt markets, developments in corporate law should also have improved the opportunities for hedge funds to push target firms into financial restructurings. In particular, reduced restrictions on share repurchases have facilitated the extraction of free cash flows (Bessler, Drobetz, and Seim, 2009). Nevertheless, several legal restrictions still impede the implementation of share repurchase programs and dividend increases. In particular, German corporate law limits share repurchases and dividend distributions to current period earnings and retained earnings and makes it difficult for companies to access other capital reserves for this purpose. Therefore, hedge funds often have to remain active in the governance of target firms for extended periods of time when they want to ensure that large amounts of cash reserves are paid out to shareholders.

This suggests that hedge funds can initiate the same type of financial restructurings which have been observable in the U.S. capital market for a long time. However, this reasoning only applies to the large German corporations. These corporations can diversify their sources of external debt financing towards market-based debt financing (Schmidt, 2004). In contrast, smaller firms still rely on their "hausbanks" and on intermediated bank financing (Hackethal, Schmidt, and Tyrell, 2004). These banks have strong incentives to resist financial restructurings because there is also the possibility that returns to hedge fund activism reflect wealth transfers from debtholders. As a result, a large fraction of German firms are still locked into lending relationships that provide creditors with the bargaining power to stop activist hedge funds from restructuring the firm's balance sheet (Renneboog and Szilagyi, 2008).

Therefore, it is difficult for hedge funds to restructure the financial policies of these firms.

b. Asset Restructuring and Mergers & Acquisitions

Activist hedge funds also try to force managers to restructure their business models and sell off non-core assets. The value that can be created by these transactions also depends on the liquidity and valuations in capital markets (Schlingemann, Stulz, and Walkling, 2002). Therefore, the recent growth in German equity capital markets, which started during the new economy period, should also have facilitated the execution of these asset restructurings. For instance, there was a growing volume of share issuance activity (Bessler and Kurth, 2007), a proliferation of mutual funds and pension funds (Bundesbank, 2001) and increased analyst coverage (Bessler and Stanzel, 2009). Similar to the case of financial restructurings, however, this reasoning mostly applies to large German corporations. In contrast, it appears difficult for hedge funds to attack smaller firms that are locked into lending relationships with their "hausbanks" (Hackethal, Schmidt, and Tyrell, 2004). These banks also have strong incentives to resist asset restructurings and break-ups because they typically benefit from the reduction in earnings volatility created by corporate diversification. Moreover, there is a risk for banks that returns to hedge fund activism reflect wealth transfers from debtholders (Renneboog and Szilagyi, 2008).

In addition to break-ups, activist hedge funds often exert influence on mergers & acquisition strategies. In the case that the hedge funds want to promote mergers & acquisitions, their influence is curtailed by the limited hostile activity on the German market for corporate control (Schmidt, 2004). This reduces the likelihood that hedge funds will gain the support of other shareholders for hostile mergers & acquisitions. In addition, it seems reasonable to assume that other hedge funds, which follow merger arbitrage strategies, can create difficulties for activist hedge funds. In particular, anecdotal evidence suggests that these hedge funds frequently take advantage of specific provisions in German takeover regulations. For instance, German acquirers can only initiate a freeze-out of remaining minority shareholders after acquiring 90% of all shares. Moreover, they need 75% in order to be able to enforce "Unternehmensverträge" that enable acquirers to integrate target firms into their own operations. These thresholds create incentives for engineering hold-up situations which enable hedge funds to force acquirers to increase their offers for target firms. This suggests that hedge funds active in merger arbitrage complicate mergers &

acquisitions and, therefore, reduce the likelihood that activist hedge funds will try to initiate takeover attempts.

III. Agency Problems between Hedge Funds and other Shareholders

The strategies pursued by activist hedge funds in Germany also have the potential to create additional agency problems with other shareholders. These problems can result from differences in disclosure regulations compared to the U.S. In particular, after reaching the threshold of 5% of outstanding shares, minority shareholders in the U.S. need to make a 13D filing with the SEC, which requires them to reveal their objectives and whether they intend to influence the firm's management. According to German securities laws (§§21/26 WpHG), minority shareholders only had to disclose the size of their stakes larger than 5% and do not have to disclose the objectives of their investment.[104] In addition, reporting lags are substantially longer in Germany compared to the U.S. (Weber and Zimmermann, 2010). This weakness in the enforcement of German disclosure rules allows hedge funds to secretly accumulate controlling positions and exploit other shareholders.[105] A similar problem is created by the use of derivatives by activist hedge funds because German disclosure regulations apparently lack the flexibility to quickly adjust to new trading tactics. In particular, German rules still do not take into account the growing use of cash-settled derivatives which can be used by hedge funds to circumvent German disclosure regulations and secretly accumulate stakes larger than 3% (5% before February 2007). Moreover, this allows hedge funds to quietly exit their positions because they do not need to report their hedging position in the cash-settled derivative. In addition, this also enables them to decouple cash-flow and voting rights which can create substantial conflicts of interests with other investors when shareholders vote on important decisions.[106] In contrast, regulatory institutions in the U.S. and the UK have reacted swiftly and expanded the scope of disclosure regulations to include cash-settled derivatives.[107]

---

[104] Since February 1, 2007, investors also need to disclose stakes larger than 3% in the firms and need to disclose their intentions when they hold more than 10% of outstanding shares.

[105] For example, the French insurer Axa was subjected to the threat of a fine of just €200,000 for violating the WpHG 21/26-rules (Börsenzeitung, August 24, 2004, p. 1, "Axa verstößt gegen Meldepflicht nach WpHG").

[106] Moreover, they can exercise voting rights without carrying the corresponding economic exposure which can create substantial problems for other shareholders during mergers & acquisitions.

[107] For instance, see the verdict on the use of cash-settled derivatives by TCI when it tried to obtain control of the U.S. railway operator CSX.

Another agency problem emerges due to the problem of "acting in concert". This occurs when a group of hedge funds explicitly or implicitly coordinates its activities against the target firm. According to German security trading laws these groups also have to adhere to the disclosure regulations contained in §§ 21/26 WpHG. In addition, these groups also have to make a mandatory takeover bid for the whole company if they collectively hold more than 30% of outstanding shares. Theoretically, these provisions by the German capital market law should help to protect other investors against the adverse selection risk of trading against a better informed counterparty and should also reduce the risk of expropriation by a new dominating shareholder. In practice, however, these regulations apparently do not achieve this objective because the track record of the German regulator BAFIN in enforcing these rules appears to be weak. In particular, the reputation of the BAFIN was damaged by the case of the hedge funds TCI and Atticus attacking the management of Deutsche Börse AG. In this case, the BAFIN did not rule that these investors engaged in "acting in concert" even though there was plausible evidence that they were following very similar objectives. In addition, this also deprived other investors of the opportunity to tender their shares to the hedge funds in a mandatory bid.

Overall, this suggests that the legal and informational environment in Germany for activist investors such as hedge funds is still different from that in the U.S. In particular, activist hedge funds can engage in trading tactics that allow them to hide for an unreasonable amount of time in order to maximize their share of the increase in shareholder value generated by their intervention.

IV. Empirical Evidence

Empirical evidence for the U.S. capital market suggests that hedge fund activism reduces agency problems and creates value. This might also apply to hedge funds targeting German firms because recent reforms have pushed the German corporate governance and capital market environment towards a more market-oriented system. However, there are still substantial differences between the U.S. and the German environment which might complicate hedge funds' restructuring attempts and even create additional agency problems. Therefore, several empirical studies analyze the valuation effects triggered by activist hedge funds in order to determine whether they also create value in Germany.

Most of these empirical studies report positive abnormal returns in both the short- and in the long-run (e.g. Bessler, Drobetz, and Holler, 2010a; Achleitner, Betzer, and Gider, 2008). This suggests that the engagement of activist hedge funds leads to sustainable increases in shareholder value and is not driven by fads or short-term buying pressure. Thus, hedge funds appear to improve corporate governance. This is also supported by evidence that the characteristics of hedge fund target companies also seem to be consistent with severe agency problems of free cash flow. For instance, Achleitner, Betzer, and Gider (2008) document that target companies hold excessive financial slack and have no controlling shareholder. Thus, they interpret hedge fund attacks on these companies as evidence that hedge funds force managers to take into account the interests of outside shareholders. In line with this interpretation, Mietzner, Schweitzer, and Tyrell (2008) report that hedge fund activism leads to an improvement in operating performance. Moreover, in contrast to targets of private equity firms, they report no impact on profit margins or on the competitive behavior of target firms, supporting the hypothesis that hedge funds become less involved with the details of the targets' operations.

However, there are also at least three studies which seem to cast some doubts on this favorable assessment of hedge fund activism in Germany. First, Bessler, Drobetz, and Holler (2010b) find that long-term valuation effects seem to depend on the market environment, as companies targeted during a down-market exhibit negative long-run returns. This suggests that the proposals of activist hedge funds only increase share prices during an up-market environment which in turn implies that the returns to hedge activisms contain a market-timing component. Second, Bessler, Drobetz, and Holler (2010a) also find a reversal in share prices for the subsample of those hedge funds that use the media to put pressure on managers and try to generate public interest for the stock. The share prices of these firms increase for approximately four months after the engagement and then start to decline. This could also be consistent with market timing behavior but might even indicate that these hedge funds pursue manipulative trading strategies. Third, Achleitner, Betzer, and Gider (2008) provide evidence that German target firms seem to have a high R&D intensity and therefore might even force growth firms to disgorge cash flows which would impair long-term shareholder value. While they do not offer an explanation for this finding, this could also be due to difficulties associated with the accounting treatment of R&D expenditures in Germany. In fact, they also report evidence that hedge funds do not target firms with high growth prospects measured by Tobin's q, which is apparently inconsistent with the finding that target firms have a high R&D-intensity.

C. Summary and Conclusion

The German corporate governance system used to be controlled by a governing coalition consisting of banks, inside shareholders and the company's workforce. This governing coalition effectively locked capital markets out of the control of German firms. Therefore, activist shareholders, such as hedge funds, were for a long time unable to implement their trading strategies in the German capital market. More recently, however, reforms in the German corporate governance system have diminished the influence of this governing coalition and have created a control vacuum in the ownership structure of many German firms. As a result, activist shareholders such as hedge funds increasingly play an active role in corporate governance and exert influence on business strategies, financial policies and governance arrangements of German firms. So far, most empirical research suggests that these interventions trigger positive valuation effects in capital markets. This can be interpreted as evidence that hedge funds also help to contain agency problems in the German corporate governance environment. However, most of these studies are restricted to the time period prior to the recent financial crisis. Therefore, it appears important to investigate in more detail whether activist hedge funds also create value during more adverse market conditions.

Part III. Empirical Analysis – The Impact of Hedge Funds on German Target Firms

The traditional German corporate governance system did not provide many opportunities for capital market investors to have any influence on important corporate decisions. Instead, the system used to be controlled by a governing coalition consisting of controlling inside shareholders such as founding families and other companies, banks as the major providers of capital (Dittmann, Maug, and Schneider, 2010) and the company's workforce. More recently, the importance of capital markets in corporate financing has grown and many firms have experienced a significant restructuring in their ownership structure. In fact, old blockholders have taken advantage of changes in tax regulations to sell their stakes. As a result, there is evidence that hedge funds have begun to fill this "control vacuum" and started to play an influential role in the corporate governance of German firms. For instance, in January 2005 the Anglo-Saxon hedge funds TCI and Atticus confronted the management of the German security exchange operator Deutsche Börse and forced it to implement several far-reaching restructuring measures. These activities indicate that a shift has occured in the German corporate governance system such that capital market investors can now also play an important role in key corporate decisions. This raises the crucial research question of whether hedge funds help to improve the quality of corporate governance, thereby contributing to a more efficient allocation of capital in the German economy.

According to empirical evidence for the U.S., hedge fund engagements are associated with strong and persistent increases in shareholder value. This is generally interpreted as evidence that hedge funds improve corporate governance by correcting inefficiencies resulting from agency problems of free cash flows. However, it is questionable whether or not these results can be transferred to the German capital market because there are still some important differences between the U.S. and the German capital market. For instance, in the U.S. there is no mandatory co-determination which enables German workers to exert influence on corporate decision-making. Moreover, although banks have reduced their corporate lending activities, in particular to large capital-market-oriented firms, there are still many bankers on the boards of German firms. Finally, capital markets are still less liquid than U.S. markets and the enforcement of regulations is less strict than in the U.S. As a result, it is not clear whether hedge funds can also successfully implement their restructuring plans in German target firms and whether the activities of hedge funds should translate into higher firm value.

In addition, existing evidence for the U.S. capital market focuses exclusively on sample periods up to the end of 2006. These can generally be characterized as "up-markets" in that share valuations were generally rising, liquidity was high and volatility was low. Thus, it is an interesting question whether those activist hedge funds who continued to attack firms during the most recent financial crisis period generated similar valuation effects. In particular, it seems reasonable to assume that hedge fund activism can only work as a state-contingent governance mechanism because the magnitude of agency problems of free cash flows should be reduced during periods of distress. Effectively, product markets working as the "ultimate drivers of economic efficiency" (Shleifer and Vishny, 1997) already put sufficient pressure on managers to improve the efficiency of their firms during these time periods.

The empirical analysis in this part of this dissertation addresses these research questions. The first chapter investigates the valuation effects of hedge fund engagements in the German capital market during the up-market period up to the end of 2006, which corresponds to the sample periods investigated by most U.S. studies. The second chapter focuses on the hedge fund engagements which occurred during the time period from 2007 to 2008 in order to analyze valuation effects during the down-market. Finally, the third chapter presents the results of several robustness checks.

Chapter I. Data Description and Methodology

This chapter describes the research design used to investigate the valuation effects of hedge fund engagements in the subsequent chapters. The first section describes the sample selection process. This is important because there is not a common database which can be used to study the activities of hedge funds in the German capital market. The second section provides an overview of the key characteristics of the resulting dataset of 404 events in which hedge funds acquired stakes in German companies for the period between the beginning of 2000 and the end of 2008. The final section provides information on the methodology used to measure short-term and long-term valuation effects as well as the robustness checks.

A. Sample Selection Approach

The objective of the empirical analysis in the following three chapters is to investigate the implications of hedge funds on the market value of German firms. The empirical analysis begins with the collection of information on hedge fund activity in Germany using the Lexis-Nexis database that contains news articles from all of the major German and international newspapers. This database is screened for all news articles containing the company name and the term "hedge fund" within a distance of 50 words for all companies that are constituents of CDAX as of June 30th, 2007. The resulting output files are then manually searched for all news items in which a stake in a company is publicly disclosed or in which the hedge fund makes other public announcements concerning the company (e.g., publication of an open letter to the CEO or board of directors, request for an extraordinary shareholder meeting, etc.). In the last step, the resulting database of events is merged with a database of filings according to §21 WpHG supplied by the "Agentur für Unternehmensdaten" (AFU) which provides the percentage of shares acquired when the fund also makes a regulatory filing.

This sample selection process led to a dataset of 469 pairs of hedge funds and target firms. From this dataset a number of events are excluded because hedge funds also pursue a large number of other strategies which do not lead to active involvement in the target firm's corporate governance. In particular, all events are excluded in which the investor pursues a similar investment approach as private equity funds in that the ultimate objective appears to be a majority stake or a full takeover of the target company. This includes events in which more than 30% of shares outstanding are acquired, as this triggers the legal requirement to make a mandatory bid for the whole company according to German security trading laws (§30 WpÜG). In addition, this includes all events in which the initial stake is used as a toehold and is followed by a subsequent takeover offer for the whole company. Furthermore, all stakes are excluded which might be acquired by a hedge fund pursuing a merger arbitrage strategy. This is the case when there is a pending takeover offer for the target company at the time when the hedge fund obtains the stake. Moreover, events are excluded when the hedge fund obtains a stake as a result of a debt-equity swap. In this case the interests of hedge funds and other shareholders are also likely to diverge because hedge funds often invest in multiple classes of securities of distressed firms. Finally, all events are eliminated from the sample where the target company has been trading on the stock market for less than 140 trading days. This minimum pre-event window is required to estimate expected returns for all sample firms and also removes any confounding events associated with initial public offerings (IPOs) such as price support by the underwriter, expiration of lock-up-periods, etc.

One advantage of this sample selection approach is that the resulting sample is not biased towards events in which the hedge fund crosses at least the initial disclosure threshold of 3% (5% up to January 31st, 2007). This problem exists in the datasets used by most other studies for the German capital market (Achleitner, Betzer, and Gider, 2008; Mietzner and Schweizer, 2007) and also for the U.S. capital market. This bias occurs because these studies exclusively rely on regulatory filings. According to Brav, Jiang, Partnoy, and Thomas (2008) this leads to a bias in the sample towards small cap firms in which hedge funds can more easily accumulate a meaningful position with a given amount of capital. Therefore, similar to the approach presented in the previous paragraph, Brav, Jiang, Partnoy, and Thomas (2008) also conduct a similar keyword search in the financial press that allows them to include those cases of hedge fund activity where regulatory disclosure thresholds are not crossed. These additional events presumably correspond to hedge fund investments in large firms. However, one caveat of using news articles from the financial press in the sample selection process is that journalists' classification of share acquisitions as engagements by hedge funds may not always be accurate. Nevertheless, the sample selection processes implemented by other studies face a similar problem which researchers try to overcome using different approaches. For instance, Brav, Jiang, Partnoy, and Thomas (2008) rely on the self-assessment of the investor in telephone calls, Mietzner and Schweizer (2007) base their classification on interviews with representatives from the association of the private equity industry and Achleitner, Betzer, and Gider (2008) use information on previous LBO activity by the investor to differentiate between hedge funds and private equity funds. However, all of these additional sources of information face their own conflicts of interests. Moreover, in the end it is not clear whether it is really possible to draw a sharp line between hedge fund activism and certain types of investments of private equity funds such as acquisitions of minority stakes that resemble hedge fund investments. This is due to the ongoing trend for a convergence in the investment approaches by activist hedge funds and private equity funds. In fact, there are an increasing number of cases where hedge funds have launched takeover offers for whole companies and also many cases where private equity firms have acquired minority stakes in target firms. Thus, when evaluating hedge fund activism in Germany, it seems most important to constrain the sample to all those cases where the investor applies "hedge fund"-like tactics. This means that the investor only holds a minority position in the target company and, therefore, never has full control over the firm's decision-making process. Consequently, he has to convince other shareholders of the merits of his proposals.[108]

B. Decription of Dataset of Hedge Fund Engagements

This section describes the key characteristics of the dataset of hedge fund engagements in the German capital market which is constructed following the approach presented in the previous section. In the first subsection, the focus is on the distribution of hedge fund activism in Germany over time and across industries. This is followed by an overview over the tactics employed by hedge funds to acquire stakes in German firms and their subsequent behavior towards the management of target companies.

I. Distribution of Events over Time, Industries and Market Segments

Overall, the sample selection process generated a sample of 404 events consisting of a pair of hedge funds and firms between January 1st, 2000 and December 31st, 2008 (Table 7). These pairs involve a total of 210 firms and 197 hedge funds. This implies that a significant number of firms were subject to multiple investments as 89 firms

[108] In fact, in order to precisely differentiate between private equity and hedge fund investors it would be necessary to obtain access to detailed information on the structure of the fund. In particular, the length of lock-up periods varies significantly between hedge funds and private equity funds. However, so far only the study by Clifford (2008) was able to assemble this data.

were targeted by at least two hedge funds over the entire sample period (Panel B). Moreover, in 41 out of these 89 firms, these multiple events apparently took place within a relatively short time period of only 3 months. This indicates that either some hedge funds coordinated their strategies or that these firms experienced significant changes in their ownership structure during relatively short time periods.

Table 7: Descriptive Statistics – Sample Composition

Panel A: Hedge Fund – Target Pairs	
Total number of hedge fund target pairs	404
Number of individual targets	210
Number of individual hedge funds	197
Panel B: Target firms	
Number of firms targeted by one hedge fund	121
Number of firms targeted by two hedge funds	37
Of which number of firms subject to "wolf packs"	10
Number of firms targeted by three or more hedge funds	52
Of which number of firms subject to "wolf packs"	31
Panel C: Hedge Funds	
Number of hedge funds with one target	131
Number of hedge funds with two targets	40
Number of hedge funds with three or more targets	26

This table provides information on the composition of the database of events. A firm is considered to be subject to a "wolf pack" attack when within three months of the first hedge fund engagement other hedge funds also acquire a position in the firm.

The information in panel C indicates that there is also a large number of hedge funds (131 out of 197) that have only one event whereas the remaining 66 hedge funds have two or more events. This is similar to the results of Boyson and Mooradian (2008) and Klein and Zur (2009) who also document that, for the U.S. market, most hedge funds only enter into their dataset one time. Moreover, there is a total of 66 hedge funds which became active on several occasions and made at least two investments in German firms. Consequently, this group of hedge funds is responsible for the largest share of events in the sample.

Due to the adjustment process of the German corporate governance system during the sample period it is also interesting to investigate the distribution of events over time. This is reported in Figure 18 which indicates that there is a significant concentration in the number of events in later parts of the sample period.

Figure 18: Distribution of Events over Time

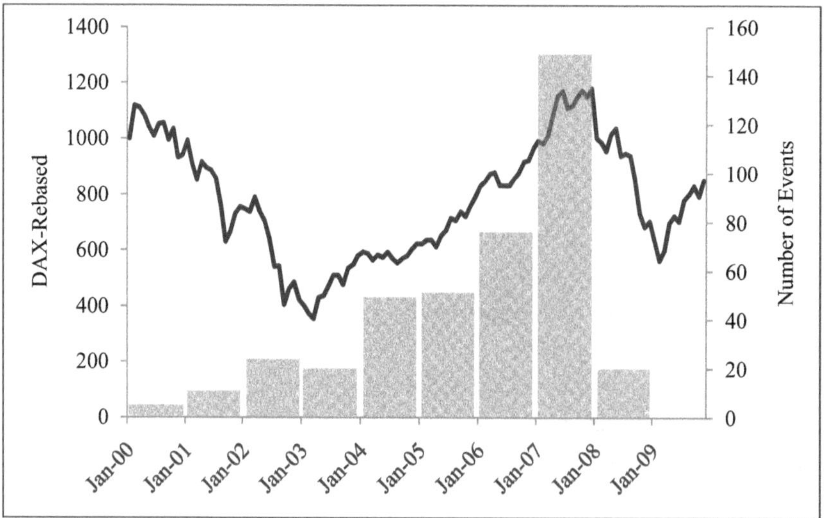

This figure plots the performance of the DAX performance index on the left-hand scale and the number of events per calendar year on the right-hand scale.

At the beginning of the sample period, there was limited hedge fund activity in Germany. In particular, there were less than 20 events per year for nearly all years prior to 2004. During the following time period there was a significant increase in the number of events which took place during a period of generally rising stock markets. Interestingly, the number of events peaked at more than 140 events in 2007 which also coincides with the peak in market valuations. However, this is probably also related to changes in disclosure rules that became effective in that year. In particular, on February 1st, 2007 the initial disclosure threshold for equity positions in German firms was lowered from 5% to 3% of voting rights. As a result, previously unobservable trading activity by hedge funds became publicly observable.

Overall, this pattern of increasing hedge fund activity over time is quite different from the roughly constant distribution of events reported by Boyson and Mooradian (2008) for the U.S. capital market. Therefore, the recent growth in activity indicates that the configuration of German capital markets and the German corporate governance system apparently underwent some significant changes during the sample period. These changes were also associated with significant shifts in the ownership structure of many companies which occurred subsequent to the enactment tax reform of 2002 in combination with the following up-market (Weber, 2008). As a result, the distribution of events over time provides some preliminary evidence that the German corporate governance adopted key elements of the U.S. system in which shareholder activism has been observed for a long time.[109]

Another interesting aspect of the dataset is the distribution of events across industries. This provides some insights into the rationale underlying hedge funds' investments and also determines whether the restructuring approach by hedge funds can be applied to target firms. According to the information in Table 8, hedge fund activity in the German capital market also appears to be concentrated in specific industries. In particular, more than 75% of all events took place within just five industries and about 50% of all events occurred within just three industries. This suggests that these industries offer interesting investment opportunities for hedge funds or in which hedge funds have specific knowledge.

More noticeably, the industry composition of the sample closely corresponds to the structure of the German industry in that about 25% of all events involve industrial firms. Furthermore, there is a fairly large number of events in financial firms which is similar to the findings reported by Boyson and Mooradian (2008) and Clifford (2008) for the U.S. capital market. However, this finding is not consistent with the characteristics of the dataset used by Klein and Zur (2009) in another study for the U.S. market. This study identifies only a limited number of events that involve financial firms. Finally, the relatively high occurence of the knowledge-based technology industry with 64 events is not in line with the characteristics of the samples compiled by studies for the U.S. market. In particular, the technology sector and other industries based on intellectual property are largely absent from the samples used by Boyson and Mooradian (2008) and by Clifford (2008). Only the sample compiled by

[109] For instance, corporate raiders attacking US firms during the 1980s usually pursued a similar investment approach as hedge funds today.

Klein and Zur (2009) contains at least some activity in the pharmaceutical industry, which is similar to the technology sector regarding its strong focus on R&D investments.

Table 8: Industry Composition

Industry	Number of pairs	Number of firms
Industrials	103	49
Financials	68	30
Technology	64	41
Consumer Services	62	28
Consumer Goods	42	23
Health Care	25	16
Basic Materials	18	10
Telecommunications	9	3
Oil & Gas	7	4
Utility	1	1
Others	5	5
Total	404	210

This table provides information on the industry composition of the sample based on the ICBIN industry classification which is obtained from the Worldscope database.

A final aspect of the dataset analyzed in Table 9 is the distribution of events across major German market segments. This provides insights into the size and transparency of German target firms.

The distribution of events is biased towards the German market segments for small and mid-caps in that only 58 out of 404 event pairs involve DAX companies. Moreover, the sample is dominated by target companies which are only included in the CDAX. This implies that German target firms are rather small in terms of market capitalization and do not have to adhere to the more strict reporting requirements imposed by the German stock exchange on companies included in higher market segments (see the homepage of the Deutsche Börse AG). Thus, hedge funds apparently prefer small and opaque target companies in the German stock market.

Table 9: Distribution of Events across Market Segments

Market Segment	Number of pairs
DAX	58
MDAX	92
SDAX	67
TecDAX	30
CDAX	157
Total	404

This table provides sample information on the market segment in which target companies are included on the event date.

This pattern is consistent with the composition of samples analyzed by studies for the U.S. market. These studies also report that hedge fund activity appears to be concentrated in small and mid-cap companies and that hedge funds appear to prefer more illiquid and opaque securities. For instance, Klein and Zur (2009) find that most events in their sample involve companies which are not included in the S&P 500, which comprises the 500 largest companies in the U.S. In fact, this is consistent with the reasoning that hedge funds should be more interested in stocks that are more likely to be mispriced and that require significantly smaller investment outlays to accumulate a meaningful position.

II. Hedge Funds' Trading Approaches and Behavior vis-à-vis Target Firms

Hedge funds use a wide range of different approaches to establish positions in target companies and rely on different tactics to convince managers to change their firm's strategy, financing or corporate governance (DAI, 2009). When investigating this aspect of hedge fund activism studies focusing on the U.S. capital market have a comparative advantage because the regulatory environment provides them with more information on the goals and objectives of hedge funds. In particular, in the U.S. all investors including hedge funds have to state their intentions upon acquiring 5% of outstanding shares in their initial 13 D filing which needs to be submitted to the SEC. Moreover, they have to revise their filing in case the investment objective changes during the course of their engagement with the company. In contrast, German security trading laws did not contain similar provisions during most of the sample period. In fact, hedge funds only had to disclose the size of their stakes. This changed only recently with the enactment of the 'Risk Limitation Act' on February 1st, 2007. This introduced the requirement of disclosing investment objectives for all investors acquiring more than 10% in a German firm.

Therefore, insights into the motivation and objectives of hedge funds investing in German target firms can only be derived from news items published in the financial press. Based on information from the Lexis-Nexis database, Table 10 differentiates the total sample of 404 events according to the trading approaches of hedge funds and their subsequent behavior vis-à-vis the management of target companies. This provides some insights into the time horizon of hedge funds and the degree to which they are committed to their investments in the firm. First of all, 365 out of 404 events are classified as "open market"-purchases which means that the first news item contains information that the investor has acquired a stake in the company and also made a regulatory filing according to §21 WpHG filing. Furthermore, 22 events are classified as an "intervention" which implies that there is only information indicating that the investor publicly put pressure on the company. For instance, this applies to the investment in Deutsche Telekom by Laxey Partners in November 2006 when the hedge fund issued public statements regarding the lack of value creation by the management of Deutsche Telekom. When the investor issues a public statement to the management of the target company, and at the same time also makes a regulatory filing of his position in the company's share, the event is assigned to the category "open market". Finally, there are 17 events which are included in the category "PIPE" ("Private Investment in Public Equity"). In these cases the hedge fund provided new financing to the firm in the form of new stocks or other equity-linked securities. This number appears to be quite small compared to the high incidence of PIPE financings involving hedge funds which has been observed in the U.S. capital market (Dai, 2007).

Table 10 also separates the total sample of 404 events into three categories, capturing the behavior of hedge funds towards the management of target companies. In particular, similar to the evidence for the U.S. capital market, most hedge funds investing in German target firms do not resort to public criticism of target management. In fact, 260 events belong to the category "communication only", which means that the hedge fund only reports its position to the capital market and does not make public statements that explicitly address problems in the company's governance, strategy or financial structure. This is surprising, given the widely held view that hedge funds always exhibit an aggressive behavior towards target firms. Moreover, 65 events are assigned to the category "aggressive in past investments" which means that the hedge fund does not exhibit any aggressive behavior towards the target company in the ongoing engagement, but has resorted to aggressive tactics in past investments when management did not implement its demands. Finally, only 79 events are assigned to the category "aggressive", indicating that the hedge fund publicly attacks target management during its engagement with the company. The resulting high number of 325 events, which does not involve public confrontations between the hedge fund and the target's management, corresponds to the proportions reported by Boyson and Mooradian (2007), Greenwood and Schoar (2009) and Brav, Jiang, Partnoy, and Thomas (2009). These studies for the U.S. market also find that in most cases hedge funds only report their positions using 13D filings, but do not include additional hostile demands to the target management.

For the subsample of 79 "aggressive" events it is interesting to investigate the nature of the hedge funds' objectives in order to infer with which aspects of corporate management and governance hedge funds are most concerned.

Table 10: Characterization of Hedge Fund Firm Pairs

		Method of Acquisition			
		Open Market	PIPE	Intervention	Total
Approach to Target Company	Communication only	251	8	1	260
	Aggressive in past investments	57	3	5	65
	Aggressive	57	6	16	79
	Total	365	17	22	404

This table provides a break-down of events according to two dimensions. First, it characterizes the method of acquisition and differentiates events into three categories. "Open Market" means that the stake was accumulated in the open market and a disclosure threshold was reached; "PIPE" implies that the stake was acquired in a PIPE transaction; and "intervention" contains those events for which there is only information regarding hedge funds' demands to target management. Second, similar to Boyson and Mooradian (2008) the table also distinguishes events into "communication only", i.e. there is only public information that the hedge funds holds a position, "aggressive in past investments" indicating that the hedge fund has engaged in hostile tactics in past investments and "aggressive", i.e. that the hedge fund directly spells out demands to the firm.

Table 11 indicates that hedge funds mostly appear to be concerned with the governance of German target firms and their strategies, which appear to be the predominant concerns of aggressive hedge funds. Moreover, there are also a meaningful number of cases in which hedge funds "want to become engaged", i.e. they make statements that firms should raise shareholder value but do not propose any concrete measures in public. This is similar to Klein and Zur (2009) and Boyson and Mooradian (2008) who also document that governance concerns and the target's strategy are the most important drivers of hedge fund activism in the U.S. However, these patterns are not consistent with other studies for the US capital market which come to different conclusions regarding hedge funds' objectives. For instance, the results from Brav, Jiang, Partnoy, and Thomas (2008) emphasize the importance of changes to financial structures while the study by Greenwood and Schor (2009) focuses on the objective of pushing target firms into mergers & acquisition. This latter aspect does not play a role in the sample of German hedge fund engagements.

Table 11: Goals of Aggressive Hedge Funds

Stated objective	Number of observation pairs
Governance	24
Strategy	26
Financing	13
"What to become engaged"	9
Multiple	7
Total	79

This table provides information on the stated objectives of aggressive hedge funds that made public statements regarding their objectives and motivations. This information is obtained from the Lexis-Nexis database.

C. Methodology

The objective of the empirical study is to determine whether hedge fund engagements have a significant impact on the market value of German firms. This type of research question is usually addressed with the event-study methodology which is described in this section. The first subsection presents the concept of cumulative abnormal returns

(CAR) and related statistical tests which are commonly used to measure short-term valuation effects triggered by corporate events. The following subsection focuses on the different methods that are available to measure the long-term performance of firms subsequent to new information. This includes buy-and-hold abnormal returns (BHAR) and more advanced methods such as the calendar-time approach (CalTime) and the generalized calendar-time approach (GCT) both of which help to address statistical and economic problems inherent in the BHAR-approach.

In addition to stock returns, the empirical analysis also investigates the operating performance of target firms. In particular, if hedge fund engagements really have a significant impact on the market value of target firms then there should also be significant shifts in measures of operating performance, such as return on equity or operating cash flows around the event date. Therefore, the final subsection presents methods that allow for the detection of shifts in measures of operating performance.

Finally, increases in stock prices subsequent to hedge fund engagements might also be related to shifts in the liquidity of target stocks. Therefore, the final section also presents an empirical approach that allows one to measure and to establish the statistical significance of time-series trends in stock liquidity.

I. Measuring Short-term Valuation Effects

1. Cumulative Abnormal Returns

The standard event-study methodology was introduced by Fama, Jensen, Fisher, and Roll (1969) and allows one to measure the short-term adjustment of security prices in response to corporate news events by estimating abnormal returns AR_{it}:

$$AR_{it} = R_{it} - E(R_{it}|\Omega) \tag{51}$$

where R_{it} is security i`s return in time period t and $E(R_{it}|\Omega)$ is the expected return based on the market's current information set Ω. This has to be estimated with an asset-pricing model (Campbell, Lo, and MacKinlay, 1997). Similar to most other studies a simple market model is employed to estimate expected returns:

$$E(R_{it}|\Omega) = \alpha_i + \beta_i \cdot R_{M,t} \tag{52}$$

where α_i and β_i are the intercept and slope estimates of a linear regression of the security's return on the market return. Thus, this simple statistical model does not impose any additional economic restrictions on the cross-section of expected returns. In the empirical application the CDAX is used as the market index because it is a value-weighted performance index that reflects the performance of the aggregate German stock market. Furthermore, the window from 140 to 81 trading days prior to the event date is used to estimate the parameters of the market model for each additional event. This choice of estimation window ensures that estimates of expected returns are not biased by pre-event abnormal trading patterns which are often observable in the case of hedge fund activism.

In the next step, the estimates of abnormal returns for each individual event are averaged in the cross-section to obtain the mean change in the market value of target firms in time period t:

$$dAR_{P,t} = \frac{1}{N}\sum_{i=1}^{N} AR_{i,t} \tag{53}$$

Finally, these daily changes in the market value of the average event firm are aggregated over multiple trading days which leads to cumulative abnormal returns (CAR):

$$CAR_{P,t} = \sum_{t=1}^{T} dAR_{P,t} \tag{54}$$

Cumulative abnormal returns can then be used to analyze the market reaction to news events for different windows before, after, and around the event date. This also requires tests for the statistical significance of estimated CARs. In general, the cross-sectional distribution of cumulative abnormal returns across individual stocks can be reasonably approximated by a normal distribution so that the statistical significance of cumulative abnormal returns can be determined with simple t-tests.

Even though the intuition of this approach is straightforward, its empirical implementation often involves a range of methodological and statistical problems. In particular, any test of market efficiency based on the event-study-approach actually tests a joint hypothesis that (1) market prices are efficient and (2) that the asset pricing model used to estimate expected returns is an accurate description of security returns (Fama, 1970). As a result, the finding that CARs are significantly different from zero is consistent with the interpretation that the news event is associated with higher firm value as well as with the interpretation that the asset pricing model employed does not capture all systematic risk factors. Therefore, it is sometimes argued that in order to incorporate additional risk factors multi-factor models should be used instead of the single-factor market model. In particular, the size factor or the value factor might bias estimates of abnormal performance when a single-factor asset pricing model is used (Dimson and Marsh, 1986; Fama and French, 1993). However, Schwert (1983) demonstrates that the intercept of the market model generally adjusts estimates of abnormal returns for the size effect. Since this reasoning should also extend to other systematic risk factors over short time periods, it is fair to assume that using a single-factor model does not lead to biases in measured short-term valuation effects.

Another problem emerges when abnormal returns are estimated for small stocks which are often subject to thin trading which can lead to biased estimates of market-model betas (Scholes and Williams, 1977). However, Jain (1986) provides empirical evidence that the impact of this infrequent trading bias on the distribution of abnormal returns is small. In fact, he shows that the differences in estimated abnormal returns are small when comparing the results based on a market model and on the approach by Scholes and Williams (1977). Therefore, in the empirical analysis the conventional market model is used to estimate abnormal returns.

In addition to biases in the size of valuation effects, it is also conceivable that a misspecified asset-pricing model that does not control for all systematic factors also leads to biased t-statistics. In particular, there can also be distortions in estimates of the cross-sectional variance when there are multiple overlapping event windows in the sample. In this case, estimates of abnormal returns for individual events can be correlated when the asset-pricing model does not contain all relevant risk factors. In this case, the central limit theorem does not apply and simple t-statistics are biased. However, CARs are commonly used to measure share price effects over relatively short time periods. Therefore, this seems to be a second-order problem. In fact, Bernard (1987) shows that this problem only becomes severe for longer sampling intervals such as weekly or monthly returns. Additional support for using a market model is provided by empirical evidence which shows that the simple market model performs just as well as more complicated multi-factor asset pricing models when daily returns are analyzed (Brown and Warner, 1980). This occurs because the marginal contribution of each factor in addition to the market risk factor, which explains total variance of stock returns, is rather small in daily data. Consequently, the additional reduction in the volatility of the abnormal return estimate is also small (Campbell, Lo, and MacKinlay, 1997).[110]

Conventional t-statistics can also be biased due to heteroscedasticity in the cross-section of cumulative abnormal returns, which occurs if the events also lead to shifts in the volatility of the stock returns of sample firms. For instance, Brown, Watts, and Wruck (1988) demonstrate that the arrival of new information can lead to an increase in the cross-sectional dispersion of abnormal returns because the valuation impact of the event often depends on firm characteristics and, therefore, differs in the cross-section. Thus, in order to take account of this "event-induced" variance different statistical methodologies have been developed which are also based on standardized stock returns. For instance, the most widely used test statistic that adjusts for "event-induced" variance has been designed by Böhmer, Masumeci, and Poulsen (1991) who constructed the following standardized time-series of returns for each individual stock in event time:

$$SR_{i,E} = A_{i,E} \Big/ \hat{S}_t \cdot \sqrt{1 + \frac{1}{T_i} + \frac{(R_{m,E} - R_m)^2}{\sum_{t=1}^{T} (R_{m,t} - \bar{R}_m)^2}} \tag{55}$$

T_i is the number of trading days in the estimation window for the market-model. In the second step, they use the cross-section of these standardized returns to calculate an adjusted t-statistic:

$$t = \frac{1}{N} \sum_{i=1}^{N} SR_{i,E} \Big/ \sqrt{\frac{1}{N(N-1)} \sum_{i=1}^{N} \left(SR_{i,E} - \sum_{i=1}^{N} \frac{SR_{i,E}}{N} \right)^2} \tag{56}$$

The final problem of the analysis of CAR concerns the exact timing of the event date as there is often uncertainty regarding the precise moment of when the information was released to the market. This is reflected in many empirical studies that document cases in which the price adjustment begins several days prior to the identified event date. This implies that either the information arrived earlier at the market or that some investors exploited inside information. In these cases estimates of abnormal returns tend to understate the complete valuation impact of the event. Therefore, different approaches can be used to take account of this problem. However, it is usually sufficient to use an ad-hoc procedure in that the event window is expanded forwards and backwards to take account of event date uncertainty. Ball and Torous (1988) show

[110] According to Campbell, Lo, and MacKinlay (1997) the advantages of multi-factor models increase when firms share a common characteristic.

that this informal approach yields the same quality of results as more sophisticated methods for incorporating event date uncertainty into the analysis.[111] Moreover, pre-event trading patterns can also distort estimates of abnormal returns by biasing estimates of expected returns. For instance, in many corporate finance studies there are pre-event run-ups in stock prices when market participants anticipate the event, when there is insider trading or when there is short-term buying/selling pressure. However, Schwert (1996) shows that this bias can be easily captured by estimating the market-model without an intercept, which is most likely to be distorted by pre-event trading patterns.

2. Abnormal Trading Volume

Information regarding the implications of corporate news events is not only included in security prices but is also included in the behavior of trading activity around the event date. In particular, the analysis of trading volume offers additional insights into the processing of new information by market participants. More precisely, while changes in stock prices reflect revisions in the market's average expectation, the dynamics of trading volume illustrate how the new information is incorporated into stock prices and how the market aggregates the information sets of all individual investors (Beaver 1968; Kim and Verrecchia, 1991). Therefore, trading volume is closely related to the diversity of opinion among market participants and information aggregation in security markets. In line with this reasoning, Chae (2005) emphasizes that trading volume increases in information asymmetry, thus an increase in trading activity might indicate insider trading prior to major news events.[112] In addition, the analysis of trading activity around corporate news events provides information on potential changes in the stocks' liquidity, which in turn might explain a fraction of the valuation effects.

However, in contrast to the analysis of asset price adjustments, there is no consensus on the correct method for measuring abnormal trading volume. Hence, many different

---

[111] According to Campbell, Lo, and MacKinlay (1997) this advantage has to be traded off with the higher volatility of estimates of abnormal returns for longer event windows.

[112] More precisely, Chae (2005) states that this is based on the assumption that noise trader demand is elastic (see the model by Kyle 1985) which allows better informed traders to exploit their informational advantage. This result does not hold if liquidity traders face some discretion in the timing of their trades.

approaches are used by different authors.[113] The approach by Brav and Gompers (2003) estimates abnormal trading activity based on equation (7):

$$AV_{i,t} = \frac{V_{i,t}}{\frac{1}{60}\sum_{\tau=-81}^{\tau=-140} V_{i,\tau}} - 1 \quad (57)$$

where V_{it} is the daily trading volume of stock i on trading day t, and the denominator is the average trading volume of stock i during the 60 day period from -140 until -81 days before the event date. Accordingly, the ratio AV_{it} relates the daily trading volume to its time-series average during the measurement period from -140 until -81 trading days before the event date.

Finally, increases in share prices can also be the result of increases in stock liquidity. Therefore, it is interesting to investigate whether increases in share prices of target firms are related to increases in their liquidity. While intuitive, the approach by Brav and Gompers (2003) presented in the previous section suffers from a serious drawback in that it is not amenable for statistical tests due to the high skewness in the time-series of trading volume.

Therefore, a measure used by Amihud (2002) is also employed. This liquidity ratio measures the dollar volume which is needed to change the share price by one percent and, therefore, can be considered as a measure of market impact. This measure is defined as

$$LR_i = \sum_t V_{i,t} / \sum_t |R_{i,t}| \quad (58)$$

Thus, the liquidity ratio is defined as the ratio between accumulated dollar trading volume over the last *t* trading days and the sum of absolute returns over the last *t* trading days. This liquidity ratio can be used for significant changes in the liquidity of stocks by using the following equation:

$$DLR_i = log\left(LR^i_{After\ Event} / LR^i_{Before\ Event}\right) \quad (59)$$

[113] More precisely, due to the conceptual difficulties in accurately measuring trading activity different authors employ a range of different approaches. In particular, they use different metrics for measuring volume including the daily number of shares traded, the dollar values of shares traded, or the fraction of shares outstanding traded. Moreover, while some authors use log or square transformations in order to address non-normality in the time-series of the volume distributions, other authors simply employ raw volume data.

This ratio is approximately normally distributed and, therefore, can be used to construct simple t-statistics that allow one to infer whether liquidity has increased on average in the cross-section of events.

II. Measuring Long-term Abnormal Performance

In addition to analyzing short-term valuation effects around the event date it is also important to evaluate the long-term performance subsequent to corporate news events because a growing amount of literature challenges the assumption that stock prices quickly adjust to new information and documents that there are often prolonged time lags before market prices fully incorporate new information (Fama 1998). Moreover, reversals in stock prices are also possible over longer time periods after the event date when the capital market initially overrates the implications of the event on firm value.

However, measuring long-run performance involves more methodological challenges as small measurement errors over short-time periods compound into large errors over longer time periods. Moreover, the assumptions underlying standard event study methodology are also more likely to be violated.[114] Therefore, empirical research has developed new approaches for measuring long-term performance. These include buy-and-hold abnormal returns (BHAR), the calendar-time approach (CalTime) and the generalized calendar time approach (GCT) proposed by Höchle, Schmid and Zimmermann (2009).

1. Buy-and-Hold Abnormal Returns

The most common approach for measuring long-run performance is the analysis of buy-and-hold abnormal returns (BHAR) which extends the intuition of cumulative abnormal returns to the perspective of a long term investor who holds a position in each event firm for a specified holding period T. The investment performance of this portfolio is given in event time by the buy-and-hold abnormal returns $BHAR_{P,T}$ which is written as:

$$BHAR_{P,T} = \frac{1}{N}\sum_{i=1}^{N}\left[\prod_{t=1}^{T}(1 + R_{i,t}) - \prod_{t=1}^{T}(1 + ER_{i,t})\right] \tag{60}$$

[114] See Fama (1998) for a general discussion of the problems involved in the analysis of long-run stock returns.

where $ER_{i,t}$ is the security's expected return which is usually approximated by a broad market benchmark index. This market benchmark is approximated by the index for the market segment (DAX, MDAX, SDAX, TecDAX, CDAX) to which the firm belonged on the event date. In contrast to short-term CARs, long-term buy-and-hold abnormal returns are based on multiplicative compounding and, therefore, accurately reflect the investment performance of an investor continuously investing in each event firm in event time. However, interpreting graphical representations of BHAR results can be difficult because multiplicative compounding can give wrong impressions on the speed of adjustment (Mitchell and Stafford, 1997; Fama 1998).

The implementation of this approach is subject to problems similar to those of the estimation of cumulative abnormal returns. However, in the case of long-run buy-and-hold abnormal returns, the joint hypothesis and the misspecification of the benchmark lead to stronger measurement errors in valuation effects and test statistics (Fama, 1970; Kurth, 2005). Effectively, small valuation errors compound over longer time periods because average returns scale with a factor N over time, whereas the associated variance only grows at $N^{1/2}$. This problem is usually the result of missing factors in the asset pricing model used to estimate expected returns. Therefore, it is most acute when a simple one-factor model is employed and when this factor does not closely correspond to the risk characteristics of event firms (Kothari and Warner, 2006). For instance, this leads to large measurement errors when event firms have significant loadings on size- and value-factors. Consequently, these problems are most severe when the sample contains a large number of small stocks for which pricing errors are higher than for large stocks (Fama, 1998). Therefore, different methods for estimating expected returns have been proposed that try to construct benchmarks with similar risk exposures and/or characteristics as the event firms. This usually includes the construction of matched samples based on firm characteristics such as market-to-book and size (Loughran and Ritter, 1995).[115] In the subsequent empirical analysis this problem is addressed by matching each event firm to the index corresponding to the market segment (DAX, SDAX, MDAX, TecDAX) to which it belonged on the event date and which should most closely reflect the risk characteristics of each target firm.

[115] The use of multi-factor models also raises an additional fundamental question regarding the interpretation of the additional factors. Should these factors really be interpreted as compensation for taking on specific risks? See Fama and French (2007) for a discussion of the major arguments in this debate.

Evaluating the statistical significance of buy-and-hold abnormal returns is also more difficult because the standard assumptions used to derive simple test statistics are more likely to be violated. In particular, the frequency of overlapping event windows increases in the case of long-term returns leading to cross-sectional dependence in estimated buy-and-hold returns for individual stocks. This will typically lead to an underestimation of standard errors and, consequently, to an upward bias in t-statistics (Brav, 1999). In addition, overlapping events appear to be related to skewness in the cross-sectional distribution of buy-and-hold abnormal returns so that statistical tests based on a normal distribution are not applicable (Kothari and Warner, 2006). Therefore, a range of other test statistics have been developed to test buy-and-hold abnormal returns. In particular, many studies use the skewness-adjusted t-test by Barber and Lyon (1997) which is given by

$$t_{sa} = \sqrt{N}\left(S + \frac{1}{3}\hat{\gamma}S^2 + \frac{1}{6n}\hat{\gamma}\right) \text{ with } S = \frac{\overline{BHAR_\tau}}{\sigma(BHAR_\tau)} \tag{61}$$

where $\overline{BHAR_\tau}$ is the cross-sectional average of BHAR estimates for all N events corresponding to an investment horizon τ, $\sigma(BHAR_\tau)$ is the associated cross-sectional standard deviation and $\hat{\gamma}$ is an estimate of the skewness of the cross-sectional distribution of buy-and-hold abnormal returns. However, this test only works in random samples so that t-statistics can be overstated if the sample is non-random and sample companies exhibit similar characteristics. This typically occurs when many sample firms operate in the same industry (Jegadeesh and Karceski, 2009). This problem might also apply to the sample investigated in this study which is biased towards small cap stocks. This bias can be reduced by using the approach of Jegadeesh and Karceski (2009) who constructed an adjusted t-statistic that accounts for heteroscedasticity and autocorrelation in buy-and-hold returns. However, the application of this approach has a significant drawback in that it is less powerful in random samples. Hence, the empirical analysis follows the conventional approach used by most empirical studies and uses the skewness-adjusted t-statistics of Barber and Lyon (1997).

A further problem in the statistical analysis of buy-and-hold abnormal returns is the assumption that events are exogenous and that all equally likely event-return histories have the same weight in the data (Schultz, 2003). Hence, if events are endogenous and their realization depends on the past path of returns then buy-and-hold returns will be biased because in small samples of up to 400 events certain types of event-return combinations will be overweighted. Viswanathan and Wei (2008) extensively analyze this problem in the case of pseudo market-timing as a potential explanation for IPO and SEO underperformance. However, they do not provide a general theory that explains how to adjust statistical tests in the presence of endogenous events. Therefore, nearly all studies of long-run BHAR do not correct for this problem and are therefore based on the implicit assumption that events are exogenous.

Overall, the preceding discussion reveals that the statistical analysis of buy-and-hold abnormal returns used in many empirical studies of long-term performance is subject to several important biases. Therefore, it is common practice to also measure long-run performance with other approaches, such as the calendar-time portfolio approach or the generalized calendar-time approach, both of which help to address these statistical biases. These methods are presented in the next two sections.

2. Calendar-Time Portfolio Approach

The calendar-time portfolio has been strongly advocated by Fama (1998) because it easily addresses several of the most important statistical problems inherent in the analysis of buy-and-hold abnormal returns. Therefore, this approach has been implemented more recently in a growing number of studies of long-run performance (e.g. Eckbo and Norli, 2005; Höchle, Schmid, and Zimmermann, 2009). This approach consists of two steps. First, a portfolio of event firms in calendar time is constructed for each month that includes all the stock returns $R_{i,t}$ of the N_t firms which experienced an event during the previous T months:

$$R_{CalTime,t} = \frac{1}{N_t}\sum_{i=1}^{N} z_{i,t} \cdot R_{i,t} \qquad (62)$$

N is the total number of firms in the sample and $z_{i,t}$ is an indicator variable equal to one if the firm had an event during the last T months, otherwise it is zero. Hence, the calendar-time portfolio replicates the investment performance of an investor who attempts to take advantage of the event in real time using a buy-and-hold strategy with an investment horizon of T months. In the second step, the time-series of returns of the calendar-time portfolio is regressed on a set of risk factor such as the Fama-French factors:

$$R_{CalTime,t} - R_{f,t} = \alpha + \beta_{Mkt}(R_{Mkt,t} - R_{f,t}) + \beta_{HML}R_{HML,t} + \beta_{SMB}R_{SMB,t} + \varepsilon_t \qquad (63)$$

In the case that the intercept α of this regression is positive and statistically significant then the event used to construct the calendar-time portfolio leads to an increase in market value.

The major problem in the application of this approach in the German capital market is the construction of the Fama-French factors. This is due to the fact that the German stock market is relatively small compared to the U.S. market. This can create problems in applying the double-sorting routine proposed by Fama and French (1993). As the first step, therefore, proxies for the Fama-French factors constructed from MSCI style indices are used. In particular, the value-factor is constructed as the return of an arbitrage portfolio which is long in the MSCI Germany Value index and short in the MSCI Germany Growth index. Similarly, the size-factor is the return of an arbitrage portfolio which exploits the small firm effect, i.e. the lack of liquidity and the information risks associated with small firms (Banz, 1981) by going long in the MSCI Germany Small index and short in the MSCI Germany Large index. This analysis is restricted to the time period starting in January 2001 because not all MSCI style indices are available prior to this date. This should not have a significant impact on the results because the calendar-time portfolios contain only a small number of stocks during the first year following their initial formation in January 2000. Furthermore, Fama-French factors which were constructed based on the sorting mechanisms proposed by Fama and French (1993) are also used. In particular, the whole CDAX universe is sorted based on the variables market capitalization and market-to-book ratio obtained from Datastream (see Bessler and Kurmann, 2010 for details).

Importantly, this approach addresses two major shortcomings of the conventional BHAR approach. From an economic point of view, this approach directly adjusts expected returns for post-event firm characteristics which are reflected in the factor exposures estimated in the time-series regression (Kothari and Warner, 2006). Moreover, the statistical reliability of this approach is not reduced by overlapping events and event-clustering because portfolio formation naturally takes account of any covariation between individual event firms' returns (Kothari and Warner, 2006, Fama 1998). However, this approach is subject to new statistical problems in that it puts excessive weights on events that take place during time periods when there is only a limited number of events (Loughran and Ritter, 2000).

Finally, in the practical implementation of this approach there are two additional parameters. First, the length of the holding period has to be determined which can influence estimates of long-run performance and which also affects the stability and the diversification properties of calendar time portfolios (Bessler, Holler, and Seim, 2010a). Second, some companies might be subject to more than one event so that it becomes important to note whether the calendar time portfolio puts excessive weight on some companies.

3. Generalized Calendar Time Approach

The calendar-time approach has several statistical advantages compared to conventional buy-and-hold abnormal returns. However, from an economic point of view, it has one major drawback in that it does not allow one to investigate the cross-section of long-run returns. In fact, it is only possible to determine the impact of dichotomous variables on the magnitude of valuation effects by constructing the corresponding long-short portfolios. This problem is overcome by Höchle, Schmid, and Zimmermann (2009) who show that a simple regression approach augmented by Driscoll-Kraay (1998) standard errors is capable of replicating the results of the calendar-time portfolio approach for the case of dichotomous variables and that this approach can be extended to incorporate continuous variables such as leverage, profitability and others.

The approach by Höchle, Schmid, and Zimmermann (2009) is based on estimating the following regression equation:

$$R_{it} - R_{ft} = [(p_{it} \otimes z_{it}) \otimes x_t] \cdot \beta + v_{it} \quad (64)$$

using pooled OLS where standard errors are estimated using the non-parametric approach proposed by Driscoll and Kraay (1998) which takes spatial correlations into account. The dependent variable $R_{it} - R_{ft}$ is a stacked vector of excess returns of all individual securities in all time periods. The vector x_t contains the set of risk factors specified by the asset pricing model used to estimate expected returns which are the same proxies as those for the Fama-French factors, which were already used in the simple calendar-time portfolio approach. Moreover, the vector z_{it} represents the set of firm characteristics used as control variables where different accounting variables obtained from the Worldscope database can be included. Finally, p_{it} contains a set of dummy variables indicating whether an event took place during specific time periods. More precisely, in the analysis in the next chapters, there is a "run-up"-dummy which is equal to one for different time periods prior to the event date and zero otherwise as well as a "drift"-dummy which is equal to one for different time periods after the event date and zero otherwise. In contrast to the simple calendar-time portfolio approach this framework also contains interaction terms between firm characteristics and the dummy variables in the vector p_{it}. This offers the opportunity to measure whether differences in abnormal returns in different time periods for hedge fund targets are related to specific firm characteristics.

Finally, the estimation of this panel requires a control group to identify all parameters (Bessler, Holler, and Seim 2010a). Therefore, all other German stocks listed in the CDAX are used as the control group.

III. Operating Performance

If hedge fund activism increases firm value, then the operating performance in terms of return on assets or operating cash flows should also improve subsequent to a hedge fund engagement. In general, this question is addressed by focusing on the abnormal operating performance which is approximated by the difference between realized operating performance of an event firm and its expected operating performance.

The practical implementation of this approach needs to address several important questions (Barber and Lyon, 1997). First, it is necessary to select a measure of operating performance. Since earnings per share can be distorted by special items, taxes and differences among firm's capital structures, Barber and Lyon (1997) emphasize that operating income-based measures should be used. In particular, they propose that researchers should use operating income and scale it by the book value or the market value of assets. Therefore, in the robustness checks the return on assets as well as the operating cash flow scaled by the book value of assets will be used. Second, a benchmark needs to be defined that captures the expected operating performance of each event company. This is often measured as the median of industry- and size-matched peer-groups.[116] However, Barber and Lyon (1997) argue that researchers should instead create matched samples based on industry and pre-event operating performance in order to adjust for mean reversion in accounting profitability. This can result from the use of specific accounting methods and/or economic forces and which also helps to account for differences in firm strategies, the nature of

[116] For instance, Fama and French (1995) show that the earnings of small firms scaled by the book value of equity tend to be systematically below the level of large cap stocks.

investment opportunities and managerial skill. However, taking differences leads to a further reduction in the number of available data points. Therefore, the robustness checks will be based on the conventional approach of industry- and size-adjusted accounting ratios. Third, researchers need to select an appropriate test statistic. Here, median-based Wilcoxon-tests appear to be superior to simple t-statistics due to the occurrence of extreme outliers in all measures of abnormal operating performance. Therefore, this test will be used in the robustness tests.

Chapter II. Hedge Fund Activism in Good Times

There is substantial evidence from countries such as the U.S. and the UK that hedge fund engagements lead to a significant increase in the equity value of target firms. Most of these studies focus on sample periods between 2000 and 2006, which generally correspond to a time period of rising share prices and favorable market conditions. However, the capital market and corporate governance system of these countries differ substantially from the German environment. Therefore, it seems interesting to investigate the performance of target companies in Germany over the same time period and evaluate whether valuation effects triggered by hedge fund engagements are different in the German capital market environment. This question is important because it helps to assess the economic implications of recent changes in the German capital market and corporate governance system. In particular, if these changes have created more opportunities for capital market influence, then investments of hedge funds in German firms should trigger similar increases in shareholder value both in the short and the long run. In contrast, if these changes in the German capital market environment did not really create opportunities for outsiders to exert influence on corporate decision-making, then it should be difficult for hedge funds to put pressure on managers which should in turn lead to smaller valuation effects as compared to the U.S. market.

Therefore, this chapter presents an analysis of the valuation effects of hedge funds engagements in German firms for the period between 2000 and 2006. This allows for a comparison with studies for the U.S. which focus on the same time period. Moreover, during good times hubris and agency problems of free cash flows should be rather high (Jensen, 2005).

A. Characteristics of Target Companies

Evidence from the U.S. capital market suggests that hedge funds' engagements appear to be concentrated in specific types of firms. In general, target firms are characterized by low stock valuations, excessive diversification of their product market strategies and conservative financial structures with low debt ratios, high liquidity reserves and low payouts to shareholders. This indicates that engagements by hedge funds in the U.S. capital market are concentrated in firms that suffer from agency problems of free cash flows. Since the German capital market environment differs substantially from the U.S. system it is interesting to investigate whether this explanation also applies to the engagements of hedge funds in Germany.

Therefore, this section investigates the key characteristics of the 235 event firms included in the sample of hedge fund investments between 2000 and 2006 to detect whether target firms also suffer from agency problems of free cash flow in Germany. In the first subsection the focus is on key accounting information which summarizes the firm`s financial policies, profitability and operating diversification. This allows one to determine whether target firms have too much financial slack or whether they are characterized by excessive diversification. The second subsection investigates the market valuation of target companies around the event date based on the reasoning that target firms should be undervalued if agency problems of free cash flows exist. In addition, this subsection also analyzes the market capitalization and liquidity of target firms which also have a systematic impact on firm valuations. Third, it summarizes key information on the ownership structure of target companies prior to the event date which determines whether hedge funds are actually able to impose substantial restructurings on target firms.

I. Financial Policies, Profitability and Diversification

This section provides an overview of the financial policies, profitability and operating diversification of target firms, based on their financial statements, in order to investigate whether German target companies suffer from the same agency problems reported for target companies in the U.S. market. For instance, Brav, Jiang, Partnoy, and Thomas (2008) provide evidence that hedge funds accumulate positions in firms that face agency problems of free cash flows which are reflected in low payouts to shareholders and substantial capital expenditures. This is confirmed by Klein and Zur (2009) who find that target firms hold more cash than comparable firms. In order to investigate whether this reasoning also applies to targets in Germany, with its distinct corporate governance system, key accounting ratios of target companies are compared to their peer group. This allows one to infer whether hedge fund engagements in German target companies are related to free-cash flow problems, to inefficient management and/or below average profitability.

The first two columns of Table 12 provide sample means and medians for eight accounting ratios at the end of the fiscal year preceding the event date. These ratios are constructed using data from the Worldscope database. Accounting ratios designed to capture the financial policies of target companies include the payout ratio defined as the ratio of total dividends paid to total earnings, the ratio of cash and cash equivalents to total assets, the gross leverage defined as total liabilities to total assets and the net leverage given by the ratio of total liabilities minus total cash and cash equivalents to total assets. Moreover, the profitability of target companies relative to their peer group is assessed using three different accounting metrics including the return on equity, the return on assets and the ratio of operating cash flow to total assets. Finally, the magnitude of ongoing investment activity is measured by the ratio of capital expenditures to total sales. In the next four columns these variables are compared to the median of their peer group in order to assess whether target companies differ systematically from their peer group. The third and fourth columns provide the mean and median of the difference of accounting ratios relative to a peer group represented by the industry median for the respective year based on all firms included in the DAX, MDAX, SDAX and TecDAX that are in the same IBC industry class. In the fifth and sixth columns the results of a matched pairs approach are presented where the peer group is constructed by matching each firm to the firm from the same industry for which the difference in firm size measured by its market capitalization is minimized. This takes into account the fact that there are often systematic differences in accounting ratios between large and small firms (see Fama and French, 1995). In order to test whether the resulting differences in means and medians are statistically significantly different from zero, simple t-statistics are used to evaluate means and Wilcoxon tests are applied to evaluate medians.

Similar to the results for the U.S. market by Brav, Jiang, Partnoy, and Thomas (2008) and Klein and Zur (2009), German target firms also seem to suffer from agency problems of free cash flows in that they exhibit significantly higher cash holdings and lower payout ratios. In particular, cash and cash equivalents make up 10.80% of total assets on average, which is significantly higher than the industry median. Moreover, target companies pay out an average 20.93% of their earnings which is significantly smaller than the industry median. In addition, the median payout is 0% suggesting that more than half of all target firms pay no dividends at all. This suggests that the managers of some target firms indeed have access to excessive free cash flow. This is also supported by the level of capital expenditures to sales which is significantly higher than the industry median. This can be interpreted as evidence for the inefficient use of free cash flows, but could also be related to the ongoing exercise of profitable growth options. At the same time, however, there are several patterns in accounting characteristics that are not consistent with this free cash flow argument. First, the leverage of target companies appears to be already high in that the means of gross leverage and net leverage are 31.19% and 19.15%, respectively, which is significantly higher than the industry median. Second, target companies are apparently not very profitable and do not generate excessive cash flows from their operations. In particular, medians of return on equity and return on assets are significantly smaller than the industry median. Similarly, means of return on assets and operating cash flow to total assets are significantly smaller than their industry peers. While this could also be related to the ongoing exercise of growth options (Bessler, Drobetz, and Holler, 2010a) this is clearly not in line with the argument that target firms suffer from free cash flow problems. Third, measured differences are no longer statistically significant for payout ratios and cash holdings when the accounting ratios are also adjusted for firm size. This suggests that perceived free cash flow problems inherent in relatively high cash holdings and low payout ratios are related to the fact that smaller firms often face more severe financing constraints and, therefore, have to adopt more conservative financial structures.

The information contained in financial statements also provides insight into the operating strategies of target companies as German firms have to report major accounting items individually for each business segment.[117] Based on information obtained from the Worldscope database, Table 13 provides some insights into the operating diversification of target companies. In the second column the percentage of firms with 1, 2,…, 10 business segments is reported which is calculated as the sum of non-zero entries in the data items "product segment sales 1",…, "product segment sales 10". Moreover, the third and fourth column use the same information to estimate mean and median Herfindahl indices of segment sales for target companies conditional on the firm having 1, 2…, 10 business segments. This concentration measure is defined as the sum of the squared fractions of segment sales to total sales. Thus, a ratio of 1 indicates that firm sales are completely concentrated in one segment and ratios close to zero indicate that sales are evenly dispersed across all business segments.

[117] This requirement was introduced with the KontraG in 1998.

Table 12: Capital Structure, Payout Policy and Profitability of Target Firms

Sample	Level		Industry Benchmarking		Industry & Size Benchmarking	
	Mean	Median	Mean	Median	Mean	Median
Payout-Ratio	20.93	0	-6.84***	-8.20***	-2.34	0
	(n=229)		(n=229)		(n=214)	
Cash to Total Assets	10.80	6.66	3.31***	-0.01	-1.51	-1.30
	(n=179)		(n=179)		(n=139)	
Leverage Net Debt	19.15	16.06	5.54*	2.88	14.47***	11.02***
	(n=179)		(n=179)		(n=139)	
Leverage Gross Debt	31.19	23.97	8.59***	4.10***	10.77***	4.25***
	(n=231)		(n=231)		(n=217)	
RoE	-4.70	8.22	-14.84	-2.53***	-9.22	-4.79***
	(n=231)		(n=231)		(n=218)	
RoA	-19.75	2.72	-4.98***	-2.14***	-4.82***	-2.46***
	(n=229)		(n=229)		(n=218)	
Oper. CF to Total Assets	4.99	6.41	-2.48*	0	-2.24	-0.25
	(n=223)		(n=223)		(n=208)	
Capex-to-Sales	6.44	3.63	2.92***	1.70***	1.00	0.55
	(n=222)		(n=222)		(n=202)	

This table provides the means and medians of several accounting ratios at the end of the fiscal year prior to the event date calculated using data from the Worldscope database. In addition, it shows the means and medians of differences relative to the industry median for all companies included in the DAX, MDAX, SDAX and TecDAX in the same year. In addition, the means and medians of differences are also calculated relative to a matched firm which is identified using industry and size as matching criteria. $^{*}/^{**}/^{***}$ indicate statistical significance at the 10%/5%/1%-levels.

Based on the definition of Höchle and Schmid (2009) that a diversified firm is a firm operating in more than one product segment, most German target firms seem to be highly diversified in that only 16.6% focus on one individual business segment and the majority of firms operate in more than 4 business segments. This is confirmed by the Herfindahl index whose median is 0.5165 for the whole sample. This also suggests that the majority of firms do not have a focused business model. However, there are some problems inherent in using accounting information to measure operating diversification. In particular, Villalonga (2004) emphasizes that firms have substantial discretionary freedom in defining business segments and that segment definitions are often inconstant and are often revised over time. Thus, these results are best interpreted as an indication that German target firms are diversified but more detailed information is needed.

Table 13: Diversification of Target Firms

Number of Business Segments	Percentage	Mean Herfindahl Index Sales	Median Herfindahl Index Sales
1	16.60%	1	1
2	7.23%	0.6676	0.7141
3	20.85%	0.6285	0.5807
4	17.87%	0.5075	0.4838
5	19.57%	0.3841	0.3557
6 or more	17.88%	0.3232	0.2727
Total	100%	0.5700	0.5165

This table provides information on the number of product segments of target companies using data on product segment sales from the Worldscope database. In addition, it reports Herfindahl indices of product segment sales which are also derived from Worldscope data.

II. Market Valuation of Target Companies

According to the hypothesis that hedge funds capitalize on valuation discounts resulting from agency problems of free cash flows or ineffective management, target companies should be trading at a discount in capital markets. This hypothesis is generally supported for target companies in the U.S. capital market. These are not only characterized by an excessive diversification strategy and accounting fundamentals which are consistent with agency problems of free cash flow, but they are also undervalued in capital markets. For instance, the results by Brav, Jiang, Partnoy, and Thomas (2008), Klein and Zur (2009) and other studies suggest that hedge fund engagements are concentrated in value firms which exhibit low market-to-book ratios. Therefore, it is interesting to investigate whether these findings also apply to target firms in Germany with its distinct corporate governance and capital market system. However, it is difficult to accurately measure undervaluation because commonly used proxies for undervaluation can also reflect additional sources of fundamental risk and, therefore, need not reflect true undervaluation. Thus, in the following analysis a range of different approaches is used to measure valuation discounts in the sample of German target firms. This includes the undervaluation index proposed by Peyer and Vermaelen (2009) and the individual components of this index which are based on market-to-book ratios, market capitalization and abnormal stock returns during time periods before the hedge fund engagement.

Figure 19 plots the distribution of the undervaluation index proposed by Peyer and Vermaelen (2009). This measure is defined as the sum of three subindices that attempt to capture different aspects of firm valuation in comparison to the aggregate stock market. In particular, these subindices assign each company a score of 1, 2,…,5 in each trading month if it belongs to the top, second-highest,…, bottom quantile respectively among all CDAX constituents in terms of the market-to-book ratio, past returns over the past six months and market capitalization. The mean of this distribution is 7.2 and the median is 7.0 which is below the average score of 9 for the whole population. Thus, the majority of target firms is apparently not undervalued according to the undervaluation index by Peyer and Vermaelen (2009). However, the distribution is rather skewed indicating that a small number of target firms exhibit a very large undervaluation prior to the event date. This can be interpreted as evidence that most hedge funds do not target undervalued stocks and that their investment strategies seem to be driven by other objectives such as market timing or capturing price and earnings momentum.

However, the application of the undervaluation index by Peyer and Vermaelen (2009) to a sample of German target firms involves some statistical problems. These problems occur because this measure was originally developed for the U.S. capital market which is more liquid and has a significantly larger number of stocks that are actively traded. For samples of U.S. stocks there is consequently a large cross-section of stocks available to determine the cut-off points within the cross-sectional distributions of each of the three underlying variables. In contrast, a large control group can only be constructed in Germany if the entire CDAX universe is used. However, this control group contains a large number of firms that are infrequently traded which creates substantial liquidity discounts. As a result, low market capitalizations and low market-to-book ratios not only reflect undervaluation but also reflect discounts for assuming liquidity risk. Moreover, hedge funds need sufficient liquidity in order to quickly accumulate and sell off substantial stakes in target companies. Thus, most of these very small CDAX companies subject to infrequent trading are not attractive targets for hedge funds and, therefore, should not be included in the control group. This is reflected in Figure 20 which shows that a large share of target firms exhibits relatively low scores in the category market capitalization. This means that their market capitalizations are in the upper percentiles of the CDAX universe:

Figure 19: Distribution of the Undervaluation Index

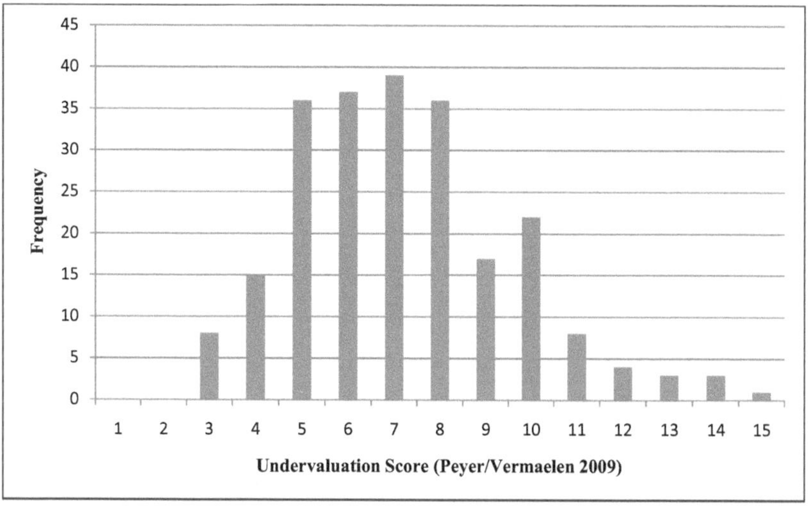

This figure plots the distribution of the undervaluation index proposed by Peyer and Vermaelen (2009). All data is used from the Worldscope database and Datastream and the whole CDAX universe of German stocks is used as a control group to estimate the cut-off points for each of the three subindices.

In order to investigate the problems related to liquidity discounts in more detail, Table 14 summarizes additional information regarding the market capitalization and liquidity of target firms. This information indicates that target firms are significantly larger in terms of market capitalization than the median across all firms included in the CDAX. At the same time, however, Table 14 also shows that target firms are not small when compared to the group of all liquid stocks approximated by the constituents of the major indices (DAX, MDAX, SDAX, TecDAX). In fact, the median of their market capitalization is 354.37 mio. € which is not statistically different from the median market capitalization of the index constituents from the same industry.

Figure 20: Distribution of the Subindices of the Undervaluation Index

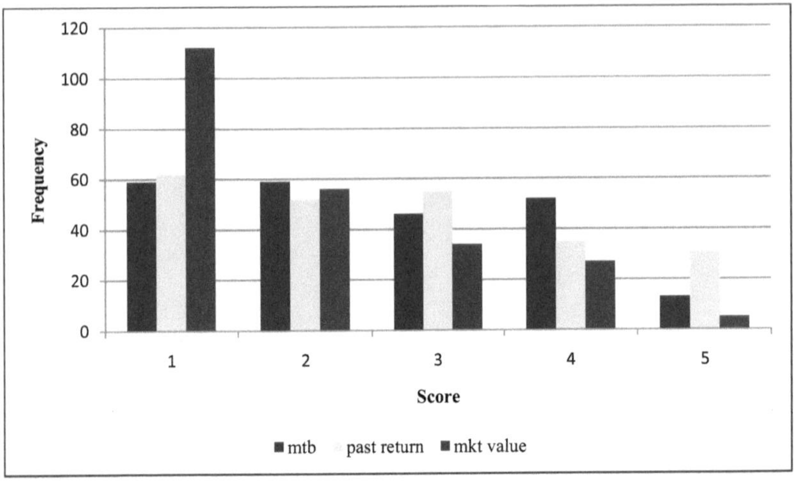

This figure plots the distribution of the subindices of the undervaluation index proposed by Peyer and Vermaelen (2009). All data is used from the Worldscope database and Datastream and the whole CDAX universe of German stocks is used as a control group in order to estimate the cut-off points for each of the three sub-indices.

Market capitalization is closely related to the liquidity of a firm's stocks. Therefore, Table 14 also contains information from the liquidity of event companies which is approximated by a liquidity measure proposed by Amihud (2002). This measures the price impact of a one-unit increase in dollar trading volume during the pre-event interval (-120,-80) so that a higher value indicates lower liquidity. This ratio can only be calculated for 156 out of 235 events because for the missing events there is at least one trading day without any trading volume. In line with the patterns identified in market capitalization of event firms, the liquidity of their stocks also seems to be located between the median liquidity of index members and the median liquidity of CDAX firms. In fact, the median liquidity ratio for sample firms is 0.0085 which is significantly larger than that for the median of all index constituents over the same time period, but it is not significantly different from the median of all firms contained in the CDAX.

Table 14: Market Capitalization and Liquidity

Statistic	Level		Difference to median for all index firms		Difference to median for all CDAX firms	
	Mean	Median	Mean	Median	Mean	Median
Market Cap	2823.86	354.37	370.03	-221.84	2737.98***	304.43***
Liquidity	0.0156	0.0085	0.0086***	0.0015***	0.0038**	-0.0028

This table summarizes information from the market capitalization of target firms 60 trading days prior to the event date as well as the average liquidity measure by Amihud (2002) in the interval (-120,-80). These variables are also compared to the median for all CDAX firms from the same industry and to the median of all index members in the DAX, MDAX, SDAX, or TecDAX. */**/*** indicate statistical significance at the 10%/5%/1%-levels.

These results indicate that German target companies are relatively small and therefore enable hedge funds to build up meaningful stakes with limited capital resources (Brav, Jiang, Partnoy, and Thomas, 2008; Bessler, Drobetz, and Holler, 2010a). Moreover, given the limited liquidity of target stocks it seems fair to assume that their valuation suffers from liquidity discounts and higher information asymmetries for outside investors. In turn, this might imply that control by outside capital markets was less effective for these firms prior to the engagement of the hedge fund (Bessler, Drobetz, and Holler, 2010a). These results also have implications for the interpretation of low average score in the category market capitalization according to the results for the undervaluation index by Peyer and Vermaelen (2009). In fact, the low score does not indicate that target firms are overvalued. Instead, it is more plausible to assume that the corresponding subindex is biased in the case of German data because the cut-off points derived from the cross-section of market caps are biased downwards by the small size and limited liquidity of many CDAX companies.

The undervaluation index by Peyer and Vermaelen (2009) also uses the market-to-book ratio to determine whether firms should be classified as "undervalued" value firms or as "overvalued" growth firms. According to the corresponding subindex in Figure 20, German firms targeted by hedge funds were also overvalued. For instance, 50% of target firms receive only a score smaller or equal to 2 on this subindex. This result might also be driven by two problems in the construction of the undervaluation index by Peyer and Vermaelen (2009). First, in German data it is likely that there is a downward bias in the cut-off points derived from the CDAX control group because it contains a large number of illiquid stocks. Second, the measure by Peyer and Vermaelen (2009) does not account for the systematic variation of market-to-book ratios across different industries. Table 15 addresses these problems and investigates the behavior of industry-adjusted market to book ratios during the time period of up to one year before the event date. In particular, the industry median is used to estimate industry-adjusted market-to-book ratios. In panel A the whole CDAX universe is used as a control group and in panel B the control group consists of all firms traded in a liquid market which is approximated by the constituents of the major German stock indices (DAX, MDAX, SDAX, and TecDAX).

Table 15: Market to Book Ratios of Target Companies

Panel A – Market to Book relative to industry median of all CDAX constituents							
Period	0	-40	-80	-120	-160	-200	-240
Mean	1.7035***	1.3119***	1.1436***	0.7622***	0.8896***	0.8264***	0.8863***
Med.	0.37***	0.2825***	0.1829***	0.1600***	0.1875***	0.2275***	0.2575***
Panel B – Market to Book relative to industry median of index members							
Period	0	-40	-80	-120	-160	-200	-240
Mean	1.1570**	0.7549*	0.6048	0.2532	0.3721**	0.3338*	0.3918**
Med.	-0.1799	-0.2499	-0.2749	-0.2900	-0.2050	-0.1850	-0.1600

In Panel A this table reports the difference in market-to-book ratios between target firms and the industry median derived from all stocks traded in a liquid market, i.e. those belonging to the DAX, MDAX, SDAX and TecDAX as a control group. The significance of these effects is tested with simple t-statistics and Wilcoxon tests, respectively. Panel B repeats this analysis using the whole CDAX universe to estimate industry medians. */**/*** indicate statistical significance at the 10%/5%/1%-levels.

The results in panel A indicate that target firms are apparently not undervalued and cannot be classified as value firms when their market-to-book ratio is compared to the industry median of all CDAX firms. In fact, the means and medians are significantly positive for all time periods prior to the event date. Moreover, there is some indication for run-up effects as the adjusted market-to-book ratio increases prior to the event date. This increase begins 120 trading days prior to the event date at a median level of 0.16 steadily increasing up to 0.37 on the event date. The results are different in panel B where the target's market-to-book ratio is compared to the industry median of the index constituents which have a fairly liquid market and whose valuation is less likely to suffer from liquidity discounts. In this case the means and medians of the adjusted market-to-book ratio are not significantly different from zero up to 80 trading days prior to the event date. Moreover, there is also a run-up effect in that only the mean of adjusted market to book ratios increases sharply starting 80 trading days prior to the event date. However, the median of the industry-adjusted market-to-book ratio does not exhibit a similar pattern. This suggests that the run-up is concentrated in a limited number of firms.

Overall, the behavior of market-to-book ratios suggests that target firms are fairly valued prior to the event date and cannot be classified as "undervalued" value firms. Moreover, these results suggest that the high fraction of "overvalued" firms, according to the corresponding subindex of the undervaluation index by Peyer and Vermaelen (2009), can be explained by liquidity discounts which affect the valuation of a large number of firms in the CDAX control group and by the fact that this index does not adjust for systematic patterns in market-to-book ratios across industries.

The final valuation metric considered by Peyer and Vermaelen (2009) is past stock returns prior to the event date. Based on the corresponding subindex in Figure 20, the fraction of target companies with above average past returns is fairly high. This is not consistent with the hypothesis that companies targeted by hedge funds should be undervalued. However, the behavior of market-to-book ratios already indicated that there are run-up effects prior to the event date which might also distort the Peyer-Vermaelen index. In order to investigate this possibility more closely, Table 16 summarizes abnormal stock returns starting two years before the event date. These are estimated with the BHAR-approach where expected stock returns are approximated by the index corresponding to the market segment (DAX, MDAX, SDAX, TecDAX, and CDAX) to which the company belonged on the event date. The statistical significance of BHAR is tested with skewness-adjusted t-statistics and Wilcoxon-tests.

Empirical results suggest that the majority of target companies exhibit a negative stock price performance that persists for up to 6 months before the event date. In fact, the median buy-and-hold abnormal return is -11.22% which is significant at the 5% level during the time period from 24 months to 6 months before the event date. In addition, for most of the firms, the initial undervaluation seems to be generated more than one year before the event date as more than 50% of target firms incur negative returns of -9.34 or even lower during the interval (-480,-160). Moreover, BHAR remain in this range up to 40 trading days before the event date. Subsequently, median buy-and-hold abnormal returns improve in that the dispersion increases indicating that a large share of target firms exhibit long run-up periods that differ in length. As a result, the median BHAR remains negative but is barely significantly different from zero. This is also supported by the patterns in the mean of buy-and-hold abnormal returns which become positive over the same time period. Thus, it seems fair to conclude that a substantial fraction of target companies are undervalued prior to the event date. However, this undervaluation is not captured by Peyer and Vermaelen's approach, which is based on past returns during the past 6 months, because these are "contaminated" by run-up effects. Unfortunately, it is difficult to adjust their measure for this effect because the length of run-up periods differs substantially between individual stocks.

Table 16: Pre-Event BHAR of Target Companies

Period	Mean	Median
(-480, 0)	0.0962*	-0.0751
(-480, -40)	0.0416	-0.1279*
(-480, -80)	0.0164	-0.1294
(-480, -120)	-0.0117	-0.1122**
(-480, -160)	-0.0279	-0.0934**
(-480, - 200)	-0.0208	-0.0413**
(-480, -240)	-0.0341	-0.0621**

This table reports the means and medians of buy-and-hold abnormal returns which are estimated using the respective market index to which the target company belonged on the event date. Mean valuation effects are tested for statistical significance using bootstrapped skewness-adjusted t-statistics and Wilcoxon tests are used to test medians. */**/*** indicate statistical significance at the 10%/5%/1%-levels.

Overall, there is some evidence for "undervaluation" of target firms prior to the event date which is in contrast to the empirical results based on the undervaluation index by Peyer and Vermaelen (2009). In particular, this is supported by patterns in buy-and-hold abnormal returns before the event date. Importantly, these BHAR can be considered as a conservative measure of undervaluation because the omission of factors capturing valuation discounts due to size effects or liquidity discounts leads to an upward bias in estimated valuations during time periods when the corresponding factor risk premia are positive.

III. Ownership Structure of Target Firms

An important determinant of the magnitude of agency problems and of the entrenchment of managers is the ownership structure of target firms. While no existing study of the U.S. market makes a detailed analysis of the ownership structure of target companies, it seems reasonable to assume that target companies should exhibit a relatively dispersed ownership structure. Furthermore, there should not be any other blockholder that also derives private benefits of control from his position in the firm (Barclay and Holderness, 1989; Dyck and Zingales, 2004a/b). In fact, even though some recent studies have questioned the assumption of fully dispersed ownership structures in the U.S. market, the predominant view in the literature is still that most U.S. firms have ownership structures that facilitate outside interference by capital markets. In Germany, however, ownership structures used to be dominated by a "governing coalition" of families, banks, and industrial owners which could easily defend itself against outside interference. More recently, this has changed (Weber, 2008) so that it is reasonable to assume that hedge fund activity should be concentrated in those German firms with restructured, i.e. sufficiently dispersed, ownership structures.

In order to investigate this hypothesis, Table 17 provides information on the concentration and the composition of the ownership structure of German target firms at the end of the fiscal year prior to the event date. Panel A analyzes the concentration of shareholdings at the end of the year prior to the event date based on attendance rates at company's general assemblies, which is provided by the "Schutzgemeinschaft der Kleinaktionäre" (www.sdk.de). Moreover, it also includes the fraction of closely held shares from the Worldscope database which measures the fraction of shares held by corporate insiders and other blockholders owning stakes larger than 5%. Consequently, it reflects the fraction of shares that are not available for trading and that are in the possession of investors who might suffer from conflicts of interest. In the third and fourth column these variables are adjusted for the median across all firms for which information is available in the same year in order to adjust for time trends in the ownership structures of German firms (Weber, 2008).

The empirical results in panel A generally provide support for the hypothesis that target companies exhibit a relatively dispersed ownership structure. In particular, the fraction of closely held shares is 33.56% on average and its median is 30.72% which is significantly lower than the median for other German firms. This implies that approximately 70% of all outstanding shares are freely traded in financial markets. In addition, the attendance rates at the general assembly of target firms appear to be significantly smaller than the median among all German firms. Since attendance rates are significantly related to the presence of large blocks of shares, this also indicates that target firms appear to have a more dispersed ownership structure. According to these results, it is fair to conclude that hedge funds can gain substantial influence over target firms even though they only acquire non-controlling blocks.

Table 17: Ownership in the Year of the Event

Panel A – Concentration of Ownership

Statistic	Sample Firms		Difference in	
	Mean	Median	Mean	Median
HV-Presence (n=130)	46.51%	44.43%	-8.59%***	-9.17%***
Closely held Shares (n=175)	33.56%	30.72%	-19.19%***	-21.15%***

Panel B – Composition of Ownership

Largest Investor	Nobs	Size of Investor Stake		Size of HF Stake	
		Mean	Median	Mean	Median
Bank	8	0.2485	0.2311	0.0541	0.0522
Corporation	51	0.6755	0.2586	0.0745	0.0560
Financial	82	0.1411	0.0904	0.2109	0.0521
Government	10	0.2026	0.1816	0.0553	0.0512
Individual	81	0.2792	0.2400	0.0998	0.0747
Total	232	0.3131	0.2052	0.1327	0.0577

This table presents information on the ownership structure of target firms. Panel A summarizes data on the ownership concentration of target firms using the mean and median of the attendance rates at annual shareholder meeting from the Schutzgemeinschaft der Kleinaktionäre and of closely held shares from the Worldscope database. These are compared to the median for all other firms in the same year. Panel B provides information on the classification of large blockholders based on the Thomson One database. */**/*** indicate statistical significance at the 10%/5%/1%-levels.

In addition, panel B contains information on the composition of the ownership structure and focuses on the identity of the largest blockholder. This determines whether hedge funds are in a position to implement their restructuring plans or whether there are other large shareholders with opposing interests. In particular, large shareholders such as banks, family investors or corporations often derive substantial private benefits of control and therefore have a vested interest in maintaining the status quo. Thus, in Panel B provides information on the identity of the largest shareholder and the size of his stake at the end of the quarter before the event date. This is based on the ownership module of the Thomson One database. There is a relatively large percentage of large non-financial shareholders present in the ownership structure of most target firms. In fact, the dominant shareholder is either an individual investor in one of the 81 companies, or a corporation (51), or a government entity (10) or a bank (8). Because each of these different types of investors can extract significant private benefits of control from their controlling position, this might create significant difficulties for hedge funds to implement their restructuring plans. In fact, hedge funds should only be able to easily implement their restructuring plans in those 82 cases in which target companies have a financial investor as the dominant shareholder. Panel B also reports information on the size of the hedge fund holdings. Overall, these figures appear to be significantly smaller than the positions held by the dominant shareholder as they barely exceed the initial reporting threshold of 5% in all categories. This indicates that hedge funds need to be confident that they would obtain the support of other outside shareholders at the company's general shareholder meeting.

However, there are several caveats in this analysis. In particular, these variables are based on public filings according to German security trading laws which require investors to publicly disclose their ownership stakes when they cross the reporting threshold of 5%.[118] Thus, these data items do not take into account smaller blockholders or informal coalitions among smaller blockholders. Moreover, these data items are not updated on a daily basis so it is not possible to obtain information on significant shifts in ownership structures between the end of the fiscal year and the event date. And finally, this analysis cannot take into account other means by which the old governing coalition can exert control. In particular, this applies to the influence of banks which still exert significant influence and hold seats on the boards of many firms (Dittmann, Maug, and Schneider, 2010).

B. Short-term Valuation Effects

In the U.S. capital market engagements by hedge funds lead to substantial increases in the share prices of target firms in the short run. For instance, Brav, Jiang, Partnoy, and Thomas (2008) document abnormal returns of 7% during the time period covering 20

[118] The reduction of this initial disclosure threshold to 3% according §§21, 22 WpHG only became effective after the end of the sample period on February 1st, 2007.

trading days before and after the event date. Similarly, Klein and Zur (2009) report substantial abnormal returns of 10.2% in the period 30 trading days before and after the event date. However, the German capital market and corporate governance systems differ from the U.S. system in some important aspects. Therefore, it is interesting to investigate whether the engagement of hedge funds leads to similar increases in the shareholder value of German target firms. This question is addressed in the following sections which present the results of an event study using the sample of 235 events taking place between January 1st, 2000 and December 31st, 2006. This roughly corresponds to the time period analyzed in studies for the U.S. market. Moreover, this time period was generally characterized by rising stock markets which increase the risk of free cash flow problems and which should also make it easier for hedge funds to implement their restructuring plans. In addition to estimating average valuation effects, the analysis also differentiates between different subsamples because the ability of hedge funds to increase firm value should depend on several factors, such as characteristics of target firms and the tactics used by the hedge funds. Finally, the magnitude of short-term valuation effects might also be related to different accounting fundamentals which implicitly measure the magnitude of agency problems of free cash flow and reflect the ability of managers to efficiently manage the firm. Therefore, the results of cross-sectional regressions are also presented in the last subsection.

I. Results for the Full Sample

The impact of hedge fund engagements on the share prices of target firms in the short-run is measured by the widely used event study approach. Following Schwert (1996) abnormal returns are estimated using a market model with the intercept constrained to zero. The estimation window for market model parameters corresponds to the interval from 140 to 81 trading days before the the event date. This approach takes into account the potential upward bias in estimates of expected returns for some target firms which might result from the run-up in their share prices during the estimation period. The results for the full sample of 235 events during the window (-80,+140) are shown in Figure 21.

Figure 21: Cumulative Abnormal Returns and Abnormal Trading Volume

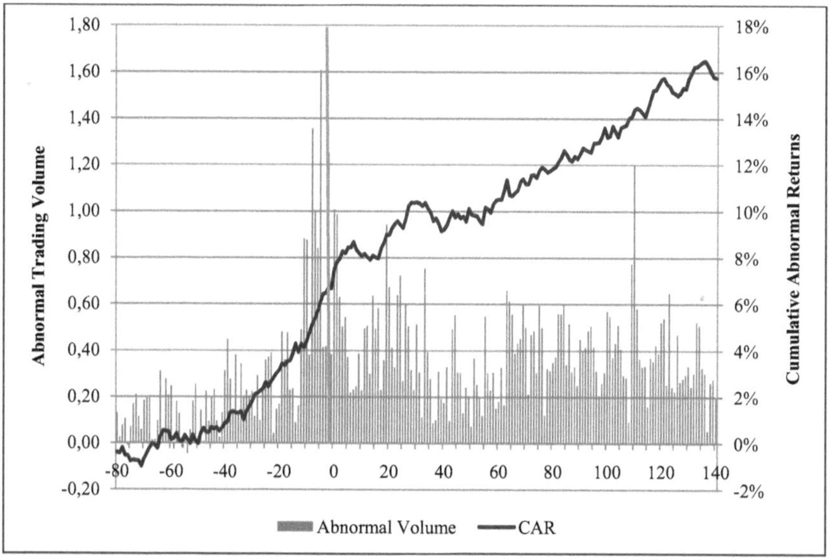

This figure presents cumulative abnormal returns on the left hand scale for the full sample of 235 events where the approach by Schwert (1996) with the estimation period (-140,-81) and the CDAX as a market proxy are used to estimate expected returns. It also shows abnormal trading volume on the right hand scale which is measured using the approach by Brav and Gompers (2003) where normal trading activity is measured in the interval (-140,-81).

The results in Figure 21 indicate that hedge fund engagements create shareholder value because investments in target companies generate cumulative abnormal returns of approximately 16% during the entire time period from 80 trading days before until 140 trading days after the event date. This valuation effect is highly significant at the 1%-level. Moreover, during the shorter window of 40 trading days before and after the event date abnormal returns accumulate to more than 9% and are also highly significant, suggesting that total valuation effects are similar in magnitude to the effects measured in the U.S. market. Apparently, other investors also expect that firms that are targeted by hedge funds will experience increases in shareholder value and push managers to adapt value-increasing changes to corporate strategies, financial policies or corporate governance.

Interestingly, a large fraction of this valuation effect is generated before the event date when the investment of a hedge fund became public information according to the information contained in the Lexis-Nexis database used to identify event dates. This is visible in Figure 21 which shows that this run-up period starts approximately 40 trading days before the event date. Moreover, the existence of this run-up effect is also supported by the estimates of abnormal returns for different windows before and after the event date which are reported in Table 18.

Table 18: Cumulative Abnormal Returns

Interval	CAR	Interval	CAR
Panel A: Intervals around the event		**Panel B: Intervals before and after the event**	
(-80,+80)	**11.84%*****	(-80,-3)	**6.47%*****
(-45,+45)	**9.41%*****	(-45,-3)	**6.00%*****
(-15,+15)	**4.45%*****	(-30,-3)	**4.89%*****
(-5,+5)	**2.76%*****	(-15,-3)	**2.90%*****
(-3,+3)	**1.85%*****	(+3,+15)	0.05%
(-1,+1)	**1.08%*****	(+3,+30)	**2.42%****
		(+3,+45)	1.91%
		(+3,+80)	**3.88%****

The table reports the mean cumulative abnormal returns for the entire sample of n=231 event firms during different time windows. The time intervals describe the number of trading days around the event date. */ **/*** implies that the mean cumulative abnormal return is significantly different from zero at the 10%, 5%, 1% level, respectively.

Using the approach by Schwert (1996), the run-up effect is 6.47% during the interval (-80, -3) which is also statistically significant at the 1%-level. In addition, this run-up effect is also observable in abnormal trading volume measured with the method by Brav and Gompers (2003). In particular, Figure 21 also shows that abnormal trading volume starts to increase substantially at the same time that share prices begin to increase. Subsequently, abnormal trading volume appears to remain at this higher level suggesting that additional investors begin to trade the stock based on the news that a hedge fund invested in the company. The results in Table 18 also suggest that abnormal returns during short announcement windows are relatively small and constitute only a small fraction of the total valuation effect. For instance, during the event window (-1, 1) cumulative abnormal returns are equal to 1.08% and during the longer window (-3, 3) cumulative abnormal return are only 1.85%. Both figures are significantly different from zero.

The statistical significance of announcement period returns might also be due to event-induced variance leading to biases in t-statistics. Therefore, similar to Bessler and Nohel (1996) Table 19 provides estimates of daily abnormal returns, conventional t-statistics and t-statistics adjusted for event-induced variance based on the approach by Böhmer, Masumeci, and Poulsen (1991) in order to check the robustness of announcement effects. According to the results in Table 19, average abnormal returns are small but positive on most individual trading days around the event date. At the same time, however, abnormal returns are not significantly different from zero when conventional t-statistics or t-statistics adjusted for event-induced variance are used. This indicates that for each individual trading day the cross-sectional variance of abnormal returns is fairly large relative to the mean. Hence, valuation effects only become statistically significant when they are accumulated over multiple trading days. This occurs because there is a slow but steady increase in share prices before the event date.

This pattern of long run-up periods before the event date is not consistent with the evidence for the U.S. capital market. For instance, Brav, Jiang, Partnoy, and Thomas (2008) and Klein and Zur (2009) both report significantly shorter run-up periods.[119] Consequently, this run-up effect should be related to differences between hedge fund engagements in Germany and in the U.S., respectively or to differences between the German and U.S. capital market environments. First, the pre-event run-up in share prices might reflect limited liquidity of target shares so that the accumulation of shares by hedge funds generates continuous buying pressure which in turn slowly pushes up the company`s share price. However, while this explanation might help to explain run-up effects in small-cap targets, it cannot explain the observation that this longer run-up period apparently also exists in large-cap stocks. Alternatively, longer run-up periods in Germany might also be the result of inefficiencies in German regulations governing the disclosure of large trading positions. In particular, German disclosure rules are based on a two-step approach in which investors first communicate the crossing of a reporting threshold to the firm which in turn is responsible for publishing this information to all market participants. Moreover, according to the empirical results by Weber and Zimmermann (2010) this system appears to be weakly enforced by the German regulator. As a result, there are often long reporting lags that create a higher risk of early leakage of inside information and insider trading than the more stringent

[119] There is only one study (Ryan 2006) for the US market that seems to report similarly long run-up periods as those in this study. However, his study is based on a relatively small sample.

U.S. disclosure regulations. These problems might also apply to "wolf pack" investing when several hedge funds implicitly coordinate their trading into target firms or "tipping" where hedge funds reveal their intentions to a limited number of other investors before making a public announcement in exchange for reciprocation of other favors (see Brav, Jiang, Partnoy, and Thomas, 2008). Moreover, this effect could be due to the circulation of rumors among market participants regarding a pending hedge fund engagement which might push up share prices prior to the official announcement of the hedge funds' position. Effectively, all of these explanations also involve event date uncertainty, meaning that it is not possible to identify the precise moment when the information became public in capital markets. This can also create run-up effects in the average performance across the whole sample of hedge fund engagements, even if the market`s response to each individual event is perfectly efficient and entails no run-up. Finally, longer run-up effects might also reflect confounding events in that hedge funds start to accumulate their stakes based on other trading signals, such as increases in dividends, that initiate an upward drift in prices even before the hedge fund starts trading in the stock.

Table 19: Abnormal Returns and Event-Induced Variance

Period	Mean AR (%)	Median AR (%)	Convent. t-stat	Event-ind. t-stat	CAR
-5	0.4077	0.0373*	1.4902	2.1816	0.4077
-4	0.3354	0	1.2338	0.17462	0.7431
-3	0.0424	-0.0228	0.1495	1.0971	0.7855
-2	0.2579	-0.0208	0.9888	-0.0598	1.0434
-1	-0.0615	0	-0.3277	-0.1182	0.9819
0	0.8302	0.2291***	3.4170	4.2622	1.8121
1	0.3114	0	1.4080	1.3330	2.1235
2	0.1609	0	0.8279	1.0210	2.2844
3	0.3118	0	1.6526	2.2026	2.5962
4	-0.0837	-0.1501	-0.4359	-0.8880	2.5125
5	0.0249	0	1.3699	1.5354	2.5374

This table reports daily abnormal returns calculated using the approach by Schwert (1996) where the estimation period ist (-140,-81) and the CDAX is the market proxy. In addition to conventional t-statistics it also shows t-statistics that are adjusted for event-induced variance based on the approach proposed by Böhmer, Masumeci and Poulsen (1991). Medians are tested for significance using the Wilcoxon test. */**/*** indicate statistical significance at the 10%/5%/1%-levels.

II. Results for Subsamples

Most hedge funds pursue the tactic of accumulating a small but meaningful stake in target companies before trying to win the support of other shareholders to force managers to make significant adjustments in the firms` strategies or financial policies. The success rate of this approach might be related to several factors. For instance, Boyson and Mooradian (2008) report that hedge funds generate higher returns in the U.S. market when they adopt a more confrontational approach towards incumbent management. Therefore, in the following subsections the full sample is differentiated into a number of different subsamples according to criteria that might affect the success rate of activist hedge funds in order to determine whether they have a significant impact on observed valuation effects. This includes the acquisition method, target firm valuations prior to the event date, firm size and the hostility of the hedge fund. Moreover, the event windows that are considered are the announcement period

(-3, 3) and the longer event window (-40, 40). Even though this is longer than the intervals analyzed in studies for the U.S. market (Brav, Jiang, Partnoy, and Thomas, 2008) which use a shorter window (-20, 20) this longer window is reasonable in this case because run-up effects are longer and more pronounced in the sample of German targets than in studies for the U.S. capital market.

1. Acquisition Method

Hedge funds use different methods, such as open market purchases or participating in secondary offerings, to acquire their stakes in target companies. These methods differ in the inherent commitment to the investment and, therefore, might affect the outcome of the hedge fund engagement. Since rational investors should be able to anticipate this effect, the acquisition method might affect the magnitude of short-term valuation effects. Therefore, the full sample is separated into three subsamples according to the method used to acquire a stake. First, there are 202 events in which the hedge fund acquires the shares in the open market and crosses the initial reporting threshold of 5% of outstanding shares which was applicable throughout the entire sample period. Importantly, this disclosure mechanism creates a lock-in effect in that the hedge fund also has to make a filing if his position falls below this threshold again. Hence, the hedge fund cannot secretly sell off his investment without notifying other capital market participants. This commits the hedge fund to his engagement so that valuation effects should be relatively strong for this subsample. In contrast, there are 19 events classified as interventions in which the hedge fund only makes public statements regarding the target firm but does not report the size of his holdings and also does not cross the initial reporting threshold of 5%. Evidently, in this case the commitment to the engagement is considerably smaller because the hedge fund can make a "quiet exit" and close out his position without notifying other investors that he has stopped his engagement. Therefore, valuation effects should be smaller for this subsample compared to the first subsample. Finally, there are 14 events classified as PIPE ("Public Investment in Private Equity") in which the hedge funds have to make a filing and acquires a large stake in the target company by participating in a secondary offering. This large stake creates an even stronger commitment effect than a simple regulatory filing. Thus, it seems reasonable to assume that short-term valuation effects should be strongest for PIPEs. The cumulative abnormal returns and test statistics for these three subsamples are reported in Figure 22 and Table 20, respectively.

Overall, valuation effects are positive and significant for almost all subsamples and event windows except for the subsample "intervention" during the event window (-40, 40) where the effect is positive but not statistically significant. Interestingly, valuation effects are relatively small for the subsamples "open market" and "intervention" which are not statistically different from each other. Thus, the hypothesis that a regulatory filing creates a lock-in effect leading to higher initial returns has to be rejected. However, the subsample "PIPE" is characterized by a significantly higher valuation effect of 5.93% in the shorter window (-3,3) and 32.09% in the longer window (-40,40) compared to the other two subsamples. Thus, commitment effects might be stronger for these transactions involving relatively large stakes from the perspective of hedge funds. However, these higher valuation effects can also be reconciled with another explanation. In particular, the signaling effect might be stronger because companies subject to PIPE`s are typically very small and unprofitable, implying substantial uncertainty and information asymmetries from the perspective of outside investors.

These results also raise some further interesting issues. First, highly positive valuation effects for PIPE-investments by hedge funds are in contrast to the empirical results of studies investigating share price reactions to other seasoned equity financings. These studies typically document negative valuation effects in the short and long run (Bessler, Drobetz, and Seim, 2009). This seems to be related to the structure of these transactions in that all new shares are placed with a supposedly sophisticated investor which seems to be a positive signal for other shareholders.

Figure 22: CARs differentiated by Acquisition Method

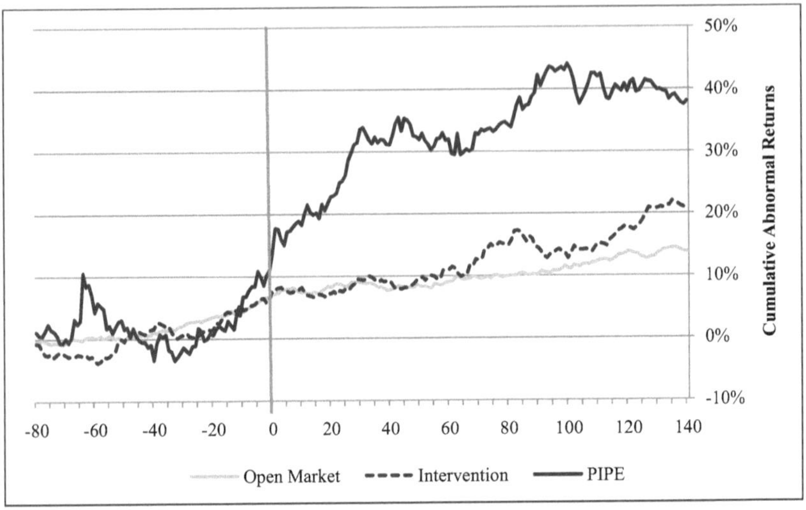

This figure reports cumulative abnormal returns differentiated by the acquisition method used by the hedge fund. CARs are calculated with the approach by Schwert (1996) where the estimation period is (-140,-81) and the CDAX is the market proxy.

Table 20: CARs differentiated by Acquisition Method

Panel A: Mean and Median Valuation Effects				
Interval	(-3, 3)		(-40, 40)	
Statistic	Mean	Median	Mean	Median
Open Market (n = 202)	0.0157^{***}	0.0097^{**}	0.0703^{***}	0.0726^{***}
Intervention (n = 19)	0.0181^{*}	0.0063	7.73	0.1108
PIPE (n = 14)	0.0593^{*}	0.0577^{**}	32.09^{**}	0.2855^{**}
Panel B: Tests for Differences				
Statistic	t-stat	z-stat	t-stat	z-stat
Open Market vs. Intervention	0.1162	0.182	0.1149	-0.253
Open Market vs. PIPE	1.8258	1.610	3.3250	2.184
Intervention vs. PIPE	1.5447	1.421	2.1308	1.858

This table reports cumulative abnormal returns differentiated by the acquisition method used by the hedge fund. CARs are calculated using the approach by Schwert (1996) where the estimation period is (-140,-81) and the CDAX is the market proxy. Means are tested for difference using a simple t-test and differences in medians are tested with the Mann-Whitney tests. $^{*}/^{**}/^{***}$ indicate statistical significance at the 10%/5%/1%-levels.

Second, positive valuation effects for PIPE-investments by hedge funds in Germany are not consistent with the results of research for the U.S. capital market which usually document negative valuation effects for PIPE-investments by hedge funds (Dai 2007; Brophy, Ouimet, and Sialm, 2009). These differences appear to be related to the structure of transactions in the U.S. which often create incentives for hedge funds to engage in simultaneous short-selling. This can put selling pressure on the share prices of target firms (Hillion and Vermaelen, 2004). In contrast, German PIPEs seem to constitute straight issues of common stock that do not confer similar repricing rights or other implicit options to the buyer.

2. Characteristics of Target Firms - Size and Technology

Hedge fund engagements occur in different types of companies. For instance, there is a wide-variation in the size of hedge fund targets in that large firms included in the DAX, as well as very small firms included in CDAX, have become targets of hedge funds. Moreover, target firms also operate in many different industries. Thus, targets operate in mature industries as well as in technology-intensive industries. The differences in the size and industry of target firms might have significant implications for the ability of hedge funds to create firm value by forcing managers to change their strategies or financial policies. Consequently, this might have implications for the magnitude of short-term valuation effects.

In order to evaluate the impact of these firm characteristics on the magnitude of short-term valuation effects, the total sample is differentiated into three subsamples using the index assignments from Deutsche Börse on the event dates. First, the category "large" comprise all 99 events involving firms that belong to the DAX or MDAX on the event date. In these cases valuation effects might be smaller for two reasons. On the one hand, it might be more difficult for hedge funds to restructure large and more complex firms. On the other hand, information asymmetries for these firms are relatively small because they are traded in liquid markets and are covered by a large number of financial analysts. This suggests that the signaling effect of a large investment by a sophisticated investor should be relatively small. Second, the category "small" contains all 119 events involving firms that are members of the SDAX or CDAX on the event date. In these cases valuation effects should be stronger since it is easier for hedge funds to restructure small firms and because higher information asymmetries result in stronger signaling effects.[120] Third, the category "technology" is composed of all 17 events where firms that belong to the TecDAX on the event date became hedge fund targets. Due to the high importance of intellectual property rights, conventional hedge fund tactics might not be well suited to increase the value of these firms. For instance, activism might destroy the value derived from the co-investment in human capital by employees and management (Zingales, 2000; Myers, 2000). As a result, valuation effects should be smaller than for the other two groups or even become negative. The results for these three subsamples are reported in Figure 23. Table 21 contains the relevant test statistics.

Short-term valuation effects are strongest when hedge funds invest in small cap stocks. In particular, for the category "small" the announcement effect in the short event window (-3, 3) reaches almost 3% and is highly significant. Moreover, small caps continue to outperform the other two subsamples after 40 trading days with cumulative abnormal returns climbing up to a highly significant 13.54%. In contrast, when hedge funds invest in large cap stocks the initial valuation effects are rather small and statistically insignificant. However, after 40 trading days, cumulative abnormal returns reach 4.89% and become significant at the 5%-level. Compared to these two groups, the subsample of technology firms exhibits a distinct pattern in that valuation effects are only positive and statistically significant during the short announcement period. Subsequently, cumulative abnormal returns deteriorate so that after 40 trading days average valuation effects are negative and insignificant.

Table 21 confirms that the differences between these subsamples are statistically significant. In particular, valuation effects are significantly larger for small capitalization firms compared to large cap stocks. This effect leads to two interpretations. First, there might be a "neglected firm" effect in that the arrival of a sophisticated investor making a substantial investment in the firm signals to other investors that the firm has been undervalued. Second, it might be easier for hedge funds to quickly restructure small firms. This is consistent with the observation from the U.S. market that hedge funds generally prefer small and more opaque targets (Klein and Zur, 2009).

[120] However, it can also be argued that it is more difficult to impose specific types of financial restructurings on small firms because these firms are usually subject to more significant financial constraints and have a smaller debt capacity.

Figure 23: Cumulative Abnormal Returns differentiated by Size and Technology

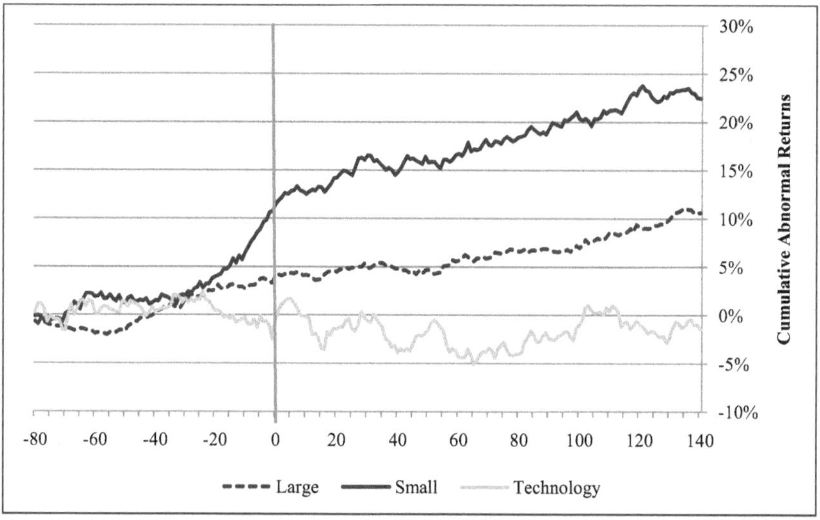

This figure reports cumulative abnormal returns differentiated by firm size and technology used by the hedge fund. CARs are calculated with the approach by Schwert (1996) where the estimation period is (-140,-81) and the CDAX is the market proxy.

Table 21: CARs differentiated by Size and Technology

Panel A: Mean and Median Valuation Effects				
Interval	(-3, 3)		(-40, 40)	
Statistic	Mean	Median	Mean	Median
Large (n=99)	0.0044	0.0089	0.0489**	0.04277***
Small (n=119)	0.0299***	0.0097***	0.1354***	0.1422***
Technology (n=17)	0.0208	0.0240	-0.0469	-0.0334
Panel B: Tests for Differences				
Statistic	t-stat	z-stat	t-stat	z-stat
Large vs. Small	2.2037	1.491	2.3217	2.395
Large vs. Technology	-0.9401	-1.058	1.6187	1.737
Small vs. Technology	0.3763	0.016	2.3838	2.839

This table reports cumulative abnormal returns differentiated by the acquisition method used by the hedge fund. CARs are calculated with the approach by Schwert (1996) where the estimation period is (-140,-81) and the CDAX is the market proxy. Means are tested for differences using a simple t-test and differences in medians are tested using Mann-Whitney tests. */**/*** indicate statistical significance at the 10%/5%/1%-levels.

Moreover, valuation effects for technology firms apparently become significantly smaller after 40 trading days in comparison to the other two groups. This result supports the notion that it is difficult to apply hedge fund tactics to firms relying on technology and intellectual property. Moreover, this result is also in line with the argument by Brav, Jiang, Partnoy, and Thomas (2008) that hedge funds should abstain from opaque and complicated businesses because the resolution of uncertainty regarding the interventions` impact on market prices may be slower.

3. Valuation of Target Firms

The valuation of target firms before the engagement of a hedge fund might also affect the magnitude of the share price response. In particular, it can be argued that short-term returns should be higher for more undervalued target companies for two reasons. First, the signaling effect generated by the arrival of a sophisticated investor making a substantial investment in the firm should be stronger. Second, low valued firms should also offer more opportunities for implementing value-enhancing measures which in turn should lead to higher short-term valuation effects. Hence, in order to test this hypothesis, the events are separated into three groups based on the percentiles of buy-and-hold abnormal returns in the time period from 48 to 6 six months prior to the event date. These returns should not be "contaminated" by pre-event run-up effects. Specifically, a stock is assigned to the category high (low) valuation if its BHAR (-48,-6) is higher (lower) than 22.3% (-37,3%). 11 events are dropped from the analysis due to a lack of share price data in the interval (-48,-6). The results are plotted in Figure 24 and Table 22 contains the corresponding test statistics.

Figure 24: CARs differentiated by Pre-Performance

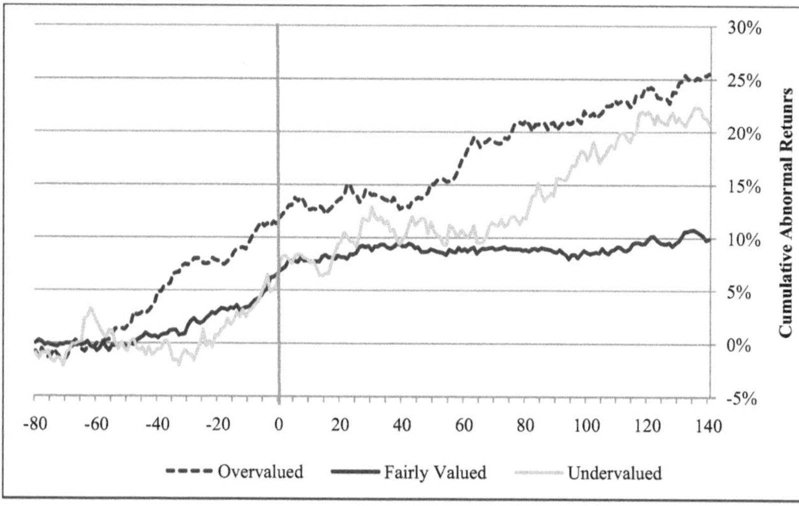

This figure reports cumulative abnormal returns differentiated by pre-performance used by the hedge fund. CARs are calculated with the approach by Schwert (1996) where the estimation period is (-140,-81) and the CDAX is the market proxy.

Table 22: Cumulative Abnormal Returns differentiated by Pre-Performance

Panel A: Mean and Median Valuation Effects				
Statistic	(-3, 3)		(-40, 40)	
Interval	Mean	Median	Mean	Median
High Valuation (n = 58)	0.0169*	0.0124	0.0897**	0.0926**
Intermediate Valuation (n=119)	0.0277***	0.0129***	0.0853***	0.0843***
Low Valuation (n = 58)	0.0143	0.0029	0.1073**	0.0681**
Panel B: Tests for Differences				
Statistic	t-stat	z-stat	t-stat	z-stat
High vs. Low	-0.1571	-0.169	0.2916	0.291
High vs. Intermediate	0.8377	0.659	-0.1058	0.061
Low vs. intermediate	-0.9413	-0.989	0.5002	0.427

This table reports cumulative abnormal returns differentiated by the acquisition method used by the hedge fund. CARs are calculated with the approach by Schwert (1996) where the estimation period is (-140,-81) and the CDAX is the market proxy. Means are tested for difference using a simple t-test and differences in medians are tested using Mann-Whitney tests. */**/*** indicate statistical significance at the 10%/5%/1%-levels.

The hypothesis that short-term valuation effects should be highest for the most undervalued firms is not supported by the empirical results. Instead, short-term valuation effects in the event window (-3, 3) are strongest for the events in the subgroup with an intermediate valuation. These generate significant abnormal returns of 2.77% which increase up to a significant 8.53% after 40 trading days. For the group of undervalued target firms, the average valuation effects in the short event window (-3, 3) are 1.43% and statistically insignificant. However, abnormal returns for events involving undervalued firms increase up to 10.73% after 40 trading days and are significant at the 5%-level. Finally, valuation effects for the group of most overvalued target companies are rather small and insignificant for the window (-3,3) and after 40 trading days.

Although the magnitude of mean and median valuation effects differs between the different subsamples, the differences in means or medians are not statistically significant. As a result, the valuation of target firms prior to the event date does not seem to have a substantial impact on short-term valuation effects. This implies that hedge funds do not predominantly target firms suffering from valuation discounts due to agency problems of free cash flows.

4. Aggressiveness

Finally, hedge funds use different approaches to convince the management of target firms to implement their proposals. While many hedge funds seem to prefer to engage privately with the management of target firms there are other hedge funds who employ more aggressive tactics and make their demands public in order to increase the pressure on management. In these cases, valuation effects might be larger for two reasons. First, more aggressive tactics should lead to superior results in that this leads to faster and more substantial changes in the governance, strategy or financial structure of target firms. Second, this approach often creates substantial public attention which can create a snowball effect which is similar to the finding by Barber and Odean (2006) that investors are more likely to trade into attention-grabbing stocks (Bessler, Drobetz, and Holler, 2010a).

In order to investigate this hypothesis in more detail, the full sample is split into three subsamples based on the approach of the hedge fund towards target management. The subsample “No activism” contains all events for which there is no public information regarding the interaction between the investor and management and where the investor has never resorted to more aggressive tactics in his past investments. The subsample "Activism" contains all events where the hedge fund explicitly spells out its demands and makes direct statements to the management of target companies using the financial media. Finally, the subsample "Reputation for Activism" contains all events where the investor has used aggressive approaches in past investments and is therefore known by market participants to resort to more activist tactics if management does not cooperate. The valuation effects and the associated test statistics for these three subsamples are reported in Figure 25 and Table 23, respectively.

The empirical evidence in Figure 25 confirms the hypothesis that short-term valuation effects in the window immediately surrounding the event date are significantly higher for the subsamples "Activist" and "Reputation for Activism" which include more aggressive and hostile hedge funds. In particular, during the short event window (-3,3) average returns are 3.57% and 4.81%, respectively which are both significant at the 1% level. This is higher than the insignificant valuation effect of 0.48% for the subsample "No Activism". However, for longer windows, valuation effects for the targets of passive hedge funds become significant and reach 7.01%. Nevertheless, CARs still remain substantially smaller for the subset of passive hedge funds for the holding period (-40,40) compared to the other two subsamples. For longer periods the differences decline as the stocks targeted by passive hedge funds continuously generate positive abnormal returns while the returns on the two subsamples of aggressive hedge funds stagnate or even decline, respectively.

Figure 25: CAR differentiated the Approach to Target Management

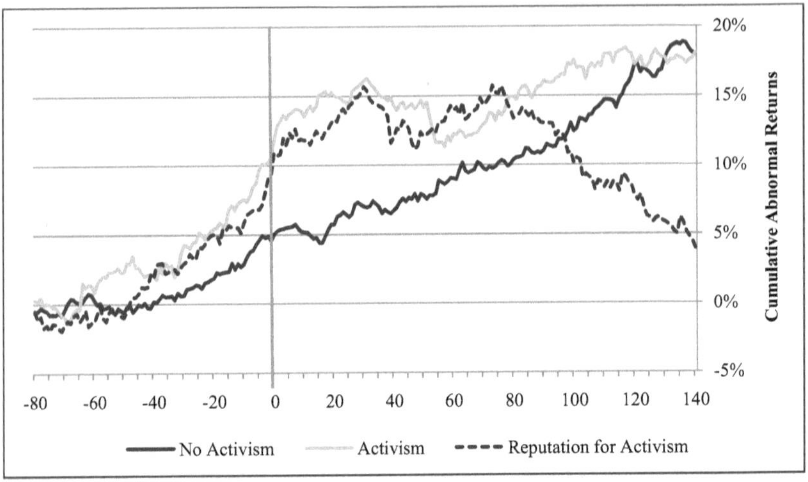

This figure reports cumulative abnormal returns differentiated by the hedge fund's approach to target management. CARs are calculated with the approach by Schwert (1996) where the estimation period is (-140,-81) and the CDAX is the market proxy.

Table 23: CARs differentiated by the Approach to Target Management

Panel A: Mean and Median Valuation Effects				
Interval	(-3, 3)		(-40, 40)	
Statistic	Mean	Median	Mean	Median
No Activism (n = 146)	0.0048	0.0054	0.0701***	0.0757***
Activism (n = 51)	0.0357***	0.0176***	0.1209***	0.0676***
Reputation for Activism (n = 38)	0.0481***	0.0226***	0.0988**	0.0926**
Panel B: Tests for Differences				
Statistic	t-stat	z-stat	t-stat	z-stat
No Activism vs. Activism	2.3498	1.884	1.1372	0.181
No Activism vs. Rep. for Activism	2.8527	2.147	0.5860	0.017
Activism vs. Rep. for Activism	0.6854	0.390	-0.3642	-0.348

This table reports cumulative abnormal returns differentiated by the acquisition method used by the hedge fund. CARs are calculated with the approach by Schwert (1996) where the estimation period is (-140,-81) and the CDAX is the market proxy. Means are tested for difference using a simple t-test and differences in medians are tested using Mann-Whitney tests. */**/*** indicate statistical significance at the 10%/5%/1%-levels.

The differences in CARs among the three subsamples are in generally significantly different from zero during the announcement period (-3, 3). This confirms the hypothesis that announcement effects should be stronger if hedge funds employ more aggressive tactics or if the hedge funds involved have gained a reputation for stepping up their campaigns when managers do not go along with their demands. Thus, the analysis seems to confirm the results of studies for the U.S. capital market. In fact, Brav, Jiang, Partnoy, and Thomas (2008) also report a highly positive and significant coefficient on a hostile dummy in cross-sectional regressions of cumulative abnormal returns on a range of explanatory variables.[121] Similarly, Clifford (2008) also indicates higher returns for hedge funds using more aggressive approaches. Moreover, Boyson and Mooradian (2008) find higher returns if hedge funds reveal their intentions upon the initial 13D filing. However, the differences become insignificant for the longer event window (-40, 40) so that the result in Table 23 also casts some doubt on this hypothesis. These doubts are reinforced when the analysis of CARs is extended up to 140 trading days after the event date. In fact, the performance of targets belonging to the category "reputation for activism" deteriorates substantially to 3.95%. This is significantly smaller than the performance of targets of passive hedge funds at the 5%-level in terms of means and at the 10%-level in terms of medians.

The finding of a strong initial boost in share prices followed by a reversal over the next half year is consistent with two alternative explanations. First, this might indicate that hedge funds successfully make a quick profit to the detriment of other shareholders. Second, other investors overrate the abilities of hedge funds to enforce value-increasing changes in corporate strategies or financial structures. In particular, this is plausible as despite recent changes in the German corporate governance system, managers still have substantial opportunities to defend their position against outside interference by capital market investors.

III. Cross-Sectional Regressions

In order to ensure that the previous findings are not driven by other variables, this section presents the results of cross-sectional regressions of cumulative abnormal returns on different sets of explanatory variables. This approach allows us to determine whether the valuation effects depend on the potential magnitude of agency problems,

[121] They did not include the full results in the final journal version of the paper. These results are included in the working paper version from the year 2006.

the valuation of the target firm or the activist's approach. The results are shown in Table 24.

The success of the hedge funds' strategies depends on the objectives of the largest shareholder of the firm who often controls a larger fraction of voting rights than the hedge funds. Therefore, a set of dummy variables is included as explanatory variables in the cross-sectional regressions which are set equal to one if the largest shareholder is a bank, corporation, government entity or individual/family investor and zero otherwise. Short-term announcement effects appear to be more negative if the dominant shareholder is a bank or an individual investor. This supports the hypothesis that these investors create conflicts of interests with other outside shareholders and, therefore, have strong incentives to oppose restructurings initiated by hedge funds. In the case of banks, however, this effect is only statistically significant in model II and is no longer significant in the full model I which includes all explanatory variables. Moreover, short-term announcement effects are significantly higher if the largest investor is another corporation. This might indicate that other investors expect the previous dominant shareholder to unwind his position in order to take advantage of the tax breaks created by the tax reform in 2002 which should lead to a more dispersed ownership structure and less rent extraction in the future.

In order to capture differences in the hedge fund behavior towards the firm management, an additional set of explanatory variables is included in the cross-sectional regressions. First, the dummy variable "wolf pack" is set equal to one if multiple hedge funds attack the same firm within the three months subsequent to the initial attack. According to the restricted model III this variable appears to have a significantly positive effect on short-term announcement effects, indicating that the formation of coalitions allows hedge funds to lever up their bargaining power against incumbent management. However, this variable ceases to have a significant impact on valuation effects in the full model I. In contrast, the ratio of the hedge funds' initial stake to the size of the largest shareholders' stake has a significantly negative impact on short-term valuation effects. Some hedge funds also try to increase their bargaining power by initiating aggressive public campaigns against managers and their current strategies. Therefore, an additional dummy variable is included which is set equal to one if the hedge fund initiates a public campaign or if the hedge fund has employed this tactic in its previous investments. In line with Boyson and Mooradian (2007) this dummy variable is highly significant and positive indicating that short-term announcement effects are approximately 3.5% higher for these events. This can be interpreted as evidence that investors have very positive expectations regarding the outcome of these hedge fund investments. However, this is also consistent with the idea that these hedge funds try to stir up public interest in their target companies in order to temporarily increase share prices. Finally, there is evidence from the U.S. that hedge funds try to create value by forcing target firms into mergers & acquisitions (Greenwood and Schoar, 2009). Therefore, an additional dummy variable is included in the cross-sectional regression which is set equal to one if the firm becomes the subject of a takeover attempt during the subsequent 3 years after the event date. This variable is also highly significant and positive indicating that investors correctly anticipate which target firms will ultimately become the subject of takeover attempts, resulting in high returns for target shareholders.

The potential influence of hedge funds might be significantly curtailed in Germany compared to other capital markets because according to German corporate law major corporate decisions can also be influenced by the company's workforce. In particular, if the firm employs between 500 and 2000 employees a third of the supervisory board consists of labor representatives. If the firm employs more than 2000 employees, then half of the seats on the supervisory board are held by labor representatives. The influence of labor representatives is captured with two dummy variables "labor 1/3 of board seats" and "labor 1/2 of board seats". Neither of these variables has a statistically significant impact on short-term announcement effects, which suggests that market participants do not expect that labor representatives can significantly constrain hedge fund activists. This belief is reasonable because shareholders elect the chairman of the board who can ultimately override labor representatives in cases of a draw between labor and shareholder representatives.

The adjusted market-to-book and adjusted market-value of target firms are also included in order to capture the impact of these variables on valuation effects. However, both of these variables are not statistically significant indicating that valuation effects are not stronger for more undervalued firms and firms with higher information asymmetries.

Table 24: Cross-Sectional Regressions – CAR (-3,+3)

	Independent Variable	I	II	III	IV	V	VI
	Constant	0.0218	0.0236***	-0.0031	0.0293*	0.0202***	0.0256**
Largest Investr	Bank	-0.0142	-0.0323*				
	Corporation	0.0411**	0.0143				
	Government	-0.0010	-0.0131				
	Individual	-0.0357**	-0.0203				
HF Behavior	Wolfpack	0.0243		0.0269*			
	HF Rel. Stake	-0.0002***		-0.0001*			
	Aggressive	0.0352***		0.0344***			
	Subsequent M&A	0.0291		0.0255**			
Cod eter.	Labor 1/3	-0.0287			-0.0246		
	Labor ½	-0.0206			-0.0114		
Mar ket	MtB adj.	0.0031				-0.0005	
	Market Value adj.	-0.0011				-0.0008	
Accounting Fundamentals	R&D	0.0142					0.0032
	Payout Ratio adj.	-0.0004					-0.0004
	Cash Hold. adj.	-0.1034					-0.1049**
	Leverage adj.	-0.0926***					-0.0718*
	RoE adj.	-0.0092					-0.0192**
	CF-to-Assets adj.	0.1766**					0.1520**
	Capex-to-Sales adj.	0.1135					0.0308
	R^2	0.2735	0.0281	0.0661	0.0091	0.0045	0.1156
	Number of Observations	150	234	203	235	229	172

The table reports coefficient estimates for the impact of firm-level fundamental characteristics in the year prior to the event on the short-run valuation effects (event returns) of the target firms, as measured using the CAR approach. The CDAX is used as a common benchmark for all firms, and the regression is estimated without a constant (Schwert, 1996). Fundamental variables are median-adjusted using all firms from the same industry. The firm universe consists of all constituents of the DAX, MDAX, SDAX or TecDAX indices. Robust standard errors are used to calculate t-statistics. */**/*** indicate statistical significance at the 10%/5%/1% level.

Variables that are presumably related to free-cash flow problems, such as the leverage ratio and the level of cash flows, apparently have a significant influence on the magnitude of abnormal returns in the event window. In line with the hypothesis that hedge funds target firms with excessive free cash flows, announcement period returns are higher if the firm uses less debt or if it generates higher cash flows. However, according to the restricted model VI lower cash holdings are associated with lower announcement period returns. Therefore, the empirical results cannot completely confirm the results of prior U.S. studies by Brav, Jiang, Partnoy, and Thomas (2008) and Klein and Zur (2009).

A. Long-Run Performance

Based on the observation that hedge fund engagements lead to significant increases in share prices in the short-run, it seems reasonable to assume that these investors help to increase shareholder value. However, high stock returns in the short-run are also consistent with several other explanations. For example, short-term buying pressure when hedge funds establish their position can temporarily push up share prices. Moreover, investors might be overly optimistic regarding the ability of hedge funds to increase firm value, which may occur when capital markets are not always perfectly efficient in the short run. If these alternative hypotheses are correct, then short-term increases in share prices are followed by reversals which correct a temporary overvaluation of target stocks. As a result, this would significantly change the conclusion from the previous sections that hedge fund investments increase firm value, thereby fulfilling a valuable function in corporate governance.

Due to the importance of this issue, this section investigates whether the short-term share price increases are persistent, and whether hedge fund engagements also create firm value in the long run. The first subsection begins with an analysis of buy-and-hold abnormal returns for the full sample of 235 events that occurred between January 1st, 2000 and December 31st, 2006. While similar studies for the U.S. market only use windows of up to 12 months after the event date to analyze long-term valuation effects, the time horizon is extended for up to 36 months after the event date. In the next subsections the calendar-time portfolio approach and the generalized calendar-time approach are implemented, which help to address statistical biases inherent in buy-and-hold-abnormal returns.

I. Buy-and-Hold Abnormal Returns

This section uses buy-and-hold abnormal returns to estimate the long-term valuation effects generated by hedge fund investments in the German capital market. This approach compares the performance of a portfolio in event time that invests in sample firms with the performance of an investment in a comparable market index over the corresponding time periods. For each target firm the market index corresponding to the market segment (DAX, MDAX, SDAX, TecDAX or CDAX) to which the firm belongs on the event date is used to estimate buy-and-hold abnormal returns. The first subsection starts with an analysis of the full sample of all events taking place between January 1st, 2000 and December 31st, 2006. The empirical results of this analysis indicate that valuation effects are persistent as there are no reversals of short-term increases in share prices and that target companies continue to beat their respective benchmarks. This confirms the general result from the analysis of short-term valuation effects, leading to the conclusion that hedge funds also boost value in the long run. Next, it seems interesting to investigate whether long-run valuation effects are also related to different event characteristics which were found to influence the magnitude of short-term valuation effects in the preceding section. Therefore, this issue is investigated in the second subsection which leads to some new insights. In particular, these empirical results indicate that some patterns which were observable in short-term CARs are reversed over longer time periods.

1. Analysis of the Full Sample

Hedge fund investments also lead to significant increases in shareholder value in the long-run based on buy-and-hold abnormal returns. Figure 26 plots the mean of buy-and-hold abnormal performance for the full sample of 235 events starting 40 trading days prior to the event date in order to capture the full valuation effect which includes the pre-event run-up. In addition, Figure 26 differentiates buy-and-hold abnormal returns into one portfolio that includes all events and one portfolio that excludes all events involving target firms classified as financials according to the ICB classification (n=195). This adjusts for the concerns of many authors that different models should be used to estimate the long-run performance of financial firms (Bessler and Kurmann, 2010).

Figure 26: BHAR (-40, 720) – Full Sample

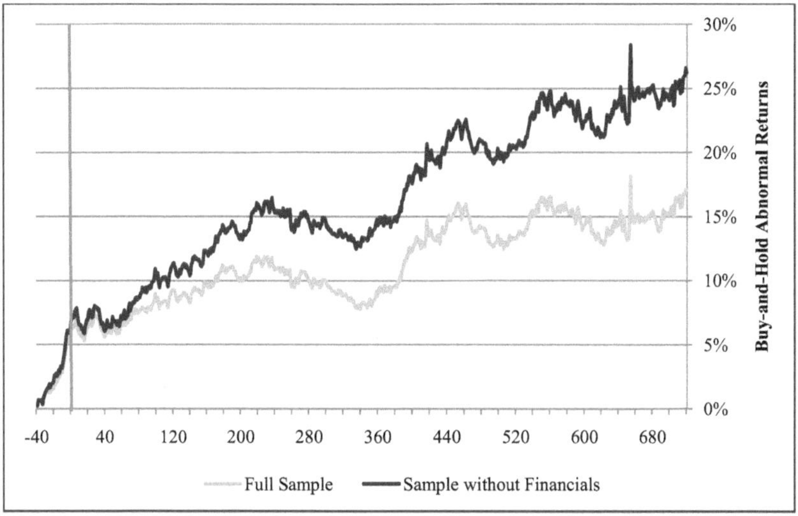

This figure reports buy-and-hold abnormal returns where expected returns are approximated with the market index corresponding to the market segment to which the target company belonged on the event date. BHAR are also differentiated into one portfolio that includes financial stocks and one portfolio that excludes financial stocks.

The results in Figure 26 indicate that BHAR are highly positive for periods of up to three years after the event date. In particular, buy-and-hold abnormal returns over the three-year period subsequent to the event date exceed 15% in the portfolio excluding financial firms and exceed 25% for the full sample. Moreover, there is a pronounced spike in BHAR after approximately 600 trading days. This reflects the manipulation of VW's share price which apparently occurred during Porsche's takeover of VW. Because this is a very special event that has a pronounced effect on BHAR it will be excluded in the subsequent analysis when BHAR for holding periods longer than two years are investigated. Furthermore, Table 25 contains the associated test statisticis in panel A. This indicates that the observed valuation effects are highly significant at the 1%-level based on skewness-adjusted t-statistics (Barber and Lyon, 1997). Interestingly, however, the median of buy-and-hold abnormal returns is only positive and statistically significant at the 1%-level for holding periods of up to to 120 trading days after the event date. For longer holding periods the median of buy-and-hold abnormal returns is not significantly different from zero.

The magnitude of BHAR changes when the run-up period is excluded from the holding period. This is illustrated in Figure 27 which plots buy-and-hold abnormal returns for the window (0,720) for the portfolios with and without financial targets.

Figure 27: BHAR (0, 720) – Full Sample

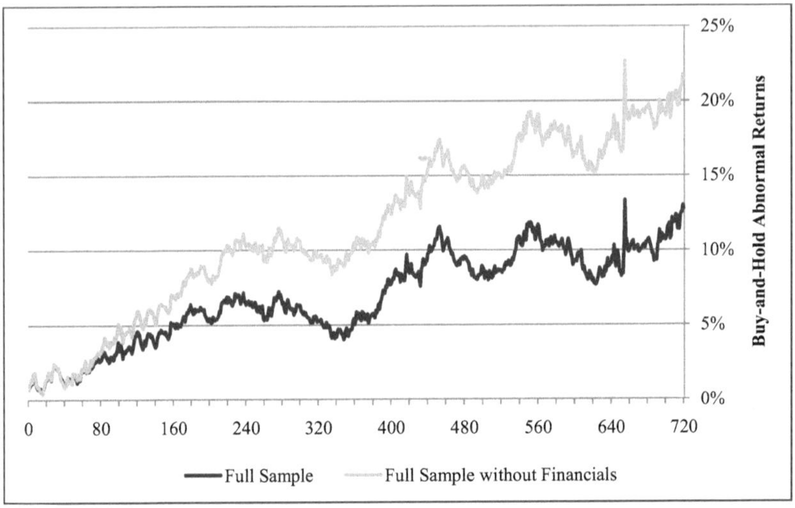

This figure reports buy-and-hold abnormal returns where expected returns are approximated with the market index corresponding to the market segment to which the target company belonged on the event date. The figure differentiates buy-and-hold returns into one portfolio including financial firms and one portfolio that excludes financial firms.

Interestingly, the magnitude of buy-and-hold abnormal returns becomes substantially smaller when the run-up period is not included. Moreover, the mean of buy-and-hold abnormal returns is only statistically significant at the 1%-level for the portfolio that excludes financial stocks and reaches 21.37% after three years. In contrast, the mean buy-and-hold abnormal return of the portfolio that includes financial firms is only statistically significant for specific holding periods (see Panel B of Table 25). In addition, the median is negative for nearly all holding periods for both portfolios. In fact, only the portfolio excluding financials generates a positive and significant median for buy-and-hold abnormal returns for the very short holding period of 120 trading days after the event date. This result indicates that the largest fraction of returns due to hedge fund involvement is earned during the run-up period.

Table 25: Buy-and-Hold Abnormal Returns

Panel A: Including Run-Up BHAR starting in t=-40				
Statistic	BHAR (full sample)		BHAR (excluding banks) – n=195	
	Mean	Median	Mean	Median
(-40, 120)	0.0933***	0.0484***	0.1133***	0.0519***
(-40, 240)	0.1086***	0.0041	0.1530***	0.0279*
(-40, 360)	0.0879**	-0.0833	0.1431***	0.0209
(-40, 480)	0.1419***	-0.0749	0.2093***	-0.0274
(-40, 600)	0.1438**	-0.0839*	0.2244***	-0.0387
(-40, 720)	0.1693**	-0.0998	0.2621***	-0.0346
Panel B: No Run-Up – BHAR starting in t=0				
Statistic	BHAR (full sample)		BHAR (excluding banks) – n=195	
	Mean	Median	Mean	Median
(0, 120)	0.0461**	0.0187	0.0598**	0.0234*
(0, 240)	0.0638*	-0.0039	0.1026***	0.0089
(0, 360)	0.0504	-0.0721	0.1010**	-0.0058
(0, 480)	0.0958*	-0.0903	0.1570***	-0.0406
(0, 600)	0.0928*	-0.1252	0.1656***	-0.0288
(0, 720)	0.1276*	-0.1778	0.2137***	-0.0924*

The table reports buy-and-hold abnormal returns for our sample of n=235 events. The intervals describe the number of trading days around the event date. The values in parentheses indicate standard deviations. */**/*** implies that the mean is significantly different from zero at the 10%/5%/1%-level, respectively, using skewness-adjusted t-statistics (Barber and Lyon, 1997).

Focusing on the mean of buy-and-hold abnormal returns, there are no reversals in buy-and-hold abnormal returns over longer time periods. Thus, the run-up effect appears to be persistent so that short-term valuation effects are apparently not driven by temporary buying pressure or overly optimistic investors overestimating the ability of hedge funds to create firm value. Furthermore, the weak upwards drift in buy-and-hold returns is consistent with the idea that the initial abnormal returns only reflect a fraction of the expected value enhancement generated by hedge funds. In fact, at early stages in their engagements there is always substantial uncertainty as to whether the hedge funds will ultimately prevail against management.[122] Moreover, these results highlight that the run-up effect is a crucial component of realized long-term returns. This can be demonstrated by focusing on buy-and-hold abnormal returns estimated for different entry points. In Figure 28 it is assumed that the investor takes a position in the target company on the following event dates: 80 and 40 trading days before the event date, at the end event date, as well as 40 trading days after the event date.

Figure 28: Buy-and-Hold Abnormal Returns for Different Entry Points

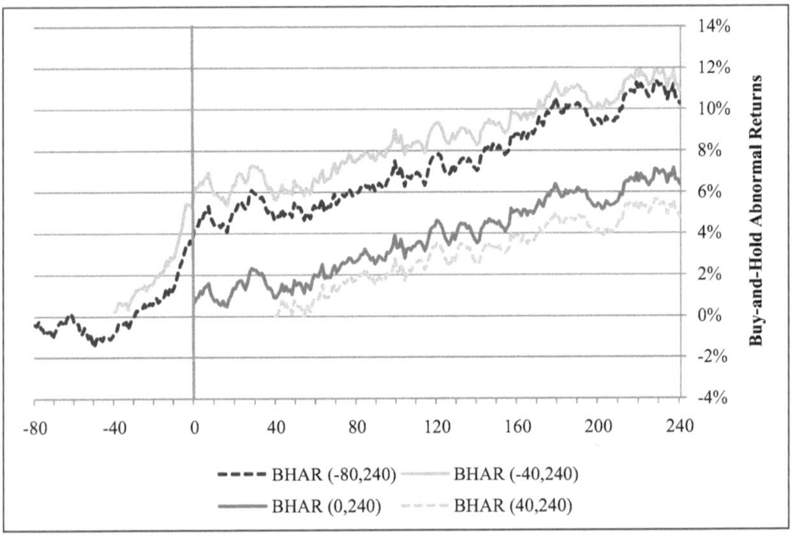

This figure reports mean buy-and-hold abnormal returns where the benchmark is the market index corresponding to the market segment to which the company belonged on the event date for different entry points.

The empirical evidence in Figure 28 indicates that the magnitude of realized buy-and-hold abnormal returns increases in proportion to the length of the run-up period

[122] However, in contrast to US studies such as Klein and Zur (2009), it is not possible to examine whether the market differentiates ex ante between successful and failed interventions because hedge funds were not required to state the goals of their investments in German target firms during the sample period.

included in the investment period. In particular, hedge funds and other investors taking an early position in target stocks realize high buy-and-hold abnormal returns of 10.26% (80 trading days before event date) or 10.86% (40 trading days before event date) after one year which are both highly significant at the 1%-level. In contrast, investors who acquire a position in a target company after observing that a hedge fund made an investment only generate weakly significant returns of 6.38%. Finally, those investors who invest in target companies with a time lag of 40 trading days after the event do not generate significantly positive returns.

However, the median of buy-and-hold abnormal returns suggests that valuation effects are negative and not statistically significant for more than 50% of individual events. This points to some biases inherent in the analysis of the sample using buy-and-hold abnormal returns in that inferences based on skewness-adjusted t-statistics should be consistent with the inferences based on non-parametric median tests, which are generally considered to be quite robust. This might be related to overlapping holding periods for some events during the sample period which seems to induce biases in the estimates of cross-sectional variance of buy-and-hold abnormal returns (see Barber and Lyon, 1997). Therefore, in the following sections the calendar-time portfolio approach and the generalized calendar-time approach are implemented, which help to address the problem of cross-correlations, thereby allowing testing for whether on average there is still an outperformance after adjusting for this problem.

Table 26: BHAR for Different Entry Points

Statistic	Mean	Median
(-80, 240)	0.1026***	-0.0212
(-40, 240)	0.1086***	0.0041
(0, 240)	0.0638*	-0.0039
(40, 240)	0.0478	-0.0214

This table reports mean and median buy-and-hold abnormal returns where the benchmark is the market index corresponding to the market segment to which the company belonged on the event date. */**/*** indicate statistical significance at the 10%/5%/1%-levels.

2. Analysis of Subsamples

The magnitude of long-run valuation effects might also be related to the characteristics of target firms and the tactics employed by the hedge funds. In fact, there is convincing evidence that the magnitude of short-term valuation effects is related to several event characteristics. Therefore, it is highly interesting to investigate whether the relationships identified in short-term CARs in the previous section are persistent and also carry over into longer-run buy-and-hold abnormal returns. Therefore, this section investigates the impact of the set of event characteristics considered in the previous section on the magnitude of buy-and-hold abnormal returns.

a. Acquisition Method

Hedge funds employ different methods to build up their positions in target companies. These may lead to a difference in the hedge funds' commitment to the investment. According to the empirical results in the previous section this has a significant impact on the magnitude of short-term valuation effects. In fact, short run valuation effects are highly positive for engagements in which hedge funds make substantial investments in target firms using PIPE-transactions. In order to detect whether the differences in valuation effects are related to differences in the acquisition method, this subsection analyzes buy-and-hold abnormal returns for each of the three categories: "acquisition", "intervention" and "PIPE". The empirical results for holding periods of up to three years are presented for each subsample in Figure 29. Table 27 contains the test statistics for mean (skewness-adjusted t-statistic) and medians (Wilcoxon-test).

According to the results in Figure 29, valuation effects reverse over longer time periods. The events classified as "PIPE", which used to outperform over short holding periods, generate an inferior performance over longer holding periods. After approximately 100 trading days buy-and-hold abnormal returns for this group fall below the level of the other two subsamples. As a result, the mean performance of events classified as "PIPE" is insignificant at only 6.25% after 240 trading days and 11.53% after 480 trading days. Eventually, BHAR for this subsample are close to zero after 720 trading days. In contrast, for the other two subsamples mean performance is significantly positive for all holding periods. This reversal in the performance of PIPEs indicates that investors are initially overly optimistic regarding the valuation impact of hedge funds investing in PIPEs. These effects are even more pronounced when looking at the median of buy-and-hold abnormal returns. They indicate that for most targets of PIPE investments buy-and-hold abnormal returns are smaller than -10.03% after 240 trading days, smaller than -22.53% after 480 trading days and smaller than -62.44% after 720 trading days. Notice that this last holding period contains the beginning of the financial crisis. This sharp drop in shareholder value indicates that these firms had problems withstanding the impact of the emerging financial crisis.

In contrast to short-term valuation effects, buy-and-hold abnormal returns are largest for events classified as interventions. In particular, after 240 trading days buy-and-hold abnormal returns are on average 20.23% (with a p-value of 12.84%) and 26.38% after 480 trading days which is significant at the 10%-level. Even for the holding period extended 720 trading days after the event date, i.e. including the beginning of the financial crisis, this subsample still generates highly positive BHAR of 37.65% which are significant at the level of 10%. Interestingly, this result is in contrast to the finding that small caps outperform, as this subsample is predominantly composed of large cap stocks.

The differences in the median BHAR between the subsamples are statistically significant when "interventions" are compared to the other two groups. The performance of events classified as "interventions" is significantly larger than buy-and-hold abnormal returns of the other two subsamples. In summation, the most interesting result is that initial market reaction to hedge funds investing in PIPEs is followed by a substantial reversal. This indicates that there indeed occur cases in which investors are overly optimistic regarding the ability of hedge funds to create value.

Figure 29: BHAR differentiated by Acquisition Method

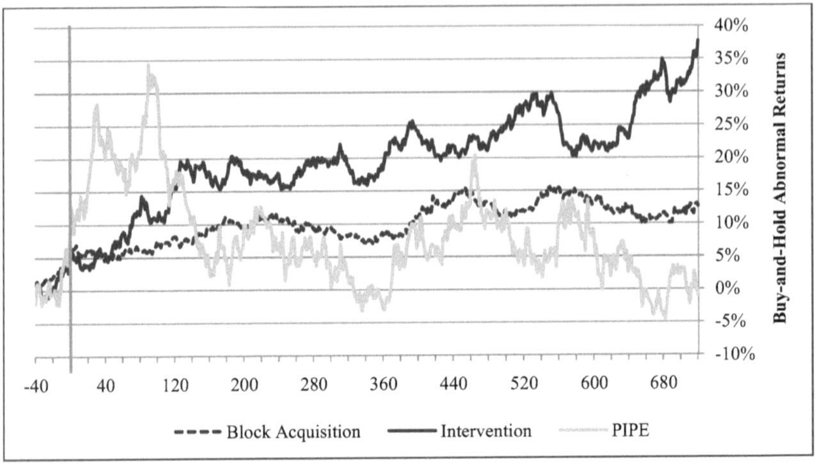

This figure reports mean buy-and-hold abnormal returns differentiated by acquisition method, where the benchmark is the market index corresponding to the market segment to which the company belonged on the event date.

Table 27: Buy-and-Hold Abnormal Returns - Acquisition Method

Panel A: Mean and Median Valuation Effects						
Interval	(-40, 240)		(-40, 480)		(-40, 720)	
Statistic	Mean	Median	Mean	Median	Mean	Median
Open Market (n = 202)	0.1029***	-0.0034	0.1323**	-0.0993	0.1261*	-0.0989
Intervention (n = 19)	0.2023	0.2465	0.2638*	0.1849*	0.3765*	0.0819
PIPE (n = 14)	0.0625	-0.1003	0.1153	-0.2253	-0.0103	-0.6244*
Panel B: Tests for Differences						
	t-stat	z-stat	t-stat	z-stat	t-stat	z-stat
Open Market vs. Interv.	0.7125	1.83	0.6310	1.818	-0.9249	-1.721
Open Market vs. Pipe	-0.2367	-1.008	0.0681	-1.030	-0.4226	-2.073
Intervention vs. Pipe	-0.5842	-1.822	-0.425	1.931	-0.8097	-2.584

This table reports mean buy-and-hold abnormal returns differentiated by the acquisition method used by the hedge fund where the benchmark is the market index corresponding to the market segment to which the company belonged on the event date. Means are tested for statistical significance using bootstrapped skewness-adjusted t-statistics and medians are tested using Wilcoxon tests. */**/*** indicate statistical significance at the 10%/5%/1%-levels.

b. Firm Characteristics - Firm Size and Technology

The ability of hedge funds to implement their restructuring plans depends on the size and industry of target firms. Therefore, valuation effects should also be related to the size of target firms and the industry in which they operate. Indeed, there is empirical evidence that short-term valuation effects are significantly larger for small cap firms which should be easier to restructure and for which signaling effects should be stronger. Moreover, short-term valuation effects are close to zero for technology firms indicating that hedge fund tactics are not suitable to increase the value of firms that rely on intellectual property and other intangible assets. Thus, in order to assess whether these short-term valuation effects also apply over longer time periods, buy-and-hold returns are differentiated into the same categories as in section B.II. Figure 30 plots mean buy-and-hold abnormal returns for these three subsamples and Table 28 reports the means and medians of buy-and-hold abnormal returns and the associated test-statistics.

Long-term buy-and-hold abnormal returns for the three subgroups are largely in line with short-term valuation effects. In particular, small caps continue to outperform the other two subsamples up to approximately 300 trading days after the event date. Afterwards, there are apparently no pronounced differences in BHAR for both subsamples for the next 300 trading days before the performance of small target firms begins to deteriorate. This can be rationalized by the beginning of the financial crisis. However, this does not apply to the median of small cap firms which apparently underperforms the median of large cap firms for all holding periods.

In addition, the subsample of events in the technology sectors continues to underperform the other two subsamples supporting the conclusion that hedge fund strategies are difficult to apply to technology firms. In fact, the performance of this subsample is highly negative. However, this effect is not statistically significant due to the small size of this subsample and the high cross-sectional variance of BHAR. Moreover, this is also consistent with the argument of Brav, Jiang, Partnoy, and Thomas (2008) that hedge funds should abstain from opaque and complicated businesses in order to avoid delays in the resolution of the intervention's impact on share prices.

Figure 30: BHAR differentiated by Size and Technology

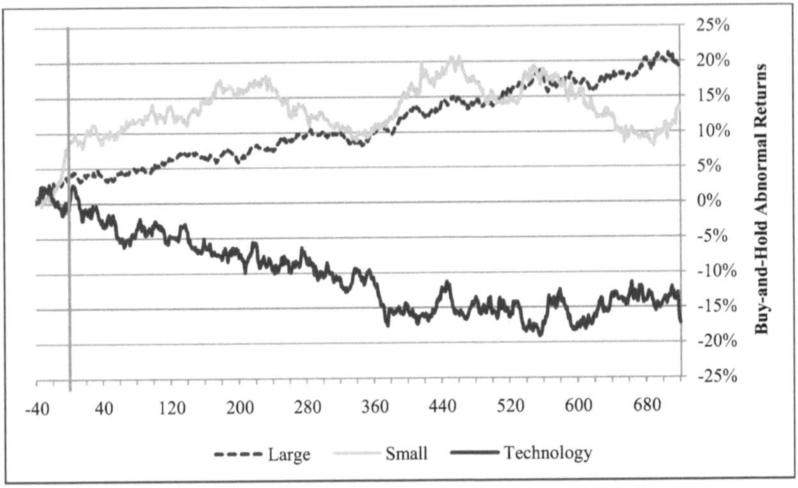

This table reports mean buy-and-hold abnormal returns differentiated by firm size and technology where the benchmark is the market index corresponding to the market segment to which the company belonged on the event date.

Table 28: BHAR – Size and Technology

Panel A: Mean and Median Valuation Effects						
Interval	(-40, 240)		(-40, 480)		(-40, 720)	
Statistic	Mean	Median	Mean	Median	Mean	Median
Large (n = 99)	0.0817**	0.0714**	0.1535***	0.0393**	0.1972**	-0.0138
Small (n = 119)	0.1594**	-0.0565	0.1719**	-0.1959	0.1303	-0.2955
Techn (n = 17)	-0.0904	-0.1525	-0.1352	-0.1912	-0.1728	-0.2861
Panel B: Tests for Differences						
	t-stat	z-stat	t-stat	z-stat	t-stat	z-stat
Large vs. Small	0.9203	-1.414	0.1501	-2.227	-0.4102	-2.543
Large vs. Techn.	1.8890	2.502	1.9310	2.088	-1.7271	-1.771
Small vs. Techn.	1.3190	0.898	1.1425	0.418	-0.8497	-0.007

This table reports mean buy-and-hold abnormal returns differentiated by the market segment of target firms where the benchmark is the market index corresponding to the market index to which the company belonged on the event date. Means are tested for statistical significance using bootstrapped skewness-adjusted t-statistics and medians are tested using Wilcoxon tests. */**/*** indicate statistical significance at the 10%/5%/1%-levels.

However, the information in panel B of Table 28 indicates that the observed differences are in most cases insignificant. In fact, there is only a significant difference between large firms and technology firms highlighting the overall negative performance of hedge fund targets operating in knowledge-intensive industries.

c. Valuation of Targets

Long-term buy-and-hold abnormal returns should also be higher for more "undervalued" firms because signaling effects should be stronger for these firms. Moreover, these firms should also offer more opportunities for value-enhancing measures. However, this reasoning is not supported by the analysis of short-term valuation effects. Thus, it is interesting to investigate whether the pre-event valuation of target firms has a significant impact on valuation effects when longer time horizons are investigated. Therefore, the analysis of the three subsamples from section B.II is extended and buy-and-hold abnormal returns are differentiated into the same three subsamples. Figure 31 plots the mean of buy-and-hold abnormal returns and Table 29 provides summary statistics.

Interestingly, long-term valuation effects are strongest for the most undervalued and for the most overvalued companies after 240 and 480 trading days. For the group of most highly valued companies before the event date the mean buy-and-hold abnormal performance is 29.09% after 240 trading days and 27.01% after 480 trading days, both of which are highly significant. In addition, medians are positive for both periods and also significant at the 10%-level for the period (-40,240). However, for the longer holding period (-40,720) BHAR decline and become smaller than the BHAR for the subsample of the most undervalued target companies. This can be reconciled with the glamour effect described by Chan, Jegadeesh, and Lakonishok (1995). For the group of the most undervalued firms, buy-and-hold abnormal returns are almost significant at the 10%-level and reach 12.92% after 240 trading days and 18.51% after 480 trading days. Interestingly, there is a sudden increase in BHAR after approximately 520 trading days. This performance persists so that after 720 trading days following the event the subsample of undervalued events achieves the highest BHAR. However, medians are close to zero or even negative for this subsample. Finally, there is no evidence for long-run outperformance for the sample of firms whose pre-event stock performance does not substantially differ from the performance of their peer group.

Figure 31: BHAR differentiated by the Valuation of Target Firms

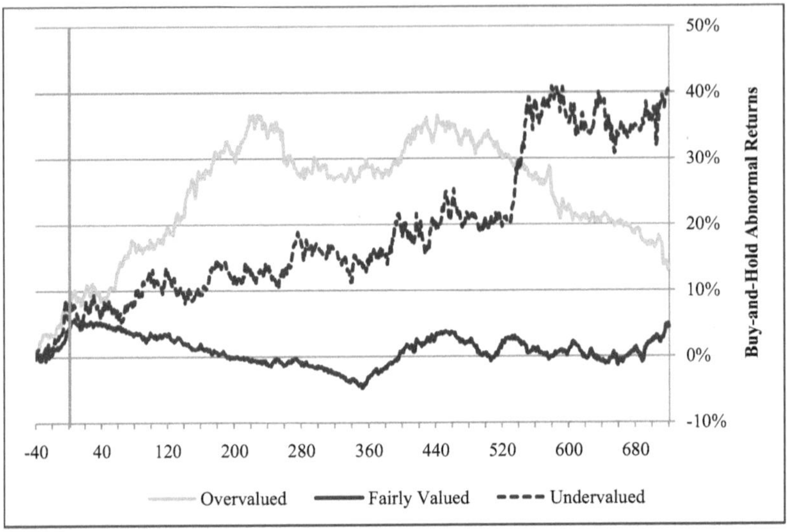

This table reports mean buy-and-hold abnormal returns differentiated by the valuation of the target firm prior to the event date where the benchmark is the market index corresponding to the market segment to which the company belonged on the event date.

Table 29: BHAR - Valuation of Target Firms prior to the Event Date

Panel A: Mean and Median Valuation Effects						
Interval	(-40, 240)		(-40, 480)		(-40, 720)	
Statistic	Mean	Median	Mean	Median	Mean	Median
High Valuation (n = 56)	0.3321***	0.0995**	0.3412***	0.1054**	0.1381	-0.1217
Low Valuation (n = 56)	0.1350	0.0135	0.0335	-0.1149	0.3984**	0.0185
Intermediate (n = 112)	-0.0061	-0.0552	0.2087*	-0.1308	0.0442	-0.1436
Panel B: Tests for Differences						
	t-stat	z-stat	t-stat	z-stat	t-stat	z-stat
High vs. Low	1.3795	1.379	0.7235	1.373	-1.1344	0.149
High vs. intermediate	3.6800	2.914	2.2483	2.446	-1.6949	-0.873
Low vs. intermediate	-1.6696	-0.895	-1.2183	-0.478	0.5546	1.288

This table reports mean buy-and-hold abnormal returns differentiated by the valuation of target firms prior to the event date where the benchmark is the market index corresponding to the market segment to which the company belonged on the event date. Means are tested for statistical significance using bootstrapped skewness-adjusted t-statistics and medians are tested using Wilcoxon tests. */**/*** indicate statistical significance at the 10%/5%/1%-levels.

However, the statistical significance of univariate valuation effects in most cases does not lead to significant differences in the mean or median performance of the different groups. In fact, only the difference between overvalued and fairly valued firms appears to be significant for the interval (-40,240). In contrast, the subsample containing the most undervalued firms does not generate superior returns compared to the subsample of fairly valued or overvalued firms.

Overall, it seems fair to conclude that the pre-event valuation of firms does not have a very high impact on the returns due to hedge fund investments in Germany. Nevertheless, there is some evidence that at least for very long holding periods the most undervalued firms begin to excel. However, this effect should be considered as an asset-pricing anomaly, which has already been identified in previous research and is not related to hedge fund investments.

d. Aggressiveness

There are also reasons to assume that the magnitude of valuation effects is related to the aggressiveness of the hedge fund approach. It could be expected that more aggressive hedge funds should generate higher returns because this should enable them to implement their strategies more quickly. This reasoning was supported by the analysis of short-term valuation effects which identified higher cumulative abnormal returns for hedge funds with a more aggressive behavior towards target management. However, this outperformance for more aggressive hedge funds apparently lasted only for a brief period of time. For some of these investors a reversal occurred within a relatively short time period of only 140 trading days after the event date. Thus, short-term valuation effects already provided preliminary evidence that the apparent outperformance of more hostile hedge funds is related to a snowball effect and higher public attention. In order to corroborate this finding this subsection extends this analysis and break down longer-run buy-and-hold abnormal returns into the subsamples investigated in section B.II.

Figure 32 reports the mean of buy-and-hold abnormal returns and Table 30 contains the associated test statistics for these three subsamples.

Overall, the results confirm the hypothesis that the high initial returns to more aggressive hedge funds should be interpreted as overly optimistic investors trading attention-grabbing stocks. In particular, Figure 32 indicates that there are reversals in buy-and-hold abnormal returns after approximately 100 trading days for both the subsample of events where the hedge fund made public demands to target management and for the subsample of events involving hedge funds that have gained a reputation for aggressive behavior in the German capital market. This is also supported by the mean buy-and-hold abnormal returns for both groups as mean valuation effects are barely positive, or even negative, and not statistically significant for all holding periods. In addition, the medians for both groups are negative. In contrast, the subsample of events involving non-hostile hedge funds generate positive buy-and-hold abnormal returns whose means (17.61% after 240 trading days, 24.94% after 480 trading days and 26.04% after 720 trading days) and medians (2.68%, 3.76% and -0.51%, respectively) are mostly significantly different from zero. However, this does not apply to medians for the three year holding period.

The empirical evidence in panel B of Table 30 indicates that the differences in buy-and-hold abnormal returns between the subsample of non-hostile hedge funds and both subsamples involving hostile hedge funds are significant. In particular, the medians of both subsamples are statistically different from each other at least at the 10% level. Similarly, the means of buy-and-hold abnormal performance are also statistically different from each other at the 10% level. In contrast, there are apparently no significant differences regarding long-term valuation effects between the two subsamples including hostile hedge funds.

Based on these empirical results, it appears that there is a group of hedge funds operating in the German capital markets that take advantage of short-term price increases which are triggered by the publicity generated by their activities.

Figure 32: BHAR differentiated by the Approach to Target Management

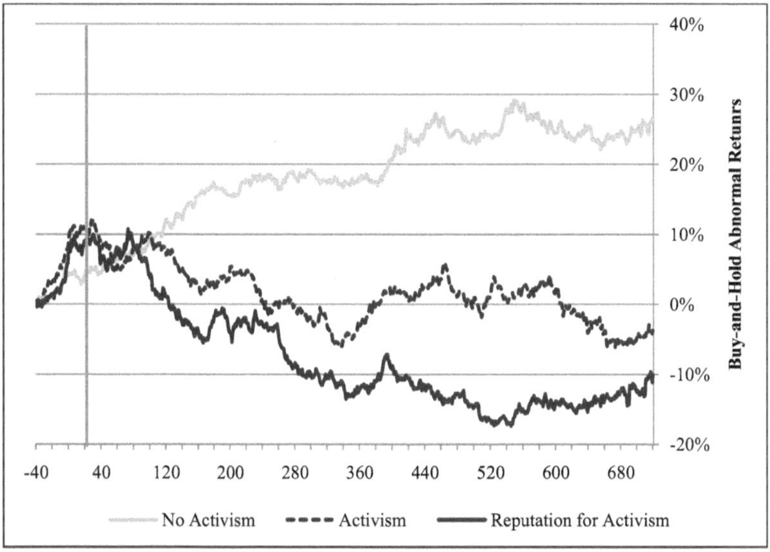

This table reports mean buy-and-hold abnormal returns differentiated by the valuation of the target firm prior to the event date where the benchmark is the market index corresponding to the market segment to which the company belonged on the event date.

Table 30: BHAR - Approach to Target Management

Panel A: Mean and Median Valuation Effects						
Interval	-40,240		-40,480		-40,720	
Statistic	Mean	Median	Mean	Median	Mean	Median
No Act. (n = 146)	0.1761***	0.0268**	0.2493***	0.0376*	0.2604***	-0.0051
Activism (n = 51)	0.0165	-0.1003	0.0349	-0.1811	-0.0373	-0.2610**
Rep. f. Act. (n = 38)	-0.0274	-0.0890	-0.1269	-0.1662	-0.1007	-0.3079
Panel B: Tests for Differences						
Statistic	t-stat	z-stat	t-stat	z-stat	t-stat	z-stat
No Act. vs. Act.	-1.6464	-2.124	-1.4465	-1.770	-1.5196	-2.342
No Act. vs. Rep. Act.	-1.8115	-2.264	2.3456	2.370	-1.6784	-2.055
Act. vs. Rep. Act.	-0.3579	-0.639	1.0177	0.713	-0.2943	-0.166

This table reports mean buy-and-hold abnormal returns differentiated by the valuation of target firms prior to the event date where the benchmark is the market index corresponding to the market segment to which the company belonged on the event date. Means are tested for statistical significance using bootstrapped skewness-adjusted t-statistics and medians are tested using Wilcoxon tests. */**/*** indicate statistical significance at the 10%/5%/1%-levels.

3. Cross-Sectional Regression

The break down of buy-and-hold abnormal returns into different subsamples in the preceding section provides evidence that long-run valuation effects are related to specific event characteristics. In order to check the robustness of these results the following section reports results from cross-sectional regressions of buy-and-hold abnormal returns on a set of explanatory variables. Table 31 summarizes the findings.

The ability of hedge funds to restructure target firms can be complicated if there are other large shareholders invested in the target company. In particular, individual/family investors and banks can capture significant private benefits from the status quo and, therefore, have strong incentives to oppose hedge funds' demands. This was reflected in significantly lower short-term announcement effects. However, this effect is not observable in long-run buy-and-hold abnormal returns in that the coefficients on both dummy variables are not statistically significant. In line with short-term cumulative abnormal returns longer-term buy-and-hold abnormal returns are significantly higher if the dominant shareholder is a corporation. This suggests that these shareholders do not oppose hedge funds' demands or sell off their positions so that the increase in share values reflects a more dispersed ownership structure.

The ability of a hedge funds to control target firms also depends on their behavior and their strategies for putting pressure on incumbent management. In order to investigate whether this also has an impact on long-term buy-and-hold abnormal returns the same variables as in the previous subsection are also added to the cross-sectional regressions of BHAR. The results in Table 31 reveal that BHAR are significantly higher in the case of "wolf packs". It seems that hedge funds have employed this strategy to increase their bargaining power against incumbent management. In addition, the hedge funds' bargaining power measured as the ratio between the size of their stakes and that of the stake of the largest shareholder also has a significantly positive impact. Interestingly, buy-and-hold abnormal returns are significantly negative for aggressive hedge funds. This is not consistent with their pronounced outperformance for short holding periods, indicating that other market participants initially overrate the ability of these hedge funds to enforce their restructuring plans and to create value. This is in sharp contrast to the evidence for the U.S. by Boyson and Mooradian (2007) who document a persistent outperformance for this group of hedge funds. Finally, buy-and-hold abnormal returns are significantly higher if the target firm ultimately becomes the subject of a takeover attempt during the three year time period starting on the event date.

It can also be argued that the influence of hedge funds is restricted for all German firms that have more than 500 employees due to mandatory co-determination. Therefore, we also add the two dummy variables from the previous section into the cross-sectional regressions of buy-and-hold abnormal returns. Interestingly, this indicates that buy-and-hold abnormal returns are significantly higher when labor representatives occupy one third of the seats on the supervisory board of the firm. In contrast, when they hold one half of the seats buy-and-hold abnormal returns become smaller and the level of statistical significance is lower in the full model I. The valuation of the firm measured by the adjusted market-to-book ratio and the market value also does not have a significant impact on the magnitude of long-term buy-and-hold abnormal returns meaning that the magnitude of value creation does not depend on the target's pre-event valuation or level of information asymmetries. Finally, the coefficients on the accounting variables indicate firms with higher payout ratios outperform in the long-run, which is consistent with lower agency problems of free cash flows. However, the coefficients in model VI also indicate that long-term returns are higher for target firms that make higher investments in R&D and in fixed assets.

Table 31: Cross-Sectional Regressions – BHAR (-40,+720)

	Independent Variable	I	II	III	IV	V	VI
	Constant	-0.5262**	-0.0368	0.1779*	-0.2493*	0.1469	-0.0624
Largest Investor	Bank	0.2352	0.1346				
	Corporation	0.7251**	0.7433**				
	Government	-0.1271	0.8087**				
	Individual	-0.1050	0.0095				
HF Behavior	Wolfpack	0.4352**		0.1266			
	HF Rel. Stake	0.0046***		0.0033***			
	Aggressive	-0.3809**		-0.4993***			
	Subsequent M&A	1.1781**		0.5880*			
Codet.	Labor 1/3	0.6730**			0.7595**		
	Labor ½	0.4738*			0.5002***		
Market	MtB adj.	-0.0078				0.0090	
	Market Value adj.	-0.0038				0.1072	
Accounting Fundamentals	R&D	0.0533					0.3686*
	Payout Ratio adj.	0.0036					0.0075***
	Cash Hold. adj.	0.2584					0.2747
	Leverage adj.	0.3209					0.5594
	RoE adj.	0.0404					-0.0274
	CF-to-Assets adj.	-0.0516					-1.0536
	Capex-to-Sales adj.	5.0553**					4.2349**
	R^2	0.3379	0.0711	0.0869	0.0869	0.0045	0.1038
	Number of Observations	150	234	203	235	229	172

The table reports coefficient estimates for the impact of firm-level fundamental characteristics in the year prior to the event on long-run valuation effects of the target firms. Long-run returns are measured using the BHAR approach. The benchmark is the market index to which the target firm belonged on the event date. Fundamental variables are median-adjusted using all firms from the same industry. The firm universe consists of all constituents of the DAX, MDAX, SDAX or TecDAX indices. Robust standard errors are used to calculate t-statistics. */**/*** indicate statistical significance at the 10%/5%/1% level.

II. Calendar-time Portfolio Approach

The analysis of BHAR indicated that hedge fund activism is generally associated with substantial increases in shareholder value. More recently, however, empirical studies of long-run stock performance also use the calendar-time portfolio approach because it addresses two problems which are a part of the BHAR-approach. First, t-statistics derived from buy-and-hold abnormal returns often overstate statistical significance, in particular for longer holding periods, due to overlapping event periods and cross-correlations (Kothari and Warner, 2006). Second, the BHAR-approach does not adjust for multiple risk factors and changes in post-event risk exposures. Therefore, it appears necessary to assess the robustness of the finding of positive long-run returns based on the BHAR-approach and to investigate the share price performance of the sample of 235 hedge fund targets between 2000 and 2006 using the calendar-time portfolio approach. The results of this analysis are presented in this section.

1. The Performance and Properties of Calendar Time Portfolios

In the first step, several calendar-time portfolios are constructed and the portfolio performance is then compared to an investment in an aggregate German stock market index. These calendar-time portfolios replicate the investment performance of a trading strategy that takes positions in target companies upon observing the entry of a hedge fund and holding these positions for a specified holding period. Thus, in contrast to the BHAR-approach, calendar-time portfolios are realistic investment opportunities in the sense that they can be implemented in real time.

Figure 33 plots the performance of a calendar-time portfolio that establishes positions in target companies two months prior to the event date and holds the position for 36 months. Hence, it assumes the perspective of a hedge fund that starts trading in the stocks of target companies approximately two months prior to the event date. In addition, if a company is subject to multiple hedge fund investments over the holding period, it is assumed that the initial holding period is extended accordingly so that the calendar-time portfolio is equally weighed across all target stocks at each point in time.

Figure 33: Calendar Time Portfolio (-2, 36)

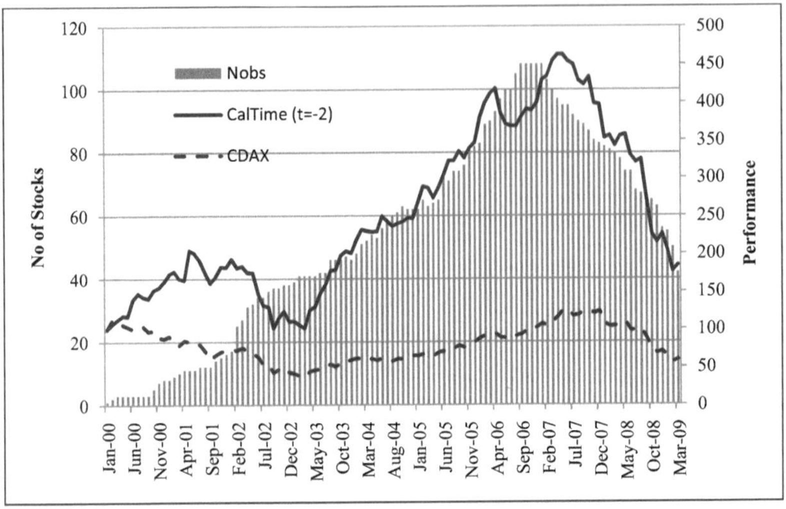

This figure reports the performance of a calendar-time portfolio that enters a position in target stocks prior to the event date and holds the position for 36 months. In the case that there are overlapping events the holding period is adjusted so that each target firm is included once in the calendar time portfolio at each point in time.

The investment strategy underlying this calendar-time portfolio outperforms the overall market index (CDAX) over the entire sample period. Starting with a net worth of 100 EUR at the beginning of the year 2000, the value of the portfolio increases to 463 EUR in the middle of the year 2007. Over the same time period, an investment in the broad German market index would only have increased to 124 EUR. However, there is a sharp decline in the value of the calendar time portfolio between the beginning of the most recent financial crisis in mid 2007 and the end of the sample period.

In addition, Figure 33 also provides information on the number of firms included in the calendar time portfolio at each point in time. Initially, the number of firms increases slowly as there is only a limited number of events during the early parts of the sample period. Along with the increase in the frequency of events starting in 2002, the number of firms included and, therefore, the diversification of the calendar time portfolio, also increases substantially. Hence, the performance of this investment strategy is significantly biased by a small number of events at the beginning of the sample period which drive the initial returns of the calendar-time portfolio. Importantly, this also influences the subsequent behavior of the investment performance of the calendar time portfolio due to multiplicative compounding (Fama, 1998).

The properties of calendar-time portfolios depend on different parameters. In particular, the holding period used to construct calendar-time portfolios affects their stability and the diversification properties and, therefore, should have a significant impact on the investment performance. In order to investigate this issue in more detail, Figure 34 plots the performance of three calendar time portfolios initiated in t=-2 with holding periods of 12, 24 and 36 months.

Figure 34: Calendar Time Portfolio – Impact of Holding Period

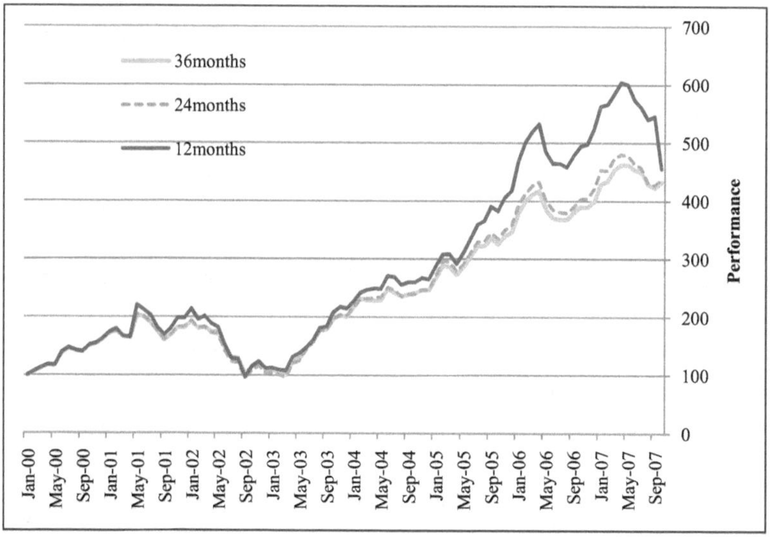

This figure reports the performance of three calendar-time portfolio that entered a position in target stocks prior to the event date and held the positions for 12, 24, or 36 months. In the case that there are overlapping events the holding period is adjusted accordingly.

Comparing the investment performance of the three calendar-time portfolios there is evidence that their investment performance is not sensitive to the choice of holding period for a large part of the sample period. However, closer to the end of the sample period starting in 2005 the calendar-time portfolio with the shortest holding periods begins to outperform the calendar time portfolios with longer holding periods. This indicates that the performance of target companies during this period is characterized by an initial outperformance for the first 12 months, which is then followed by lower returns subsequent to this initial increase in share prices. Importantly, as most events actually take place during this time period, this effect should apply to most events included in the sample.

Another important parameter in the construction of calendar-time portfolios is the starting point. In fact, the calendar-time portfolio approach actually allows the investigation of the differences in returns that result from hedge funds taking an early position in target stocks as well as the performance of other investors who try to participate in the value creation by the hedge fund in that they trade on publicly available information. This difference in returns is an important determinant of the ability of hedge funds to coordinate stable investor coalitions because it determines the willingness of other investors to follow the hedge funds lead. Therefore, Figure 35 compares the investment performance of three calendar time portfolios. In particular, the different portfolios initiate a position in target stocks two months prior to the event date, on the event date and one month after the event date holding this position for 36 months.

According to the empirical results in Figure 35, there are significant differences in realized investment performances between the hedge funds who effectively create the event and trade the stock early on, and other investors who try to participate in the increases in firm value based on publicly observable information. The calendar-time portfolio investing in target stocks two months prior to the public dissemination of this information generates substantially higher returns than the calendar-time portfolio reflecting the investment performance of other investors "tracking" hedge funds. Moreover, the majority of long-run returns is driven by the initial run-up effect which is only captured by the hedge funds. This is supported by the observation that the difference between investors trading the target stock in t=0 or t=1 are neglible.

Figure 35: Calendar Time Portfolio – Impact of Entry Points

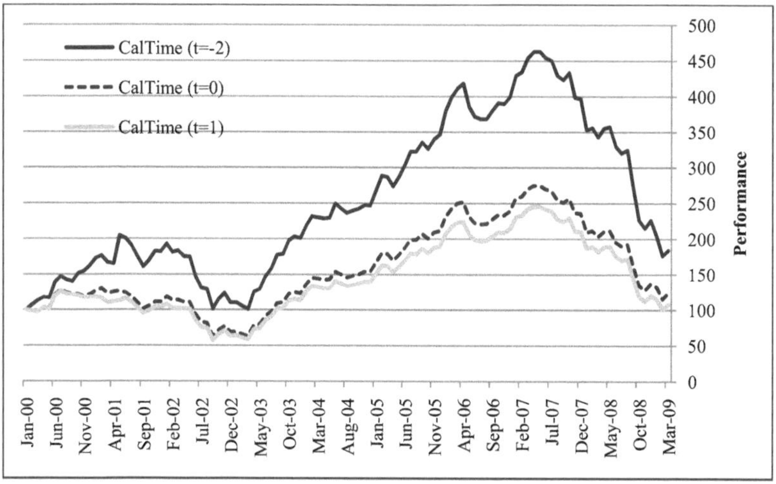

This figure reports the performance of three calendar-time portfolio that entered a position in target stocks 2 months prior to the event date, on the event date and one month after the event date. The holding period is 36 months and if there are overlapping events the holding period is adjusted accordingly.

Finally, in the analysis of long-run stock returns financial companies are often analyzed separately because these stocks might be driven by other risk factors. For instance, it is reasonable to assume that their stock returns are driven by variables such as the dynamics of interest rates and credit spreads (Bessler and Kurmann, 2010). Therefore, Figure 36 compares two calendar time portfolios establishing positions in target stocks in t=-2 and holding the position for 36 months. One calendar-time portfolio contains all stocks and the other calendar-time portfolios excludes firms operating in the financial industry.

Overall, both portfolios behave similarly during most of the sample period, but the portfolio excluding financial stocks outperforms during the latter stages of the sample period. This can be interpreted as evidence that hedge fund investments in the financial industry perform below average. Nevertheless, the visual analysis of buy-and-hold returns implicit in the calendar-time approach can easily lead to wrong conclusions (Fama, 1998). Therefore, the next step of the calendar-time portfolio approach consists of time-series regressions using an asset pricing model. This analysis is presented in the next section.

Figure 36: Calendar Time Portfolio – Impact of Financial Stocks

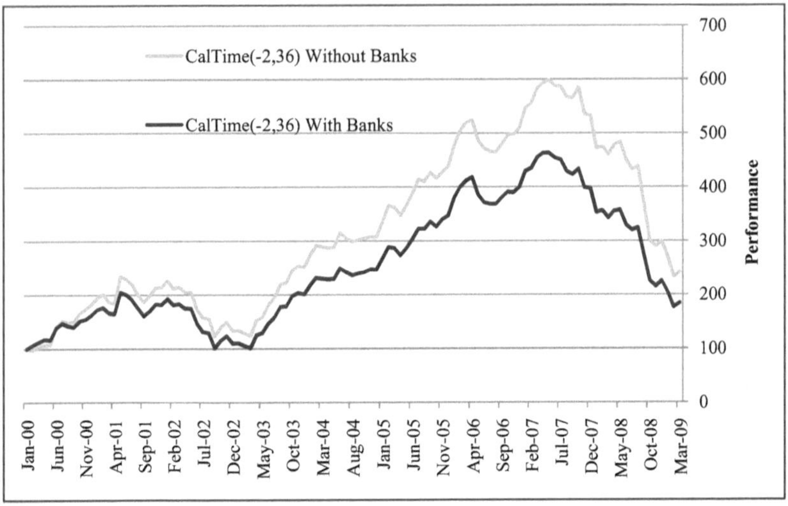

This figure reports the performance of two calendar-time portfolio – one with and one without financial stocks (n=195) - that entered a position in target stocks 2 months prior to the event date and held the position for 36 months. If there are overlapping events the holding period is adjusted accordingly.

2. Fama-French Regressions

The investment performance of calendar-time portfolios reflecting the investment strategy of hedge funds suggests that hedge fund targets generate an outperformance. However, this apparent outperformance might be driven by below average market risk exposures of target firms or exposures to other risk factors such as the HML and SMB-factors of Fama and French (1993). Therefore, the next step of the calendar-time portfolio approach consists of time-series regressions of calendar-time portfolio returns on a set of risk factors in order to test whether the apparent outperformance of hedge fund targets really is statistically significant. The results of these time-series regressions are presented in this section, where two different sets of Fama-French factors are used as measures of systematic risk. The first set is constructed based on MSCI style indices (MSCI-factors). The second set is derived from sorts of the CDAX universe of German stocks based on the criterias market capitalization and market-to-book ratio (CDAX-factors)[123].

Table 32 reports the results of the time-series regressions for a one-factor specification with the CDAX performance index as the market risk factor and for a three-factor-model with the CDAX-factors as proxies for the Fama-French factors. The results in Table 32 indicate that hedge funds can generate an outperformance because they establish their positions in target stocks before other investors take notice. For instance, from the perspective of hedge funds, the estimated alpha in the time-series regressions is positive and significant as long as they hold their positions for less than two years. More precisely, based on a market model, the estimate of alpha is weakly significant at 1.01% per month for a one year holding period and declines to 0.78% per month for a two year holding period, which is still weakly significant. These alpha estimates decline if the Fama-French factors are also included in the regression equation. In particular, alpha estimates decline to 0.92% and 0.75%, respectively. However, for longer investment horizons estimated alphas are no longer statistically significant. In addition, other investors entering into a position in target stocks in t=0 or in t=1 based on the news release that a hedge fund has established a position in a target firm apparently do not achieve an outperformance. In fact, estimated alphas for all of the corresponding regressions are not significant and in many specifications even become negative.

Hedge funds might outperform the general market by taking on systematic risks. In particular, it has often been argued that hedge funds invest in value stocks and opaque securities so that their investment performance might be driven by the value- and size-factors. This issue can also be investigated with the calendar-time approach because the estimated loadings on the Fama-French factors provide information on additional systematic components in the returns of hedge funds` investment strategies. In line with evidence for the U.S. market, these loadings suggest that hedge funds target small cap stocks as estimated coefficients on the SMB factor vary around 0.50 and are highly statistically significant at the 1%-level. At the same time, in contrast to evidence for the U.S. market that hedge funds invest in value stocks, loadings on the HML factors are very small and negative and not statistically significant. However, the results also indicate that taking the Fama-French factors into account apparently does not lead to material changes in conclusions regarding abnormal performance.

---

[123] See Bessler and Kurmann (2010) for a detailed description of the construction of these factors.

Table 32: Time-Series Regression – CDAX-Factors

Holding Period	Alpha	Market	HML	SMB	R^2
(-2, 10)	**0.0130**	**0.8189**			0.3481
	(1.95)	***(6.29)***			
	0.0048	**1.1852**	**0.5371**	**0.9230**	0.4764
	(0.78)	***(9.89)***	***(3.62)***	***(4.71)***	
(-2, 22)	0.0091	**0.8597**			0.4613
	(1.73)	***(7.76)***			
	0.0030	**1.1295**	**0.5970**	**0.8388**	0.6215
	(0.66)	***(12.55)***	***(5.40)***	***(5.76)***	
(-2, 34)	0.0086	**0.8433**			0.4674
	(1.74)	***(8.83)***			
	0.0040	**1.0841**	**0.4641**	**0.8082**	0.6059
	(0.91)	***(13.69)***	***(3.87)***	***(5.64)***	
(0, 12)	0.0085	**0.9519**			0.5179
	(1.62)	***(7.42)***			
	-0.0009	**1.2098**	**0.5807**	**0.7294**	0.6282
	(-0.16)	***(10.04)***	***(3.97)***	***(4.77)***	
(0, 24)	0.0079	**0.9259**			0.5433
	(1.67)	***(9.21)***			
	0.0013	**1.1056**	**0.5574**	**0.7055**	0.6676
	(0.28)	***(12.56)***	***(5.02)***	***(5.98)***	
(0, 36)	0.0050	**0.8973**			0.5934
	(1.24)	***(10.32)***			
	-0.0004	**1.0655**	**0.4460**	**0.6368**	0.6988
	(-0.11)	***(13.50)***	***(4.03)***	***(5.67)***	
(1, 13)	0.0073	**0.9594**			0.5599
	(1.45)	***(8.14)***			
	-0.0015	**1.1699**	**0.5417**	**0.6175**	0.6500
	(-0.26)	***(10.64)***	***(3.79)***	***(4.24)***	
(1, 25)	0.0056	**0.9150**			0.5761
	(1.25)	***(9.50)***			
	-0.0014	**1.0665**	**0.5559**	**0.5967**	0.6898
	(-0.32)	***(12.97)***	***(5.07)***	***(5.35)***	
(1, 37)	0.0045	**0.8908**			0.5771
	(1.11)	***(10.18)***			
	-0.0015	**1.0583**	**0.4679**	**0.6185**	0.6836
	(-0.38)	***(13.31)***	***(4.45)***	***(5.07)***	

This table reports the results from a time-series regression of different calendar-time portfolios returns during good times on our proxies for the Fama-French-factors, which are constructed based on the CDAX universe. For details see Bessler and Kurmann (2010). The values in parentheses indicate t-values based on Newey-West standard errors.

An important, but often neglected, aspect of long-run performance evaluation with the calendar-time portfolio approach is the choice of Fama-French factors. This is important because their properties can differ substantially depending on the methodology used. For example, Fama and French (2008) note that very small "micro cap" stocks can distort the properties of the size-factor even in the highly liquid U.S. capital market. These problems should become even more pronounced in the German capital market with its limited number of listed firms. Therefore, Table 33 provides the results of time-series regressions when the MSCI-factors are used to approximate the Fama-French factors.

The empirical results in Table 33 based on the MSCI-factors do not support all of the major conclusions that were obtained based on the CDAX-factors in Table 32. These indicated that hedge funds can generate alpha as long as they held their positions only for a limited time period because they invested in the firm before the publication of their stake and captured the full run-up effect. Specifically, estimates of alpha are not significant anymore from the perspective of hedge funds. Moreover, from the perspective of other investors trying to capitalize on hedge funds activities estimated alphas actually become negative when they enter the target stocks on or after the event date and hold their positions for long time periods. In addition, the market exposure of the calendar-time portfolio becomes significantly higher in that its market beta increases from around 0.90 to between 1.13 and 1.31, depending on the entry point and holding period. At the same time, the loadings on the SMB factors increase in particular for calendar-time portfolios replicating the investment performance of hedge funds who take positions in target stocks two months before the event date. Finally, the loadings on the HML factor are positive when the MSCI-factors are used and become highly significant at the 1%-level. This supports the result of U.S. studies that hedge funds seem to target value stocks. This shift in results emphasizes that the method used to construct Fama-French factors can have a significant impact on empirical results.

Table 33: Time-Series Regressions – MSCI-Factors

Holding Period	Alpha	Market	HML	SMB	R^2
(-2,10)	0.0092 *(1.46)*	**1.0057** ***(13.53)***	-0.1644 *(-1.02)*	**0.7767** ***(4.28)***	0.5830
(-2,22)	0.0077 *(1.80)*	**0.9466** ***(15.42)***	-0.0777 *(-0.78)*	**0.6590** ***(5.19)***	0.7162
(-2,34)	0.0049 *(1.17)*	**0.9028** ***(16.15)***	-0.1141 *(-1.25)*	**0.5462** ***(4.88)***	0.6796
(0,12)	0.0051 *(1.14)*	**1.0650** ***(12.90)***	-0.0675 *(-0.37)*	**0.7047** ***(4.73)***	0.7361
(0,24)	0.0057 *(1.54)*	**0.9616** ***(14.28)***	-0.0776 *(-0.74)*	**0.6365** ***(4.89)***	0.7632
(0,36)	0.0011 *(0.38)*	**0.9055** ***(16.23)***	-0.0922 *(-1.11)*	**0.5005** ***(5.24)***	0.7923
(1,13)	0.0058 *(1.48)*	**1.0471** ***(14.70)***	-0.1386 *(-1.00)*	**0.6470** ***(4.17)***	0.7814
(1,25)	0.0045 *(1.34)*	**0.9418** ***(16.19)***	**-0.1617** ***(-2.12)***	**0.5536** ***(4.94)***	0.7896
(1,37)	0.0016 *(0.51)*	**0.9056** ***(16.91)***	-0.0980 *(-1.41)*	**0.5422** ***(4.70)***	0.7819

This table reports the results from time-series regression on different calendar-time portfolios on proxies for the Fama-French factors during the good times period. The Fama-French factors are constructed from MSCI Value, Growth, Large and Small Cap indices from sorts on the universe of German stocks. The values in parentheses indicate t-values based on Newey-West standard errors.

Another important issue that might have substantial implications for empirical results is the industry composition of calendar-time portfolios. Many studies that focus on long-run stock returns differentiate between financial and non-financial firms because the stock returns of financial firms might be driven by risk factors other than the stocks of industrial firms (Bessler and Kurmann, 2010). This might lead to large distortions in measured long-run performance because the omission or misspecification of risk factors can lead to large pricing errors when abnormal returns for individual time periods are aggregated over longer time periods. Therefore, Table 34 repeats the same time-series regressions for the sample restricted to the 195 events involving non-financial target firms. Overall, the results are in line with the results for the full sample. In particular, based on the MSCI-factors estimated abnormal performance becomes even more pronounced for short holding periods and for calendar-time portfolios that initiate positions two months prior to the event date. This provides additional support for the conclusion that hedge funds can generate returns that substantially exceed the returns earned by other shareholders. For longer investment horizons and portfolios taking a position on or after the event date there is only weak evidence for abnormal performance. In addition, estimated factor loadings of calendar time portfolios are also in line with previous results as there are highly significant exposures on SMB but no statistically significant exposures on HML.

Table 34: Time-Series Regressions – Without Financial Stocks (MSCI-Factors)

Holding Period	Alpha	Market	HML	SMB	R^2
(-2,10)	**0.0145**	**0.9970**	-0.1338	**0.7431**	0.6005
	(2.43)	***(13.33)***	*(-0.82)*	***(4.18)***	
(0,12)	**0.0099**	**1.0443**	-0.0773	**0.6564**	0.7302
	(2.28)	***(13.12)***	*(-0.44)*	***(4.43)***	
(1,13)	**0.0093**	**1.0445**	-0.1098	**0.6648**	0.7447
	(2.18)	***(14.08)***	*(-0.78)*	***(4.06)***	
(-2,22)	**0.0099**	**0.9255**	-0.0688	**0.6648**	0.6510
	(2.14)	***(13.83)***	*(-0.58)*	***(4.75)***	
(0,24)	0.0065	**0.9187**	-0.0874	**0.5586**	0.7592
	(1.81)	***(13.87)***	*(-0.86)*	***(5.16)***	
(1,25)	0.0060	**0.9281**	-0.1480	**0.5325**	0.7652
	(1.69)	***(15.40)***	*(-1.72)*	***(4.54)***	
(-2,34)	0.0043	**0.9010**	-0.0634	**0.6119**	0.6984
	(1.08)	***(16.34)***	*(-0.63)*	***(5.13)***	
(0,36)	0.0023	**0.9093**	-0.0166	**0.5280**	0.7870
	(0.73)	***(16.22)***	*(-0.18)*	***(5.22)***	
(1,37)	0.0018	**0.9092**	-0.0246	**0.5239**	0.7993
	(0.60)	***(17.59)***	*(-0.32)*	***(4.95)***	

This table reports the results from a time-series regression of calendar portfolio returns of the good times events. Factors based on MSCI Style Indices are used. The values in parentheses indicate t-values.

Moreover, using the CDAX-factors estimated alphas again become statistically insignificant for calendar-time portfolios with a short investment horizon and for portfolios that take early positions in target companies. Additionally, similar to the full sample, there are still positive exposures on SMB and on HML. Thus, in line with the previous analysis that included financial stocks, the empirical evidence indicates that the CDAX-factors lead to a more conservative assessment of the performance of hedge fund targets.

Table 35: Time-Series Regressions – Without Financial Stocks (CDAX-Factors)

Holding Period	Alpha	Market	HML	SMB	R^2
(-2,10)	0.0085	**1.1267**	**0.7073**	**0.9132**	0.4373
	(1.20)	***(8.37)***	***(4.58)***	***(4.37)***	
(0,12)	0.0052	**1.1466**	**0.6095**	**0.6925**	0.5357
	(0.76)	***(8.59)***	***(3.89)***	***(3.92)***	
(1,13)	0.0028	**1.1236**	**0.5950**	**0.6063**	0.5271
	(0.40)	***(8.37)***	***(3.88)***	***(3.42)***	
(-2,22)	0.0053	**1.0383**	**0.6966**	**0.8318**	0.4951
	(0.96)	***(10.16)***	***(5.70)***	***(5.39)***	
(0,24)	0.0034	**1.0244**	**0.5865**	**0.6591**	0.5792
	(0.66)	***(10.61)***	***(4.91)***	***(5.29)***	
(1,25)	0.0051	**1.0269**	**0.6236**	**0.5906**	0.5890
	(0.10)	***(11.24)***	***(5.49)***	***(4.94)***	
(-2,34)	0.0036	**1.0334**	**0.5751**	**0.8053**	0.5296
	(0.71)	***(10.98)***	***(4.15)***	***(5.22)***	
(0,36)	0.0021	**1.0405**	**0.4910**	**0.6434**	0.5977
	(0.44)	***(11.32)***	***(3.91)***	***(4.95)***	
(1,37)	-0.0002	**1.0197**	**0.5034**	**0.5547**	0.5959
	(-0.04)	***(11.02)***	***(4.38)***	***(4.45)***	

This table reports the results from a time-series regression of calendar portfolio returns of the good times events. Factors derived from sorts on market-to-book and size are used. The values in parentheses indicate t-values.

Overall, the time-series regressions create some significant doubts as to the findings from the analysis of buy-and-hold abnormal returns that hedge fund targets outperform in the long run. This favorable assessment of hedge fund engagements appears to be related to the high frequency of overlapping events and the resulting cross-correlations in the sample. After correcting for these correlations by forming calendar-time portfolios there is no convincing empirical evidence that the hedge fund targets outperform on a risk-adjusted basis. Rather, there is only limited evidence for alpha which is restricted to the calendar-time portfolios with a short investment horizon and which assumes the perspective of a hedge fund investing in target stocks prior to the event date. In addition, these findings in favor of positive alphas are still not robust as they are substantially affected by the specification of Fama-French factors. In addition, there is evidence that a fraction of the outperformance measured by the BHAR-approach appears to be related to omitted risk factors. In particular, there is strong evidence supporting a size effect as loadings on SMB are significantly positive in all time-series regressions. This suggests that the evidence for the U.S. market by Griffin and Xu (2007) and Brav, Jiang, Partnoy, and Thomas (2008) also applies to the German market as hedge funds generate some returns by taking on risks related to smaller and more illiquid firms. Furthermore, in line with evidence for the U.S. capital market (Brav, Jiang, Partnoy, and Thomas, 2008) there is some evidence that hedge funds also assume the risks associated with value firms because the time-series regressions using one set of Fama-French factors consistently indicate significantly positive loadings on the HML-factor.

III. Robustness Check - Generalized Calendar Time Portfolio Approach

Another approach which is used by some researchers to investigate long-run stock returns is the generalized calendar time portfolio approach (GCT-approach) by Höchle, Schmid, and Zimmermann (2009). While it can be shown that this approach is equivalent to the simple calendar time portfolio approach that was used in the previous section in specific settings, the GCT-approach offers some additional advantages. In particular, it is more flexible and allows breaking down valuation effects further into several components. This allows one to investigate the implications of the run-up effect on long-run returns in more detail and to incorporate information on pre-event firm fundamentals into the analysis of long-term returns. Due to these advantages this section presents the empirical results of an application of the GCT-approach on the sample of 235 events in which hedge funds acquired stakes in German firms between 2000 and 2006.

1. Long-Run Performance

The empirical results of the GCT-approach are presented in Table 36 in which the excess stock return of all firms in the sample and the control group is regressed on a set of risk factors, a dummy variable labeled “drift” and a full set of interaction terms. The dummy “drift” equals 1 for an event firm if a hedge fund engagement occurred during the previous 12, 24, or 36 months which is equivalent to the holding period in the calendar-time portfolio approach. The coefficients in the columns “all” measure the impact of the respective variable on the full set of firms, including the control group which is given by the whole CDAX universe of German stocks. The coefficients in the columns ”delta” measure the differential impact of the respective variable on target firms over different investment horizons. Consequently, the most interesting coefficients are reported in the column "delta" and in the row "alpha" which measures the abnormal performance of target firms over different holdings periods.

According to the results in Table 36, Table 37 and Table 38, the GCT-approach does not indicate that target firms generate statistically significant alpha when the MSCI-factors are used as risk factors. Moreover, based on the CDAX-factors estimated alphas become negative and statistically significant for longer holding periods when the investor is assumed to initate a position in t=0 or in t=1. This confirms the results from the calendar-time portfolio approach that after taking additional risk factors into account, such as the value- and small-firm-effect, and after adjusting t-statistics for cross-correlations, hedge fund engagements do not generate a significant outperformance. In fact, there is only weak evidence for an outperformance on a risk-adjusted basis from the hedge fund perspective. Thus, overall the GCT-approach confirms the doubts raised by the simple calendar time approach regarding the hypothesis that hedge funds also increase firm value over longer time periods.

In addition, the coefficients on the risk factors in the columns "delta" measure the difference in factor loadings between the sample of hedge fund targets and the average company traded on the German stock market. Based on the MSCI-factors the estimated coefficients suggest that the market exposures of target firms are significantly higher than in the control group. In particular, this applies when the holding period is short. This effect diminishes for longer holding periods, suggesting that hedge fund interventions are initially associated with an increase in systematic risk. Finally, the exposures of target firms on size and market-to-book effects seem to be in line with average German stocks. However, when the CDAX-factors are used the market exposure is no longer significantly larger for target firms. Instead, the exposures on SMB (HML) are significantly smaller (larger) relative to the control group. Thus, based on these proxies for the Fama-French factors, hedge fund targets seem to be bigger than the average company traded in the German stock market and appear to have a larger exposure on the value effect.

Table 36: Run-Up Effects and Post-Event Abnormal Performance – 12 Month Drift

Panel A – Fama French Factors – CDAX-Factors						
Entry	t=-2		t=0		t=1	
	All	Delta	All	Delta	All	Delta
Alpha	-0.0008 *(-0.26)*	0.0024 *(0.40)*	-0.0016 *(-0.57)*	-0.0020 *(-0.35)*	-0.0029 *(-1.07)*	-0.0017 *(-0.31)*
Mkt	**1.3257** ***(18.55)***	-0.0308 *(-0.25)*	**1.3225** ***(18.79)***	0.0216 *(0.19)*	**1.3061** ***(18.32)***	0.0114 *(0.10)*
SMB	**1.0324** ***(8.59)***	**-0.3725** ***(-2.37)***	**1.1001** ***(9.69)***	**-0.4806** ***(-3.60)***	**1.0964** ***(9.57)***	**-0.4743** ***(-3.34)***
HML	0.1173 *(1.20)*	0.2867 *(1.53)*	0.1338 *(1.39)*	0.2733 *(1.42)*	0.1891 *(1.77)*	0.2361 *(1.19)*
R2	0.0767		0.0775		0.0762	
Nobs	56565		57039		56781	
Panel B – Fama French Factors – MSCI-Factors						
Entry	t=-2		t=0		t=1	
	All	Delta	All	Delta	All	Delta
Alpha	0.0004 *(0.09)*	0.0074 *(1.26)*	0.0001 *(0.02)*	0.0028 *(0.51)*	0.0002 *(0.04)*	0.0021 *(0.40)*
Mkt	**0.9222** ***(14.08)***	0.1289 *(1.33)*	**0.9191** ***(14.24)***	0.1804 (1.83)	**0.9189** ***(14.41)***	0.1627 *(1.75)*
SMB	**0.7850** ***(5.29)***	-0.0986 *(-0.62)*	**0.7963** ***(5.44)***	-0.0651 *(-0.38)*	**0.7946** **(5.42)**	-0.0189 *(-0.10)*
HML	-0.0394 *(-0.46)*	-0.1549 *(-1.20)*	-0.0367 *(-0.44)*	-0.1272 *(-0.78)*	-0.0384 *(-0.46)*	-0.1266 *(-0.74)*
R2	0.0645		0.0639		0.0638	
Nobs	48431		49859		50578	

This table reports estimates for run-up effects and post-event abnormal performance using a panel regression approach that corrects for spatial correlations by calculating Driscoll-Kraay standard errors (Höchle, Schmid, and Zimmermann, 2009). See text for the details of the implementation.

Table 37: Run-Up Effects and Post-Event Abnormal Performance – 24 Month Drift

Panel A – Fama French Factors – CDAX-Factors						
Entry	t=-2		t=0		t=1	
	All	Delta	All	Delta	All	Delta
Alpha	0.0001	-0.0045	-0.0001	-0.0060	-0.0023	-0.0039
	(0.02)	*(-0.98)*	*(-0.02)*	*(-1.38)*	*(-0.95)*	*(-0.96)*
Mkt	1.2570	-0.0677	1.2440	-0.0849	1.2366	-0.0867
	(15.28)	*(-0.83)*	*(15.43)*	*(-1.03)*	*(15.20)*	(-1.01)
SMB	0.9706	-0.2637	1.0242	-0.3651	1.0375	-0.3755
	(7.98)	*(-2.21)*	*(8.85)*	*(-3.18)*	(9.02)	*(-3.15)*
HML	0.1126	0.3834	0.1275	0.3786	0.2028	0.3037
	(1.09)	*(2.43)*	*(1.25)*	*(2.49)*	*(1.84)*	*(2.08)*
R2	0.0727		0.0736		0.0723	
Nobs	65215		65707		65453	

Panel B – Fama French Factors – MSCI-Factors						
Entry	t=-2		t=0		t=1	
	All	Delta	All	Delta	All	Delta
Alpha	-0.0004	0.0029	0.0000	0.0010	0.0001	0.0007
	(-0.10)	*(0.73)*	*(0.00)*	(0.27)	*(0.03)*	*(0.19)*
Mkt	0.8926	0.0850	0.8875	0.0688	0.8870	0.0632
	(14.36)	*(1.10)*	*(14.78)*	*(0.85)*	*(14.84)*	*(0.80)*
SMB	0.7786	-0.0133	0.7762	-0.0389	0.7713	-0.0244
	(5.87)	*(-0.11)*	*(5.85)*	*(-0.30)*	*(6.00)*	*(-0.18)*
HML	-0.0553	-0.0337	-0.0637	-0.0578	-0.0657	-0.0716
	(-0.69)	(-0.31)	*(-0.82)*	(-0.48)	(-0.85)	*(-0.59)*
R2	0.0622		0.0624		0.0624	
Nobs	57081		58527		59250	

This table reports estimates for run-up effects and post-event abnormal performance using a panel regression approach that corrects for spatial correlations by calculating Driscoll-Kraay standard errors (Höchle, Schmid, and Zimmermann, 2009). See text for the details of the implementation.

Table 38: Run-Up Effects and Post-Event Abnormal Performance – 36 Month Drift

Panel A – Fama French Factors – CDAX-Factors						
Entry	t=-2		t=0		t=1	
	All	Delta	All	Delta	All	Delta
Alpha	0.0026	-0.0058	0.0029	-0.0057	0.0013	-0.0052
	(0.88)	*(-1.64)*	*(0.97)*	*(-1.63)*	*(0.42)*	*(-1.54)*
Mkt	1.1338	0.0154	1.1309	0.0125	1.1159	0.0207
	(14.26)	*(0.20)*	*(13.85)*	*(0.17)*	*(13.38)*	*(0.26)*
SMB	0.8681	-0.2146	0.9048	-0.2798	0.9196	-0.2922
	(7.81)	*(-1.96)*	*(7.60)*	(-2.35)	*(7.47)*	*(-2.27)*
HML	0.0540	0.3136	0.0399	0.3308	0.0976	0.2874
	(0.53)	*(2.41)*	*(0.35)*	(2.74)	*(0.77)*	*(2.34)*
R2	0.0747		0.0766		0.0750	
Nobs	78215		74377		74121	
Panel B – Fama French Factors – MSCI-Factors						
Entry	t=-2		t=0		t=1	
	All	Delta	All	Delta	All	Delta
Alpha	-0.0001	0.0001	0.0002	-0.0002	-0.0001	-0.0011
	(-0.01)	(0.04)	*(0.05)*	*(-0.06)*	*(-0.01)*	(-0.33)
Mkt	0.8129	0.1363	0.8173	0.1250	0.8114	0.1283
	(14.82)	*(2.24)*	*(15.19)*	*(2.04)*	*(15.18)*	(2.05)
SMB	0.6684	-0.0191	0.6725	-0.0088	0.6805	-0.0089
	(6.29)	*(-0.23)*	*(6.51)*	*(-0.10)*	*(6.62)*	*(-0.10)*
HML	-0.1845	0.0735	-0.1841	0.0193	-0.1855	0.0171
	(-2.45)	*(1.03)*	*(-2.41)*	*(0.25)*	(-2.45)	*(0.22)*
R2	0.0691		0.0689		0.0685	
Nobs	65755		67197		67918	

This table reports estimates for run-up effects and post-event abnormal performance using a panel regression approach that corrects for spatial correlations by calculating Driscoll-Kraay standard errors (Höchle, Schmid, and Zimmermann, 2009). See text for the details of the implementation.

The stock returns of financial firms might be driven by a different set of risk factors than industrial firms. Hence, the preceding results might be affected by the presence of financial firms in the sample. Thus, in the next step, all financial firms are removed from the sample of target firms and from the control group. This leaves 195 events in the sample and 605 firms in the control group. Overall, the results remain qualitatively the same for most holding periods. Only in the case of the portfolios investing in target stocks two months before the official event date and with short holding periods of 12 and 24 months are there significant differences if the MSCI-factors are used. In particular, estimated alphas become positive and statistically significant. However, this effect diminishes if CDAX-factors are used. Finally, the shifts in risk factor exposures between sample firms and the control group are no longer statistically significant if the MSCI-factors are used. In contrast, these shifts remain qualitatively the same if the CDAX-factors are employed.

Overall, the GCT-approach leads to similar conclusions as the simple calendar-time portfolio approach. In particular, there are some concerns regarding the important issue as to whether hedge fund targets truly experience an outperformance. Given the empirical evidence documented in this section, it seems plausible that the high BHAR are the result of omitted risk factors. In particular, this concerns the size-factors which are reliably significant in all time-series regressions.

Table 39: Run-Up Effects and Post-Event Drift – 12 Months - Without Financial Stocks

Panel A – Fama French Factors – CDAX-Factors						
Entry	t=-2		t=0		t=1	
	All	Delta	All	Delta	All	Delta
Alpha	-0.0006 *(-0.18)*	0.0030 *(0.49)*	-0.0015 *(-0.51)*	-0.0010 *(-0.17)*	-0.0015 *(-0.53)*	-0.0020 *(-0.34)*
Mkt	**1.3672** ***(17.90)***	-0.0833 *(-0.64)*	**1.3636** ***(18.07)***	-0.0401 *(-0.34)*	**1.3526** ***(17.80)***	-0.0496 (-0.41)
SMB	**1.0460** ***(8.44)***	**-0.3214** ***(-1.99)***	**1.1199** ***(9.84)***	**-0.4665** ***(-3.27)***	**1.0927** ***(9.32)***	**-0.4133** ***(-2.67)***
HML	0.0931 *(0.94)*	**0.4170** ***(2.07)***	0.1119 *(1.14)*	0.3772 *(1.79)*	0.1254 *(1.24)*	0.3911 *(1.81)*
R2	0.0787		0.0793		0.0787	
Nobs	48159		48550		48741	
Panel B – Fama French Factors – MSCI-Factors						
Entry	t=-2		t=0		t=1	
	All	Delta	All	Delta	All	Delta
Alpha	0.0004 *(0.09)*	0.0095 *(1.62)*	0.0000 *(0.00)*	0.0049 *(0.91)*	0.0002 *(0.05)*	0.0044 *(0.82)*
Market	**0.9507** **(13.13)**	0.0951 *(0.92)*	**0.9469** ***(13.22)***	0.1486 *(1.47)*	**0.9449** ***(13.28)***	0.1364 *(1.37)*
SMB	**0.8041** **(5.24)**	-0.0951 *(-0.58)*	**0.8175** **(5.39)**	-0.0717 *(-0.39)*	**0.8150** ***(5.37)***	-0.0041 *(-0.02)*
HML	-0.0632 *(-0.71)*	-0.0936 *(-0.73)*	-0.0606 *(-0.70)*	-0.0646 *(-0.40)*	-0.0647 *(-0.75)*	-0.0634 *(-0.37)*
R2	0.0661		0.0655		0.0653	
Nobs	41229		42422		43023	

This table reports estimates for run-up effects and post-event abnormal performance using a panel regression approach that corrects for spatial correlations by calculating Driscoll-Kraay standard errors (Höchle, Schmid, and Zimmermann, 2009). See text for the details of the implementation.

Table 40: Run-Up Effects and Post-Event Drift – 24 Months - Without Financial Stocks

Panel A – Fama French Factors – CDAX-Factors

Entry	t=-2		t=0		t=1	
	All	Delta	All	Delta	All	Delta
Alpha	0.0002	-0.0035	0.0001	-0.0046	-0.0010	-0.0036
	(0.07)	*(-0.76)*	*(0.05)*	*(-1.07)*	(-0.40)	*(-0.84)*
Mkt	**1.2972**	-0.1159	**1.2823**	-0.1210	**1.2835**	-0.1272
	(14.83)	*(-1.35)*	***(14.89)***	*(-1.42)*	***(14.92)***	*(-1.42)*
SMB	**0.9850**	**-0.2588**	**1.0434**	**-0.3752**	**1.0350**	**-0.3582**
	(7.83)	**(-2.14)**	***(8.95)***	***(-3.52)***	***(8.66)***	**(-3.16)**
HML	0.0913	**0.4848**	0.1068	**0.4614**	0.1422	**0.4333**
	(0.87)	**(2.93)**	*(1.02)*	**(2.92)**	*(1.35)*	***(2.89)***
R2	0.0754		0.0761		0.0757	
Nobs	55394		55802		55997	

Panel B – Fama French Factors – MSCI-Factors

Entry	t=-2		t=0		t=1	
	All	Delta	All	Delta	All	Delta
Alpha	-0.0006	0.0054	-0.0001	0.0036	0.0000	0.0034
	(-0.14)	*(1.37)*	*(-0.03)*	*(1.00)*	*(0.00)*	*(0.94)*
Market	**0.9216**	0.0575	**0.9152**	0.0516	**0.9144**	0.0511
	(13.50)	*(0.73)*	***(13.80)***	*(0.63)*	***(13.83)***	*(0.63)*
SMB	**0.8112**	-0.0473	**0.8083**	-0.0769	**0.8023**	-0.0491
	(5.96)	*(-0.40)*	***(5.94)***	*(-0.58)*	***(6.08)***	*(-0.35)*
HML	-0.0768	0.0101	-0.0879	-0.0040	-0.0899	-0.0173
	(-0.94)	*(0.10)*	*(-1.11)*	*(-0.04)*	*(-1.14)*	*(-0.15)*
R2	0.0648		0.0650		0.0649	
Nobs	48464		49674		50279	

This table reports estimates for run-up effects and post-event abnormal performance using a panel regression approach that corrects for spatial correlations by calculating Driscoll-Kraay standard errors (Höchle, Schmid, and Zimmermann, 2009). See text for the details of the implementation.

Table 41: Run-Up Effects and Post-Event Drift – 36 Months - Without Financial Stocks

Panel A – Fama French Factors – CDAX-Factors						
Entry	t=-2		t=0		t=1	
	All	Delta	All	Delta	All	Delta
Alpha	0.0032	-0.0053	0.0033	-0.0051	0.0024	-0.0052
	(1.01)	*(-1.40)*	*(1.07)*	*(-1.43)*	*(0.79)*	*(-1.46)*
Mkt	1.1615	-0.0187	1.1598	0.0027	1.1533	-0.0089
	(13.16)	*(-0.22)*	*(12.99)*	*(0.03)*	*(12.82)*	*(-0.09)*
SMB	0.8485	-0.1580	0.9109	-0.2628	0.9130	-0.2682
	(6.68)	*(-1.33)*	*(7.18)*	*(-2.20)*	*(7.04)*	*(-2.19)*
HML	-0.0017	0.4660	0.0101	0.4075	0.0354	0.3969
	(-0.01)	*(3.43)*	*(0.09)*	(3.18)	*(0.28)*	*(3.18)*
R2	0.0781		0.0785		0.0778	
Nobs	62652		63056		63249	
Panel B – Fama French Factors – MSCI-Factors						
Entry	t=-2		t=0		t=1	
	All	Delta	All	Delta	All	Delta
Alpha	-0.0002	0.0024	0.0002	0.0016	-0.0001	0.0010
	(-0.04)	(0.67)	*(0.05)*	*(0.48)*	*(-0.02)*	*(0.29)*
Market	0.8373	0.1072	0.8402	0.1161	0.8345	0.1100
	(14.03)	*(1.69)*	*(14.21)*	*(1.67)*	*(14.23)*	*(1.57)*
SMB	0.6923	-0.0254	0.6977	-0.0197	0.7058	-0.0132
	(6.27)	*(-0.30)*	*(6.51)*	*(-0.23)*	*(6.61)*	*(-0.14)*
HML	-0.2064	0.1408	-0.2100	0.1350	-0.2108	0.1242
	(-2.81)	*(1.99)*	*(-2.77)*	*(1.60)*	*(-2.81)*	*(1.41)*
R2	0.0712		0.0711		0.0706	
Nobs	55722		56928		57531	

This table reports estimates for run-up effects and post-event abnormal performance using a panel regression approach that corrects for spatial correlations by calculating Driscoll-Kraay standard errors (Höchle, Schmid, and Zimmermann, 2009). See text for the details of the implementation.

2. Target Firm Characteristics and Performance

The empirical analysis of BHARs indicates that long-run valuation effects depend on event and firm characteristics. However, the BHAR-approach does not control for additional systematic risk factors, such as the value- and size-factors. Moreover, due to overlapping event periods and the resulting cross-correlations, this approach is also subject to statistical biases. Therefore, the GCT-approach is used in this section as a robustness check. This pooled regression model is specified with a 12-month drift-period and is estimated using monthly data and all non-financial CDAX firms as the control group. To save space, not all coefficients of the model are reported. Table 42 summarizes the empirical results.

Regarding the interaction terms, an emphasis is put on the interaction between the drift-dummy variable and the lagged fundamental variables. Although firm characteristics are able to explain a substantial part of the return in the year subsequent to the event, 98 basis points in the monthly excess return remain unexplained, as indicated by the significant coefficient on the drift-dummy variable. The results also corroborate the findings from the cross-sectional regressions of buy-and-hold abnormal returns (BHAR). After controlling for additional risk factor exposures there is an underperformance of target firms if a bank or government entity used to be the dominant shareholders. This is consistent with the idea that these investors derive private benefits from their controlling position and, therefore, are likely to resist hedge funds' restructuring plans. Moreover, returns are significantly higher if hedge funds push firms into mergers & acquisitions. Finally, the proportion of supervisory seats held by the firm's workforce apparently does not have a significant impact on valuation effects estimated by the GCT-approach. Finally, focusing on the lagged accounting fundamentals, the target's share price performance appears to be higher if the payout ratio is higher. Again, this is consistent with the hypothesis that hedge funds target companies with agency problems of free cash flows.

Table 42: Generalized Calendar Time Approach – Target Firm Characteristics

	Independent Variable	I	II	III	IV	V
	Abnormal Return	0.0072	0.0123	0.0100	0.0081	0.0098
Largest Investor	Bank	0.0019				-0.0172*
	Corporation	0.0099				0.0002
	Government	-0.0086				-0.0156**
	Individual	-0.0002				-0.0074
HF Behavior	Wolfpack		-0.0027			0.0082
	HF Rel. Stake		-0.0001			0.0001
	Aggressive		-0.0099			-0.0004
	Subsequent M&A		0.0123			0.0310***
Cod eter.	Labor 1/3			0.0043		-0.0064
	Labor ½			-0.0014		-0.0007
Accounting Fundamentals	R&D				-0.0033	-0.0045
	Payout Ratio adj.				0.0003**	0.0003**
	Cash Holdings adj.				0.0032	-0.0024
	Leverage adj.				-0.0315	-0.0304
	RoE adj.				-0.0054	-0.0051
	CF-to-Assets adj.				0.0454	0.0464
	Capex-to-Sales adj.				0.0210	0.0341
	R^2	0.0657	0.0656	0.0656	0.1292	0.1310
	Number of Observations	44835	44835	44835	27173	27173

This table reports estimates of the impact of firm-level fundamental characteristics in the year prior to the engagement of a hedge fund on the performance of their target firms using the generalized calendar time approach (Höchle, Schmid, and Zimmermann, 2008). The dependent variable is each stock's return in excess of the risk-free rate which is regressed on the Fama-French factors (market factor, SMB and HML), a dummy variable that captures a target firm's abnormal performance subsequent to the event ("drift"), and a set of interaction terms between the different industry-adjusted fundamental variables and the drift-dummy. The drift-dummy variable is set equal to one for the all monthly return observations in the window between the event date and 12 months subsequent to the event date, otherwise it is zero; it captures the abnormal performance of hedge fund targets compared to the universe of CDAX control firms. */**/*** indicate statistical significance at the 10%/5%/1% level.

B. Summary and Conclusion

According to the empirical results presented in this chapter, hedge fund activism in Germany is characterized by some important differences as compared to the U.S. In particular, there is no convincing evidence that hedge fund activism in Germany is driven by corporate governance problems. For instance, the analysis on the capital structure and profitability of target firms does not provide strong evidence that German target firms suffer from agency problems of free cash flows. Moreover, in contrast to evidence for the U.S. there are pronounced run-up effects which begin approximately two months before the event date. Most importantly, positive short-term valuation effects do not lead to positive long-term abnormal returns. In fact, after adjusting stock returns for post-event risk characteristics using proxies for the Fama-French factors, there is no significant outperformance for most events. This can be explained by significantly positive exposures to the size-factor. However, even after adjusting for these factors, target firms generate a strong outperformance when they subsequently become takeover targets. This is similar to evidence for the U.S. capital market (Greenwood and Schor, 2009). Finally, differentiating the sample of hedge fund events into different subsamples also leads to interesting results which are not in line with the U.S. evidence. In particular, more aggressive hedge funds who publicly attack target management only generate superior returns during short event windows before and after the event date. This initial outperformance is reversed over longer holding periods so that the subsample of passive hedge funds actually outperforms its more activist peer group. This might indicate that these aggressive hedge funds are most interesting when expropriating the firm's long-term shareholders and try to generate temporary increases in share prices that allow them to sell out at higher prices.

These results have some important implications for the debate on the role of hedge funds in corporate governance. It is important to note that not all hedge funds possess superior information on how to create shareholder value, as activist hedge funds do not always improve corporate governance. However, this does not imply that hedge funds need to be regulated and prevented from making their voice heard in corporate governance. Rather, it seems more important to strengthen the disclosure regulations so that other investors obtain better information on hedge funds' true objectives and can make a better evaluation of their activities in the company's share price. This applies in particular to the subset of more aggressive hedge funds. Given the reversal effects in the share prices of their target firms it appears reasonable to assume that these hedge funds are often not truly interested in restructuring target firms. Instead, they seem to exploit long reporting lags and weak enforcement to quietly sell off their positions before other shareholders are fully aware of what is happening.

Chapter III. Hedge Fund Investments in the Down-Market

The predominant view presented in most academic studies is that hedge fund activity in target firms helps to improve corporate governance, thereby increasing shareholder value. This hypothesis is supported by a large body of empirical evidence for the U.S. capital market based on short- and long-term returns (e.g. Klein and Zur, 2009; Brav, Jiang, Partnoy, and Thomas, 2009). Moreover, this hypothesis is also supported by several studies for the German market, at least for short holding periods (Achleitner, Betzer, and Gider, 2008). However, a significant drawback in all of these studies is that they do not take into account the time-variation in capital market conditions and their implications for hedge fund investments. In fact, almost all of these studies focus exclusively on the valuation effects triggered by events which took place up to the end of 2006. The time period between 2002 and 2006 was characterized by favorable conditions in capital markets including high liquidity, low volatility and generally rising share prices. This is highlighted in Figure 37 which shows the DAX performance index which is representative of the aggregate German stock market and the credit spread measured by Barclay Capital's European corporate bond index with a maturity of 1-5 years for the time period from the end of 1999 to the end of 2009.

Therefore, it is interesting to investigate the valuation effects of active hedge fund investments during the more challenging times in 2007 and 2008. This time period covers the most recent financial crisis and was characterized by adverse market conditions with low liquidity, high volatility and sharply declining share prices. In principle, it should be possible for hedge funds to apply the same approaches during this more challenging market environment. This is because other investors also search for opportunities to increase or at least limit the decrease in the value of their portfolio holdings. Thus, other investors should be highly interested in supporting hedge fund restructuring demands. However, there are several reasons for why hedge funds could trigger different valuation effects in such a down market. First, most of the restructuring measures typically proposed by activist hedge funds can only be profitably executed during stable market conditions. For example, firms are only able to sell off non-core assets and business units at favorable prices if markets offer fair valuations and sufficient liquidity. Similarly, it is only possible to increase the leverage of target firms to finance share repurchases and dividend increases if debt markets are fairly liquid and allow firms to raise debt at low credit spreads. Thus, firms targeted during these challenging market conditions are more likely to suffer from other types of inefficiencies such as below-average management etc. Second, the need for hedge funds to act as monitors in corporate governance during down-markets should actually be limited. The reason is that an economic recession puts managers under pressure to boost the efficiency of their firms. Effectively, product markets can be considered as the ultimate drivers of economic efficiency (Shleifer and Vishny, 1997). Therefore, it is reasonable to assume that hedge fund activism should be regarded as a state-contingent governance device, which is mostly required to raise firm value during favorable market conditions when free cash-flow problems are most severe. Finally, during more adverse market conditions hedge funds' performance problems might spill over into the share price performance of target firms in that expected fire sales by liquidity constrained hedge funds can put downward pressure on the share prices of target firms.

Figure 37: DAX Performance Index and Credit Spread – 1999 - 2009

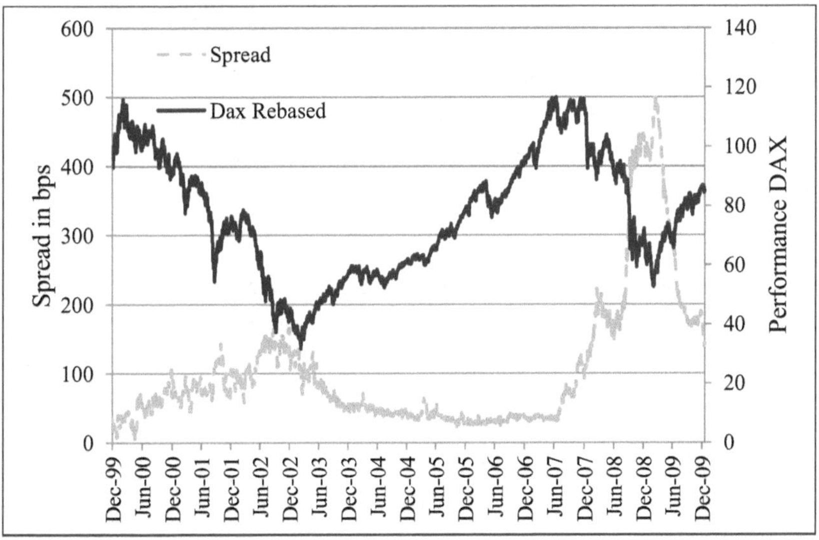

This figure reports the performance of the DAX performance index and the level of credit spreads between 1999 and 2009. The credit spread is measured Barclay Capital's European corporate bond index with a maturity of 1-5 years.

This chapter evaluates the hypothesis that valuation effects are smaller during the down-market based on the sample of 169 events in the German stock market between

January 1st, 2007 and December 31st, 2008. The first section describes the market environment during the sample period and summarizes the distribution of events over time during this distressed market environment. The next section investigates the characteristics of target firms and focuses on key accounting ratios summarizing their financial structure and profitability. This allows one to infer whether target firms suffer from agency problems of free cash flows. Finally, the last section, and main part of the analysis, is focused on short- and long-term valuation effects. This includes the standard event study approach based on cumulative abnormal returns as well as the more advanced calendar-time and generalized calendar-time approaches.

A. Hedge Fund Investments during the Recent Financial Crisis

Most studies of hedge fund activism for the U.S. and German capital markets focus on the time period before the end of 2006, which can be characterized as a quiet market environment with high liquidity, low volatility and generally rising share prices. Some hedge funds continued to accumulate stakes in German firms after this period and acquired shares in target companies after the beginning of the recent financial crisis. This is depicted in Figure 38 which plots the number of hedge fund investments per month relative to the performance of the DAX performance index and the credit spread measured by Barclay Capital's European corporate bond index with a maturity of one to five years.

Based on the distribution of events and the behavior of the DAX performance index and credit spreads the period from 2006 and 2008 can be differentiated into two subperiods which closely correspond to the two major stages of the subprime crisis.[124] The first stage covers the first half of 2007 when the first signs of the emerging subprime crisis became visible. In particular, there were losses and falling asset values in the U.S. market for subprime real estate. This began to decrease in late 2006 falling from par value in October 2006 to a level of 80 cents on the dollar in February 2007 (Economist, Feb 15th 2007). This downward spiral in asset values began to accelerate in the first half of 2007 before in May 2007 when the rating agency Moody's eventually put several structured credit products based on subprime assets on "downgrade review". This was followed by the first actual downgrades in June 2007 which in turn lead to the failure of two hedge funds managed by Bear Stearns that

[124] See Brunnermeier (2009) for a more detailed discussion of the dynamics of the recent financial crisis.

specialized in investments in credit markets. Interestingly, the declining asset values in these large markets had no significant effects on the pricing of other asset classes and accumulating losses on subprime debt did not spill over into other asset classes. For instance, the S&P 500 stock index continued to increase during most of this period and was not significantly affected by these initial credit events. This suggests that investors were apparently not aware of the potential problems in other asset classes, and in particular on the balance sheets of many large financial intermediaries, which would ultimately turn into the center of the financial crisis.

Figure 38: Distribution of Events during the Bad Times Period

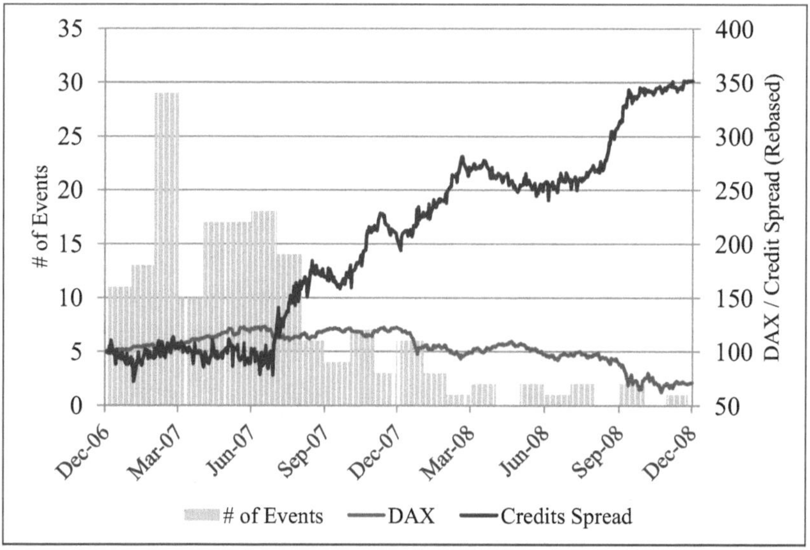

This figure reports the performance of the DAX performance index, the level of credit spreads and the number of events per month during the bad times period between January 2007 and December 2009. The credit spread is measured by Barclay Capital's European corporate bond index with a maturity of one to five years.

During the second stage the financial crisis began to spread to all other sectors of the financial system as investors began to realize the potential implications for other asset classes. In particular, in July 2007 the asset-backed commercial paper market began to dry up subsequent to bad news regarding the value of structured products. This triggered the collapse of the mid-sized bank IKB in Germany in July 2007. In August

2007 quantitatively oriented hedge funds suffered huge losses and interbank money markets started to freeze up leading to the failure of the commercial bank Northern Rock in England.[125] Next, the crisis almost led to a failure of U.S. Monoline insurers between January and February 2008 due to their exposure to the U.S. subprime debt market. In March 2008 Bear Stearns experienced problems and was forced into a merger with JP Morgan then in June 2008 Fannie Mae and Freddie Mac also began to suffer substantial problems as a result of their dominant market position in the U.S. real estate market. Finally, the crisis fully unfolded in September 2008 when the U.S. investment bank Lehman Brothers failed and subsequently the pressure on the insurance company AIG began to increase. This ultimately led to the $ 700 billion bailout of the U.S. financial industry in the same month.

B. Characteristics of Target Companies during the Down-Market

The characteristics of firms targeted by hedge funds can provide information on the investment strategy pursued by the hedge fund. In particular, information on the financial structure, profitability, pre-event valuation and on the ownership structure of target firms helps to determine whether they suffer from agency problems of free cash flows or ineffective management. For this reason, it is highly interesting to investigate these variables for the subsample of events taking place during the down-market because this helps to establish whether hedge fund investments are driven by the same objectives in up- and down-markets.

Therefore, this section focuses on the characteristics of firms targeted by hedge funds during the down-market. The first subsection analyzes fundamental accounting ratios which provide insights into the financial policies, profitability and operating diversification of target firms. These variables are closely related to the efficiency of corporate management and to the magnitude of agency problems of free cash flows. The second subsection investigates the valuation of target companies prior to the hedge fund investment. The key hypothesis is that hedge fund targets should be undervalued if they suffer from agency problems of free cash flows or from inefficient management. This analysis is based on the undervaluation index developed by Peyer and Vermaelen (2009) and its subcomponents which are derived from market capitalizations, market-to-book ratios and past stock returns. Moreover, the analysis of

[125] For a detailed discussion of this event see Lo and Khandani (2007).

market capitalization is combined with an evaluation of the liquidity of target shares. This provides further information regarding the potential price impact of hedge fund engagements and whether they are able to acquire controlling stakes with a limited amount of capital. Third, the final subsection focuses on the ownership structure of target companies prior to the event date. This has significant implications on the magnitude of agency problems affecting the ability of hedge funds to impose their restructuring plans on target firms.

I. Financial Policies, Profitability and Diversification

This section analyzes the financial policies, profitability and operating diversification of target firms during the down-market in order to determine whether there are systematic differences in the business fundamentals of firms targeted during up- and down-market environments. In particular, it is plausible to expect that target firms during more adverse market conditions should not differ systematically from their control group. This may be due to the fact that only a few firms will truely suffer from agency problems of free cash flow during an adverse market environment, putting sufficient pressure on their cash flows. Moreover, holding financial slack also becomes valuable for many firms during market down-turns because it insures them against refinancing risks. Therefore, it may be optimal for most firms to adopt more conservative financial structures during recessionary periods. Thus, the main hypothesis is that there should only be limited evidence for excessive financial slacks in the form of high cash holdings, low payout ratios or small leverage ratios. At the same time, however, it is conceivable that hedge funds focus on firms with ineffective management during down-market periods. This is most likely to be reflected in the profitability ratios of target firms. In order to test these hypotheses Table 43 provides summary statistical information on key accounting ratios of target firms in the year prior to the engagement of the hedge funds based on data from the Worldscope database.

Table 43: Capital Structure, Payout Policy and Profitability

Variable	Level		Industry Benchmarking		Industry & Size Benchmarking	
	Mean	Median	Mean	Median	Mean	Median
Payout-Ratio	22.91	17.99	-8.49***	-9.08***	-4.33	0
	(n=168)		(n=168)		(n=148)	
Cash to Total Assets	14.42	8.66	6.54***	0.78***	1.93	1.02
	(n=133)		(n=133)		(n=102)	
Leverage Net Debt	7.47	11.32	-6.06**	-0.75**	-0.47	4.31
	(n=133)		(n=133)		(n=102)	
Leverage Gross Debt	23.33	17.41	1.89	-0.42	5.79***	3.50**
	(n=164)		(n=164)		(n=149)	
Return on Equity	11.28	13.99	-4.03**	-1.30**	24.38**	-0.27
	(n=167)		(n=167)		(n=146)	
Return on Assets	6.56	6.22	10.47	-19.99	4.18*	0.12
	(n=161)		(n=161)		(n=149)	
Operating CF to Total Assets	5.31	6.12	-1.56**	-0.83**	-0.81	-1.32*
	(n=163)		(n=163)		(n=148)	
Capex-to-Sales	12.91	3.17	9.35**	-0.25	0.74	-0.29
	(n=157)		(n=157)		(n=139)	

This table provides the means and medians of several accounting ratios at the end of the fiscal year prior to the event date calculated using data from the Worldscope database. In addition, it shows the means and medians of difference relative to the industry median which is estimated by taking all companies from the DAX, MDAX, SDAX and TecDAX in the same year and the means and medians of differences relative to a matched firm constructed using industry and size as matching criteria. */**/*** indicate statistical significance at the 10%/5%/1%-levels.

The first two columns in Table 43 provide sample means and medians for eight accounting ratios at the end of the fiscal year before the event date. Accounting ratios designed to capture the financial structure of target companies include the payout ratio, defined as the ratio of total dividends to total earnings, the ratio of cash and cash equivalents to total assets, gross leverage defined as total liabilities to total assets and net leverage given by the ratio of total liabilities minus total cash and cash equivalents to total assets. Moreover, the profitability of target companies relative to their peer group is assessed using three different ratios including the return on equity, the return on assets and the ratio of operating cash flow to total assets. Finally, the investment activity of target firms prior to the hedge fund active involvement is measured by the ratio of capital expenditures to total sales. In the next four columns these variables are compared to the median of two peer groups to assess whether target companies differ systematically from comparable companies. The third and fourth columns contain abnormal accounting ratios, i.e. differences to a peer group represented by the industry median for the respective year based on all constituents of the DAX, MDAX, SDAX and TecDAX from the same IBC industry class. This control group adjusts for industry-specific effects in accounting ratios. In the fifth and sixth column a matched pairs approach is implemented where a peer group is constructed by matching each sample firm to the firm from the same industry in the CDAX universe for which the absolute difference in terms of size (market capitalization) is minimized. This takes account into the fact that there are often systematic differences in accounting ratios between large and small firms. In order to test whether the observed differences in the means and medians are statistically significant, t-tests are used for means and Wilcoxon tests are applied for medians.

The empirical results for the payout-ratios and cash holdings of target firms indicate that target firms suffer from agency problems of free cash flow. In particular, the median payout ratio is 17.99% of total earnings which is significantly smaller than the median for the industry peer group. Moreover, the median level of cash holdings is 8.66% of total assets which is significantly higher than the median for the target firms' industry peer group. However, these findings appear to be related to the small size of target firms in that the differences are no longer statistically significant if the ratios are also adjusted for firm size. Thus, after adjusting for the magnitude of financing constraints and information asymmetries resulting from small firm size, there are no significant differences between target firms and their control group. In addition, target firms apparently do not generate large free cash flows as the level of operating cash flows is smaller than that for their peer group. The median operating cash flow is 6.12% of total assets which is significantly lower than their peer group at the 10% level when operating cash flows are also adjusted for firm size. In addition, the firm's gross leverage with a median of 17.41% also appears to be significantly higher if it is also adjusted for firm size. Profitability measures, such as return on equity and return on assets, provide no clear evidence. In fact, these measures even change signs depending on the methodology used for benchmarking. Therefore, it appears that the overall profitability of target firms does not differ systematically between target firms and their peer groups. Thus, target firms do not have a more robust business model which allows them to generate profits during adverse market conditions and enables them to increase leverage and make large payouts to shareholders during down-turns.

Overall, the empirical results for accounting ratios is similar to the results for the good times period as there is no clear evidence that target companies suffer from agency problems of free cash flows. For instance, while target firms during the up-market were characterized by higher cash holdings and lower payout ratios, there was also evidence that these firms made more aggressive use of leverage prior to the hedge fund engagement and were not generating large amounts of free cash flows. Moreover, higher cash holdings and lower dividend payments were also related to the small size of target firms during the up-market. Thus, in both up- and down-markets there is no convincing evidence for agency problems of free cash flows. In addition, lower leverage and higher cash holdings might be beneficial during bad times because financial slack helps to protect the company against temporary drops in earnings and cash flows. Therefore, it is unclear whether value can be increased by taking cash flows out of companies during distressed market conditions. However, there is also no convincing evidence for lower profitability of target companies which could be interpreted as evidence for ineffective management.

Another interesting characteristic of target firms is the diversification of their product market strategies which affects the stability of their business model to external shocks but also provides insights into the potential magnitude of agency problems of free cash flows. Therefore, it is interesting to investigate whether firms that are targeted during a down-market differ from firms targeted during up-markets in terms of their operating diversification strategies. This question can be addressed by using the break-down of segment sales obtained from firms' financial statements. Defining a diversified firm as a firm with more than one product segment in its financial statements (Höchle and Schmid, 2009), there was evidence that target firms during up-markets were mostly diversified firms. In general, a large body of empirical evidence indicates that diversification can be detrimental to shareholder value.[126] However, operating diversification might also be beneficial during a down-market in that it increases the robustness of the firm's business model which might help to protect shareholder value. Table 44 reports the percentage of firms with 1, 2, etc. business segments and the dispersion of segment sales based on the Herfindahl index of segment sales.

[126] See Ammann, Hoechle, and Schmid (2009) for a review of this literature.

Table 44: Operating Diversification of Target Firms

Number of Business Segments	Percentage	Mean Herfindahl Index Sales	Median Herfindahl Index Sales
1	18.93%	1	1
2	10.65%	0.6751	0.6349
3	20.71%	0.6734	0.6664
4	21.30%	0.4989	0.4547
5	14.79%	0.4557	0.4262
6 or more	13.62%	0.3570	0.3117
Total	100%	0.6230	0.5630

This table provides information regarding the number of product segments of target companies using data on product segment sales from the Worldscope database. In addition, it reports Herfindahl indices of product segment sales which are also derived from Worldscope data.

Based on the definition by Höchle and Schmid (2009) the fraction of diversified firms is high, as more than 80% of firms report segment sales for more than one business segment and the median Herfindahl index across all target firms in the year prior to the hedge fund engagement is 0.5630. This is significantly less than the threshold for fully concentrated sales which is equal to 1. Thus, one might argue that there is scope for activist hedge funds to force firms to refocus the business model of target firms. Nevertheless, the same caveats as in the previous chapter apply to this measurement of diversification based on accounting data in that firms have substantial discretionary freedom in defining business segments and often tend to change them (Villalonga, 2004a). This problem could be reduced only with access to internal data, which is however not available for a broad cross-section of stocks. Therefore, this result should only be taken as a preliminary indication that German target firms pursue operating diversification strategies.

II. Market Valuation of Target Companies

Based on the assumption that hedge funds actively invest in firms that are inefficiently managed, or that are subject to agency problems of free cash flows, the market valuations of target firms should suffer from valuation discounts relative to their peer group. These discounts have indeed been identified in different studies such as Brav,

Jiang, Partnoy, and Thomas (2008) and Klein and Zur (2009) that investigate hedge fund activism during the up-market period. For the same period there are also some studies for the German market which tend to find only mixed evidence for undervaluation of target firms. Nevertheless, when hedge funds act as corporate governance activist then target firms should also be undervalued relative to their peer group during the more challenging down-market environment. Therefore, the working hypothesis of this section is that hedge fund engagements should be concentrated in the most undervalued firms in the bad times subperiod between 2007 and 2008.

This hypothesis is investigated for the German capital market in more detail based on the sample of 169 German events taking place during the down-market period between 2007 and 2008. In the first step, the valuation level of target firms is investigated with the undervaluation index developed by Peyer and Vermaelen (2009). The distribution of this index is plotted in Figure 39 for the full sample. This compound index aggregates different aspects of undervaluation and is defined as the sum of three subindices including the market-to-book ratio, past returns and market capitalization which are each compared to a broad control group consisting of all CDAX firms.

The mean and median of the index are 7.08 and 7.0, respectively, for the sample of German firms targeted during the down-market. The shape of the distribution in Figure 39 is similar to the shape for the subsample of events taking place during the up-market environment. In particular, it is also highly skewed towards the right tail. This indicates that there is only a small number of firms that are truly undervalued. This finding can be interpreted as evidence that most hedge fund investments are not driven by the objective of restructuring undervalued firms and improving their corporate governance. Instead many hedge funds apparently pursue other objectives such as market timing or capturing price and earnings momentum.

Figure 39: Distribution of the Undervaluation Index

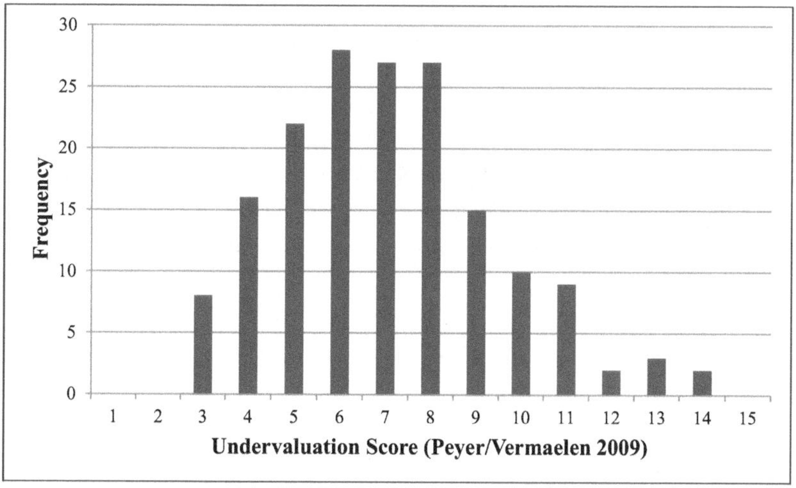

This figure plots the distribution of the undervaluation index proposed by Peyer and Vermaelen (2009). All data used is from the Worldscope database and Datastream and the whole CDAX is used as a control group in order to estimate the cut-off points.

However, the undervaluation index by Peyer and Vermaelen (2009) may be biased upwards when applied to a sample of German firms. This is because a control group of accurately valued firms is needed to assign scores to target firms in each individual category. In the broad and active U.S. capital market this is not a problem because there is a large number of firms which are actively traded, have a liquid market and should therefore be fairly valued. However, in Germany a large fraction of publicly traded firms are quite small and their stocks offer investors only limited liquidity which leads to infrequent trading biases and liquidity discounts. Therefore, the valuation of a large fraction of the firms used to construct the control group are biased downwards which in turn leads to a downward bias in the cut-off points used to assign scores on each of the three sub-criteria. As a result, the undervaluation index by Peyer and Vermaelen (2009) does not properly adjust for liquidity discounts and, thus, does not accurately reflect the valuation level of German firms. The magnitude of this problem may become even more substantial during adverse market conditions when there are often periods of flight to quality when the liquidity of the most risky asset classes is low. This might impose additional liquidity discounts on the valuation of the large fraction of very small firms. This effect might also be reinforced by increasing information asymmetries during down-market environments which also mostly concern small firms. Overall, it can be concluded that the undervaluation index by Peyer and Vermaelen (2009) assigns too high valuations to the sample of German target firms.

Due to this bias in the compound undervaluation index by Peyer and Vermaelen (2009) it is interesting to investigate the potential magnitude of this bias in its individual sub-indices. The distributions of these sub-indices are depicted in Figure 40 for the sample of 169 German events during the down-market.

Figure 40: Distribution of the Subindices of the Undervaluation Index

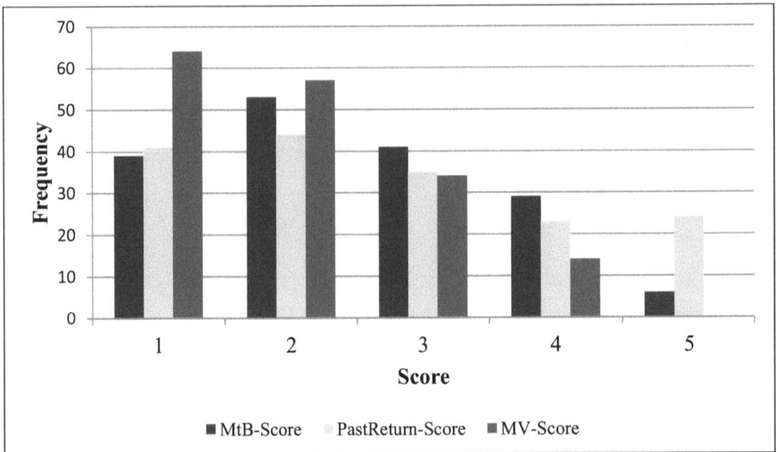

This figure plots the distribution of the subindices of the undervaluation index proposed by Peyer and Vermaelen (2009). All data used is from the Worldscope database and Datastream and the whole CDAX is used as a control group in order to estimate the cut-off points.

According to the distribution of the subindices in Figure 40 a substantial fraction of target firms exhibit relatively low scores in the market capitalization category which means that their market capitalizations are in the upper percentiles of the CDAX universe. This is consistent with the fact that hedge funds need a sufficient amount of liquidity in order to be able to acquire a sufficiently large position in target firms. Similarly, most target firms appear to have above average market-to-book ratios and past returns. Thus, the results indicate that each of the three subindices points towards an overvaluation of target firms.

The bias seems to be the result of problems when defining an adequate control group of firms that are fairly valued in the German stock market. Therefore, it is interesting to investigate in more detail the behavior of each of the three variables used to construct the subcomponents of the undervaluation index by Peyer and Vermaelen (2009).

Table 45: Market Capitalization and Liquidity

Variable	Level		Difference to median for all index firms		Difference to median for all CDAX firms	
	Mean	Median	Mean	Median	Mean	Median
Market Cap	2775.62	407.34	-225.68	-862.86***	2626.15***	314.01***
Liquidity	0.0116	0.0075	0.0049***	0.0015***	0.0004	-0.0028

This table provides information summarizing the market capitalization of target firms 60 trading days prior to the event date as well as the average liquidity measure by Amihud (2002) in the interval (-120,-80). The Amihud measure can only be calculated for 118 events because for the remaining events there is at least one day with no trading activity in the interval. These variables are also compared to the median for all CDAX firms from the same industry and to the median of all index members in the DAX, MDAX, SDAX, or TecDAX from the same industry. */**/*** indicate statistical significance at the 10%/5%/1%-levels.

The first row in Table 45 focuses on the market capitalization of target firms and indicates that the median market capitalization of target firms is 407 m €. This lies between the market capitalization of the median firm in the entire CDAX universe and the market capitalization of the median firm included in the DAX, MDAX, SDAX or TecDAX. In particular, similar to the results for the good times sample, there is empirical evidence that the median difference between the market capitalization of target firms and the median market capitalization of all CDAX firms is significantly positive. Thus, target firms apparently cannot be characterized as small or micro cap stocks. In addition, target stocks are also significantly smaller than the median firm included in the major German stock indices. Therefore, due to their limited size, target firms appear to be subject to higher information asymmetries from the perspective of outside capital markets. This is in line with evidence for the events occurring during good times. This leads to additional valuation discounts which are necessary to protect investors against the adverse selection risks inherent in these stocks. Moreover, this implies that control by outside capital markets might be less effective prior to the active involvement of the hedge fund. Furthermore, this allows hedge funds to build up positions in target firms by committing limited capital resources (Brav, Jiang,

Partnoy, and Thomas, 2008). Regarding the undervaluation index by Peyer and Vermaelen (2009) these results imply that the low score of target firms in terms of market capitalizations does not truly reflect an undervaluation of target firms. Similar to the good times subsample, this is due to problems in constructing a broad control group for the German stock market which contains only a limited number of publicly traded firms.

The market capitalization of a firm is closely related to the liquidity of its shares which can also lead to additional valuation discounts. Therefore, the second row in Table 45 compares the liquidity of target firms to the median liquidity of all firms from the CDAX universe and the median liquidity of all firms listed in the DAX, MDAX, SDAX and TecDAX. Liquidity is measured using the approach proposed by Amihud (2002) which approximates the price impact of a one-unit increase in dollar trading volume so that a higher price impact indicates lower liquidity. The median of this measure is 0.0075 for target firms which is smaller than the median of all CDAX firms. However, the difference is not statistically significant at any conventional level. Thus, target companies do not really offer hedge funds a fairly liquid market which would allow them to trade in and out of the stocks of target companies. This is in sharp contrast to the result for the good times period where hedge fund targets were characterized by fairly liquid stocks. As a result, the short run-up in stock returns followed by a quick reversal in stock prices identified in the next section might not reflect the arrival of new information, but could instead be the result of short-term buying pressure. The absolute level of the mean and median of liquidity appear to be similar for the subsamples of events during the good and bad times period. Thus, the absolute level of liquidity of target stocks is approximately similar in both time periods.

The distribution of the subindex corresponding to the market-to-book ratio of target firms in Figure 40 also indicates that the majority of target firms is overvalued. Again, this might reflect the fact that the construction of this subindex does not take some problems into account. In particular, market-to-book ratios are systematically related to the liquidity of a firm's stock and also vary systematically across different industries. This can lead to biases in valuation scores because the procedure to construct cut-off points, according to Peyer and Vermaelen (2009), does not take these patterns into account. In order to provide insights into the implications of these two problems Table 46 reports information regarding the time-series patterns of market-to-book ratios before the event date and also compares them to two industry peer groups.

The first of these groups is based on all firms included in the CDAX universe and the second is based on the subset of stocks that belong to the major indices of the Deutsche Börse (DAX, MDAX, SDAX, and TecDAX) and are therefore traded in a liquid market.

Table 46: Valuation of Target Companies

Panel A – Market to Book relative to industry median of all CDAX constituents							
t	0	-40	-80	-120	-160	-200	-240
Mean	0.3487	0.1913	0.2171	0.1745	0.4547***	0.4737***	0.4883***
Med.	0.4075***	0.3900***	0.2575***	0.2750***	0.3750***	0.3350***	0.3275***
Panel B – Market to Book relative industry median of index members							
t	0	-40	-80	-120	-160	-200	-240
Mean	-0.5089	-0.6423*	-0.6654**	-0.6643*	-0.3575**	-0.2919*	-0.2480
Med.	-0.2375*	-0.2475**	-0.3350***	-0.3675***	-0.2950***	-0.2850***	-0.2600**

In Panel A this table reports the difference in market-to-book ratios between target firms and the industry median derived from all stocks traded in a liquid market, i.e. those belonging to the DAX, MDAX, SDAX and TecDAX as a control group. The significance of these effects is tested with simple t-statistics and Wilcoxon tests, respectively. Panel B repeats this analysis using the whole CDAX universe to estimate industry medians. */**/*** indicate statistical significance at the 10%/5%/1%-levels.

The signs of the median of the adjusted market to book ratios generally exhibit the same behavior as in the good times subsample. In particular, the classification of target firms as under- or overvalued depends on the peer group used to benchmark market-to-book ratios. Based on an industry peer group drawn from all firms included in the CDAX there is evidence for an overvaluation of target firms. Thus, in line with the Peyer-Vermaelen index, target firms should not be classified as value firms. However, based on the industry median of all liquid stocks which are constituents of the major indices the median of the adjusted market-to-book ratios is significantly negative. Again, this finding can be reconciled considering differences in the liquidity of the two control groups. As a result, classifications according to the subindex "market-to-book" from the undervaluation index by Peyer and Vermaelen (2009) are biased upwards. Consequently, in order to determine whether firms are truly under- or overvalued it would be necessary to benchmark firms' market-to-book ratios to an industry- and liquidity-adjusted control group. Moreover, similar to the results for the good times subsample there is evidence for a run-up effect in adjusted market to book ratios which exhibits a similar pattern for both peer groups. Thus, the application of the Peyer-

Vermaelen undervaluation index should be adjusted to take these run-up effects into account. However, this is not possible to do in an objective manner because the run-up effects differ in their length and timing across individual event firms.

Finally, Table 47 focuses on the pre-event stock returns from target firms which are used to define the last subindex of the undervaluation index by Peyer and Vermaelen (2009). This subindex also indicates that there is a large fraction of target companies with above average past returns, which is also inconsistent with the hypothesis that firms targeted by hedge funds should be undervalued. Therefore, Table 47 contains buy-and-hold abnormal returns for different pre-event time periods where the respective market index to which the firm belonged on the event date is used as a market benchmark. Statistical significance is tested with skewness-adjusted t-statistics for means and Wilcoxon-tests for medians.

In the case of the good times subsample this analysis indicated that the median BHAR was negative up to 6 months prior to the event date when the dispersion of stock returns also began to increase. The same analysis for the bad times subsample reveals that this reversal in prices and the associated run-up begin at a later stage. In particular, the mean of buy-and-hold abnormal returns begins to increase 80 trading days prior to the event date, whereas median buy-and-hold abnormal returns only begin to increase 40 trading days prior to the event date. Moreover, pre-event buy-and-hold abnormal returns are also negative, but less so than for the good times subsample and the largest share of the undervaluation is generated in the interval (-480, -40). Thus, buy-and-hold abnormal returns indicate some weak evidence for the undervaluation of target firms. However, during a down-market environment buy-and-hold abnormal returns are likely to be biased downwards indicating undervaluation because there is a large fraction of target firms that should have high liquidity risk exposures. This additional risk exposure is not captured by a simple one-factor model leading to an overstatement of expected returns during time periods when the realized liquidity risk premia are likely to be negative.

Table 47: BHAR before the Event Date

Period	Mean	Median
(-480, 0)	0.1329**	-0.0135
(-480, -40)	0.0819*	-0.0314
(-480, -80)	0.0662	-0.0162
(-480, -120)	0.0660*	-0.0014
(-480, -160)	-0.0638*	-0.0072
(-480, -200)	0.0670**	-0.0155
(-480, -240)	0.0658**	0.0047

This table reports the means and medians of buy-and-hold abnormal returns which are estimated using the respective market index to which the target company belonged on the event date. Mean valuation effects are tested for statistical significance using bootstrapped skewness-adjusted t-statistics and Wilcoxon tests are used to test medians. */**/*** indicate statistical significance at the 10%/5%/1%-levels.

Overall, it is reasonable to conclude that there is no convincing evidence that firms are undervalued before the active involvement of hedge funds during the down-market environment of 2007/2008. Above all, this is due to the difficulties inherent in establishing the "fair" valuation level for the shares of each firm.

III. Ownership Structure of Target Firms

The potential magnitude of agency problems and the entrenchment of managers is closely related to the ownership structure of target firms which determines whether activist hedge funds can control target firms. In particular, results for the good times subsample reveal that most target firms appear to have a relatively dispersed ownership structure as the fraction of closely held shares is smaller than for the average German firm, and as managers and other firms do not hold significant stakes in most target firms. In principle, these results should also apply during down-markets since the ownership structure of a firm is a rather sticky variable. In order to investigate whether this reasoning is correct this section also provides information on the concentration, as well as on the composition, of the ownership structure of target firms at the end of the fiscal year prior to the event date.

Panel A of Table 48 summarizes the concentration of shareholdings in the year prior to the event date based on the attendance rates at the annual shareholder assembly of individual companies provided by the Schutzgemeinschaft der Kleinaktionäre (www.sdk.de) and based on the fraction of closely held shares according to the corresponding data items in the Worldscope database. Both of these variables are adjusted for the median across all firms for which information is available in the same year in order to adjust for time trends in the behavior of ownership structures of German firms (Weber, 2008).

The ownership structures of firms targeted during the down-market period are indeed similar to the ownership structures of firms targeted during the good times period. In particular, the median of the fraction of closely held shares is significantly smaller than the median for all German firms included in the CDAX. Moreover, the median attendance rate at the annual shareholder meeting is also smaller than for the control group. Thus, there are apparently no significant blockholders in most target firms, which is supported by the results in panel B, which summarizes the distribution of the data items measuring management/employee and corporate ownership, respectively. In particular, the percentiles of both of these distributions imply that the majority of target firms do not have controlling shareholders. Thus, activist hedge funds might be able to exert significant influence on corporate control.

The ownership structure of target companies determines whether hedge funds are in a position to implement their restructuring plans. In particular, large shareholders often have a vested interest in maintaining the status quo. Therefore, Panel B provides information on the identity of the largest shareholder and the size of his stake at the end of the quarter before the event date. This is based on the ownership module of the Thomson One database. The results indicate that there is a relatively large percentage of large non-financial shareholders present in the ownership structure of most target firms. In fact, the dominant shareholder is an individual investor in 56 companies, a corporation (37), a government entity (4) or a bank (1). These dominant shareholders might limit the ability of hedge funds to implement their restructuring plans. In fact, hedge funds should only be able to easily implement their restructuring plans in those 70 cases in which a financial investor is the dominant shareholder. Panel B also contains information on the size of the hedge fund holdings. Overall, these figures appear to be significantly smaller than the positions held by the dominant shareholder. In fact, the median of the hedge fund stake is only marginally higher than the initial reporting threshold of 3%. Therefore, hedge funds have to be confident that they would obtain the support of other outside shareholders.

Table 48: Ownership Structure of Target Firms

Panel A – Concentration of Ownership

Statistic	Sample Firms		Difference in	
	Mean	Median	Mean	Median
HV-Presence (n=71)	52.09%	50.62%	-6.64%***	-7.51%***
Closely held Shares (n=111)	32.52%	30.46%	4.54%***	0%

Panel B – Composition of Ownership

Largest Investor	Nobs	Size of Investor Stake		Size of HF Stake	
		Mean	Median	Mean	Median
Bank	1	0.1097	0.1097	0.0301	0.0301
Corporation	37	0.3177	0.2844	0.0652	0.0341
Financial	70	0.1034	0.0913	0.0527	0.0343
Government	4	0.2565	0.2789	0.0302	0.0302
Individual	56	0.2421	0.2279	0.0556	0.0324
Total	168	0.2005	0.1308	0.0560	0.0334

This table presents information on the ownership structure of target firms. Panel A summarizes data on the ownership concentration of target firms using the mean and median of the attendance rates at annual shareholder meetings from the Schutzgemeinschaft der Kleinaktionäre and of closely held shares from the Worldscope database. These are compared to the median for all other firms in the same year. Panel B provides information on the classification of large blockholders based on the Thomson One database. */**/*** indicate statistical significance at the 10%/5%/1%-levels.

Nevertheless, the same caveats as those in the same analysis in the previous chapter reduce the significance of these results. In particular, the data items obtained from Datastream cannot take into account smaller blockholders or informal coalitions of shareholders because they are based on regulatory filings and only capture stakes larger than 3% and 5% of voting rights for events taking place in January 2007. Moreover, these data items are not updated on a daily basis so there is the possibility that significant shifts in the ownership structure might occur between the end of the last year when this information was updated in the database and the event date. Finally, the analysis of ownership data does not capture all measures which can be used by the old governing coalition to entrench its controlling position. For instance, there is some evidence that banks still exert substantial influence on firms and often hold seats on the boards of German firms (Dittmann, Maug, and Schneider, 2010).

C. Valuation Effects in the Down-Market

There is a large body of empirical evidence for the U.S. and German capital markets that the engagements of hedge funds lead to substantial increases in shareholder value when conditions in financial markets are favorable. In particular, there are positive announcement effects which are generally followed by an upward drift in share prices as uncertainty regarding the implications of the hedge funds' active involvement gradually declines over time. This can be explained by the fact that favorable market conditions enable firms to implement most of the demands imposed on them by activist hedge funds. This includes sufficient liquidity in asset markets to sell off non-core assets and liquid capital markets to raise additional leverage to finance large-scale refinancing and cash distributions to shareholders in the form of higher dividends and share repurchases. In addition, during such time periods investors might become highly optimistic, and overrate the ability of hedge funds to create firm value.

During periods of market distress, however, there is no need for hedge fund activism since the economic recession already puts managers under pressure to improve the efficiency of their firms' operations. Therefore, it is interesting to investigate whether investments by hedge funds also trigger similar increases in share prices during more adverse financial market environments when liquidity is lower and investors are more pessimistic. Consequently, this section investigates valuation effects for the sample of 169 events taking place in the time period from 2007 to 2008 which can generally be characterized as a down-market environment.

I. Valuation Effects in the Down-Market – Full Period

This section provides empirical evidence on short- and intermediate-term valuation effects for all 169 events taking place between January 1st, 2007 and December 31st, 2008 based on the standard event study approach. Following Schwert (1996) abnormal returns are calculated based on a market model with the intercept constrained to zero and that is estimated in the window from 140 to 81 trading days prior to the event date. This takes into account potential upward bias in estimates of expected returns resulting from a run-up in share prices for some target firms during the estimation period. The empirical results for all 169 events during the window (-80,+140) are contained in Figure 41, which also includes the cumulative abnormal returns for the "good times"-sample (n=235) and the full sample (n=404).

Figure 41: Cumulative Abnormal Returns

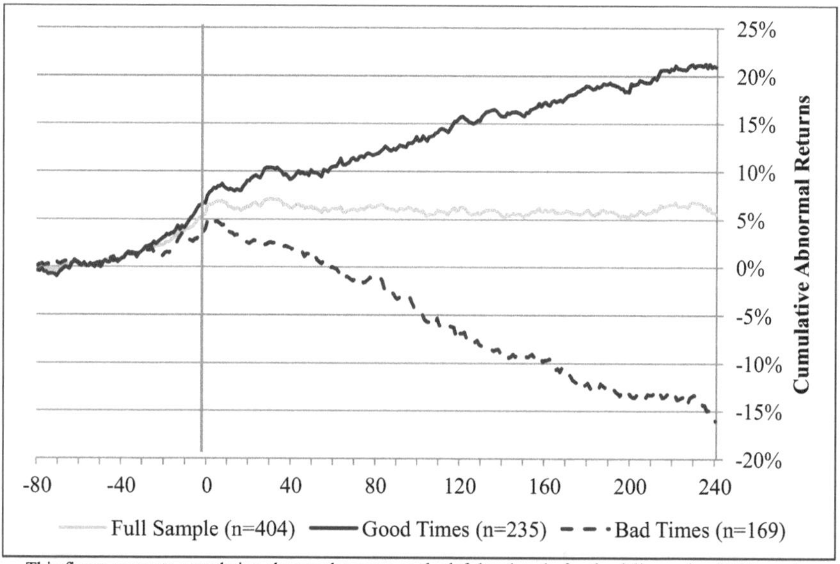

This figure presents cumulative abnormal returns on the left hand scale for the full sample of 404 events differentiated into a good times and a bad times subsample. The approach by Schwert (1996) with the estimation period (-140,-81) and the CDAX as a market proxy is used in order to estimate normal performance.

The empirical evidence in Figure 41 provides clear evidence that firms targeted by hedge funds during the down-market environment significantly underperform as CARs are highly negative and amount to -15% for the entire sample period (-80,240). In particular, according to the results in Table 49, CARs are only statistically significant when the short announcement period (-5, 5) is used. These positive valuation effects in short windows around the event date are quickly reversed after the event date when CARs become negative. In particular, CARs are -1.88% for the period (+3, +30) decling to -5.79% for the period (+3, +80). These effects are statistically significant at the 5%- and even 1%-levels. These findings support the hypothesis that hedge funds have a limited ability to create firm value during periods of market distress when there is limited liquidity, high volatility and investor sentiment is rather pessimistic. Thus, the success of hedge fund investments is apparently closely related to capital market conditions.

Similar to the empirical results for the good times period, however, there is also a pronounced run-up effect before the event date. In particular, according to the results in Figure 41, this run-up begins approximately 40 trading days before the event date. However, the information in Table 49 indicates that CARs during the pre-event windos are not statistically significant. This weak run-up effect might also be driven by the same factors that apparently generated similar patterns in share prices during the up-market environment. This includes the lower liquidity of German target companies and inefficiencies in the German disclosure system for large positions. In contrast to the evidence from the good-times-period, however, the run-up effect has no persistent impact on share prices during the down-market. This supports the explanation that the run-up is driven by the limited liquidity of target shares in combination with buying pressure generated by the hedge fund trading activity.

Overall, the behavior of cumulative abnormal returns suggests that capital markets do not expect hedge fund activity to create firm value during periods of distress in financial markets. However, there are some very short intervals around the news announcement during which hedge fund targets generate significantly positive abnormal returns according to the results in Table 49. However, the statistical significance of these announcement effects might also be due to statistical biases created by event-induced variance. Therefore, Table 50 presents estimates of daily abnormal returns around the event date with t-statistics corrected for event-induced variance based on the method developed by Böhmer, Masumeci, and Poulsen (1991).

Table 49: Cumulative Abnormal Returns

Interval	CAR	Interval	CAR
Panel A: Intervals around the event		**Panel B: Intervals before and after the event**	
		(-80,-3)	3.14%
(-80,+80)	-1.30%	(-45,-3)	2.22%
(-45,+45)	0.61%	(-30,-3)	1.60%
(-15,+15)	1.11%	(-15,-3)	0.88%
(-5,+5)	**1.81%****	(+3,+15)	-1.10%
(-3,+3)	**1.03%***	(+3,+30)	**-1.88%****
(-1,+1)	**1.03%****	(+3,+45)	**-2.94%****
		(+3,+80)	**-5.79%*****
		(+3,+240)	**-10.83%*****

This table reports the mean cumulative abnormal returns for the entire sample of n=231 event firms during different time windows. The time intervals describe the number of trading days around the event date. */**/*** implies that the mean cumulative abnormal return is significantly different from zero at the 10%, 5%, 1% level, respectively. For all subperiods starting after t = -15, the t-statistics are calculated using the volatility of abnormal returns during the time interval (-60,-15).

According to the empirical results in Table 50 the finding of significantly positive announcement period returns in the interval (-1,1) is robust and does not change when t-statistics are adjusted for event-induced variance. Moreover, the results in Table 50 also indicate that average abnormal returns are positive and quite small on most other individual trading days in the 10-day interval around the event date. However, for some trading days these effects are not statistically significant. This suggests that for individual trading days the cross-sectional variance in abnormal return estimates is fairly large relative to the mean abnormal return. Hence, the valuation effects can only become statistically significant when abnormal returns are aggregated across individual trading days which in turn leads to the slow increase in share prices prior to the event date.

Additional interesting insights can be gained by comparing the patterns in cumulative abnormal returns to the behavior of abnormal trading volume which can be estimated based on the approach of Brav and Gompers (2003). These results are reported in Figure 42 which reveals that trading volume starts to pick up long before the official event date. However, the increase in trading activity is substantially smaller than during the good-times periods. Interestingly, trading volume increases sharply during the later parts of the sample period, when the event-time periods for most events substantially overlap with the time period for when the crisis had reached its second stage and had begun to affect the stock market.

Table 50: Cumulative Abnormal Returns – Time Periods around the Event Date

Period	Mean AR (%)	Median AR (%)	Convent. t-stat	Event-ind. t-stat	CAR
-5	0.0003	-0.0004	0.1718	0.2678	0.0003
-4	0.0041	-0.0028	1.4539	1.1174	0.0044
-3	-0.0023	-0.0013	-0.8546	-1.0021	0.0021
-2	0.0055	0.0012	2.0721**	1.7140*	0.0076
-1	0.0031	0.0014	1.5224	1.8830*	0.0107
0	0.0083	0.0033	3.0358***	2.3783**	0.0190
1	-0.0012	-0.0039	-0.5521	-0.1726	0.0178
2	-0.0024	-0.0010	-1.2125	-1.1616	0.0154
3	-0.0008	-0.0014	-0.3792	-1.0492	0.0146
4	0.0035	0.0008	1.1990	1.1305	0.0181
5	-0.0002	0.0000	-0.1232	0.1231	0.0179

This table reports cumulative abnormal returns calculated using the approach by Schwert (1996) where the estimation period is (-140,-81) and the CDAX is the market proxy. In addition to conventional t-statistics, it also shows t-statistics that are adjusted for event-induced variance based on the approach proposed by Böhmer, Masumeci, and Poulsen (1991). Medians are tested for significance using the Wilcoxon test. */**/*** indicate statistical significance at the 10%/5%/1%-levels.

To sum up, positive valuation effects are rather short-lived during the down-market. Moreover, the humped-shape behavior of cumulative abnormal returns can only be reconciled with short-term buying pressure, driving the share prices up during the run-up period before the event date which is also consistent with the low liquidity of the targets' stocks. This was already identified in the previous section which focused on the characteristics of target firms. Thus, the market expects that hedge fund activity will not create, but will rather destroy shareholder value. This raises some intriguing questions. In particular, this creates doubts as to whether hedge funds can generate any positive returns for themselves based on these investments because they cannot exploit private benefits by holding small blocks in target companies. Therefore, it does not seem plausible to assume that hedge funds systematically expropriate other shareholders and reduce shareholder value. Rather, it seems more realistic to assume that hedge fund targets are also exposed to additional risk factors besides the market risk factor. For instance, due to their small average size, their negative abnormal returns might reflect exposures to other risk factors such as liquidity risk or a financial distress factor which should have realized negative returns during the down-market. A final explanation is that some problems at the level of the hedge funds might have translated to the firm's stock price if other market participants were assuming that hedge funds might have to make fire sales.

Figure 42: CAR and Trading Volume

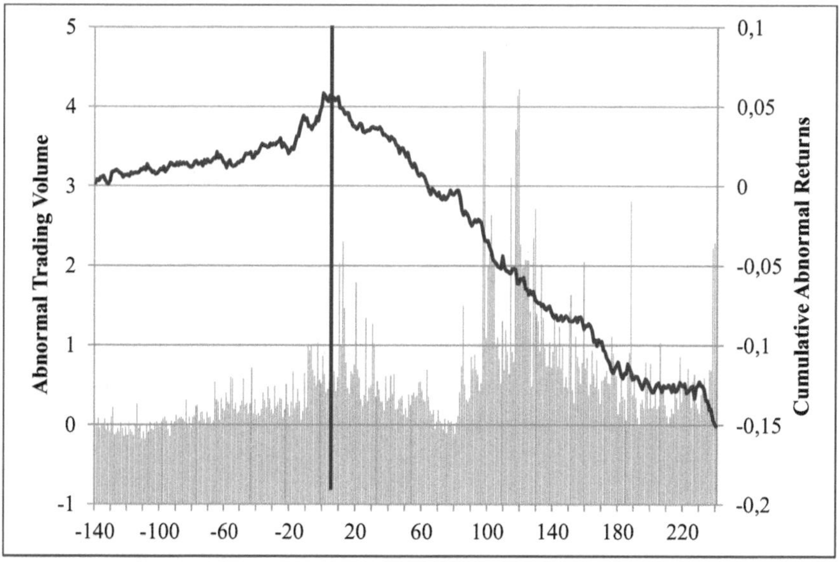

This figure presents cumulative abnormal returns based on a market model estimated with CDAX-benchmark during the estimation window (-140,-81) following the approach by Schwert (1996). Moreover, on the left-hand side, it also plots the level of abnormal trading volume which is estimated based on the approach by Brav and Gompers (2003).

II. Valuation Effects at different Stages of the Subprime Crisis

There were substantial differences in the severity of the recent financial crisis at different points in time between 2007 and 2009. Therefore, it seems plausible to assume that the magnitude of valuation effects differs between events taking place at different stages of the crisis. In particular, for events occurring during the first-stage of the crisis up to the end of June 2007, the run-up in stock returns should be similar to the pre-event patterns in stock prices during the preceding up-market. This occurs because up to this point in time the pricing of stocks was apparently not significantly affected by the emerging financial crisis and the DAX performance index still continued to deliver positive returns throughout this period. However, the post-event performance of nearly all events between 2007 and 2008 should be characterized by an underperformance. This occured because hedge funds' holding periods partially overlapped with the time period when the crisis spread to the stock markets and affected other asset classes.

In order to investigate these hypotheses, Figure 43 reports CARs differentiated by the stage of the financial crisis when the event took place. According to the empirical evidence provided in Figure 43, the magnitude of run-up effects differs substantially depending on the stage of the crisis. In particular, there are no pronounced run-up effects in the case of those events which took place during the second stage of the crisis, i.e. when the crisis had already spread to the stock market. Indeed, there is a downward trend in CARs which is only briefly interrupted by a very short period of small increases in share prices around the event date. There is only evidence for run-up effects for those events occurring during the first-stage of the financial crisis. However, in the case of both subsamples the negative post-event drift starts immediately after the event. This is interesting as a large number of events occured in the early parts of 2007 which is several months before the second stage of the financial crisis began and the crisis spread to the stock market.

Figure 43: CARs at different Stages of the Financial Crisis

This figure presents cumulative abnormal returns with market model with a CDAX benchmark using the approach by Schwert (1996). The estimation period is set equal to the interval (-140,-81).

III. Subsamples based on event characteristics

Hedge funds accumulate small stakes in target companies and try to rally for the support of other shareholders in order to push managers into significant restructurings of their firms' strategies or financial policies. In general, this approach should be applicable independent of the market environment. In fact, it might be easier during periods of market distress because many other investors are also under pressure to generate returns during these market environments and should be highly likely to support value-enhancing measures. Therefore, in the following subsections cumulative abnormal returns are differentiated according to a variety of criteria which effectively capture the ability of hedge funds to successfully implement their strategy. This includes the acquisition method, target firm valuation prior to the event, firm size and the hostility of the hedge fund towards incumbent management. Abnormal returns are investigated for the short event windows (-3, 3) and (-40, 40) and for the longer windows (-40, 120) and (-40, 240). In particular, the event window (-40, 40) is chosen instead of the shorter window (-20, 20) which is used by Brav, Jiang, Partnoy and

Thomas (2008) because run-up effects begin significantly earlier in Germany compared to the U.S. capital market.

1. Acquisition Method

Hedge funds use different approaches to acquire stakes in target companies. These approaches differ in the degree to which they commit hedge funds to their investments and to continuously work to implement their proposed restructuring plans. Therefore, these methods might affect the success of hedge fund investments which in turn should be related to valuation effects. This reasoning is supported by empirical evidence for the good times sample. In particular, valuation effects are strongest when hedge funds participate in "PIPE"-financings. This can be explained by strong signaling effects as hedge funds, who are sophisticated investors, commit a relatively large amount of capital. Moreover, there is also a lock-in effect as disclosure requirements prevent hedge funds from quietly selling off their positions. However, during the bad times period, valuation effects might actually become lower for PIPE-transactions. This occurs because stronger lock-in effects also increase the risk that hedge funds might have to prematurely unwind their leveraged positions. In contrast, valuation effects should become stronger for "interventions" because the investor remains below the publication thresholds defined in §§ 21/22 WpHG and can therefore exit from his position without being noticed. As a result, the major hypothesis investigated in this subsection is that valuation effects should be highest for interventions, followed by acquisitions and PIPE-investments.

Table 51 presents the empirical results and differentiates cumulative abnormal returns for the subsamples of PIPE-investments, interventions and acquisitions for both the good and bad times market environments.

In contrast to the up-market period, investments by hedge funds in PIPE's are no longer characterized by the strongest short-term announcements during the down-market. In particular, cumulative abnormal returns for the window (-3,3) are negative and insignificant whereas the subsample "intervention" generates a weakly significant announcement period effect of 4.79% during the down-market. Moreover, the announcement period return of the subsample "acquisitions" is also weakly significant and equal to 1.05% during the down-market. However, the differences between the good times and bad times subsamples for most categories are not significant for this very short window. These differences in returns between the three subsamples become even more pronounced over longer time periods. More precisely, after 240 trading days, the CARs of "acquisitions" are -17.05%, the CARs of "interventions" are -11.34%, and the CARs of "PIPEs" are -69.80%. This is consistent with a strong lock-in effect pushing down share prices in the subsample of "PIPEs", because of the risk of early fire sales. Moreover, the differences between the good times and bad times subsamples become strongly significant for longer holding periods. An exemption is the subsample "interventions" in which CARs are not statistically different from other subsamples for all holding periods. This might be related to the small number of events belonging to this category. However, this is also consistent with the idea that the lock-in effect is weakest for the events belonging to this subsample.

Table 51: Cumulative Abnormal Returns differentiated by Acquisition Method

Sample	Stat.	CAR (-3,3)		CAR (-40,-40)		CAR (-40,+120)		CAR (-40,+240)	
		Good	Bad	Good	Bad	Good	Bad	Good	Bad
Stake	Mean	0.0157	0.0105	0.0703	0.0134	0.1315	-0.0768	0.1911	-0.1705
		(2.626)	(1.858)	(3.855)	(0.599)	(4.920)	(-2.407)	(5.204)	(-3.687)
		-0.631		-1.9916		-5.0429		-6.2048	
	Med.	0.0097	0.0042	0.0726	0.0009	0.1192	-0.0386	0.1179	-0.1348
		(2.300)	(1.156)	(4.602)	(0.636)	(5.508)	(-2.273)	(5.240)	(-3.773)
		-0.503		-2.926		-5.611		-6.364	
Inter.	Mean	0.0181	0.0479	0.0773	0.0063	0.1633	-0.0549	0.2465	-0.1134
		(1.705)	(1.649)	(1.563)	(0.058)	(1.6512)	(-0.339)	(2.437)	(-0.678)
		1.0318		-0.5373		-0.8393		-1.3533	
	Med.	0.0063	0.0225	0.1108	-0.0856	0.1614	-0.1659	0.2272	-0.0634
		(1.127)	(1.604)	(1.570)	(0.000)	(2.173)	(0.000)	(2.415)	(-0.535)
		1.292		-0.718		-1.101		-1.579	
PIPE	Mean	0.0594	-0.0361	0.3209	-0.2638	0.4057	-0.2300	0.3180	-0.5830
		(2.137)	(-0.809)	(2.778)	(-2.075)	(2.921)	(-0.904)	(1.647)	(-3.863)
		-1.4892		-2.2401		-1.9597		-2.0849	
	Med.	0.0577	-0.0212	0.2855	-0.2423	0.2006	-0.4275	0.0582	-0.6980
		(1.978)	(-0.535)	(2.292)	(-1.604)	(2.731)	(-1.069)	(1.413)	(-1.604)
		-1.513		-2.017		-1.639		-2.269	

This table reports cumulative abnormal returns differentiated by the acquisition method used by the hedge fund. CARs are calculated using the approach by Schwert (1996) where the estimation period is (-140,-81) and the CDAX is the market proxy. Means are tested for difference using a simple t-test and differences in medians are tested using Mann-Whitney tests. */**/*** indicate statistical significance at the 10%/5%/1%-levels.

Overall, it appears that the implicit lock-in effect created by disclosure regulations can explain a substantial fraction of the negative cumulative abnormal returns as PIPE investments and acquisitions generate the lowest returns during distressed market environments. However, this finding might also be related to other factors. For instance, characteristics of companies receiving PIPE-financing might differ between different market environments as hedge funds provide capital to growth firms during favorable market environments whereas during bad times PIPEs by hedge funds target distressed firms. Nevertheless, there are only a small number of events in these categories which further restricts the empirical analysis of this interesting question.

2. Characteristics of Target Firms - Size and Technology

The magnitude of valuation effects should also depend on the size of the target firms and the importance of technology for their business model, both of which have significant implications for the success of the approach pursued by activist hedge funds. This was confirmed by evidence from the sample of events taking place during the up-market lasting until the end of 2006. In particular, short-term valuation effects were highest for small cap stocks due to strong signaling effects. Also, cumulative abnormal returns for technology firms were negative but insignificant over longer holding periods. This reflects the difficulty for hedge funds to create value in industries that rely on intellectual property (Brav, Jiang, Partnoy, and Thomas, 2008). However, during bad times share price reactions might be different for several reasons. In particular, small firms and firms from the technology sector might have less robust business models and face stronger financing constraints. Consequently, there is less scope for restructuring during down-markets of these firms as CARs are expected to be more negative for small firms and for technology firms during the down-market.

In order to investigate this hypothesis in more detail, Table 52 presents cumulative abnormal returns separately for the group of small firms defined as all targets belonging to the CDAX or SDAX on the event date, the group of big firms defined as the targets belonging to the DAX and MDAX on the event date and the group of technology firms defined as the targets belonging to the TecDAX on the event date.

Table 52: Cumulative Abnormal Returns differentiated by Size & Technology

Sample	Stat.	CAR (-3,3)		CAR (-40,-40)		CAR (-40,+120)		CAR (-40,+240)	
		Good	Bad	Good	Bad	Good	Bad	Good	Bad
Big	Mean	0.0044	0.0147	0.0489	-0.0296	0.0926	-0.0787	0.1550	-0.1075
		(0.644)	(1.368)	(2.115)	(-0.975)	(2.815)	(-2.093)	(4.232)	(-1.963)
		0.840		-2.018		-3.220		-4.076	
	Med.	0.0090	0.0083	0.0428	-0.0253	0.1104	-0.0535	0.1248	-0.0391
		(1.058)	(1.069)	(2.604)	(-0.890)	(3.679)	(-1.772)	(4.586)	(-1.481)
		0.296		-2.299		-3.862		-4.100	
Small	Mean	0.0299	0.0084	0.1354	0.0334	0.2222	-0.0778	0.2762	-0.2107
		(3.352)	(1.194)	(4.828)	(1.051)	(5.327)	(-1.676)	(4.677)	(-3.201)
		-1.861		-2.418		-4.821		-5.522	
	Med.	0.0097	0.0031	0.1422	0.0064	0.1921	-0.0247	0.1820	-0.1589
		(2.869)	(1.095)	(4.988)	(1.328)	(5.436)	(-1.450)	(4.381)	(-3.400)
		-1.427		-3.048		-5.098		-5.554	
Techn	Mean	0.0208	0.0085	-0.0469	-0.0447	-0.0162	-0.0918	-0.0273	-0.1756
		(1.467)	(0.607)	(-0.985)	(-2.103)	(-0.404)	(-1.826)	(-0.358)	(-1.560)
		-0.604		0.0347		-1.188		-1.131	
	Med.	0.0240	0.0067	-0.0334	-0.0246	-0.0846	-0.0804	-0.1393	-0.2706
		(1.491)	(1.153)	(-0.734)	(-1.852)	(-0.544)	(-1.572)	(-0.450)	(-1.293)
		-0.523		-0.356		-0.732		-1.067	

This table reports cumulative abnormal returns differentiated by the acquisition method used by the hedge fund. CARs are calculated using the approach by Schwert (1996) where the estimation period is (-140,-81) and the CDAX is the market proxy. Means are tested for difference using a simple t-test and differences in medians are tested using Mann-Whitney tests. */**/*** indicate statistical significance at the 10%/5%/1%-levels.

The empirical results in Table 52 indicate that there are significant differences in valuation effects between the good and bad times subsamples. In particular, announcement period returns during the window (-3, 3) are highest for big firms which also outperform small cap targets over longer holding periods. Small firms only briefly outperform the other two subsamples as they generate the highest returns in the window (-40, 40). However, all subsamples generate negative cumulative abnormal returns for longer holding periods. For the subsamples “small” and “big” these are significantly smaller than cumulative abnormal returns for the corresponding subsamples during the up-market. In addition, and in line with the evidence for the up-market period, the subsample “technology” generates only positive returns during the announcement period. These abnormal returns are also insignificant for the bad times subsample. For longer holding periods, CARs for events belonging to the category “technology” become negative. Thus, in line with the arguments by Zingales (2000) and Brav, Jiang, Partnoy, and Thomas (2008), technology firms are also not suitable targets for hedge funds during the down-market period. In addition, the differences in valuation effects between most groups during good and bad times are statistically significant except for the differences relative to the subsample "technology" which includes only a small number of events.

Overall, this empirical evidence indicates that during adverse market conditions "big" firms generate less negative CARs than the other two subsamples. This might be explained by the fact that they tend to have more robust business models. Moreover, for small firms there is no strong signaling effect and, instead, the potential threat of disruptions to the firms' operations by activist hedge funds during down-markets seems to trigger stronger declines in share prices.

3. Valuation of Target Firms

Based on the argument that hedge fund engagements raise the value of undervalued firms it seems reasonable to assume that short- and long-term share price reactions should be most positive for the most undervalued target firms. Nevertheless, even during good times this argument is not convincingly supported by the empirical evidence. Moreover, it is presumably even more difficult to restructure undervalued firms during periods of distress in financial markets. Therefore, it seems reasonable to assume that there should be no significant differences in share price reactions that can be explained by the target firms' pre-event valuation.

In order to investigate this hypothesis, Table 53 reports cumulative abnormal returns for three subsamples which break down the full sample according to the target's valuation level before the event date. In particular, events are assigned to the category "high" when their BHAR during the interval from 48 months before to 6 months before the event date are higher than 14.29% and the category "low" when the corresponding BHAR are smaller than -15.66%. Due to missing BHAR for this holding period, 18 events are not included in this analysis.

The empirical results in Table 53 indicate that the most undervalued firms do not generate significantly higher returns than target firms which belong to the other two categories. In particular, announcement effects for the group of target firms with a low valuation are negative and not significantly different from zero. Moreover, they become even more negative over time and accumulate to -18.48% after 240 trading days. In contrast, the group of firms with a high valuation does not generate significant announcement period returns. However, their cumulative abnormal returns remain close to zero and do not become significantly negative even for holding periods of 240 trading days. Thus, target firms in the category "high valuation" that have already exhibited an upward trend in their share price performance prior to the event date continue to outperform. Finally, in line with the results in the previous sections, target firms from all three categories deliver lower abnormal returns compared to the corresponding groups in the good times sample.

Overall, it can be concluded that the valuation level of target companies has no impact on post-event stock returns. In particular, the hypothesis has to be rejected that hedge funds help to raise the value of the most undervalued firms that often suffer most from agency problems and inefficient management.

Table 53: Cumulative Abnormal Returns differentiated by Pre-Performance

Sam.	Stat.	CAR (-3,3)		CAR (-40,-40)		CAR (-40,+120)		CAR (-40,+240)	
		Good	Bad	Good	Bad	Good	Bad	Good	Bad
High	Mean	0.0169 (1.682)	0.0073 (0.963)	0.0897 (2.261)	0.0190 (0.692)	0.2023 (3.853)	-0.0122 (-0.249)	0.3204 (4.633)	-0.0395 (-0.571)
		-0.7089		-1.3375		-2.855		-3.562	
	Med.	0.0124 (1.387)	0.0037 (0.907)	0.0926 (2.472)	0.0090 (0.907)	0.2169 (3.467)	0.0891 (0.433)	0.3046 (4.062)	-0.0169 (-0.447)
		-0.469		-1.354		-2.724		-3.215	
Inter.	Mean	0.0277 (3.693)	0.0134 (1.827)	0.0854 (4.046)	0.0169 (0.461)	0.0919 (3.099)	-0.0777 (-1.882)	0.0887 (2.262)	-0.2292 (-3.357)
		-1.299		-1.7343		-3.422		-4.325	
	Med.	0.0129 (3.527)	0.0079 (1.894)	0.0843 (4.239)	-0.0249 (-0.272)	0.1014 (4.273)	-0.0840 (-2.378)	0.0888 (2.996)	-0.1475 (-3.741)
		-0.682		-2.894		-4.419		-4.839	
Low	Mean	0.0143 (1.080)	-0.0024 (-0.150)	0.1073 (2.347)	-0.0250 (-0.458)	0.2285 (3.215)	-0.1283 (-1.451)	0.3269 (3.543)	-0.1848 (-1.703)
		-0.805		-1.851		-3.160		-3.5702	
	Med.	0.0029 (1.060)	-0.0141 (-0.863)	0.0681 (2.537)	-0.0138 (0.022)	0.1387 (3.222)	-0.0503 (-1.661)	0.2348 (3.345)	-0.1644 (-1.748)
		-1.371		-1.972		-3.490		-3.590	

This table reports cumulative abnormal returns differentiated by the acquisition method used by the hedge fund. CARs are calculated using the approach by Schwert (1996) where the estimation period is (-140,-81) and the CDAX is the market proxy. Means are tested for difference using a simple t-test and differences in medians are tested using Mann-Whitney tests. */**/*** indicate statistical significance at the 10%/5%/1%-levels.

4. Aggressiveness

Finally, it is often argued that more aggressive hedge funds should generate higher returns than hedge funds pursuing less confrontational tactics vis-à-vis the management of target firms. This occurs because more aggressive campaigns should in general lead to more successful restructurings and also generate more publicity, which in turn attracts additional investors to the company's stock. This is confirmed for events during the good times period where short-term valuation effects are stronger for more aggressive hedge funds indicating that investors expect them to quickly restructure inefficiently managed firms. However, during adverse market conditions it seems questionable whether more aggressive hedge funds can create similar valuation effects. In particular, from the perspective of other investors, there is less reason to be optimistic that the hedge fund will actually be able to quickly restructure the target. In fact, the associated recession in product markets already puts sufficient pressure on incumbent management so that there is only limited need for outside interference and additional disruptions by outside shareholders. This leads to the hypothesis that there are no significant differences in CARs that can be explained by differences in the level of the hedge fund's aggressiveness.

In order to investigate this hypothesis, Table 54 breaks down cumulative abnormal returns into three subsamples. An event is classified as "no hostility" if the hedge fund only acquires a stake in the target firm and generates no additional news; an event is classified as "aggressive" if the hedge fund also makes public disclosure about its intention regarding the target firm; and an event is classified as "reputation for activism" if the hedge fund has on previous occasions employed an aggressive approach towards another German target company.

Apparently, there is a similar "overreaction"-effect during the bad times period in that announcement period returns are strongest for the subsample of aggressive events. In particular, for the subsample of aggressive hedge funds mean CARs in the interval (-3, 3) are equal to 4.12% which is significant at the 1%-level. In contrast, for the other two subsamples, CARs are not significant. However, for longer holding periods the performance of this subsample deteriorates relative to the events included in the category "no hostility" and even becomes negative when the interval (-40, 40) is analyzed. Thus, in line with the empirical evidence for the good times sample there is a reversal in share prices. This can be interpreted as evidence that hedge funds deliberately generate investor interest in the stocks of target companies in order to engineer temporary increases in share prices (Barber and Odean, 2008). However, compared to the events classified as "aggressive" during the up-market, the duration of the positive drift is significantly shorter. This suggests that it should be rather difficult for hedge funds to exploit this overreaction effect and sell out to make a quick profit at the expense of other shareholders.

Table 54: Cumulative Abnormal Returns differentiated by Aggressiveness

Sample	Stat.	CAR (-3,3)		CAR (-40,-40)		CAR (-40,+120)		CAR (-40,+240)	
		Good	Bad	Good	Bad	Good	Bad	Good	Bad
No Hostile	Mean	0.0048	0.0029	0.0701	0.0212	0.1750	-0.0353	0.2550	-0.1478
		(0.711)	(0.460)	(3.154)	(0.913)	(5.396)	(-1.112)	(5.938)	(-3.201)
		-0.201		-1.504		-4.554		-6.347	
	Med.	0.0054	0.0033	0.0757	-0.0034	0.1391	-0.0238	0.1848	-0.1447
		(0.825)	(0.623)	(4.090)	(0.174)	(5.825)	(-1.062)	(5.715)	(-3.411)
		-0.168		-3.032		(-5.129)		-6.396	
Aggr.	Mean	0.0357	0.0412	0.1210	-0.0007	0.1499	-0.1788	0.1730	-0.1992
		(3.208)	(2.743)	(2.947)	(-0.011)	(3.119)	(-1.577)	(2.5810)	(-1.5768)
		0.289		-1.641		-3.104		-2.863	
	Med.	0.0176	0.0163	0.0676	0.0045	0.1028	-0.0718	0.0888	-0.0601
		(2.906)	(2.573)	(2.634)	(0.660)	(3.159)	(-1.776)	(2.897)	(-1.412)
		0.328		-1.332		-3.311		-2.778	
Rep. for Act.	Mean	0.0481	0.0095	0.0988	-0.0367	0.0565	-0.1611	0.0447	-0.2759
		(3.258)	(0.649)	(2.247)	(-0.542)	(0.739)	(-2.086)	(0.457)	(-1.755)
		-1.797		-1.754		-1.948		-1.822	
	Med.	0.0226	-0.0030	0.0926	-0.0281	0.0811	-0.2370	0.0762	-0.2316
		(2.618)	(0.360)	(2.125)	(-0.168)	(0.819)	(-2.066)	(0.457)	(-1.538)
		-1.611		-1.345		-1.850		-1.558	

This table reports cumulative abnormal returns differentiated by the acquisition method used by the hedge fund. CARs are calculated using the approach by Schwert (1996) where the estimation period is (-140,-81) and the CDAX is the market proxy. Means are tested for difference using a simple t-test and differences in medians are tested using Mann-Whitney tests. */**/*** indicate statistical significance at the 10%/5%/1%-levels.

IV. Cross-Sectional Regressions

This section presents the empirical results of cross-sectional regressions of cumulative abnormal returns in order to check the robustness of the results of the previous subsections. It starts with an analysis of short-run valuation effects by regressing the cross-section of CARs during the event window (-3; +3) on the same set of explanatory variables as in the previous chapter. The results are shown in Table 55.

The success of the hedge funds' strategies might depend on the ownership structure of the target firm. Therefore, a set of dummy variables is included. These are set equal to one if the largest shareholder is a bank, corporation, government entity or individual/family investor and zero otherwise. However, none of these dummy variables appears to have a significant impact on the magnitude of short-term valuation effects during the down-market environment. In fact, the highly significant coefficient on the dummy for bank ownership only reflects the high returns of one single event. The success of activist hedge funds is also related to their behavior towards the firm's management. In contrast to the subsample of events occurring during good times, most variables are not statistically significant. In fact, there is only evidence for higher initial returns for more aggressive events in the restricted model III. This is in line with Boyson and Mooradian (2008) and suggests that investors have very positive expectations regarding the outcome of these hedge fund investments. However, this might also indicate that these hedge funds try to stir up public interest in their target companies in order to temporarily increase share prices. Moreover, the coefficient on the dummy for subsequent mergers & acquisitions is also high in magnitude. However, it is not significant due to the high volatility of CARs for these events. This is in direct contrast to the results for the subsample of events occurring during the good times period and to the empirical evidence for the U.S. (Greenwood and Schoar, 2009). The influence of activist hedge funds might also be reduced by the influence of the workforce on the board of directors in some firms. Interestingly, coefficients on the dummy variables "labor 1/3 of board seats" and "labor 1/2 of board seats" are both positive and significant. During the period of the financial crisis, this might indicate that firms with many employees had a higher chance of receiving government bailout funds. Moreover, this might also reflect the larger size of these firms, which increases their ability to withstand the shocks generated by the financial crisis. However, this is not supported by model V which does not document a statistically significant impact of the target firm's market capitalization on announcement period returns. Finally, among the accounting variables only the level of capital expenditures has a significant impact. This is negative indicating that higher spending leads to lower returns.

There are some changes in empirical results when longer term cumulative abnormal returns during the window (-40, 240) are used as the dependent variable. Importantly, this window covers the run-up periods, thereby capturing the full valuation effect. Table 56 contains these results.

Table 55: Cross-Sectional Regressions – CAR (-3,+3)

	Independent Variable	I	II	III	IV	V	VI
	Constant	-0.0143	0.0100	-0.0029	-0.0124	0.0102*	0.0080
Largest Shareholde	Bank	0.2740***	0.2545***				
	Corporation	-0.0040	-0.0012				
	Government	-0.0431	-0.0271				
	Individual	0.0043	-0.0011				
HF Behavior	Wolfpack	0.0030		0.0116			
	HF Rel. Stake	-0.0057		0.0001			
	Aggressive	0.0066		0.0243*			
	Subsequent M&A	0.0487		0.0212			
Cod er.	Labor 1/3	0.0253			0.0298*		
	Labor ½	0.0392**			0.0334**		
Mar ket	MtB adj.	0.0006				0.0008	
	Market Value adj.	-0.0009				-0.0001	
Accounting Fundamentals	R&D	-0.0025					0.0106
	Payout Ratio adj.	-0.0001					-0.0001
	Cash Holdings adj.	-0.0095					-0.0419
	Leverage adj.	0.0194					0.0130
	RoE adj.	0.0128					0.0006
	CF-to-Assets adj.	-0.0520					-0.0544
	Capex-to-Sales adj.	-0.0085**					0.0094
	R^2	0.2533	0.0786	0.0361	0.0425	0.0027	0.0366
	Nobs	125	169	164	169	168	129

This table reports coefficient estimates for the impact of firm-level fundamental characteristics in the year prior to the event on the short-run valuation effects (event returns) of the target firms, as measured using the CAR approach. The CDAX is used as a common benchmark for all firms, and the regression is estimated without a constant (Schwert, 1996). Fundamental variables are median-adjusted using all firms from the same industry. The firm universe consists of all constituents of the DAX, MDAX, SDAX or TecDAX indices. Robust standard errors are used to calculate t-statistics. */**/*** indicate statistical significance at the 10%/5%/1% level.

Table 56: Cross-Sectional Regressions – CAR (-40,+240)

	Independent Variable	I	II	III	IV	V	VI
	Constant	-0.4040**	-0.2397***	-0.1749***	-0.2583***	-0.2008***	-0.3852***
Largest Investor	Bank	1.2915***	0.4998***				
	Corporation	-0.0257	0.0978				
	Government	0.1418	0.3085*				
	Individual	0.0577	0.0943				
HF Behavior	Wolfpack	-0.0325		0.0559			
	HF Rel. Stake	-0.3426**		-0.0634			
	Aggressive	-0.2570*		-0.0726			
	Subsequent M&A	0.3972*		0.4579***			
Codet.	Labor 1/3	0.1462			-0.0656		
	Labor ½	0.4242***			0.2111**		
Market	MtB adj.	-0.0164				-0.0105	
	Market Value adj.	-0.0076				0.0090*	
Accounting Fundamentals	R&D	0.2554**					0.3656***
	Payout Ratio adj.	-0.0006					0.0009
	Cash Holdings adj.	0.1047					-0.1840
	Leverage adj.	-0.3998					-0.4259
	RoE adj.	-0.3423					-0.5956**
	CF-to-Assets adj.	0.9898					1.0152
	Capex-to-Sales adj.	-0.0590					0.0155
	R^2	0.3835	0.0141	0.0808	0.0442	0.0119	0.1436
	Nobs	125	169	164	169	168	129

This table reports coefficient estimates for the impact of firm-level fundamental characteristics in the year prior to the event on long-run valuation effects of the target firms. Long-run returns are measured using the BHAR approach. The benchmark is the market index to which the target firm belonged on the event date. Fundamental variables are median-adjusted using all firms from the same industry. The firm universe consists of all constituents of the DAX, MDAX, SDAX or TecDAX indices. Robust standard errors are used to calculate t-statistics. */**/*** indicate statistical significance at the 10%/5%/1% level.

Long run abnormal returns are higher when the government or a bank is the dominant shareholder. This is consistent with the idea that these firms should have better access to additional funding during crisis periods. However, long run abnormal returns are lower if the hedge funds' stake is larger. This might be due to the risk of distressed hedge funds engaging in fire sales. This "share overhang" might have put downward pressure on stock returns during the crisis environment. Furthermore, there is still evidence that more aggressive hedge funds generate lower long run returns which is consistent with the findings for the sample of events occurring during good times. Similarly, events are characterized by superior long-run returns if target firms are acquired in a subsequent takeover. Long run abnormal returns are also higher for larger firms. This is supported by the positive coefficients on market capitalization and on the dummy "labor ½ of board seats". However, the positive coefficient on labor board representation is also consistent with the idea that it should be easier for these firms to obtain access to government funds during the financial crisis. Finally, among the accounting ratios the dummy for R&D is significantly positive and the coefficient on the adjusted return on equity is statistically signicant. This suggests that returns are higher for target firms that invest in R&D and for target firms that are characterized by below average profitability.

V. Calendar Time Approach

The analysis of cumulative abnormal returns indicates that firms targeted by hedge funds between 2007 and 2008 generated significantly negative abnormal returns during the down-market environment. However, both cumulative abnormal returns and buy-and-hold abnormal returns are subject to several economic and statistical biases if they are used to analyze stock returns over longer horizons, such as one year or more. Problems include overlapping event periods which lead to spatial correlations and distorted estimates of standard errors. Also, the risk profile of target firms may change after the event date leading to shifts in their expected returns. This applies, in particular, to longer run returns such as the CARs (-40, 240) which were evaluated in the previous section.

These problems can be overcome by the calendar time portfolio approach which is applied to the sample of 169 events during the down-market period in this section. In the first step portfolios of target stocks are formed in calendar time and their returns are analyzed in the first subsection. In the second step the time-series of returns of these portfolios is regressed on a set of risk factors specified by an asset pricing model, such as the three-factor model of Fama and French (1993). The empirical results of these regressions are summarized in the second subsection.

1. The Performance and Properties of Calendar Time Portfolios

In the first step, it is interesting to investigate the performance of the calendar-time portfolios based on the 169 events that occurred during the down-market. This approach can be used to approximate the investment performance of different investors trading stocks targeted by hedge funds. These calendar-time portfolios replicate the performance of a trading strategy that enters into a position in a target company upon the entry of a hedge fund and holds the target company in an equally weighted portfolio for a specified holding period. If a firm is subject to multiple hedge fund investments over the holding period, it is assumed that the initial holding period is extended accordingly. Thus, the calendar-time portfolio always remains an equally weighted average across all target stocks at each point in time.

Previous results indicate that hedge funds begin to accumulate their blocks at least two months before they ultimately make a public disclosure of their position to capital markets. Based on this assumption the calendar-time portfolio approach can approximate the investment strategy and performance of a hedge fund. This is achieved by constructing a calendar-time portfolio that takes a position in target companies two months prior to the event date and holds the position for 12 months. The performance of this portfolio is shown along with the CDAX performance index in Figure 44.

Figure 44: Performance CalTime (-2,10) – Bad Times

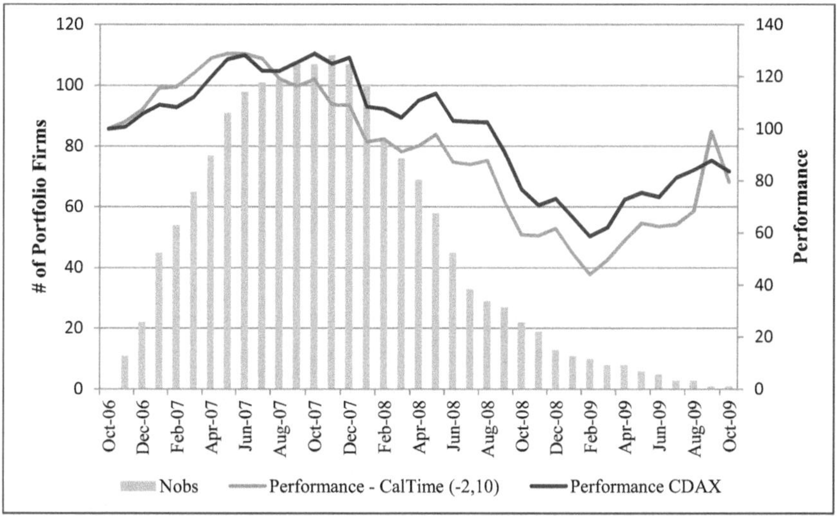

This figure reports the investment performance of the calendar-time portfolio taking a position in target stocks two months before the event date and holding the position for the next 12 months. It also contains the performance of the CDAX performance index and the number of firms included in the calendar-time portfolio in each month.

The empirical results in Figure 44 show that the calendar-time portfolio replicating the hedge funds' investment strategy closely tracks the performance of the CDAX performance index. In particular, there is an increase in portfolio value during the first half of 2007, in line with the last upward movement of the German stock market before it began to decline during the financial crisis. This reveals that hedge funds were not able to achieve superior returns by capitalizing on the run-up effects that occurred prior to the event date during the down-market. This suggests that for most events during this time period run-ups in share prices are quickly followed by reversals. After a brief period of stagnation during the later part of 2007, both the calendar-time portfolio as well as the CDAX decline sharply. However, the drop of the calendar-time portfolio appears to be more pronounced. Thus, in line with the conclusions derived from the analysis of CARs hedge fund targets had a weak performance during the financial crisis. Moreover, Figure 44 also contains information regarding the number of events included in the calendar-time portfolio at each point in time. This indicates that the composition and, therefore, the performance of the calendar-time portfolio is significantly affected by the concentration of events in the first half of 2007. In particular, the number of firms included in the portfolio increases sharply during this initial time period and declines slowly but steadily afterwards because there are only a limited number of events during the later stages of the financial crisis. As a result, the calendar-time portfolio can only be considered to be diversified up to February 2009. For this time period there are always more than 10 events in the portfolio. Therefore, the sharp rebound in the calendar-time portfolio cannot be generalized as it is generated by the pre-event run-up of one single event.

Other market participants can only invest in hedge fund targets upon observing the public news that a hedge fund has acquired an active stake in a firm. However, hedge funds can only execute their strategies profitably if other investors also share in the returns and are therefore willing to support the hedge funds. Thus, it is highly relevant to investigate returns accruing to other shareholders. This issue is investigated in Figure 45, which compares the investment performance of three calendar-time portfolios that differ with respect to the time for when they initiated positions in target firms. In addition to the hedge funds investing two months prior to the public announcement, it also contains two "tracker portfolios" which invest in the target firms in either the same month or one month after the public announcement. The empirical results in Figure 45 differ substantially from the performance of the corresponding portfolios during the good times period. In particular, during good times there was a tremendous outperformance of the hedge fund portfolio. In contrast, during the down-market, the entry point of the different portfolios only makes a small difference because when the calendar time portfolio takes a position prior to the official announcement, it generates marginally higher, i.e. less negative, returns. This suggests that hedge funds do not achieve higher returns than the supporting investors who follow the lead of hedge funds and trade the stocks targeted by hedge funds in a down market. This is in sharp contrast to the empirical findings for the good times subsample where the hedge funds generated substantially higher returns because they were able to capitalize on strong run-up effects. This empirical result can be explained by the finding in the analysis of cumulative abnormal returns that pre-event run-ups only exist during the early stages of the financial crisis and are quickly reversed by post-event declines in share prices.

Figure 45: CalTime-Portfolios for different Entry Points – Bad Times

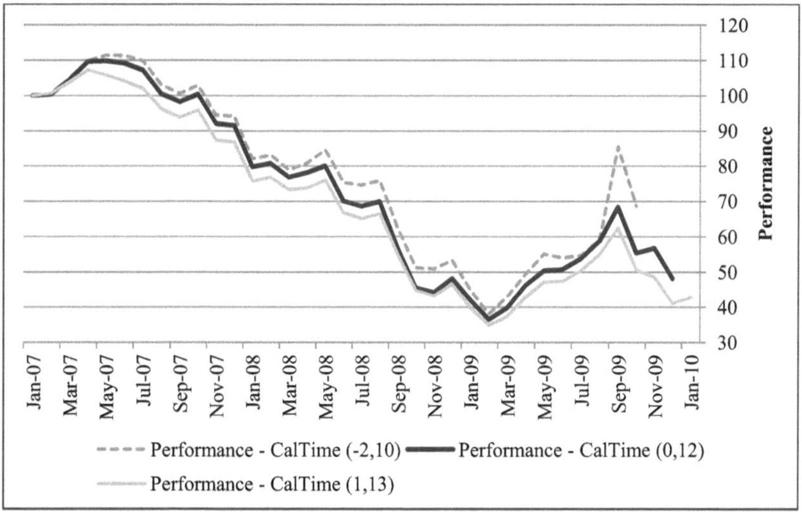

This figure reports the investment performance of three calendar-time portfolios. These take positions in target stocks two months before the event date, in the month of the event and in the subsequent month, respectively and hold the position for the next 12 months.

Another important issue in the analysis of long-term stock performance is whether financial stocks are included in the analysis. In particular, many authors argue that financial stocks are driven by a distinct set of risk factors because the structure of their balance sheets differs substantially from industrial firms (Bessler and Kurmann, 2010). In fact, this issue appears to be even more important for the sample of hedge fund targets during the down-market because during the recent financial crisis the share prices of banks were hit particularly hard by declining asset values in real estate and other asset markets. Therefore, Figure 46 compares the investment performance of a calendar-time portfolio which includes financial stocks with the investment performance of a calendar-time portfolio that does not include any financial stocks. Both assume the perspective of a hedge fund that begins to invest in event firms two months before the official announcement date.

Figure 46: CalTime Portfolios with/without Financial Stocks

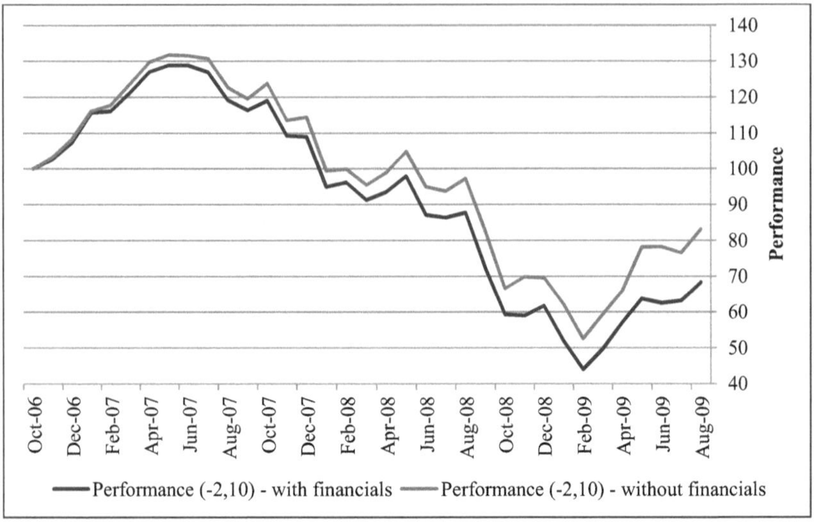

This figure reports the investment performance of two calendar-time portfolios that took positions in target stocks two months before the event date and held the position for the next 12 months. The first portfolio contains financial stocks and in the second portfolio financial stocks are excluded.

The empirical results in Figure 46 indicate that there are some differences in investment performance during the later stages of the financial crisis. In particular, the calendar-time portfolio which includes financial stocks appears to underperform more during the time period when financial stocks generated strongly negative returns. However, this difference occurs during a time period when there are only a small number of stocks in the respective calendar-time portfolios. Therefore, it is not possible to draw strong conclusions or to generalize these findings.

Overall, the investment performance of calendar-time portfolios in the down-market differs substantially from their performance during the preceding up-market environment. In particular, in line with the results based on cumulative abnormal returns, they generate negative returns, particularly during the later stages of the financial crisis. Moreover, there are no strong differences in the realized investment performance of hedge funds capitalizing on the pre-event run-up and the returns generated by other investors that attempt to track the portfolio composition of hedge funds.

2. Fama-French Regressions

The observed differences between the performance of calendar-time portfolios and the overall stock market do not necessarily imply that there is an underperformance of hedge fund targets from an economic and statistical point of view. In fact, these differences might not be statistically significant and could also be the result of exposures to additional risk factors, such as the value or size effects. Therefore, the second step of the calendar-time portfolio approach consists of a time-series regression of the returns of calendar-time portfolios on a set of risk factors. Only if the estimated alpha from this regression is significantly different from zero then is there a statistical under- or outperformance.

Table 57 reports the empirical results for time-series regressions using the CDAX-factors which were already used in the previous chapter. These are constructed by sorting the entire CDAX universe of German stocks according to the variables market capitalization and market-to-book ratio following the procedure described in Fama and French (1993).[127] The empirical results in Table 57 confirm the conclusion from the simple comparison of the investment performance of calendar-time portfolios and the CDAX performance index. In particular, there is apparently no significant under- or outperformance after adjusting for post-event risk exposures because alphas are negative, yet not statistically significant at any conventional level. Nevertheless, the pre-event run-up still increases the estimated abnormal performance because alphas become more negative and approach the margins of statistical significance for later entry points. Thus, even though the difference in the performance of the corresponding calendar-time portfolios appears to be neglible in the visual analysis, the time-series regressions indicate that the associated differences in their returns are stronger. This finding might be related to the adjustment for post-event risk characteristics and spatial correlations. Thus, there is at least some support for the idea that hedge funds generate higher returns than other investors trying to replicate their portfolio holdings because they can capitalize on the most likely self-created pre-event run-up in share prices.

---

[127] See Bessler and Kurmann (2010) for the details on the construction methodology.

Table 57: Time-Series Regressions – CDAX-Factors

Holding Period	Alpha	Market	HML	SMB	R^2
(-2,10)	0.0050	**1.4036**			0.4920
	(0.34)	***(5.64)***			
	-0.0005	**1.3840**	0.7461	0.4581	0.5480
	(-0.04)	***(6.52)***	*(1.30)*	*(1.26)*	
(0,12)	-0.0107	**1.2237**			0.5850
	(-1.03)	***(7.16)***			
	-0.0113	**1.2489**	**0.5606**	**0.7199**	0.6676
	(-1.05)	***(7.63)***	***(2.12)***	***(2.20)***	
(1,13)	-0.0144	**1.0874**			0.5173
	(-1.35)	***(6.75)***			
	-0.0151	**1.1431**	**0.5727**	**0.7657**	0.6240
	(-1.33)	***(7.40)***	***(2.33)***	***(2.33)***	

This table reports the results from the time-series regression of different calendar-time portfolio returns based on events from the bad times sample on the CDAX-factors. The values in parentheses indicate t-values based on Newey-West standard errors.

These findings should also be reflected in the factor loadings of the calendar time portfolios. In particular, in all time-series regressions the market risk exposure is substantially higher than one, indicating that target firms had a higher exposure to the market return during a time period when stock markets were falling. This helps to explain a fraction of the underperformance reported in CARs which only adjust for pre-event risk characteristics of target firms. Moreover, after excluding the run-up period from the holding period of the calendar time portfolio, there are significant exposures to the size- and value factors. However, the total impact of these additional risk exposures on the performance of calendar-time portfolio returns appears to be quite small because there is only a small increase in the R^2 when the size- and value-factors are added to the calendar-time regressions. These findings can be reconciled with two explanations: Either hedge funds target firms which have higher exposures to these risks factors in the first place – or target firms' exposures to these risk factors begin to increase subsequent to the hedge funds' interference which, therefore, makes target firms riskier than the average German firm.

Several recent papers indicate that the properties of Fama-French factors can change substantially depending on the details of the construction methodology (e.g. Fama and French, 2008). Therefore, it is necessary to investigate the robustness of the results to the construction method of Fama-French factors. Consequently, the returns of calendar time portfolios are also regressed on another set of Fama-French factors which are constructed based on MSCI style indices. In particular, the value factor is constructed as the difference in the returns of the MSCI Value index and the MSCI Growth index and the size factor are constructed as the difference in the returns of the MSCI Large index and the MSCI Small Cap index. The empirical results are reported in Table 58.

Table 58: CalTime Portfolio and Fama-French Regression – MSCI Factors

Holding Period	Alpha	Market	HML	SMB	R^2
(-2,10)	-0.0008 *(-0.07)*	**1.2021** ***(5.12)***	-0.4731 *(-0.91)*	**1.3141** ***(1.91)***	0.6301
(0,12)	-0.0141 *(-1.71)*	**0.9824** ***(8.76)***	-0.0615 *(-0.38)*	**0.9138** ***(4.13)***	0.7542
(1,13)	**-0.0184** ***(-2.15)***	**0.8715** ***(7.35)***	0.0131 *(0.07)*	**0.8306** ***(3.61)***	0.7031

This table reports the results from the time-series regression of different calendar-time portfolios returns for the bad times events on proxies for the Fama-French factors. These are constructed by using the MSCI Value, Growth, Large and Small Cap indices and by sorting the universe of German stocks. The values in parentheses indicate t-values based on Newey-West standard errors.

In contrast to the empirical results presented in Table 57, the empirical evidence based on this other set of Fama-French factors indicates that investors generate significantly negative abnormal returns when they replicate the portfolio composition of hedge funds based on publicly observable information. In particular, the estimate of alpha equals -1.41% per month, which is significant at the 10%-level in the case that the investor acquires a position in the same month that the hedge fund disclosed its position. Moreover, the alpha decreases further to -1.84%, which is significant at the 5%-level when the investor acquires a position in the subsequent month. Additionally, using this other set of Fama-French factors also leads to changes in the factor loadings of the calendar-time portfolios. In particular, the estimated market risk exposure becomes significantly smaller compared to the results when the CDAX-factors are used. Furthermore, the market risk exposure of the calendar-time portfolio becomes substantially higher if the two trading months covering the run-up period are included. Finally, only the coefficient on the SMB-factor remains positive and significant while the coefficient on the HML-factor becomes negative and is no longer significant. Thus, there are significant differences in empirical results depending on the method used to construct Fama-French factors that have substantial implications in that they affect whether target firms should be classified as value stocks or not. Overall, these results suggest that the method used to construct and estimate Fama-French factors can have a significant impact on the conclusions that are drawn from empirical studies investigating the stock price performance of German firms.

A final issue which has also been addressed in previous sections is the effect of the industry composition of calendar-time portfolios on empirical results. Therefore, Table 59 presents the results of time-series regressions of calendar-time portfolios when financial stocks are excluded from the sample. According to the results in Table 59, there are no significant changes in the estimates of alpha and factor loadings of calendar-time portfolios for different holding periods when financial stocks are excluded from the sample. Panel A shows the empirical results based on the CDAX-factors. Again, the estimated alphas are statistically significant and decline when the run-up period is excluded. Moreover, the market beta of the calendar time portfolios is larger than one, indicating that target firms are riskier than the average German firm. However, there is a difference in results in that the loading on the HML-factor is no longer statistically significant and the loadings on the SMB-factor are only significant for some holding periods. A similar pattern is observable in Panel B where the MSCI-factors are used. The estimates for alpha are negative and decline if the run-up period is excluded. Moreover, the behavior of estimated factor loadings across the different calendar-time portfolios is also broadly in line with their behavior in the time-series regressions including financial stocks.

Overall, the calendar-time portfolio approach which controls for post-event risk characteristics and spatial correlations casts some doubts on the finding that hedge fund active involvements during the down-market trigger negative share price performance. In fact, in contrast to the results based on cumulative abnormal returns, there is only significant underperformance in those regressions which use the MSCI style indices to adjust for value- and size-effects. Thus, this suggests that the risk factor exposures of target firms explain a substantial fraction of the underperformance of target firms during the recent crisis period. However, it remains an open question whether target firms already had these high loadings on some risk factors prior to the hedge fund engagement or whether they were the result of hedge funds forcing managers to make significant changes in their firm's strategies and financial structures. Moreover, these findings might also be the result of contagion effects as other investors refrain from investing in the stocks of hedge fund targets due to the risk of fire sales by hedge funds suffering their own performance problems. An additional insight provided by this analysis is that accurately measuring these risk factors seems to pose the biggest problem when investigating long-run stocks returns. In particular, according to the results of Fama and French (2008) for the U.S. capital market, the risk-return characteristics of value- and size-factors can be significantly affected by "micro-caps". Due to the large number of very small and very illiquid stocks in the German capital market, this problem might actually be even more relevant for measuring abnormal long-term performance in Germany.

Table 59: Time-Series Regressions – Without Financial Stocks

Holding Period	Alpha	Market	HML	SMB	R^2
Panel A – CDAX-Factors					
(-2,10)	0.0077 *(0.70)*	1.0711 *(5.58)*	0.0649 *(0.22)*	0.9235 *(2.69)*	0.6458
(0,12)	-0.0038 *(-0.37)*	1.1709 *(8.81)*	0.2309 *(0.88)*	0.5657 *(1.70)*	0.7054
(1,13)	-0.0103 *(-0.83)*	1.0821 *(7.53)*	0.3694 *(1.45)*	0.4574 *(1.18)*	0.6277
Panel B – MSCI-Factors					
(-2,10)	-0.0004 *(-0.05)*	0.8567 *(5.30)*	-0.0044 *(-0.02)*	0.7084 *(2.40)*	0.7141
(0,12)	-0.0074 *(-1.10)*	0.9069 *(9.45)*	0.0873 (0.53)	0.5529 *(3.00)*	0.7982
(1,13)	-0.0123 *(-1.59)*	0.8225 *(7.23)*	0.1500 *(0.76)*	0.4824 *(2.14)*	0.7171

This table reports the results from the time-series regression of calendar portfolio returns for the bad times sample events on two sets of proxies for the Fama-French-factors. In Panel A, factors derived from sorts on market-to-book and size are used and in Panel B factors based on MSCI Style Indices are used. The values in parentheses indicate t-values.

VI. Robustness Check - Generalized Calendar Time Approach

The calendar-time portfolio approach is not suitable for further analyzing the underlying drivers of long-term valuation effects. Therefore, the final section applies the generalized calendar time portfolio approach (GCT-approach) by Höchle, Schmid, and Zimmermann (2009) to the sample of 169 events occurring during the down-market period. This relatively new approach can also differentiate valuation effects into the relative contributions of pre-event run-up effects and post-event drift effects. In addition, it also facilitates the investigation of the impact of different event and firm characteristics on the magnitude of long-run valuation effects while still controlling for post-event risk characteristics as well as spatial correlations.

1. Long-Run Performance

In the first step, the GCT-approach is compared to the results derived from the simple calendar-time approach by regressing monthly excess stock returns on a "drift"-dummy capturing event firms for defined holding periods and on a set of risk factors. In particular, the dummy variable "drift" is set equal to one from time period t = -2 (t = 0, t = 1) and the subsequent 12 trading months. Otherwise it is set to zero for all other trading months and to zero for all return observations in the control group used to estimate this panel regression. The coefficients in the column "all" measure the impact of each variable on the full set of firms including the control group which is composed of all firms listed in the CDAX. The coefficients in the columns "delta" measure the differential impact of the respective variable for event firms compared to the control group. The coefficient "alpha" measures the abnormal performance of target firms and the coefficient "market" measures the average loading on the market factor between target firms and the control group. The empirical results are presented in Table 60.

Panel A contains the empirical results based on the CDAX-factors as measures of systematic risk exposures. Overall, these results indicate that hedge fund targets generate negative abnormal returns. In particular, when the run-up period prior to the event date is not contained in the holding period defined by the "drift"-dummy, then estimated abnormal performance is highly significant and negative at -0.93% and -1.12% per month, respectively. This confirms the results from the calendar time portfolio approach that after taking additional risk factors into account and after adjusting t-statistics for spatial correlations, target companies generate a significant underperformance. Moreover, similar to the results for the calendar-time portfolio approach, the average target firm seems to be characterized by a significantly higher market risk exposure because the coefficient on the interaction term between the "drift"-dummy and the market factor is positive and highly significant.

These results are broadly confirmed in Panel B where the MSCI-factors are used to measure the systematic risk exposures of stocks. In particular, if the run-up period is not included in the holding period specified by the "drift"-dummy then there is a significantly negative abnormal performance of -0.59% and -0.89% per month, respectively. Moreover, the average beta of target firms appears to be significantly higher than the average beta of the firms in the control group in that all interaction terms between the "drift"-dummy and the market risk factor are positive and highly significant. Interestingly, estimates for the market beta for the control group are rather low. This seems to be related to difficulties in constructing sufficiently broad control groups when using German capital market data.

Many researchers remove financial stocks from the analysis of long-run performance because their returns are apparently driven by a distinct set of risk factors (see Bessler and Kurmann, 2010). Therefore, it also seems necessary to check the robustness of the results of the GCT-approach to the industry composition of the sample of hedge fund targets and the control group. Table 61 reports the results from the same regression specification used above when all stocks classified as financials according to the ICB industry classification are removed from the control group and the sample of target stocks.

Panel A contains the results based on the CDAX-factors. These empirical results are broadly in line with the results in Table 60 where financial stocks are included in the sample of target stocks and in the control group. In particular, hedge funds trading in target stocks two months before the event date do not generate significant alpha and the investors trying to replicate hedge funds' positions based on publicly observable information generate significantly negative abnormal returns. However, these results become weaker for investors establishing positions in t = 0 and t = 1 when the set of MSCI-factors is used to capture systematic risk exposures of target stocks. In this case estimates of alpha are still negative but not statistically significant. Thus, it appears fair to conclude that the results are not substantially affected by the industry composition of the sample. Apparently, the behavior of financial stocks does not differ substantially from the stock price patterns of target firms operating in other industries.

Table 60: Run-Up Effects and Post-Event Abnormal Performance

Panel A: CDAX-Factors						
Window	12m Drift					
Entry Point	t=-2		t=0		t=1	
	All	Delta	All	Delta	All	Delta
Alpha	0.0017	-0.0069	0.0013	**-0.0093**	0.0006	**-0.0112**
	(0.38)	(-1.42)	*(0.31)*	***(-2.54)***	*(0.13)*	***(-2.70)***
Market	**0.8012**	**0.2815**	**0.7878**	**0.3379**	**0.7887**	**0.2952**
	(15.83)	***(3.94)***	***(15.84)***	***(4.48)***	***(14.81)***	***(3.65)***
SMB	**0.7841**	0.1637	**0.7774**	0.1962	**0.7287**	0.1828
	(9.40)	*(0.87)*	**(2.16)**	*(1.26)*	***(7.63)***	*(1.24)*
HML	**0.2037**	0.1381	**0.2202**	0.1504	**0.2168**	0.1120
	(1.98)	*(0.66)*	***(2.16)***	*(0.90)*	***(2.07)***	*(0.65)*
R^2	0.0676		0.0681		0.0650	
Nobs	25871		25915		25932	
Panel B: MSCI-Factors						
Window	12m Drift					
Entry Point	t=-2		t=0		t=1	
	All	Delta	All	Delta	All	Delta
Alpha	-0.0043	-0.0014	-0.0044	-0.0059	-0.0050	**-0.0089**
	(-1.37)	*(-0.58)*	*(-1.27)*	(-1.79)	*(-1.71)*	***(-2.51)***
Market	**0.6522**	**0.3081**	**0.6385**	**0.3078**	**0.6218**	**0.2668**
	(19.03)	***(5.04)***	***(16.31)***	***(5.36)***	***(14.93)***	***(4.01)***
SMB	**0.6810**	0.1694	**0.6685**	0.1151	**0.6223**	0.1032
	(9.02)	*(1.12)*	***(8.41)***	*(0.78)*	***(8.16)***	*(0.69)*
HML	**-0.1756**	0.0364	**-0.1650**	0.1402	-0.1196	0.1161
	(-2.15)	*(0.26)*	***(-1.95)***	*(1.04)*	*(-1.32)*	*(0.77)*
R^2	0.0712		0.0716		0.0696	
Nobs	25871		25915		25932	

This table provides results for the generalized calendar-time approach by Höchle, Schmid, and Zimmermann (2009) where monthly excess stock returns are regressed on a "drift"-dummy, a set of risk-factors designed to approximate the Fama-French Factors and a full set of interaction terms. The "drift-dummy" is set equal to one for time periods corresponding to the defined holding periods, and is otherwise set to zero.

Table 61: GCT-Approach - Without Financial Stocks

Panel A: CDAX-Factors						
Window	12m Drift					
Entry Point	t=-2		t=0		t=1	
	All	Delta	All	Delta	All	Delta
Alpha	0.0020 *(0.45)*	-0.0029 *(-0.54)*	0.0018 *(0.41)*	**-0.0070** ***(-2.00)***	0.0009 (0.21)	**-0.0090** ***(-2.18)***
Market	**0.8070** ***(15.08)***	**0.2319** ***(2.70)***	**0.7959** ***(15.15)***	**0.2811** ***(3.82)***	**0.7969** ***(14.17)***	**0.2331** ***(2.64)***
SMB	**0.8120** ***(9.64)***	0.0942 *(0.46)*	**0.8072** ***(9.60)***	0.0474 *(0.29)*	**0.7580** ***(7.97)***	0.0207 *(0.14)*
HML	0.1781 *(1.57)*	0.0982 *(0.36)*	0.1920 *(1.72)*	0.0880 *(0.42)*	0.1888 (1.65)	0.0638 *(0.31)*
R^2	0.0707		0.0714		0.0680	
Nobs	21652		21684		21696	
Panel B: MSCI-Factors						
Window	12m Drift					
Entry Point	t=-2		t=0		t=1	
	All	Delta	All	Delta	All	Delta
Alpha	-0.0044 *(-1.37)*	0.0032 *(0.95)*	-0.0044 *(-1.25)*	-0.0032 *(-0.92)*	-0.0051 *(-1.74)*	-0.0056 (-1.50)
Market	**0.6522** ***(18.13)***	**0.2789** ***(3.32)***	**0.6407** ***(16.01)***	**0.2813** ***(4.03)***	**0.6222** ***(14.38)***	**0.23005** ***(2.60)***
SMB	**0.6950** ***(7.70)***	0.1726 *(1.10)*	**0.6864** ***(7.42)***	0.0613 *(0.42)*	**0.6377** ***(7.27)***	0.0464 *(0.30)*
HML	**-0.1690** ***(-1.99)***	0.0378 (0.22)	-0.1588 *(-1.83)*	0.0868 *(0.64)*	-0.1093 *(-1.18)*	0.0856 *(0.54)*
R^2	0.0746		0.0753		0.0733	
Nobs	21652		21684		21696	

This table provides results for the generalized calendar-time approach by Höchle, Schmid, and Zimmermann (2009) where monthly excess stock returns are regressed on a "drift"-dummy, a set of risk-factors designed to approximate the Fama-French Factors and a full set of interaction terms. The "drift-dummy" is set equal to one for time periods corresponding to the defined holding periods, and is otherwise set to zero.

2. Target Firm Characteristics and Long-Run Performance

According to the empirical results in the previous sections, the magnitude of long-term valuation effects is related to event and target firm characteristics. However, findings based on CARs and BHARs suffer from some economic and statistical problems because they do not control for post-event risk characteristics and spatial correlations. In contrast, the GCT-approach can also be used to investigate the impact of these variables while at the same time taking these problems into account. This pooled regression model is specified with a 12-month drift-period and is estimated with monthly data. The control group used in the estimation consists of all non-financial CDAX firms. The results are displayed in Table 62.

The results corroborate some of the findings from the cross-sectional regressions of buy-and-hold abnormal returns (BHAR). In particular, the size of the hedge funds stake has a negative impact on returns supporting the hypothesis that this "share overhang" puts downward pressure on stock prices during a depressed market environment. Morevoer, more aggressive hedge funds are associated with lower returns and subsequent mergers & acquisitions lead to higher returns of target companies. Furthermore, firms with labor representation on the board of directors achieve higher returns. Interestingly, in the case of the ownership and the accounting variables, there are some differences between the restricted models and the full model V. In particular, the dummies for corporate and bank ownership have a significantly positive impact on returns in the restricted model but do not have a significant influence in the full model. Similarly, the payout ratio has no significant impact in the restricted model IV but a negatively significant impact in the full model. This might reflect the fact that the full model can only be estimated with a smaller sample of firms for which all data items are available.

Table 62: Generalized Calendar Time Approach

	Independent Variable	I	II	III	IV	V
	Abnormal Return	-0.0092*	0.0043	-0.0046	-0.0040	-0.0080
Largest Investor	Corporation	0.0265***				-0.0002
	Government	0.0290**				0.0021
	Individual	0.0057				-0.0055
HF Behavior	Wolfpack		0.0040			-0.0041
	HF Rel. Stake		-0.0058***			0.0404***
	Aggressive		-0.0063			-0.0215***
	Subsequent M&A		0.0319***			0.0404***
Cod et.	Labor 1/3			0.0071		0.0198**
	Labor ½			0.0134**		0.0379***
Accounting Fundamentals	R&D				0.0084	0.0050
	Payout Ratio adj.				-0.0001	-0.0003***
	Cash Holdings adj.				-0.0277	-0.0026
	Leverage adj.				-0.0397*	-0.0199
	RoE adj.				0.0032	0.0022
	CF-to-Assets adj.				0.0310	0.0357
	Capex-to-Sales adj.				0.0685	0.0719
	R^2	0.0751	0.0754	0.0751	0.1358	0.1380
	Nobs	21652	21652	21652	12401	12401

This table reports summarizes the impact of firm-level fundamental characteristics in the year prior to the engagement of a hedge fund on the performance of their target firms using the generalized calendar time approach (Höchle, Schmid, and Zimmermann, 2008). The dependent variable is each stock's return in excess of the risk-free rate which is regressed on the Fama-French factors (market factor, SMB and HML), a dummy variable that captures a target firm's abnormal performance subsequent to the event ("drift"), and a set of interaction terms between the different industry-adjusted fundamental variables and the drift-dummy. The drift-dummy variable is set equal to one for the all monthly return observations in the window between the event date and 12 months subsequent to the event date, and is otherwise set to zero; it captures the abnormal performance of hedge fund targets compared to the universe of CDAX control firms. The table provides coefficient estimates only for selected interaction terms. */**/*** indicate statistical significance at the 10%/5%/1% level.

D. Conclusion

All existing studies on hedge fund activism analyze events which took place during time periods with favorable capital market conditions when share prices were generally rising, liquidity was high, and there was low limited asset price volatility. However, there are several reasons to expect that hedge fund activism only works as a state-contingent governance mechanism and that valuation effects should be smaller during time periods of distress in financial markets. This hypothesis has been strongly supported by the empirical analysis in this chapter which focused on those hedge fund investments in the German capital market taking place during the recent financial crisis. In particular, the results find only limited support for positive share price reactions in the short and in the longer run. In fact, there are only significantly positive abnormal returns immediately around the event date. For longer time periods there is a pronounced underperformance compared to the aggregate German stock market. This can be partially explained by the small size of sample firms which is reflected in significant exposures to the size-factor. Thus, the underperformance can be explained by higher information asymmetries and financing constraints of target firms which become particularly severe in down-market environments.

The empirical finding is that hedge fund engagements can only create value during up-markets. This result raises further interesting research questions. In particular, this empirical result could be driven by three different mechanisms. First, during down-markets hedge funds cannot successfully implement their restructuring measures because capital markets do not offer attractive valuations and sufficient liquidity to sell-off non-core assets or to raise additional debt financing. Second, the magnitude of agency problems of free cash flows is relatively small during down-markets since the economic recession already puts managers under pressure to increase the efficiency of their firm's operations. And third, the risk that leveraged hedge funds have to prematurely unwind their positions due to their own performance problems might generate significant downward pressure on the stocks of target companies. Thus, differentiating among these three mechanisms appears to be an interesting question which is left for future research.

Chapter IV. Robustness Checks

The previous two chapters focused on the valuation effects triggered by hedge fund engagements in the German capital market. However, if hedge funds pursue the objective of improving corporate strategies, financial structures and governance then their engagements should also affect several other variables. In particular, the operating performance of target companies should improve when the hedge funds interference increases the efficiency of corporate investment decisions. This occurs because hedge funds typically ask managers to spin-off non-core assets, to break-up value-destroying conglomerates and to increase leverage which imposes additional discipline on corporate managers. Consequently, if this hypothesis is correct, then future operating performance should improve in line with current period increases in share prices as the market expects future increases in earnings and cash flows. Additionally, hedge fund engagements might also affect the liquidity of target stocks. In particular, before the event date there is a run-up in share prices which might be related to hedge funds accumulating shares in target companies. This in turn might temporarily extract liquidity out of the market for the company's shares. After the event date, liquidity may increase because the presence of sophisticated investors in their ownership structure might spark the interest of other investors in the firm leading to an increase in trading activity. This increase in liquidity would help to reduce the firm's cost of capital, which should in turn be associated with a permanent increase in share prices.

It is interesting to analyze these hypotheses in more detail because this might help to explain the patterns in stock prices identified in the previous two chapters. Therefore, this chapter presents the results of a series of robustness checks which focus on the operating performance and liquidity of target companies. The first section focuses on the operating performance and the second section investigates the time-series behavior of the liquidity of target stocks.

A. Operating Performance

If hedge funds really increase the fundamental value of target firms then their engagements should not only be associated with increases in share prices but should also lead to improvements in their operating performance in future time periods. In particular, it can be argued that target firms should be among the underperformers in their industries and exhibit below average operating performance during the time period before the hedge fund investment. After the hedge fund engagements, however, their operating performance should improve continuously due to more efficient investment decisions. This assumes that hedge funds help to discipline managers and force them to sell off non-core assets, to break-up value-destroying conglomerates and to increase leverage.

The hypothesis of improvements in operating performance is investigated in this section which analyzes the return on equity and operating cash flows for all of the 404 events occurring in the German capital market between 2000 and 2008. In line with the approach in the previous chapters, the first subsection focuses on the 235 events which took place during the up-market period from 2000 to 2006 and the second subsection investigates the 169 events that occurred during the down-market period from 2007 to 2008.

I. Good Times

During good times hedge funds can more easily restructure the business models of target firms and force incumbent managers to increase leverage. This occurs because capital markets offer sufficient liquidity to sell off non-core assets and also enable firms to raise additional leverage at low credit spreads. Moreover, agency problems of free cash flow are likely to be most pronounced during these time periods because firms typically generate higher profits and cash flows during expansionary time periods. Consequently, hedge funds can play an important role in curbing managerial moral hazard during these time periods. Assuming that hedge funds play a valuable role in corporate governance the operating performance of target firms should therefore be characterized by two properties. First, they should only achieve below-average operating performance compared to their peer group prior to the hedge fund engagement. Second, their operating performance should begin to improve over the time period after the hedge funds' investments when their measures begin to have positive effects on the firms' earnings.

This hypothesis is investigated in Table 63, which presents empirical evidence for the operating performance of target firms in the accounting periods from two years before until one year after the event date. Operating performance is measured by a return on equity and the ratio of operating cash flows to total assets. These two variables are benchmarked against two control groups in order to estimate the abnormal operating performance of event firms. The first control group is represented by the industry median based on all firms included in the major indices of the Deutsche Börse. The second control group is given by a matched firm approach such that each firm is matched according to its industry and size so that the absolute deviation in terms of market capitalizations is minimized.

Overall, the empirical evidence indicates that target firms suffer from below-average operating performance for a long time before the event date. For instance, the abnormal return on equity relative to the industry control group is -3.04% in the accounting period two years before the event date for the whole sample in panel A. This is significant at the 1%-level. This finding also applies when operating cash flows are used as a measure of operating performance. In particular, the operating cash flow of event firms is 0.93% below the operating cash flows of the industry control group. This finding is significant at the 10%-level. However, these effects are no longer significant when the measures of operating performance are also adjusted for firm size. Thus, the finding of below-average operating performance can be explained by a size-effect in firm profitability which has already been identified by other studies. Furthermore, these effects persist in the operating performance of event firms in the year before the event and in the year in which the event takes place. In addition, the differences also become significant in those periods when the control group is also adjusted for firm size. Importantly, however, these effects also carry over into the post-event period when all measures of abnormal operating performance remain significantly negative. Therefore, the hypothesis that hedge fund engagements help to improve the operating performance of target firms cannot be supported by the empirical findings.

It is often argued that more aggressive hedge funds should lead to quicker improvements in the operating performance of target firms because they put more pressure on managers to adjust business strategies, financial structure or corporate governance. Therefore, it is interesting to differentiate operating performance according to the hostility of the hedge funds' approach. The empirical results are reported in panels B and C. Overall, this analysis provides evidence that there are no meaningful differences in patterns of operating performance for the subsamples of hostile and non-hostile events. In particular, measures of abnormal operating performance are negative in both subsamples in the accounting periods before the event date and also remain negative in subsequent accounting periods. In fact, the only difference is that firms targeted by non-hostile hedge funds are characterized by a more negative level of operating performance. Overall, these results provide evidence that more aggressive hedge funds do not substantially affect the operating performance of target companies. This finding is consistent with the below-average share price performance documented in previous chapters for the subsamples of aggressive hedge funds over longer time periods. This reinforces the conclusion that more aggressive hedge funds are not interested in improving corporate governance and in increasing shareholder value. Instead, they seem to focus on short-term price effects generated by their high-profile public campaigns and expropriate other shareholders who help to increase the target's share price in the erroneous belief that the hedge fund is truly interested in creating firm value.

The previous analysis indicated that hedge fund engagements are not associated with improvements in operating performance. However, there is also the possibility that hedge funds have superior skills in timing shifts in the operating performance of target firms which allows them to generate short-term trading gains. This hypothesis is investigated in Table 64 which presents empirical results based on the GCT-approach. In particular, excess stock returns for sample firms and the control group are regressed on changes in operating performance in the concurrent accounting period. The terms in the columns labeled "all" measure the impact of contemporaneous changes in accounting fundamentals on the stock returns of all firms, i.e. sample firms and the firms in the control group, and the interaction terms in the columns "delta" measure their incremental impact on the target firms' share price performance. Thus, a positively significant coefficient in this column indicates that hedge funds profited from a positive trend in this variable. The drift dummy is set equal to 1 for the holding period (-2, 10) for each target firm and is otherwise set to zero. The CDAX-factors from the previous chapter are used to measure the systematic risk of target companies.

The empirical results in Table 64 indicate that all firms, i.e. sample firms and firms in the control group, generate higher returns during periods when their return on equity increases. Moreover, this effect is significantly larger for the subsample of firms that were targeted by hedge funds during the holding period (-2,10). This is demonstrated by the positive coefficient on the interaction term which is 0.0041 and highly significant at the 1%-level. In addition, this incremental effect appears to be largely driven by the subsample of more hostile hedge fund engagements, which becomes visible when comparing the empirical results in panels B and C. In particular, the level and statistical significance of the interaction term is substantially higher in the GCT-regressions for the subsample of hostile hedge funds compared to the subsample of non-hostile hedge funds. Thus, hostile hedge funds apparently can capitalize on short-term improvements in the return on equity of target firms. However, these effects are not supported by the same regression specifications when the operating cash flow is used as the measure of operating performance. Moreover, it is surprising to note that an increase in this measure of operating performance appears to be inversely related to stock returns over the same accounting period.

Overall, these findings do not support the notion that hedge fund engagements are related to improvements in future operating performance during the good times period which generally provides favorable market conditions for implementing restructuring plans designed to improve firm efficiency. Thus, hedge funds apparently do not use their stakes in order to play an influential role in corporate governance and improve the firm's operations and financial structure. Thus, they do not earn rents for restructuring firms and, instead, the largest fraction of their returns has to be interpreted as taking on the systematic risk exposures identified with the calendar-time portfolio- and the GCT-approach.

Table 63: Operating Performance Good Times

Period		t-2	t-1	t	t+1
Panel A: Full Sample					
Industry	RoE	-0.0304***	-0.0253***	-0.0408***	-0.0357***
	Difference to (t-1)	-	-0.0120**	-0.0171**	0.0051
	Op. CF to Assets	-0.0093*	0	-0.0109**	-0.0121***
	Difference to (t-1)	-	-0.0062	-0.0022	-0.0064
Industry & Size	RoE	-0.0120	-0.0496**	-0.0319***	-0.0292***
	Difference to (t-1)	-	-0.0229**	-0.0512***	-0.0289
	Op. CF to Assets	-0.0168	-0.0051*	-0.0116**	-0.0062*
	Difference to (t-1)	-	0	-0.0064	-0.0063
Panel B: No Hostile					
Industry	RoE	-0.0367***	-0.0322***	-0.0513***	-0.0234**
	Difference to (t-1)	-	-0.0148**	-0.0302**	0.0151
	Op. CF to Assets	-0.0085*	-0.0001	-0.0055	-0.0162**
	Difference to (t-1)	-	-0.0076	0.0071	-0.0047
Industry & Size	RoE	-0.0012	-0.0707**	-0.0522***	-0.0335**
	Difference to (t-1)	-	-0.0216**	-0.0575***	-0.0258
	Op. CF to Assets	-0.0254**	-0.0231**	-0.0098*	-0.0175*
	Difference to (t-1)	-	0.0026	0.0080	-0.0032
Panel C: Hostile					
Industry	RoE	-0.0024**	-0.0088*	-0.0331***	-0.0496***
	Difference to (t-1)	-	0	0	0
	Op. CF to Assets	-0.0098	0	-0.0207**	-0.0082*
	Difference to (t-1)	-	0	-0.0174**	-0.0079
Industry & Size	RoE	-0.0150	-0.0283	-0.0209	-0.0192**
	Difference to (t-1)	-	-0.0297	0	-0.0298
	Op. CF to Assets	0.0006	0	-0.0153*	0
	Difference to (t-1)	-	-0.0035	-0.0201**	-0.0087

This table summarizes the abnormal operating performance of the sample of 169 events which occurred during the down-market. This is measured by the return on equity and the ratio of operating cash flows to assets. These performance measures are compared to two peer groups. The first consists of the industry median for all firms that are also included in the major German stock indices (DAX, MDAX, SDAX, TecDAX) and the second is based on a matched firm approach in that each event firm is also matched to that firm in the CDAX universe for which the absolute difference in terms of market capitalization is minimized. */**/*** indicate statistical significance at the levels of 10%/5%/1%.

Table 64: Abnormal Performance and Operating Performance

Panel A: Whole Sample				
Variable	All	Delta	All	Delta
Constant	0.0005 *(0.23)*	0.0006 *(0.11)*	0.0006 *(0.27)*	0.0004 *(0.09)*
RoE_adj	**0.0003** ***(1.95)***	**0.0041** ***(2.53)***		
CF_to_Assets_adj			**-0.0005** ***(-6.14)***	0.0650 *(1.31)*
R2	0.1098		0.1212	
Nobs	51317		49120	
Panel B: No Hostile				
Constant	0.0004 *(0.20)*	0.0032 *(0.47)*	0.0005 *(0.23)*	0.0048 *(0.69)*
RoE_adj	**0.0003** ***(2.04)***	0.0029 *(1.23)*		
CF_to_Assets_adj			**-0.0004** **(-5.96)**	0.0511 *(0.77)*
R2	0.1100		0.1216	
Nobs	51317		49120	
Panel C: Hostile				
Constant	0.0006 *(0.29)*	-0.0038 *(-0.73)*	0.0007 *(0.34)*	-0.0063 *(-1.13)*
RoE_adj	**0.0003** ***(2.09)***	0.0039 *(1.85)*		
CF_to_Assets_adj			**-0.0005** ***(-5.36)***	0.0658 *(0.80)*
R2	0.1091		0.1200	
Nobs	51317		49120	

This table summarizes the results of GCT-regressions in which monthly excess stock returns are regressed on a set of proxies for the Fama-French factors (CDAX-factors), contemporaneous changes in measures of operating performance over the corresponding accounting period, a "drift"-dummy which is set equal to 1 if an event occurred during the interval (-2, 10) and a full set of interaction terms. The values in parentheses indicate t-statistics based Driscoll-Kraay standard errors.

II. Bad Times

During periods of distress in financial markets there is only a small need for hedge funds to impose discipline on incumbent management. This occurs because recessionary environments already put pressure on corporate earnings and cash flows and thereby forcing managers to enhance the efficiency of their firms' operations. Moreover, it becomes increasingly more difficult to implement hedge funds' restructuring plans during these market environments which do not offer firms liquid markets to sell off non-core assets at attractive valuations and to raise more debt at low credit spreads. Thus, it is less likely that the hedge funds attacking firms during these market periods are able to target firms with below-average operating performance and to restructure their operations. Therefore, it seems fair to assume that there should be no pronounced changes in the time-series of operating performance for this subsample.

This hypothesis is investigated in Table 65, which focuses on the operating performance of the 169 events occurring during the down-market environment between 2007 and 2008. According to the empirical results in Table 65, the operating performance of target firms in terms of return on equity and operating cash flows deteriorates substantially subsequent to the hedge fund engagement. This is in sharp contrast to the conventional view that hedge fund engagements create value and help to improve the efficiency of a firm's operations. In particular, two years prior to the event date both return on equity and the ratio of operating cash flows to assets are either not significantly different from zero or are even significantly positive. However, operating performance continuously deteriorates over the next accounting periods. As a result, many measures of operating performance become significantly negative in the year following the hedge fund engagement. However, this result is generally less pronounced when the control group is also adjusted for firm size. In particular, in this case return on equity also deteriorates in t+1 but operating cash flows actually improve in t+1. A possible explanation for this mixed evidence is that operating performance deteriorates more sharply for all small cap firms during the down-market due to the lower robustness of their business models. As the sample is also biased towards small caps this leads to an apparent deterioration in operating performance when the return on equity and operating cash flows are compared to an industry peer group. Finally, the level of aggressiveness of the hedge funds is related to operating performance during the down-market, which is not consistent with the findings for the up-market period. In particular, events classified as "non hostile" experience a more pronounced downward trend in operating performance while "hostile" events only exhibit strong negative operating performance in the event year. Overall, the major conclusion from this analysis is that hedge fund targets are apparently quite vulnerable to the down-market because the operating performance is below-average for all subsamples.

During the bad times period there is also the possibility that hedge funds might have superior skills in timing shifts in the operating performance of target firms. Therefore, Table 66 provides information regarding the relationship between the stock returns of hedge fund targets and simultaneous changes in measures of operating performance based on the GCT-approach.

According to the empirical results in Table 66, there are substantial differences in the relationship between stock returns and simultaneous changes in measures of operating performance between the periods of good and bad times. In particular, the interaction terms do not have a significant impact on contemporaneous share price performance anymore. Thus, improvements in operating performance do not have a stronger impact on stock returns for those firms which were targeted by hedge funds. Moreover, the coefficient on "all" firms for the return on equity has a significant impact on share price indicating that firms with a more (less) robust business model generate higher (lower) shareholder returns. This is consistent with more cyclical stocks generating higher losses during a down-turn.

Table 65: Operating Performance Bad Times

Panel A: Full Sample					
Periode		t-2	t=-1	t	t+1
Industry	RoE	-0.0016	-0.0130**	-0.0249***	-0.0277***
	Difference to (t-1)	-	-0.0140**	-0.0253**	-0.0371***
	Op. CF to Assets	-0.0042	-0.0083**	-0.0120***	-0.0102*
	Difference to (t-1)	-	-0.0033	-0.0074	0
Industry & Size	RoE	0.0156**	-0.0027	0.0085	-0.0381
	Difference to (t-1)	-	-0.0079	-0.0260	-0.0688*
	Op. CF to Assets	-0.0025	-0.0132*	0.0064	0.0059
	Difference to (t-1)	-	-0.0059	0.0102	-0.0111
Panel B: No Hostile					
Industry	RoE	0	-0.0134*	-0.0219**	-0.0408***
	Difference to (t-1)	-	-0.0170***	-0.0316**	-0.0371***
	Op. CF to Assets	-0.0117**	-0.0128**	-0.0134***	-0.0102
	Difference to (t-1)	-	0.0011	-0.0071	0.0007
Industry & Size	RoE	0.01556**	0.0164	0.0204	-0.0381
	Difference to (t-1)	-	-0.0057	-0.0142**	-0.0688*
	Op. CF to Assets	-0.0076	-0.0160*	0.0077	0.0059
	Difference to (t-1)	-	0.0103	0.0111	-0.0047
Panel C: Hostile					
Industry	RoE	-0.0025	-0.0117	-0.0490**	-0.0077
	Difference to (t-1)	-	0.0019	-0.0216	-0.0112
	Op. CF to Assets	0.0006	-0.0017	-0.0109	-0.0095
	Difference to (t-1)	-	-0.0091	-0.0101	-0.0017*
Industry & Size	RoE	0.0115	-0.0150	-0.0468	-0.0232
	Difference to (t-1)	-	-0.0227*	-0.0460	-0.0701
	Op. CF to Assets	0.0080	0.0065	0.0003	0.0065
	Difference to (t-1)	-	-0.0179	0.0072	-0.0256

This table summarizes the information on the abnormal operating performance for the sample of 169 events which occurred during the down-market. This is measured by the return on equity and the ratio of operating cash flows to assets. These performance measures are compared to two peer groups. The first consists of the industry median for all firms that are also included in the major German stock indices (DAX, MDAX, SDAX, TecDAX) and the second is based on a matched firm approach in that each event firm is also matched to that firm in the CDAX universe for which the absolute difference in terms of market capitalization is minimized. */**/*** indicate statistical significance at the levels of 10%/5%/1%.

Table 66: Abnormal Performance and Operating Performance

Panel A: Whole Sample				
Variable	All	Delta	All	Delta
Constant	0.0063 *(1.31)*	**-0.0091** ***(-2.26)***	0.0061 *(1.27)*	**-0.0086** ***(-1.97)***
RoE_adj	**0.0012** ***(2.42)***	-0.0015 *(-0.98)*		
CF_to_Assets_adj			-0.0021 *(-0.74)*	0.0140 *(0.44)*
R2	0.1209		0.1209	
Nobs	17840		17579	
Panel B: No Hostile				
Constant	0.0060 *(1.23)*	-0.0080 *(-1.43)*	0.0058 *(1.20)*	-0.0077 *(-1.30)*
RoE_adj	**0.0011** **(2.37)**	-0.0013 *(-1.47)*		
CF_to_Assets_adj			-0.0029 *(-1.04)*	-0.0172 *(-0.53)*
R2	0.1206		0.1205	
Nobs	17840		17579	
Panel C: Hostile				
Constant	0.0059 *(1.24)*	**-0.0088** ***(-2.50)***	0.0057 *(1.21)*	**-0.0088** ***(-2.24)***
RoE_adj	**0.0011** ***(2.27)***	0.0008 *(0.06)*		
CF_to_Assets_adj			-0.0022 *(-0.75)*	0.0595 *(1.40)*
R2	0.1212		0.1213	
Nobs	17840		17579	

This table summarizes the results of the GCT-regressions in which monthly excess stock returns are regressed on a set of proxies for the Fama-French factors (CDAX-factors), simultaneous changes in measures of operating performance over the corresponding accounting period, a "drift"-dummy which is set equal to 1 if an event occurred during the interval (-2, 10) and a full set of interaction terms. The values in parentheses indicate t-statistics based on Driscoll-Kraay standard errors.

B. Liquidity of Target Stocks

The analysis of stock returns in the previous two chapters indicated that stocks targeted by hedge funds experience strong run-up effects. These are an important determinant of the investment performance achieved by hedge funds and explain why investors trying to track a hedge funds' portfolio holdings based on publicly observable information achieve significantly lower returns. Consequently, it appears important to investigate the drivers of this run-up effect in more detail. Based on the results in the previous section, it can be concluded that this effect is not related to expected improvements in future operating performance after the hedge fund engagement. Therefore, this section focuses on changes in the liquidity of target stocks as another possible explanation. This is based on the reasoning that the run-up could also be the result of buying pressure or increased liquidity which reduces the cost of capital and thereby increasing share prices.

This section investigates this hypothesis using the liquidity measure of Amihud (2002) for the full set of 404 events occurring between 2000 and 2008. In line with the approach in the previous section the analysis is composed of two sections. The first focuses on the good times periods between 2000 and 2006 and the second investigates the bad times period between 2007 and 2008.

I. Good Times

For the events taking place during the good times period there is strong evidence for a run-up in share prices which has a persistent impact on share valuations and is not reversed after the event date. Moreover, this effect cannot be explained by expected improvements in operating performance because the results in the previous section did not provide any evidence for increases in operating performance. Therefore, it appears interesting to investigate whether this boost in share prices is related to changes in the liquidity of target stocks. This question is addressed by the liquidity measure by Amihud (2002) which is calculated as the median over the past 40 trading days. The empirical results are reported in Figure 47 which contains the time-series of this measure for the full sample and for the subsamples of "hostile" and "non-hostile" events.

Figure 47: Liquidity Measure by Amihud (2002) - Good Times

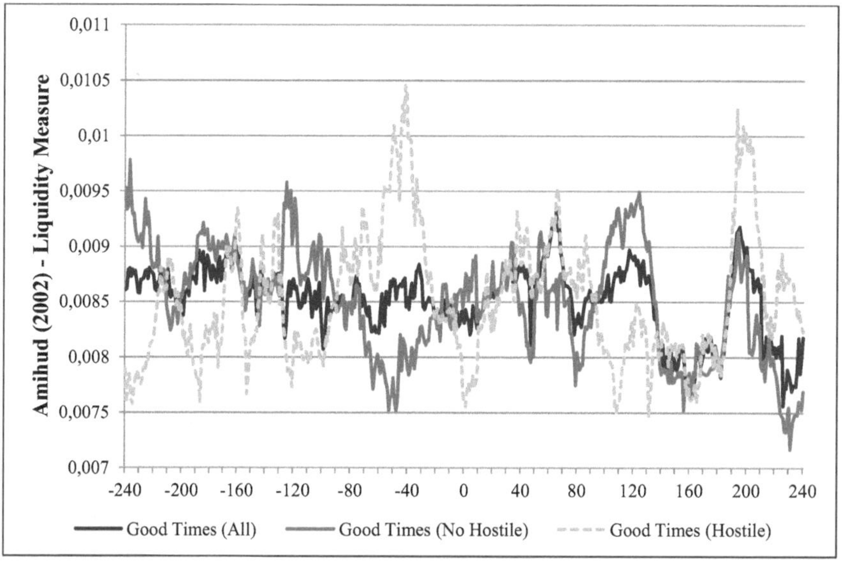

This figure plots the liquidity ratio by Amihud (2002) for the time period from 240 trading days before until 240 trading days after the event date. A window of 40 trading days is used in order to estimate the median for each stock. The resulting time-series is plotted for three subsamples. The first includes all events, the second only contains the events involving passive hedge funds and the third only includes events involving aggressive hedge funds.

The liquidity of target shares should experience a structural break approximately 40 trading days before the event, assuming that the run-up in share prices is related to changes in liquidity. However, according to the results in Figure 47, the liquidity measure by Amihud (2002) does not experience any significant patterns during this time period. In fact, it fluctuates in a relatively narrow band ranging from 0.0075 to 0.01. Hence, it is not possible to identify significant movements in the liquidity of target firms. Interestingly, however, for the subsample of "hostile" events the liquidity ratio experiences a pronounced peak approximately 40 trading days before the event date. This indicates that the price impact of a given level of dollar trading volume increases sharply during this time period. This can be interpreted as evidence that the persistent buying of shares by the hedge funds extracts liquidity out of the order book for the company's stock. However, according to the test statistics in Table 67, this effect is not statistically significant as there is no significant difference between the liquidity ratio in t = -40 and at the beginning of the observation period in t = -240.

Moreover, there should be a significant downward shift in the liquidity ratio if the increase in valuation levels generated by the run-up effect is related to improvements in the liquidity of target stocks. However, this cannot be identified in the empirical results reported in Figure 47 and Table 67.

Table 67: Changes in Liquidity – Good Times

	(t=-240)	(t=-80)	(t=-40)	(t=0)	t=40	t=80	t=240
Panel A: Full Sample							
Median Liquidity	0.0086	0.0085	0.0085	0.0083	0.0088	0.0083	0.0082
Difference to (t-1)	-	0.0002	-0.0001	-0.0001	-0.0001	0.0001	-0.0001
Panel B: No Hostile							
Median Liquidity	0.0095	0.0085	0.0079	0.0086	0.0084	0.0080	0.0077
Difference to (t-1)	-	-0.0003	-0.0003	-0.0003	0.0002	0.0000	-0.0004
Panel C: Hostile							
Median Liquidity	0.0079	0.0086	0.0099	0.0076	0.0088	0.0085	0.0082
Difference to (t-1)	-	0.0000	0.0000	0.0002	-0.0002	0.0001	0.0003

This table summarizes the information on the liquidity ratio by Amihud (2002) for the time period from 240 trading days before until 240 trading days after the event date. A window of 40 trading days is used in order to estimate the median for each stock. The resulting time-series is plotted for three subsamples. Panel A includes all events; Panel B only contains the events involving passive hedge funds; and Panel C only includes events involving aggressive hedge funds.

Based on this empirical evidence for the good times period, it seems fair to conclude that there is no systematic relationship between the run-up effect and the increasing valuation level of target firms around the event date.

II. Bad Times

The properties of the run-up effect and the subsequent behavior of stock returns are different for the subsample of events during the bad times period. In particular, the run-up effect does not have a persistent impact on share valuations and is quickly reversed after the event date. Therefore, it seems very likely that this humped-shaped pattern in share prices is generated by temporary buying pressure generated by hedge funds accumulating their position in target shares. This question is also investigated by using the liquidity measure of Amihud (2002) which is calculated as the median over the past 40 trading days. The empirical results are plotted in Figure 48, which contains the time-series of this measure for the full sample and for the subsamples of "hostile" and "non-hostile" events.

Figure 48: Liquidity Measure by Amihud (2002) - Bad Times

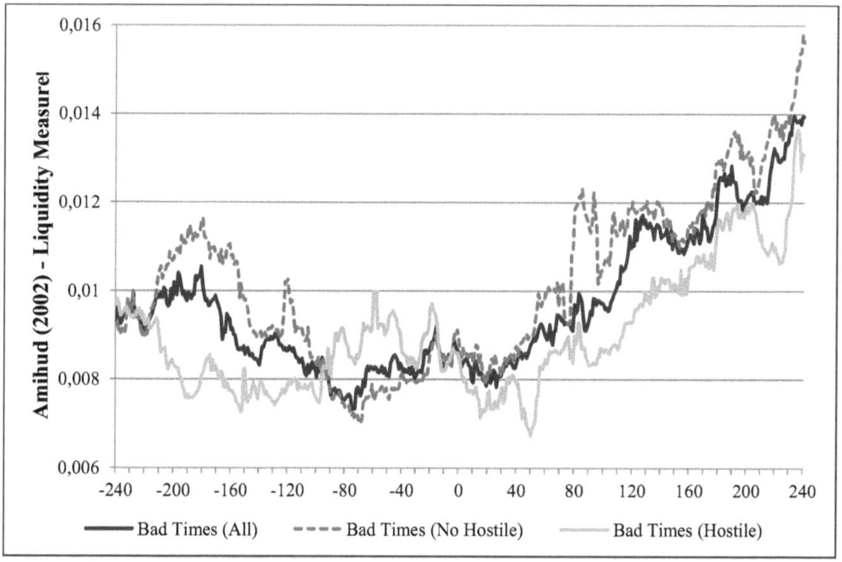

This figure plots the liquidity ratio by Amihud (2002) for the time period from 240 trading days before until 240 trading days after the event date. A window of 40 trading days is used in order to estimate the median for each stock. The resulting time-series is plotted for three subsamples. The first includes all events, the second only contains the events involving passive hedge funds and the third only includes events involving aggressive hedge funds.

If the humped-shaped pattern in share prices is related to the liquidity of target shares then there should be a temporary shift in the liquidity measure during the time period corresponding to the run-up effect. However, Figure 48 provides only limited evidence that such a shift in the liquidity ratio occurs during the 40 trading days immediately prior to the event date, as there is a small spike in the liquidity measure approximately 20 trading days before the event date. Thus, there is only weak evidence that the combination of pre-event run-up and post-even reversal is related to limited liquidity in combination with buying pressure.

Another interesting result in Figure 48 is that the liquidity of target shares apparently declines sharply for all subsamples for longer holding periods. In particular, the liquidity ratio is smaller than 0.01 for most subsamples for most of the time. However, starting approximately 40 trading days after the event date it begins to increase sharply and reaches a maximum of 0.014 after 240 trading days. Interestingly, according to the test statistics in Table 68, this shift is statistically significant for all subsamples.

Table 68: Changes in Liquidity – Bad Times

	(t=-240)	(t=-80)	(t=-40)	(t=0)	t=40	t=80	t=240
Panel A: Full Sample							
Median Liquidity	0.0093	0.0075	0.0083	0.0085	0.0084	0.0097	0.0135
Difference to (t-1)	-	-0.0003	-0.0002	-0.0004	0.0004	0.0010**	0.0048***
Panel B: No Hostile							
Median Liquidity	0.0093	0.0074	0.0081	0.0089	0.0088	0.0119	0.0156
Difference to (t-1)	-	0.0002	-0.0002	-0.0001	0.0004	0.0012***	0.0061***
Panel C: Hostile							
Median Liquidity	0.0098	0.0089	0.0086	0.0085	0.0079	0.0090	0.0131
Difference to (t-1)	-	-0.0003	-0.0004	-0.0010	0.0005	0.0008	0.0032***

This table summarizes the information on the liquidity ratio by Amihud (2002) for the time period from 240 trading days before until 240 trading days after the event date. A window of 40 trading days is used in order to estimate the median for each stock. The resulting time-series is plotted for three subsamples. Panel A includes all events; Panel B only contains the events involving passive hedge funds; and Panel C only includes events involving aggressive hedge funds.

In particular, the median for the full sample is 0.0093 in t = 240 and reaches a level of 0.0135 which is significantly higher at the 1%-level. This finding helps to explain the strong underperformance of firms targeted by hedge funds during the down-market. In fact, these target firms suffer from a substantial reduction in the liquidity of their shares during the financial crisis. This puts high pressure on their share prices explaining the strongly negative returns earned by hedge fund targets during this time period. This can be interpreted as evidence that the hedge funds were also caught off guard by the break-out of the financial crisis.

III. Summary

The analysis in the previous three chapters has revealed that hedge fund active investments in the German capital market generate some interesting valuation effects. In particular, valuations effects appear to be stronger for firms that become takeover targets subsequent to the hedge fund engagements. This is similar to evidence for the U.S. capital market (Greenwood and Schoar, 2009). Morever, more aggressive hedge funds only lead to superior returns for short holding periods. This is not consistent with evidence for the U.S. market (Boyson and Mooradian, 2007). However, while the short-term stock price performance of firms targeted during the up-market period was generally positive, there is empirical evidence that target firms during the subsequent down-market experienced a substantial underperformance relative to the broad German stock market index. Importantly, the valuation effect can be at least partially explained by exposures to the size-factor for longer holding periods. Thus, after adjusting for post-event risk characteristics there is no significant out- or underperformance of target firms.

In order to check whether these valuation effects are consistent with changes in firm characteristics over the same time period this chapter presents the results of several robustness checks. Most importantly, there is empirical evidence that target firms do not achieve a superior operating performance compared to their peer group during the time periods before and after the hedge fund engagements. This confirms the findings from the analysis of long-term valuation effects which did not identify significant alphas based on the Fama-French three-factor model. Moreover, there are also no structural breaks in the liquidity of target stocks before and after the event date which is consistent with the finding of no significant out- or underperformance in the short- or long-run. Surprisingly, however, there are also no temporary shifts in liquidity during the run-up period. Thus, temporary buying pressure cannot be used to explain the pre-event run-up. However, during the down-market period there is a pronounced decrease in liquidity for longer holding periods which extends into the crisis period. This might also help to explain the below-average share price performance of hedge fund targets during this time period.

Part IV. Conclusion and Outlook

The total amount of capital managed by hedge funds has grown significantly over the last decade. Therefore, understanding hedge funds is important for investors, regulators and politicians because they differ in many important aspects from conventional mutual funds and pension funds. In particular, they are not subject to regulatory restrictions on their investment strategies and can therefore implement sophisticated dynamic trading strategies using leverage and derivative instruments. Moreover, their managers face high-powered incentives to generate returns which also might have substantial implications on their trading behavior. Due to these special characteristics, the growth of hedge funds has important implications for nearly all dimensions of financial intermediation. This dissertation focuses on two of these aspects, including the implications of hedge funds for asset management and for corporate governance.

The first part of this dissertation investigates hedge funds from an asset management perspective and focused on an important trade-off facing hedge fund investors. On the one hand, hedge funds generate additional portfolio benefits in the form of alpha, alternative risk premia and low correlations. On the other hand, hedge fund investments expose investors to additional risks such as phase-locking correlations, lock-up restrictions and higher-order moment risks. Determining the value-maximizing trade-off between these benefits and costs appears to be an important research question from the perspective of asset management. However, this issue is still largely unresolved for a variety of reasons. Most importantly, it is still not clear how to appropriately define investor preferences for higher-order moments and how to model the associated trade-offs. As a result, different studies rely on different models and come to widely differing conclusions regarding the optimal size of the allocation to hedge funds. Moreover, existing research neglects other important determinants of optimal asset allocations which have been thoroughly addressed for other asset classes. For instance, even though it is well-known that optimal allocations depend on the investment horizon, there is only one study so far which addresses this research question. Instead, all other studies rely on single-period models which do not help most institutional and retail investors who tend to have rather long investment horizons. Moreover, optimal asset allocations also depend on investor characteristics including their background risks, the risks contained in their liabilities and differences in regulation and sophistication. These important issues have not yet been satisfactorily addressed. Therefore, it is not surprising that the current state of research cannot explain why only one class of institutional investors, namely U.S. university endowments, make large allocations to hedge funds. Moreover, other important issues have also not yet been satisfactorily addressed by existing research. This includes the value of hedge funds to long-term investors and the value of hedge funds to different types of investors such as pension funds, endowments, insurance companies and retail investors all of whom differ substantially in their ability and willingness to take on the risks of hedge fund investments. Consequently, it is not surprising that the allocations to hedge funds by most institutional and retail investors are small. Moreover, the growth and increasing institutionalization of hedge funds also creates new challenges for research and asset management in that they might have significant repercussions on the investment properties of hedge funds. Thus, existing empirical research has not addressed all important research questions so far. Therefore, in order to address one gap in the existing literature, the last chapter in this part presents the results of an empirical study investigating the portfolio contribution of hedge funds in different market environments. This provides strong evidence for time-variation in the portfolio benefits of hedge funds. In particular, hedge funds add significant value to investors' portfolios during time periods of rising stock markets. This casts some doubt on the hedge funds' proposition that they really deliver returns that are independent of market conditions.

The second part of this dissertation focuses on the implications of hedge funds on corporate governance. This is particularly important in Germany and other Continental European countries which, unlike the market-based systems of the U.S. and UK, have not traditionally experienced active interference by capital markets in corporate governance. Consequently, the German business establishment, regulators and politicians were surprised by the first high-profile incident of hedge fund activism involving the Anglo-Saxon hedge funds TCI and Atticus attacking the management of the German security exchange operator Deutsche Börse. Ultimately, this attack had a substantial impact on the subsequent development of the firm in that the hedge funds made significant adjustments to the firm's corporate governance and actively interfered in its investment decisions and financial policies. In particular, they forced the Deutsche Börse to abandon its takeover bid for the London Stock Exchange, to implement several efficiency programs and to recapitalize its balance sheets by distributing its liquidity reserves to shareholders. This new form of shareholder activism raises the fundamental question of whether hedge funds make corporate governance more efficient. In fact, the activist campaigns by hedge funds can have positive as well as negative implications on corporate governance and consequently on the creation of firm value. The conventional view is that these shareholder activists help to reduce agency problems of free cash flow, thereby increasing firm value. This is based on the reasoning that they attack mature value firms whose management would otherwise use the large amounts of free cash flows generated by these firms to build overly diversified "corporate empires". Therefore, hedge funds seem to raise value by forcing these firms to break-up inefficient conglomerates and by forcing managers to distribute excessive liquidity reserves and/or to increase leverage. At the same time, however, the tactics employed by these activist hedge funds can create additional agency problems. In particular, these measures can also be used by hedge funds to increase the operating and financial risk of target firms. This might enable them to capitalize on the resulting risk shifting effects reducing the value of debtholders' claims on the firm's cash flows. Moreover, there are also agency problems with other shareholders because hedge funds frequently trade in derivatives. This allows hedge funds to hide their true position in the target firm preventing other investors from making a fair assessment of the activists' true objectives. Furthermore, additional agency problems can emerge with other shareholders if capital markets are inefficient. In this case hedge funds might be able to engineer temporary boosts in share prices which help them to capitalize on short-term gains in share prices. These can come at the expense of long-term shareholders if these measures force companies to abandon investment projects with a positive net present value and cut capital expenditures or investments in R&D.

From a theoretical point of view, it is a-priori not clear which of these effects dominates. Therefore, it is necessary to conduct an empirical analysis to detect which issues are most important in practice. This is performed in the second half of the second part of this dissertation. This presents the result of an empirical study of the performance of a sample of 404 events in which hedge funds acquired stakes in German companies between January 1st, 2000 and December 31st, 2008. Compared to other studies for the German capital market, this empirical study offers the advantage that it investigates a longer time period including time periods of both rising and falling stock markets. This is important because the value of hedge fund activism as a corporate governance mechanism should differ significantly depending on aggregate market and economic conditions. The empirical study has three major results. First, even though hedge fund engagements are associated with significantly positive cumulative abnormal returns over short holding periods the empirical evidence for longer term abnormal performance is less convincing. In particular, more advanced methods such as the calendar-time portfolio approach and the generalized calendar-time approach provided strong evidence that the apparent outperformance based on buy-and-hold abnormal returns is due to omitted risk factors. Specifically, hedge fund targets outperform the general market because they have high loadings on the size-factor which compensates investors for the limited liquidity and the high information risks associated with investments in intransparent small cap firms. Thus, hedge funds acquiring stakes in German firms do not always assume the role of corporate governance activists earning monitoring rents. Second, there is a strong relationship between realized valuation effects and the capital market environment which has not been thoroughly investigated by other studies. In particular, target companies generate significantly negative returns during down-markets. In fact, it seems that during the down-market the associated real economic recession already puts sufficient pressure on managers to improve the efficiency of their firms. This suggests that hedge fund activism can only be interpreted as a state-contingent corporate governance device which can only be effective during good times. Third, there is strong evidence that hedge funds expropriate other shareholders. In particular, there are long and pronounced run-up periods prior to the event date when hedge funds disclose their position to the public capital market. In addition, there are several more aggressive hedge funds operating in the German capital market who apparently generate temporary boosts in share prices in order to make a quick exit. This can impose additional losses on other "naïve" shareholders who trade the stocks targeted by these activists based on the belief that hedge funds were truly interested in restructuring these firms.

These findings have important implications for the regulatory debate on hedge funds. In particular, the major problem is not the conflict between hedge funds and incumbent management. Rather, the most important issue is the conflict between other shareholders and the hedge funds who actively take advantage of loopholes in disclosure regulations. This prevents other investors from discerning the true economic exposure of hedge funds to the target firm's share price and infering their true motivation. Consequently, other investors cannot differentiate between those hedge funds which have value-increasing proposals and those which try to expropriate them. This is due to three problems in the details of German disclosure regulations which are responsible for the low degree of transparency concerning hedge funds' activities. First, the enforcement of German disclosure rules is rather weak (Weber and

Zimmermann, 2010). As a result, the reporting lags are fairly long compared to the reporting regime in the U.S. This provides hedge funds with substantial time to build up and sell off their positions before they need to disclose their positions to other investors. Second, new amendments introduced into German disclosure regulations in 2007 only require investors to state their intentions upon crossing the threshold of 10% of voting rights, whereas the corresponding rules in the U.S. require the disclosure of this information upon crossing the initial 5%-threshold. Thus, as most hedge funds rely on significantly smaller stakes to initiate their campaigns, they are effectively not covered by this amendment. Third, German disclosure rules do not include cash-settled derivatives which are frequently used by hedge funds to disguise their trading activities. This is also in contrast to the reporting regime in the U.S. which has already reacted and closed this loophole.

Finally, there are still many interesting research questions regarding the implications of hedge funds on financial markets. In particular, their contribution to the liquidity of financial markets and their impact on the efficiency of asset prices are still unresolved issues. Moreover, there is still no solid empirical evidence indicating whether the presence of hedge funds really increases the level of systemic risk. This analysis will require a comprehensive approach, simultaneously considering the behavior and interactions among all the important players in financial markets. This will be necessary because the balance sheets of many other financial intermediaries are characterized by similar risk exposures and because they also face similar incentive mechanisms as hedge funds. This important issue is left for future research.

Bibliography

Achleitner, Ann-Kristin, Andres, Christian, Betzer, André and Charlie Weir (2010), Wealth Effects of Private Equity Investments on the German Stock Market, in: European journal of Finance, forthcoming.

Achleitner, Ann-Kristin, Betzer, André and Bastian Hinterramskogler (2009), Private Equity Investors as Corporate Governance Mechanism in Continental Europe, Working Paper.

Achleitner, Ann-Kristin, Betzer, André und Jasmin Gider (2008), Do Corporate Governance Motives Drive Hedge Funds and Private Equity Activities, Working Paper.

Ackermann, Carl, McEnally, Richard and David Ravenscraft (1999), The Performance of Hedge Funds: Risk, Return and Incentives, in: Journal of Finance 54, 833-874.

Adams, Michael (1999), Cross Holdings in Germany, in: Journal of Institutional and Theoretical Economics 155, 80-109.

Admati, Anat R. and Paul Pfleiderer (2009), The "Wall Street Rule" and Shareholder Activism: Exit as a Form of Voice, in: Review of Financial Studies 22, 2645-2685.

Adrian, Tobias and Markus K. Brunnermeier (2007), Hedge Fund Tail Risk, Working Paper.

Adrian, Tobias and Markus K. Brunnermeier (2009), CoVar, Working Paper.

Agarwal, Vikas and Narayan Y. Naik (2000): Multi-Period Performance Persistence Analysis of Hedge Funds, in: Journal of Financial and Quantitative Analysis 35, 327-342.

Agarwal, Vikas and Narayan Y. Naik (2004), Risks and Portfolio Decisions involving Hedge Funds, in: Review of Financial Studies 17, 63-98.

Agarwal, Vikas, Daniel, Naveen D. and Narayan Y. Naik (2007), Why is Santa so Kind to Hedge Funds? The December Puzzle, Working Paper.

Agarwal, Vikas, Daniel, Naveen D. and Narayan Y. Naik (2009), Role of Managerial Incentives and Discretion in Hedge Fund Performance, in: Journal of Finance 64, 2221-2256.

Agarwal, Vikas, Fung, William H., Loon, Yee Cheng and Narayan Y. Naik (2009), Risk and Return in Convertible Arbitrage: Evidence from the Convertible Bond Market, Working Paper.

Aggarwal, Raj and Shelly Zhao (2009), The Diversification Discount Puzzle: Evidence from a Transaction-Cost Resolution, in: Financial Review 44, 113-135.

Aggarwal, Rajesh K. and Philippe Jorion (2010), The Performance of Emerging Hedge Funds and Managers, in: Journal of Financial Economics 96, 238-256.

Aggarwal, Reena, Erel, Isil, Stulz, René M. and Rohan Williamson (2009), Differences in Governance Practices between U.S. and Foreign Firms:

Measurement, Causes, and Consequences, in: Review of Financial Studies 22, 3131-3169.

Ahn, Seougpil, Denis, David J. and Diane K. Denis (2006), Leverage and Investment in Diversified Firms, in: Journal of Financial Economics 79, 317-337.

Akdogu, Evrim (2009), Gaining a Competitive Edge through Acquisitions: Evidence from the Telecommunications Industry, in: Journal of Corporate Finance 15, 99-112.

Alexander, Gordon J. and Alexandre M. Baptista (2002), Economic Implications of Using a Mean-VaR Model for Portfolio Selection: A Comparison with Mean-Variance Analysis, in: Journal of Economic Dynamics & Control 26, 1159-1193.

Allen, Franklin and Douglas Gale (1995), A Welfare Comparison of Intermediaries and Financial Markets in Germany and the US, in: European Economic Review 39, 179-209.

Allen, Franklin and Douglas Gale (1999), Diversity of Opinion and Financing of New Technologies, in: Journal of Financial Intermediation 8, 68-89.

Allen, Franklin and Roni Michaely (2003), Payout Policy, in: Constantinides, George M., Harris, Milton and René M. Stulz (eds), Handbook of the Economics of Finance, Elsevier, North Holland, 337-429.

Allen, Jeffrey W. and John J. McConnell (1998), Equity Carve-Outs and Managerial Discretion, in: Journal of Finance 53, 163–186.

Almeida, Heitor V. and Thomas Philippon (2007), The Risk-Adjusted Cost of Financial Distress, in: Journal of Finance 62, 2557-2586.

Almeida; Heitor V. and Daniel Wolfenzon (2006), A Theory of Pyramidial Ownership and Family Business Groups, in: Journal of Finance 61, 2637-2680.

Althayde, Gustavo M. de and Renato G. Flôres Jr (2004), Finding a Maximum Skewness Portfolio – A General Solution to Three-Moments Portfolio Choice, in: Journal of Economic Dynamics & Control 28, 1335-1352.

Amenc, Noel and Lionel Martellini (2002), Portfolio Optimization and Hedge Fund Style Allocation Decisions, in: Journal of Alternative Investments 5, Winter, 7-20.

Amenc, Noel, El Bied, Sina, and Lionel Martellini (2003), Predictability in Hedge Fund Returns, in: Financial Analysts Journal 59, Sept/Oct, 32-46

Amihud, Yakov (2002), Illiquidity and Stock Returns: Cross-Section and Time-Series Effects, in: Journal of Financial Markets 5, 31-56.

Amihud, Yakov and Baruch Lev (1981), Risk Reduction as a Managerial Motive for Conglomerate Mergers, in: Bell Journal of Economics 12, 605-617.

Amihud, Yakov and Haim Mendelson (1986), Asset Pricing and the Bid-Ask Spread, in: Journal of Financial Economics 17, 223-249.

Amin, Gaurav S. and Harry M. Kat (2002), Hedge Fund Attrition and Survivorship Bias Over the Period 1994-2001, Working Paper.

Amin, Gaurav S. and Harry M. Kat (2003), Hedge Fund Performance 1990-2000: Do the 'Money Machines' really Add Value?, in: Journal of Financial and Quantitative Analysis 38, 251-274.

Amin, Gaurav S. and Harry M. Kat (2003), Stocks, Bonds, and Hedge Funds, in: Journal of Portfolio Management 29, 113-120.

Ammann, Manuel, Hoechle, Daniel and Markus Schmid (2009), Is There really no Diversification Discount? Working Paper.

Ammann, Manuel, Oesch, David and Markus M. Schmid (2009), Corporate Governance and Firm Value: International Evidence, in: Working Paper.

Anderson, Ronald C., Bates, Thomas W., Bizjak, John M. and Michael L. Lemmon (2000), Corporate Governance and Firm Diversification, in: Financial Management 29, 5-22.

Andrade, Gregor and Erik Stafford (2002), Investigating the Economic Role of Mergers, in: Journal of Corporate Finance 10, 1-36.

Andrade, Gregor and Steven N. Kaplan (1998), How Costly is Financial (Not Economic) Distress? Evidence from Highly Leverage Transactions that Became Distressed, in: Journal of Finance 53, 1443-1493.

Andrade, Gregor, Mitchell, Mark and Erik Stafford (2001), New Evidence and Perspectives on Mergers, in: Journal of Economic Perspectives 15, 103-120.

Andres, Christian, Betzer, André and Charlie Wei (2007), Shareholder Wealth Gains Through Better Corporate Governance – The Case of European LBO Transactions, in: Financial Markets and Portfolio Management 21, 403-424.

Ang, Andrew and Geert Bekaert (2002), International Asset Allocation with Regime Shifts, in: Review of Financial Studies 15, 1137-1187.

Ang, Andrew, Hodrick, Robert J., Xing, Yuhang, and Xiaoyan Zhang (2006), The Cross-Section of Volatility and Expected Returns, in: Journal of Finance 61, 259-299.

Aragon, George O. (2007), Share Restrictions and Asset Pricing: Evidence from the Hedge Fund Industry, in: Journal of Financial Economics 83, 33-58.

Arditti, Fred D. (1967), Risk and the Required Return on Equity, in: Journal of Finance 22, 19-36.

Ataullah, Ali, Davidson, Ian and Hang Le (2010), Large Shareholder, the Board of Directors and the Allocation of Cash Proceeds from Corporate Asset Sell-Offs, in: European Financial Management 16, 271-295.

Atennassov, Julian and E. Han Kim (2009), Labor and Corporate Governance: International Evidence from Restructuring Decisions, in: Journal of Finance 64, 341-374.

Avramov, Doron, Barras, Laurent and Robert Kosowski (2008), Understanding Hedge Fund Return Predictability: A Comprehensive Outlook Using a Fund-by-Fund Analysis, Working Paper.

Avramov, Doron, Kosowski, Robert, Naik, Narayan Y. and Melvyn Teo (2007), Investing in Hedge Funds When Returns are Predictable, Working Paper.

Avramow, Doron and Russ Wermers (2006), Investing in Mutual Funds When Returns are Predictable, in: Journal of Financial Economics 81, 339-377.

Bae, Kee-Hong and Vidhan K. Goyal (2009), Creditor Rights, Enforcement, and Bank Loans, in: Journal of Finance 64, 823-860.

Bagwell, Laurie S. (1991), Shareholder Heterogeneity: Evidence and Implications, in: American Economic Review 81, 218-221.

Baker, Malcolm and Jeffrey Wurgler (2004a), A Catering Theory of Dividends, in: Journal of Finance 59, 1125-1165.

Baker, Malcolm and Jeffrey Wurgler (2004b), Appearing and Disappearing Dividends: The Link to Catering Incentives, in: Journal of Financial Economics 73, 271-288.

Baker, Malcolm and Serkan Savasoglu (2002), Limited Arbitrage in Mergers & Acquisitions, in: Journal of Financial Economics 64, 91-115.

Baks, Klaas P., Metrick, Andrew and Jessica Wachter (2001), Should Investors Avoid All Actively Managed Mutual Funds? A Study in Bayesian Performance Evaluation, in: Journal of Finance 56, 45-85.

Bali, Turan G., Gokcan, Suleyman and Bing Liang (2007), Value at Risk and the Cross-Section of Hedge Fund Returns, in: Journal of Banking & Finance 31, 1135-1166.

Ball, Clifford A. and Walter N. Torous (1988), Investigating Security-Price Performance in the Presence of Event-date Uncertainty, in: Journal of Financial Economics 22, 123-153.

Bange, Mary M. and Werner F.M. De Bondt (1998), R&D Budgets and Corporate Earnings Targets, in: Journal of Corporate Finance 4, 153-184.

Banz, Rolf W. (1981), The Relationship between Return and Market Value of Common Stock, in: Journal of Financial Economics 9, 3-18.

Baquero, Guillermo, ter Horst, Jenke and Marno Verbeek (2005), Survival, Look-Ahead Bias, and the Persistence in Hedge Fund Performance, in: Journal of Financial and Quantitative Analysis 40, 493-517.

Barber, Brad M. and John D. Lyon (1996), Detecting Abnormal Operating Performance: The Empirical Power and Specification of Test Statistics, in: Journal of Financial Economics 41, 359-399.

Barber, Brad M. and John D. Lyon (1997), Detecting Long-run Abnormal Stock Returns: The Empirical Power and Specification of Test Statistics, in: Journal of Financial Economics 43, 341-372.

Barber, Brad M. and Terrance Odean (2008), All That Glitters: The Effect of Attention and News on the Buying Behavior of Individual and Institutional Investors, in: Review of Financial Studies 21, 785-818.

Barberis, Nicholas, Huang, Ming and Tano Santos (2001), Prospect Theory and Asset Prices, in: Quarterly Journal of Economics 141, 1-53.

Barca, Marco and Marco Becht (2001), The Control of Corporate Europe, Oxford University Press, Oxford.

Barclay, Michael J. and Clifford G. Holderness (1989), Private Benefits from Control of Public Corporations, in: Journal of Financial Economics 25, 371-395.

Barclay, Michael J. and Clifford W. Smith (2005), The Capital Structure Puzzle: The Evidence Revisited, in: Journal of Applied Corporate Finance 17, 8-17.

Barclay, Michael, Holderness, Clifford G. and Dennis P. Sheehan (2009), Dividends and Corporate Shareholders, in: Review of Financial Studies 22, 2423-2455.

Barès, Pierre-Antoine, Gibson, Rajna and Sebastien Gyger (2003), Performance in the Hedge Fund Industry: An Analysis of Short and Long Term Persistence, in: Journal of Alternative Investments 6, Winter, 25-41.

Barry, Ross (2003), Hedge Funds: A Walk through the Graveyard, Working Paper.

Basak, Suleyman, Pavlova, Anna and Alexander Shapiro (2007), Optimal Asset Allocation and Risk Shifting in Money Management, in: Review of Financial Studies 20, 1583-1621.

Bates, Thomas W. (2005), Asset Sales, Investment Opportunities, and the Use of Proceeds, in: Journal of Finance 60, 105-135.

Bates, Thomas W., Lemmon, Michael L. and James S. Linck (2006), Shareholder Wealth Effects and Bid Negotiation in Freeze-Out Deals: Are Minority Shareholders Left Out in the Cold?, in: Journal of Financial Economics 81, 681-708.

Bauguess, Scott W., Moeller, Sara B., Schlingemann, Frederik P. and Chad J. Zutter (2009), Ownership Structure and Target Returns, in: Journal of Corporate Finance 15, 48-65.

Baums, Theodor and Philipp von Randow (1995), Der Markt für Stimmrechtsvertreter, in: Die Aktiengesellschaft 40, 97-112.

Baur, Dirk G. and Brian M. Lucey (2009), Flights and Contagion – An Empirical Analysis of Stock-Bond Correlations, in: Journal of Financial Stability 5, 339-352.

Beaver, William H. (1968), The Information Content of Annual Earnings Announcements, in: Journal of Accounting Research 6, 67-92.

Bebchuk, Lucian A. (1994), Efficient and Inefficient Sales of Corporate Control, in: Quarterly Journal of Economics 103, 957-993.

Becht, Marco, Franks, Julian, Mayer, Colin and Stefano Rossi (2009), Returns to Shareholder Activism: Evidence from a Clinical Study of the Hermes UK Focus Fund, in: Review of Financial Studies 22, 3093-3129.

Becker, Bo, Cronqvist, Henrik and Rüdiger Fahlenbrach (2010), Estimating the Effects of Large Shareholders Using a Geographic Instrument, Working Paper

Beiner, Stefan, Drobetz, Wolfgang, Schmid, Markus M. and Heinz Zimmermann (2006), An Integrated Framework of Corporate Governance and Firm Valuation, in: European Financial Management 12, 249-283.

Bekaert, Geert and Campbell R. Harvey (1995), Time-Varying World Market Integration, in: Journal of Finance, 50, 403-444.

Bekaert, Geert and Michael S. Urias (1996), Diversification, Integration and Emerging Market Closed-End Funds, in: Journal of Finance 51, 835-869.

Ben-David, Itzhak and Darren T. Roulstone (2008), Why Do Small Stock Acquierers Underperform in Long Term?, Working Paper.

Benmelech, Efraim and Nittai K. Bergman (2009), Collateral Pricing, in: Journal of Financial Economics 91, 339-360.

Berger, Philip G. and Eli Ofek (1995), Diversification's Effect on Firm Value, in: Journal of Financial Economics 37, 39-65.

Berger, Philip G. and Eli Ofek (1996), Bustup Takeovers of Value-Destroying Diversified Firms, in: Journal of Finance 51, 1175-1200.

Berger, Philip G., Ofek, Eli and David L. Yermack (1997), Managerial Entrenchment and Capital Structure Decisions, in: Journal of Finance 52, 1411-1438.

Berglöf, Erik and Mike Burkart (2003), European Takeover Regulation, in: Economic Policy 18, 171-213.

Berk, Jonathan B. and Richard C. Green (2004), Mutual Fund Flows and Performance in Rational Markets, in: Journal of Political Economy 112, 1269-1295.

Berkovitch, Elazar and M.P. Narayanan (1993), Motives for Takeovers: An Empirical Investigation, in: Journal of Financial & Quantitative Analysis 28, 347-362.

Bernanke, Ben S. and Kenneth N. Kuttner (2005), What Explains the Stock Market's Reaction to Federal Reserve Policy?, in: Journal of Finance 60, 1221-1257.

Bernard, Victor (1987), Cross-Sectional Dependence and Problems in Inference in Market-based Accounting Research, in: Journal of Accounting Research 25, 1-48.

Bessler, Wolfgang (1989), Zinsrisikomanagement in Kreditinstituten, DUV, Wiesbaden.

Bessler, Wolfgang and Andreas Kurth (2007), Agency Problems and the Performance of IPOs in Germany: Venture Capital, Lock-Up Periods and Bank Ownership, in: European Journal of Finance 13, 29-63.

Bessler, Wolfgang and Claudia Bittelmeyer (2008), Patents and the Performance of Technology Firms: Evidence from Initial Public Offerings in Germany, in: Financial Markets and Portfolio Management 22, 323-356.

Bessler, Wolfgang and Heiko Opfer (2005), Macroeconomic Factors and Stock Returns in Germany, in: Daniel Baier and Klaus-Dieter Wernecke (eds.), Innovations in Classification, Data Science, and Information Systems, Springer, 419-426.

Bessler, Wolfgang and Julian Holler (2009), Hedge Funds and Asset Allocation: Investor Confidence, Diversification Benefits, and a Change in Investment Style Composition, in: Fink, Andreas, Lausen, Berthold, Seidel, Wilfried and Alfred Ultsch (eds.), Advances in Data Analysis, Data Handling and Business Intelligence, Springer, Berlin, 441-450.

Bessler, Wolfgang and Julian Holler (2010), Corporate Governance and Corporate Control: A Case Study on the Impact of Hedge Funds on the Strategy and Performance of the German Stock Exchange 'Deutsche Börse'.

Bessler, Wolfgang and Matthias Stanzel (2009), Conflicts of Interest and Research Quality of Affiliated Analysts in the German Universal Banking System: Evidence from IPO Underwriting, in: European Financial Management 15, 757-786.

Bessler, Wolfgang and Philipp Kurmann (2010), Conditonal Factor Models for European Bank Returns, Working Paper.

Bessler, Wolfgang and Thomas Book (2001), Elektronischer Handel und Globale Märkte: Motive, Strukturen und Zielkonfigurationen von internationalen Börsenkooperationen, in: Buhl, Hans U., Kreyer, Nina and Werner Steck (eds.), e-Finance: Innovative Problemlösungen für Informationssysteme in der Finanzwirtschaft, Springer, Berlin, 155-174.

Bessler, Wolfgang and Tom Nohel (1996), The Stock-Market Reaction to Dividend Cuts and Omissions by Commercial Banks, in: Journal of Banking & Finance 20, 1485-1508.

Bessler, Wolfgang and Tom Nohel (2000), Asymmetric Information, Dividend Reductions, and Contagion Effects in Bank Stock Returns, in: Journal of Banking & Finance 24, 1831-1848.

Bessler, Wolfgang and Wolfgang Drobetz (2008), Editorial, in: Financial Markets and Portfolio Management 22, 95-99.

Bessler, Wolfgang and Peter Lückoff (2007): Performancemaße und Performancemessung, in: Thießen, Friedrich (eds.), Knapps Enzyklopädisches Lexikon des Geld-, Bank- und Börsenwesens, Schriftleitung, Fritz Knapp Verlag, Frankfurt.

Bessler, Wolfgang, Becker, Christoph and Daniil Wagner (2007), Ausgestaltung und Anreizwirkung von Aktienoptionsplänen für Mitarbeiter junger innovativer Unternehmen – Eine empirische Untersuchung für den Neuen Markt, in: Andreas Langenohl und Kerstin Schmidt-Beck (eds.), Die Markt-Zeit der Finanzwirtschaft, Metropolis Verlag, Marburg.

Bessler, Wolfgang, Blake, David, Lückoff Peter, and Ian Tonks (2010), Why is Persistent Mutual Fund Performance so Difficult to Achieve? The Impact of Fund Flows and Manager Turnover, Working Paper.

Bessler, Wolfgang, Book, Thomas and Andreas Preuss (2006), Elektronischer Handel versus Parketthandel: Der Wechsel in der Marktführung im Bund-Future-Handel von der LIFFE zur DTB/Eurex, in: Bessler, Wolfgang (ed.), Börsen, Banken und Kapitalmärkte, Duncker & Humblot, Berlin, 157-186.

Bessler, Wolfgang, Drobetz, Wolfgang and Jan Zimmermann (2010), Financing Corporate Mergers and Acquisitions, in: Baker, Kent H. and Gerald S. Martin (eds.), Capital Structure and Financing Decisions, Wiley, Hoboken, forthcoming.

Bessler, Wolfgang, Drobetz, Wolfgang and Julian Holler (2007), Hedge Funds, in: Knapps Enzyklopädisches Lexikon des Geld-, Bank- und Börsenwesens, Thießen, Friedrich (ed.), Fritz Knapp Verlag, 2007.

Bessler, Wolfgang, Drobetz, Wolfgang and Julian Holler (2010a), The Returns to Hedge Funds Activism in Germany, Working Paper.

Bessler, Wolfgang, Drobetz, Wolfgang and Julian Holler (2010b), The Performance of Hedge Fund Targets in Good and Bad Times – A Comparison of Short- and Long-Term Valuation Effects before and after the Financial Crisis, Working Paper.

Bessler, Wolfgang, Drobetz, Wolfgang and Martin Seim (2009), Financing Activities and Payout Policies of Entrepreneurial Firms: Empirical Evidence from German Initial Public Offerings, Working Paper.

Bessler, Wolfgang, Drobetz, Wolfgang and Pascal Pensa (2008), Do Managers Adjust the Capital Structure to Market Value Changes? Evidence from Europe, in: Zeitschrift für Betriebswirtschaft, Special Issue: 50 Years after Modigliani & Miller, Recent Developments in Corporate Finance, 113-145.

Bessler, Wolfgang, Drobetz, Wolfgang und Jacqueline Henn (2005), Hedge Funds: Die „Königsdisziplin" der Kapitalanlage, in: Dichtl, Hubert, Kleeberg, Jochen M.

and Christian Schlenger (eds.), Handbuch Hedge Funds – Chancen, Risiken und Einsatz in der Asset Allocation, Uhlenbruch Verlag, Bad Soden, 3-54.

Bessler, Wolfgang, Holler, Julian and Martin Seim (2010), An Analysis of Alternative Methods for Measuring Long-Run Performance: An Application to Share Repurchase Announcements, in: Locarek-Junge, Hermann and Claus Weihs (eds.), Classification as a Tool for Research, Springer, Berlin, forthcoming.

Bessler, Wolfgang, Holler, Julian and Martin Seim (2010), Venture Capital and Private Equity in Germany, in: Cumming, Douglas (ed.), Private Equity – Fund Types, Risks and Returns, and Regulation, Wiley, Hoboken, 511-554.

Bessler, Wolfgang, Holler, Julian and Philipp Kurmann (2010), Hedge Funds and Optimal Asset Allocation, Bayesian Expectations, Time Varying Investment Opportunities and Mean-Variance Spanning, Working Paper.

Bessler, Wolfgang, Kaen, Fred R. and Heidemarie C. Sherman (1998), Going Public: A Corporate Governance Perspective, in: Hopt, Klaus J., Kanda, Hideki, Roe, Mark J., Wymeersch, Eddy and Stefan Prigge (eds.), Comparative Corporate Governance – The State of the Art and Emerging Research, Clarendon Press, 569-605.

Bethel, Jennifer E., Hu, Gang and Qinghai Wang (2009), The Market for Shareholder Voting Rights around Mergers and Acquisitions: Evidence from Institutional Daily Trading and Voting, in: Journal of Corporate Finance 15, 129-145.

Betton, Sandra, Eckbo, B. Espen, and Karin S. Thorburn (2008), Corporate Takeovers, in: B. Espen Eckbo (eds.), Handbook of Corporate Finance: Empirical Corporate Finance, Volume 2, Elsevier, North-Holland, 291-430.

Bhagat, Sanjai and Richard Jefferis (2002), The Econometrics of Corporate Governance Studies, MIT Press, Cambridge.

Bigelli, Marco, Mehrotra, Vikas and P. Raghavendra Rau (2008), Expropiation, Unification, and Corporate Governance in Italy, Working Paper.

Billet, Matthew T. and Hui Xue (2007), The Takeover Deterrent Effect of Open Market Share Repurchases, in: Journal of Finance 62, 1827-1850.

Billett, Matthew T., King, Tao-Hsien Dolly and David C. Mauer (2004), Bondholder Wealth Effects in Mergers and Acquistions: New Evidence from the 1980s and 1990s, in: Journal of Finance 59, 107-135.

Bittelmeyer, Claudia (2007), Patente und Finanzierung am Kapitalmarkt, DUV, Wiesbaden.

Black, Fischer and Myron Scholes (1973), The Pricing of Options and Corporate Liabilities, in: Journal of Political Economy 81, 637-654.

Blanchard, Olivier J. (1981), Output, the Stock market, and Interest Rates, in: American Economic Review 71, 132-143.

Blanchard, Olivier J., Lopez-de-Silanes, Florencio and Andrei Shleifer (1994), What Do Firms Do with Cash Windfalls? in: Journal of Financial Economics 36, 337-360.

Bodie, Zvi, Merton, Robert C., and William Samuelson (1992), Labor Supply Flexibility and Portfolio Choice in a Life-Cycle Model, in: Journal of Economic Dynamics and Control 16, 427-449.

Böhmer, Ekkeahrd (2001), Germany, in: Gugler, Klaus (Ed.), Corporate Governance and Economic Performance, Oxford University Press, New York, 96-120.

Böhmer, Ekkehard (2000), Business Groups, Bank Control, and Large Shareholders: An Analysis of German Takeovers, in: Journal of Financial Intermediation 9, 117-148.

Böhmer, Ekkehart, Masumeci, Jim and Annette B. Poulsen (1991), Event-study Methodology under Conditions of Event-induced Variance, in: Journal of Financial Economics 30, 253-272. Brown, Stephen J. and Mark I. Weinstein (1985), Derived Factors in Event Studies, in: Journal of Financial Economics 14, 491-495.

Bollen, Nicholas P.B. and Jeffrey A. Busse (2005), Short-Term Persistence in Mutual Fund Performance, in: Review of Financial Studies18, 569-597.

Bollen, Nicholas P.B. and Veronika K. Pool (2008a) Conditional Return Smoothing in the Hedge Fund Industry, in: Journal of Financial and Quantitative Analysis 43, 267-298.

Bollen, Nicholas P.B. and Veronika K. Pool (2008b), Do Hedge Fund Managers Misreport Returns? Evidence from Pooled Distribution, in: Journal of Finance 64, 2257-2288.

Bollen, Nicolas P.S. and Robert E. Whaley (2009), Hedge Fund Risk Dynamics: Implications for Performance Appraisal, in: Journal of Finance 64, 985-1035.

Bolton, Patrick and Ernst-Ludwig von Thadden (1998), Blocks, Liquidity, and Corporate Control, in: Journal of Finance 53, 1-25.

Bondarenko, Oleg (2004), Market Price of Variance Risk and Performance of Hedge Funds, Working Paper.

Bontschev, Georgi and Martin Eling (2008), Wo investieren Distressed-Securities-Hedgefonds? Ein Asset-Based Style-Faktorenmodell, Working Paper.

Book, Thomas (2001), Elektronischer Börsenhandel und globale Märkte. Eine ökonomische Analyse der Veränderungen an Terminbörsen, DUV Verlag, Wiesbaden.

Bookstaber, Richard and Jeremy Gold (1988), In Search of the Liability Asset, in: Financial Analysts Journal 44, Jan/Feb, 70-80.

Boone, Audra L. and J. Harold Mulherin (2008a), Do Auctions Induce a Winner's Curse? New Evidence from the Corporate Takeover Market, in: Journal of Financial Economics 89, 1-19.

Boone, Audra L. and J. Harold Mulherin (2008b), Do Private Equity Consortiums Impede Takeover Competition?, Working Paper.

Boot, Arnoud, Gopalan, Radhakrishnan and Anjan Thakor (2006), The Entrepreneur's Choice between Private and Public Ownership, in: Journal of Finance 61, 803-835.

Bott, Claudia (2002), Aktionärsstruktur, Kontrolle und Erfolg von Unternehmen, DUV Verlag, Wiesbaden.

Bowman, Christa H.S., Fuller, Kathleen and Amrita S. Nain (2009), Market Valuation and Acquisition Quality: Empirical Evidence, in: Review of Financial Studies 22, 633-679.

Boyd, John H., Hu, Jian and Ravi Jagannathan (2005), The Stock Market's Reaction to Unemployment News: Why Bad News is Usually Good for Stocks, in: Journal of Finance 60, 649-672.

Boyson, Nicole M. (2008), Hedge Fund Performance Persistence: A New Approach, in: Financial Analysts Journal 64, 6, 27-44.

Boyson, Nicole M. and Robert M. Mooradian (2008), Hedge Funds as Shareholder Activists from 1994-2005, Working Paper.

Bradley, Michael, Brav, Alon, Goldstein, Itay and Wei Jiang (2010), Activist Arbitrage: A Study of Open-Ending Attempts of Closed-End Funds, in: Journal of Financial Economics 95, 1-19.

Brav, Alon (1999), Inference in Long-Horizon Event Studies: A Bayesian Approach with Application to Initial Public Offerings, in: Journal of Finance 55, 1979-2016.

Brav, Alon and Paul A. Gompers (2003), The Role of Lock-Ups in Initial Public Offerings, in: Review of Financial Studies 16, 1-29.

Brav, Alon and Richmond D. Mathews (2011), Empty Voting and the Efficiency of Corporate Governance, in: Journal of Financial Economics 99, 289-307.

Brav, Alon, Jiang, Wie, Partnoy, Frank and Randall S. Thomas (2008), Hedge Fund Activism, Corporate Governance, and Firm Performance, in: Journal of Finance 63, 1729-1775.

Brav, Alon, Jiang, Wei, and Hyunseob Kim (2009), Hedge Fund Activism – A Review, in: Foundations and Trends in Finance 4, 185-246.

Brennan, Michael J. (2003), Corporate Investment Policy, in: Constantinides, George M., Harris, Milton and René M. Stulz (eds), Handbook of the Economics of Finance, Elsevier, North Holland, 167-214.

Brocato, Joe and Steve Steed (1998), Optimal Asset Allocation over the Business Cycle, in: Financial Review 33, 129-148.

Brockman, Paul and Emre Unlu (2009), Dividend Policy, Creditor Rights, and the Agency Costs of Debt, in: Journal of Financial Economics 92, 276-299.

Brophy, David J., Ouimet, Paige P. and Clemens Sialm (2009), Hedge Funds as Investors of Last Resort?, in: Review of Financial Studies 22, 541-574.

Brown, Jerold B., Watts, Ross L. and Karen H. Wruck (1988), Stock Prices and Top Management Changes, in: Journal of Financial Economics 20, 461-492.

Brown, Keith C., Dittmar, Amy and Henri Servaes (2005), Corporate Governance, Incentives, and Industry Consolidations, in: Review of Financial Studies 18, 241-270.

Brown, Keith C., Garlappi, Lorenzo and Cristian Tiu (2007), The Troves of Academe: Asset Allocation, Risk Budgeting and the Investment Performance of University Endowment Funds, Working Paper.

Brown, Stephen J. and Jerold B. Warner (1980), Measuring Security Price Performance, in: Journal of Financial Economics 8, 205-258.

Brown, Stephen J. and William N. Goetzmann (2003), Hedge Funds with Style, in: Journal of Portfolio Management 29, 101-112.

Brown, Stephen J. and Willianm N. Goetzmann (1995), Performance Persistence, in: Journal of Finance 50, 679-698.

Brown, Stephen J., Goetzmann, William N. and James Park (2001), Careers and Survival: Competition and Risk in the Hedge Fund and CTA Industry, in: Journal of Finance 56, 1869-1886.

Brown, Stephen J., Goetzmann, William N. and Roger G. Ibbotson (1999), Offshore Hedge Funds: Survival and Performance 1989-95, in: Journal of Business 72, 91-117.

Brown, William O., Mulherin, Harold and Marc D. Weidenmier (2008), Competing with the New York Stock Exchange, in: Quarterly Journal of Economics 123, 1679-1719.

Brunnermeier, Markus K. (2001), Asset Pricing under Asymmetric Information: Bubbles, Crashes, Technical Analysis and Herding, Oxford University Press, Oxford.

Brunnermeier, Markus K. (2009), Deciphering the Liquidity and Credit Crunch 2007-2008, in: Journal of Economic Perspectives 23, 77-100.

Brunnermeier, Markus K. and Lasse Heje Pedersen (2005), Predatory Trading, in: Journal of Finance 60, 1825-1863.

Brunnermeier, Markus K. and Stefan Nagel (2004), Hedge Funds and the Technology Bubble, in: Journal of Finance 59, 2013-2040.

Bundesbank (2001), Rolle und Verhalten deutscher Fondsmanager auf dem Aktienmarkt, Monatsbericht April, 45-61.

Bushee, Brian J. (1998), The Influence of Institutional Investors on Myopic R&D Investment Behavior, in: Accounting Review 73, 305-333.

Calamos, Nick P. (2003), Convertible Arbitrage: Insights and Techniques for Successful Hedging, Wiley Finance, Hoboken.

Campa, Jose Manuel and Simi Kedia (2002), Explaining the Diversification Discount, in: Journal of Finance 57, 1731-1762.

Campbell, John Y. and Luis M. Viceira (2002), Strategic Asset Allocation: Portfolio Choice for Long Term Investors, Oxford University Press, Oxford.

Campbell, John Y. and Luis M. Viceira (2005), The Term Structure of the Risk-Return Trade-Off, in: Financial Analysts Journal 61, 1, 34-44.

Campbell, John Y., Lo, Andrew W. and A. Craig MacKinlay (1997), The Econometrics of Financial Markets, Princeton University Press.

Capocci, Daniel and Georges Hübner (2004), Analysis of Hedge Fund Performance, in: Journal of Empirical Finance 11, 55-89.

Capon, Noel, Fitzsimons, Gavan J. and Russ Alan Prince (1996), An Individual Level Analysis of the Mutual Fund Investment Decision, in: Journal of Financial Services Research 10, 59-82.

Carr, Peter and Liuren Wu (2009), Variance Risk Premiums, in: Review of Financial Studies 22, 1311-1341.

Chae, Joon (2005), Trading Volume, Information Asymmetry, and Timing Information, in: Journal of Finance 60, 413-442.

Chan, Konan, Ikenberry, David L., Lee, Inmoo, and Yanzhi Wang (2010), Share Repurchases as a Potential Tool to Mislead Investors, in: Journal of Corporate Finance 16, 137-158.

Chan, Nicholas, Getmansky, Mila, Haas, Shane M. and Andrew Lo (2006), Systemic Risk and Hedge Funds, in: Carey, Mark and René Stulz (eds.), The Risks of Financial Institutions, University of Chicago Press, 235-340.

Chan, Su Han, Martin, John D. and John W. Kensinger (1990), Corporate Research and Development Expenditures and Share Value, in: Journal of Financial Economics 26, 255-276.

Chang, Saeyoung and Michael Hertzel (2004), Equity Ownership and Firm Value: Evidence from Targeted Stock Repurchases, in: Financial Review 39, 389-407.

Chay, J.B. and Jungwon Suh (2009), Payout Policy and Cash-Flow Uncertainty, in: Journal of Financial Economics 93, 88-107.

Chen, Peng and Roger G. Ibbotson (2006), The A, B, Cs of Hedge Funds: Alphas, Betas, and Costs, Working Paper.

Chen, Peng, Feldman, Barry and Chandra Goda (2002), Portfolios with Hedge Funds and Other Alternative Investments, Ibbotson Associates.

Chen, Xia, Harford, Jarrad and Kai Li (2007), Monitoring: Which Institutions Matter?, in: Journal of Financial Economics 86, 279-305

Cheng, Shijun, Nagar, Venky and Madhav V. Rajan (2004), Identifying Control Motives in Managerial Ownership: Evidence from Antitakeover Legislation, in: Review of Financial Studies 18, 637-672.

Cheung, C. Sherman and Peter Miu (2010), Diversification Benefits of Commodity Futures, in: Journal of International Financial Markets, Institutions, and Money, 20, 451-474.

Chiang, Kevin C.H. and Ming-Long Lee (2007), Spanning Tests on Public and Private Real Estate, in: Journal of Real Estate Portfolio Management 13, 7-15.

Chiou, Wan-Jiun Paul, Alice C. Lee, Chiu-Chi A. Chang (2009), Do Investors still Benefit from International Diversification with Investment Constraints?, in: The Quarterly Review of Economics and Finance, 49, 448-483.

Chou, De-Wai, Liu, Yi and Zaher Zantout (2009), Long-Term Stock Performance Following Extraordinary and Special Cash Dividends, in: Quarterly Journal of Economics and Finance 49, 54-73.

Christie-David, Rohan and Mukesh Chaudhry (2001), Coskewness and Cokurtosis in Futures Markets, in: Journal of Empirical Finance 8, 55-81.

Christoffersen, Susan E.K., Geczy, Christopher C., Musto, David K. and Adam V. Reed (2007), Vote Trading and Information Aggregation, in: Journal of Finance 62, 2897-2929.

Chun, Gregory H., Ciocchetti, Brian A., and James D. Shilling (2000), Pension-Plan Real Estate Investment in an Asset-Liability Framework, in: Real Estate Economics 28, 467-491.

Clayton, Jim and Gregory H. MacKinnon (2001), The Time-Varying Nature of the Link between REIT, Real Estate and Financial Returns, in: Journal of Real Estate Portfolio Management 7, 43-55.

Clifford, Christopher P. (2008), Value Creation or Destruction? Hedge Funds as Shareholder Activists, in: Journal of Corporate Finance 14, 323-336.

Cocco, Joao F., Gomes, Francisco J., Pascal J. Maenhout (2005), Consuption and Portfolio Choice over the Life Cycle, in: Review of Financial Studies 18, 491-533.

Cochrane, John H. (1999), Portfolio Advice for a Multifactor World, in: Economic Perspective Federal Reserve Bank of Chicago 23, 59-78.

Cochrane, John H. (2005), Asset Pricing, Princeton University Press, Princeton.

Colak, Gönül (2010), Diversification, Refocusing and Firm Value, in: European Financial Management 16, 422-448.

Conner, Andrew (2003), Asset Allocation Effects of Adjusting Alternative Assets for Stale Pricing, in: Journal of Alternative Investments 5, 42-52.

Cornelli, Francesca and David D. Li (2002), Risk Arbitrage in Takeovers, in: Review of Financial Studies 15, 837-868.

Cornelli, Francesca and Oguzhan Karakas (2008), Private Equity and Corporate Governance: Do LBOs Have More Effective Boards?, Working Paper.

Craft, Timothy M. (2005), Impact of Pension Plan Liabilities on Real Estate Investment, in: Journal of Portfolio Management 32, 23-31.

Cremers, K.J. Martijn, Nair, Yinay B. and Chenyang Wei (2007), Governance Mechanisms and Bond Prices, in: Review of Financial Studies 20, 1359-1388.

Croci, Ettore (2007), Corporate Raiders, Performance and Governance in Europe, in: European Financial Management 13, 949-978.

Cronqvist, Henrik, Heyman, Fredrik, Nilsson, Mattias, Svaleryd, Helena and Jonas Vlachos (2009), Do Entrenched Managers Pay Their Workers More?, in: Journal of Finance 64, 309-339.

Cvitanic, Jaksa, Lazrak, Ali, Martellini, Lionel, and Fernando Zapatero (2003), Optimal Allocation to Hedge Funds: An Empirical Analysis, in: Quantitative Finance 3, 1-12.

Cvitannic, Jaksa, Polimenis, Vassilis and Fernando Zapatero (2007), Optimal Portfolio Allocation with Higher Moments, in: Annals of Finance 4, 1-28.

DAI and McKinsey (2009), Investorendialog im Umbruch, Frankfurt a. Main.

Dai, Na (2007), Does Investor Identity Matter? An Empirical Examination of Investments by Venture Capital Funds and Hedge Funds in PIPEs, in: Journal of Corporate Finance 13, 538-563.

Dai, Zhonglan, Maydew, Edward, Shackelford, Douglas A. and Harold H. Zhang (2008), Capital Gains Taxes and Asset Prices: Capitalization or Lock-In?, in: Journal of Finance 63, 709-742.

Daniel, Kent, Grinblatt, Mark, Titman, Sheridan, and Russ Wermers (1997), Measuring Mutual Fund Performance with Characteristics-Based Benchmarks, in: Journal of Finance 52, 1035-1058.

Dann, Larry Y. and Harry DeAngelo (1983), Standstill Agreements, Privately Negotiated Stock Repurchases, and the Market for Corporate Control, in: Journal of Financial Economics 11, 275-300.

Darolles, Serge and Christian Gourieroux (2010), Conditionally Fitted Sharpe Performance with an Application to Hedge Fund Rating, in: Journal of Banking & Finance 34, 578-593.

Das, Sanjiv Ranjan and Raman Uppal (2004), Systemic Risk and International Portfolio Choice, in: Journal of Finance 59, 2809-2834.

Datta, Sudip, Mai Iskandar-Datta, and Kartik Raman, 2001, Executive compensation and corporate acquisition decisions, Journal of Finance 56, 2299–2336.

David, Alexander (2001), Pricing the Strategic Value of Putable Securities in Liquidity Crisis, in: Journal of Financial Economics 59, 63-99.

Davies, Ryan J., Kat, Harry M. and Sa Lu (2003), Higher Moment Portfolio Analysis with Hedge Funds, Stocks, and Bonds, Working Paper.

Davies, Ryan J., Kat, Harry M. and Sa Lu (2005), Fund of Hedge Funds Portfolio Selection: A Multiple-Objective Approach, Working Paper.

De Jong, Frank and Frans A. De Roon (2005), Time-Varying Market Integration and Expected Returns in Emerging Markets, in: Journal of Financial Economics, 78, 583-613.

De Roon, Frans A., Nijman, Theo E. and Bas J.M. Werker (2001), Testing for Mean-Variance Spanning with Short Sales Constraints and Transaction Costs: The Case of Emerging Markets, in: Journal of Finance 56, 721-742.

DeAngelo, Harry and Linda DeAngelo (1991), Union Negotiations and Corporate Policy – A Study of Labor Concessions in the Domestic Steel Industry during the 1980s, in: Journal of Financial Economics 30, 3-43.

DeAngelo, Harry and Linda DeAngelo (2006), The Irrelevance of the MM Dividend Irrelevance Theorem, in: Journal of Financial Econoics 79, 293-315.

DeAngelo, Harry, DeAngelo, Linda and René M. Stulz (2006), Dividend Policy and the Earned/Contributed Capital Mix: A Test of the Life-Cycle Theory, in: Journal of Financial Economics 81, 227-254.

Del Guercio, Diane and Jennifer Hawkins (1999), The Motivation and Impact of Pension Fund Activism, in: Journal of Financial Economics 52, 293-340.

Del Guercio, Diane and Paula A. Tkac (2008), Star Power: The Effect of Morningstar Ratings on Mutual Fund Flow, in: Journal of Financial & Quantitative Analysis 43, 907-936.

Demsetz, Harold (1983), The Structure of Ownership and the Theory of the Firm, in: Journal of Law and Economics 26, 375-390.

Demsetz, Harold and Kenneth Lehn (1985), The Structure of Corporate Ownership: Causes and Consequences, in: Journal of Political Economy 93, 1155-1177.

Denis, David J. (1990), Defensive Changes in Corporate Payout Policy: Share Repurchases and Special Dividends, in: Journal of Finance 45, 1433-1456.

Denis, David J. and Igor Osobov (2008), Why do Firms Pay Dividends? International Evidence on the Determinants of Dividend Policy, in: Journal of Financial Economics 89, 62-82.

Denis, David J., Denis, Diane K. and Atulya Sarin (1997), Agency Problems, Equity Ownership, and Corporate Diversification, in: Journal of Finance 52, 135-160.

Desai, Hemang and Prem C. Jain (1999), Firm Performance and Focus: Long-Run Stock Market Performance Following Spinoffs, in: Journal of Financial Economics 54, 75–101.

Devos, Erik, Kadapakkam, Palani-Rajan and Srinivasan Krishnamurthy (2009), How Do Mergers Create Value? A Comparison of Taxes, Market Power, and Efficiency Improvements as Explanations for Synergies, in: Review of Financial Studies 22, 1179-1211.

Diamond, Douglas W. (1984), Financial Intermediation and Delegated Monitoring, in: Review of Economic Studies 51, 393-414.

Dietz, Stephanie (2004), Aktienoptionsprogramme und Corporate Governance, DUV Verlag, Wiesbaden.

Dimmock, Stephen G. (2010), Background Risk and University Endowment Funds, Working Paper.

Dimson, Elroy and Paul Marsh (1986), Event Study Methodology and the Size Effect: The Case of UK Press Recommendations, in: Journal of Financial Economics 17, 113-142.

Ding, Bill and Hany A. Shawky (2007), The Performance of Hedge Fund Strategies and the Asymmetry of Return Distributions, in: European Financial Management 13, 309-331.

Dittmann, Ingolf, Maug, Ernst and Christoph Schneider (2010), Bankers on the Boards of German Firms: What They Do, What They are Worth, and Why They Are (Still) There, in: Review of Finance 14, 35-71.

Dittmar, Amy and Jan Mahrt-Smith (2007), Corporate Governance the the Value of Cash Holdings, in: Journal of Financial Economics 83, 599-634.

Dobler, René, Häring, Mirko, Kolberg, Marcus and Alexander Müller (2002), Hedge Funds – Anlageverhalten deutscher Versicherungsgesellschaften, in: Absolut Report 10/11, 34-37.

Driessen, Joost, Maenhout, Pascal J. and Grigory Vilkov (2009), The Price of Correlation Risk: Evidence from Equity Options, in: Journal of Finance 64, 1377-1406.

Driscoll, John C. and Art Kraay (1998), Consistent Covariance Matrix Estimation with Spatially Dependent Panel Data, in: Review of Economics and Statistics 80, 549-560.

Drobetz, Wolfgang, Schillhofer, Andreas and Heinz Zimmermann (2004), Corporate Governance and Expected Stock Returns: Evidence from Germany, in: European Financial Management 10, 267-293.

Drukarczyk, Jochen (1993), Theorie und Politik der Finanzierung, Vahlen, München, 2nd Ed.

Duarte, Jefferson, Longstaff, Francis A. and Fan Yu (2007), Risk and Return in Fixed-Income Arbtirage: Nickels in Front of a Steamroller?, in: Review of Financial Studies 20, 769-811.

Dunn, Kenneth B. and Chester S. Spatt (1999), Call Options, Points, and Dominance Restrictions on Debt Contracts, in: Journal of Finance 54, 2117-2337.

Dutz, Mark A. (1989), Horizontal Mergers in Declining Industries – Theory and Evidence, in: International Journal of Industrial Organization 7, 11-33.

Dybvig, Philip H. and Stephen A. Ross (1985), Differential Information and Performance Measurement Using a Security Market Line, in: Journal of Finance 40, 383-399.

Dyck, Alexander and Luigi Zingales (2004a), Control Premiums and the Effectiveness of Corporate Governance Systems, in: Journal of Applied Corporate Finance 59, 51-72.

Dyck, Alexander and Luigi Zingales (2004b), Private Benefits of Control: An International Comparison, in: Journal of Finance 59, 537-600.

Dyck, Alexander, Volchkova, Natalya and Luigi Zingales (2008), The Corporate Governance Role of the Media: Evidence from Russia, in: Journal of Finance 63, 1093-1135.

Easterbrook, Frank H. (1984), Two Agency-Cost Explanations of Dividends, in: American Economic Review 74, 650-659.

Eckbo, B. Espen (2009),Bidding Strategies and Takeover Premiums: A Review, in: Journal of Corporate Finance 15, 149-178.

Eckbo, Espen B. and Oyvind Norli (2005), Liquidity Risk, Leverage and Long-Run IPO Returns, in: Journal of Corporate Finance 11, 1-35.

Ederington, Louis H. and Jae Ha Lee (1993), How Markets Process Information: News Releases and Volatility, in: Journal of Finance 48, 1161-1191.

Ederington, Louis H. and Jae Ha Lee (1996), The Creation and Resolution of Market Uncertainty: The Impact of Information Releases on Implied Volatility, in: Journal of Financial & Quantitative Analysis 31, 513-539.

Edmans, Alex (2009), Blockholder Trading, Market Efficiency, and Managerial Myopia, in: Journal of Finance 64, 2481-2513.

Edwards, Franklin R. and Mustafa Onur Caglayan (2001a), Hedge Fund Performance and Manager Skill, in: Journal of Futures Markets 21, 1003-1028.

Edwards, Franklin R. and Mustafa Onur Caglayan (2001b), Hedge Fund and Commodity Fund Investments in Bull and Bear Markets, in: Journal of Portfolio Management 27, 97-108.

Ehrhardt, Olaf, Kuklinski, Jan and Eric Nowak (2004), Unifications of Dual-Class Shares in Germany – Empirical Evidence on the Effects of Related Changes in Ownership Structure, Market Value, and Bid-Ask Spreads from the German Stock Market, Working Paper.

Eisdorfer, Assaf (2008), Empirical Evidence of Risk Shifting in Financially Distressed Firms, in: Journal of Finance 63, 609-637.

Eling, Martin (2006), Hedgefonds-Strategien und ihre Performance, Eul-Verlag, Lohmar.

Eling, Martin (2009), Does Hedge Fund Performance Persist? Overview and New Empirical Evidence, in: European Financial Management 15, 362-401.

Eling, Martin and Roger Faust (2010), The Performance of Hedge Funds and Mutual Funds in Emerging Markets, in: Journal of Banking & Finance 34, 1993-2009.

Elsas, Ralf and Yvonne Löffler (2008), Universal Banks, Corporate Control, and Equity Carve-out in Germany, in: Kredit und Kapital 41, 557-587.

Elsland, Silvia and Martin Weber (2004), Squeeze-Outs in Germany: Determinants of the Announcement Effects, Working Paper.

Elston, Julie A. and Lawrence G. Goldberg (2003), Executive Compensation and Agency Costs in Germany, in: Journal of Banking & Finance 27, 1391-1410.

Elton, Edwin J. and Martin J. Gruber (1992), Optimal Investment Strategies with Investor Liabilities, in: Journal of Banking & Finance 16, 869-890.

Elton, Edwin J. and Martin J. Gruber (1995), Modern Portfolio Theory and Investment Analysis, Wiley, New York, 5. Ed.

Emmons, William R. and Frank A. Schmid (1998), Universal Banking, Allocation of Control Rights and Corporate Finance in Germany, Federal Reserve Bank of St. Louis Review 80, 19-42.

Erb, Claude B., Harvey, Campbell R. And Tadas E. Viskanta (1994), Forecasting International Equity Correlations, in: Financial Analysts Journal 50, Nov/Dec, 32-45.

Errunza, Vihang and Oumar Sy (2005), A Three-Moment International Asset-Pricing Model: Theory and Evidence, Working Paper.

Faccio, Mara and David Stolin (2006), Expropiation vs. Proportional Sharing in Corporate Acquisitions, in: Journal of Business 79, 1413-1444.

Faccio, Mara and Larry H.P. Lang (2002), The Ultimate Ownership of Western European Corporations, in: Journal of Financial Economics 65, 365-395.

Falaye, Olubunmi, Mehrotra, Vikas and Randall Morck (2006), When Labor Has a Voice in Corporate Governance, in: Journal of Financial & Quantitative Analysis 41, 489-510.

Faleye, Olubunmi (2004), Cash and Corporate Control, in: Journal of Finance 59, 2041-2060.

Faleye, Olubunmi (2007), Classified Boards, Firm Value and Managerial Entrenchment, in: Journal of Financial Econmics 83, 501-529.

Fama, Eugene F. and Kenneth R. French (1995), Size and Book-to-Market Factors in Earnings and Returns, in: Journal of Finance 50, 131-155.

Fama, Eugene F. (1970), Efficient Capital Markets: A Review of Theory and Empirical Work, in: Journal of Finance 25, 383-417.

Fama, Eugene F. (1980), Agency Problems and the Theory of the Firm, in: Journal of Political Economy 88, 288-307.

Fama, Eugene F. (1996), Multifactor Portfolio Efficiency and Multifactor Asset Pricing, in: Journal of Financial & Quantitative Analysis 31, 441-465.

Fama, Eugene F. (1998), Market Efficiency, Long-term Returns, and Behavioral Finance, in: Journal of Finance 49, 283-306.

Fama, Eugene F. and David G. Booth (1992), Diversification Returns and Asset Contributions, in: Financial Analysts Journal, 48, 26-32.

Fama, Eugene F. and Kenneth R. French (1989), Business Conditions and Expected Returns on Stocks and Bonds, in: Journal of Financial Economics 25, 23-49.

Fama, Eugene F. and Kenneth R. French (1993), Common Risk Factors in the Returns on Stocks and Bonds, in: Journal of Financial Economics 33, 3-56.

Fama, Eugene F. and Kenneth R. French (2006), Tilted Portfolios, Hedge Funds, and Portable Alpha, Report, Dimensional Fund Advisors.

Fama, Eugene F. and Kenneth R. French (2007), Migration, in: Financial Analysts Journal 63, 48-58.

Fama, Eugene F. and Kenneth R. French (2008), Dissecting Anomalies, in: Journal of Finance 63, 1653-1678.

Fama, Eugene F., Jensen, Michael C., Fisher, Lawrence and Richard Roll (1969), The Adjustment of Stock Prices to New Information, in: International Economic Review 10, 1-21.

Fang, Hsing and Tsong-Yue Lai (1997), Co-Kurtosis and Capital Asset Pricing, in: Financial Review 32, 293-307.

Fang, Lily and Joel Press (2009), Media Coverage and the Cross-Section of Stock Returns, in: Journal of Finance 64, 2023-2052.

Fauver, Larry and Michael E. Fuerst (2006), Does Good Corporate Governance Include Employee Representation? Evidence from German Corporate Boards, in: Journal of Financial Economics 82, 673-710.

Favre, Laurent and José-Antonio Galeano (2002), Mean-Modified Value-at-Risk Optimization with Hedge Funds, in: Journal of Alternative Investments 5, Fall, 21-25.

Fee, C. Edward, Hadlock, Charles J. and Shawn Thomas (2006), Corporate Equity Ownership and the Governance of Product Market Relationships, in: Journal of Finance 61, 1217-1251.

Ferson, Wayne E. and Campbell R. Harvey (1991), The Variation of Economic Risk Premiums, in: Journal of Political Economy 99, 385-415.

Ferson, Wayne E. and Rudi W. Schadt (1996), Measuring Fund Strategy and Performance in Changing Economic Conditions, in: Journal of Finance 51, 425-461.

Fich, Eliezer, Starks, Laura T. and Adam S. Yore (2008), CEO Deal-Making Activity, CEO Compensation and Firm Value, Working Paper.

Fishman, Michael J. and Kathleen M. Hagerty (1992), Insider Trading and the Efficiency of Stock Prices, in: RAND Journal of Economics 23, 106-122.

Frank, Murray and Vidhan Goyal (2008), Tradeoff and Pecking Order Theories of Debt, in: Espen Eckbo (ed.), The Handbook of Empirical Corporate Finance, Elsevier, 135-197.

Franks, Julian and Colin Mayer (1998), Bank Control Takeovers and Corporate Governance in Germany, in: Journal of Banking & Finance 22, 1385-1403.

Franks, Julian and Colin Mayer (2001), Ownership and Control of German Corporations, in: Review of Financial Studies 14, 943-977.

Franks, Julian, Mayer, Colin and Stefano Rossi (2009), Ownership: Evolution and Regulation, in: Review of Financial Studies 22, 4009-4056.

French, Kenneth R. (2008), Presidential Address: The Cost of Active Investing, in: Journal of Finance 63, 1537-1573.

Frino, Alex and Amelia Hill (2001), Intraday Futures Market Behavior around Major Scheduled Macroeconomic Announcements: Australian Evidence, in: Journal of Banking & Finance 25, 1319-1337.

Froot, Kenneth A. (1995), Hedging Portfolios with Real Assets, in: Journal of Portfolio Management 21, 60-77.

Froot, Kenneth A., Scharfstein, David S. and Jeremy C. Stein (1992), Herd on the Street: Informational Inefficiencies in a Market with Short-Term Speculation, in: Journal of Finance 47, 1461-1484.

Füss, Roland, Rehkugler, Heinz and Wolfgang Disch (2005), Hedge Funds als Anlagealternative, in: Finanzbetrieb 01/2005, 40-56.

Fugazza, Carolina, Guidolin, Massimo, and Giovanna Nicodano (2007), Investing for the Long-run in European Real Estate, in: Journal of Real Estate Finance and Economics 34, 35-80.

Fung, William and David A. Hsieh (1999a), A Primer on Hedge Funds, in: Journal of Empirical Finance 6, 309-331.

Fung, William and David A. Hsieh (1999b), Is Mean-Variance Analysis Applicable to Hedge Funds?, in: Economics Letters 62, 53-58.

Fung, William and David A. Hsieh (2000), Performance Characteristics of Hedge Funds and Commodity Funds: Natural vs. Spurious Biases, in: Journal of Financial & Quantitative Analysis 35, 291-307.

Fung, William and David A. Hsieh (2001), The Risk in Hedge Fund Strategies: Theory and Evidence from Trend Followers, in: Review of Financial Studies 14, 313-341.

Fung, William and David A. Hsieh (2002a), Asset-Based Style Factors for Hedge Funds, in: Financial Analysts Journal 58, Sept/Oct, 16-27.

Fung, William and David A. Hsieh (2002b), Risk in Fixed-Income Hedge Fund Styles, in: Journal of Fixed Income 12, 6-27.

Fung, William and David A. Hsieh (2004a), Extracting Portable Alphas From Equity Long/Short Hedge Funds, in: Journal of Investment Management 2, 1-19.

Fung, William and David A. Hsieh (2004b), Hedge Fund Benchmarks: A Risk-Based Approach, in: Financial Analysts Journal 60, 5, 65-80.

Fung, William and David A. Hsieh (2006), The Risk in Hedge Fund Strategies: Theory and Evidence from Long/Short Equity Hedge Funds, Working Paper.

Fung, William, Hsieh, David A., Naik, Narayan Y. and Tarun Ramadorai (2008), Hedge Funds: Performance, Risk, and Capital Formation, in: Journal of Finance 63, 1777-1803.

Galai, Dan and Ronald W. Masulis (1976), The Option Pricing Model and the Risk Factor of Stock, in: Journal of Financial Economics 3, 53-81.

Gamba, Andrea and Alexander Triantis (2008), The Value of Financial Flexibility, in: Journal of Finance 58, 2263-2296.

Garvey, Gerald T. and Gordon Hanka (1999), Capital Structure and Corporate Control: The Effect of Antitakeover Statutes on Firm Leverage, in: Journal of Finance 54, 519-546.

Gaspar, José-Miguel, Massa, Massimo and Pedro Matos (2005), Shareholder Investment Horizons and the Market for Corporate Control, in: Journal of Financial Economics 76, 135-165.

Gatev, Evan, Goetzmann, William N. and K. Geert Rouwenhorst (2006), Pairs Trading: Performance of a Relative-Value Arbitrage Rule, in: Review of Financial Studies 19, 797-827.

Gebhardt, William R., Hviskjaer, Soeren and Bhaskaran Swaminathan (2005), Stock and Bond Market Interaction: Does Momentum Spill Over?, in: Journal of Financial Economics 75, 651-690.

Getmansky, Mila, Lo, Andrew W. and Igor Makarov (2004), An Econometric Model of Serial Correlation and Illiquidity in Hedge Fund Returns, in: Journal of Financial Economics 74, 529-609.

Ghemawat, Pankaj and Barry Nelebuff (1990), The Devolution of Declining Industries, in: Quarterly Journal of Economics 105, 167-186.

Giamouridis, Daniel and Ionnis D. Vrontos (2007), Hedge Fund Portfolio Construction: A Comparison of Static and Dynamic Approaches, in: Journal of Banking & Finance 31, 199-217.

Gillan, Stuart L and Laura T. Starks (1998), A Survey of Shareholder Activism: Motivation and Empirical Evidence, in: Contemporary Finance Digest 2, 10-34.

Gillan, Stuart L. and Laura T. Starks (2000), Corporate Governance Proposals and Shareholder Activism: The Role of Institutional Investors, in: Journal of Financial Economics 57, 275-305.

Glosten, L.R. and Ravi Jagannathan (1994), A Contingent Claim Approach to Performance Evaluation, in: Journal of Empirical Finance 1, 133-160.

Goergen, Marc, Martynova, Marina and Luc Renneboog (2005), Corporate Governance Convergence: Evidence From Takeover Regulation Reforms in Europe, Working paper.

Goetzmann, William N., Li, Lingfend and K. Geert and Rouwenhorst (2005), Long-Term Global Market Correlations, in: Journal of Business 78, 1-38.

Goetzmann, William, Ingersoll, Jonathan E. and Stephen A. Ross (2003), High-Water Marks and Hedge Fund Management Contracts, in: Journal of Finance 58, 1685-1717.

Gomes, Armando R. (2001), Takeovers, Freezeouts, and Risk Arbitrage, Working Paper.

Gompers, Paul A., Kovner, Anna, Lerner, Josh and David Scharfstein (2008), Venture Capital Investment Cycles: The Impact of Public Markets, in: Journal of Financial Economics 87, 1-23.

Gompers, Paul, Ishii, Joy and Andrew Metrick (2003), Corporate Governance and Equity Prices, in: Quarterly Review of Economics 118, 107-155.

Gordon, Lilli A. and John Pound (1990), ESOPs and Corporate Control, in: Journal of Financial Economics 27, 525-555.

Gorton, Gary and K. Geert Rouwenhorst (2006), Facts and Fantasies About Commodity Futures, in: Financial Analysts Journal 62, 47-68.

Graham, John R., Lemmon, Michael L. and Jack G. Wolf (2002), Does Corporate Diversification Destroy Value?, in: Journal of Finance 57, 695-720.

Greenwood, Robin and Michael Schoar (2009), Investor Activism and Takeovers, in: Journal of Financial Economics 92, 362-375.

Griffin, John M. and Jin Xu (2009), How Smart are the Smart Guys? A Unique View from Hedge Fund Stock Holdings, in Review of Financial Studies 22, 2531-2570.

Grinblatt, Mark and Sheridan Titmann (1987), The Relation Between Mean-Variance Efficiency and Arbitrage Pricing, in: Journal of Business 60, 97-112.

Grossman, Sanford J. and Oliver D. Hart (1980), Takeover Bids, the Free-Rider Problem, and the Theory of the Corporation, in: Bell Journal of Economics 11, 42-64.

Gupta, Anurag and Bing Liang (2005), Do Hedge Funds Have enough Capital? A Value-at-Risk Approach, in: Journal of Financial Economics 77, 219-253.

Gupta, Bhaswar, Cerrahoglu, Burak and Alper Daglioglu (2003), Hedge Fund Strategy Performance: Using Conditional Approaches, Working Paper.

Gupta-Mukherjee, Swasti (2008), When Active Fund Managers Deviate from Their Peers: The Impact on Performance, Working Paper.

Guse, Frank (2005), Portfoliooptimierung unter Berücksichtigung höherer Momente, Eul-Verlag, Lohmar.

Hackethal, Andreas, Schmidt, Reinhard H. and Marcel Tyrell (2004), Banks and German Corporate Governance: On the Way to a Capital Market-Based System?, Working Paper.

Hafner, Reinhold and Martin Wallmeier (2007), Optimal Investments in Volatility, in: Financial Markets and Portfolio Management 22, 147-167.

Hagelin, Niclas, Pramborg, Bengt, and Fredrik Stenberg (2006), Gains from Adding Funds of Hedge Funds to Portfolios of Traditional Assets: An International Perspective, in: Gregoriou, Greg N. (ed.), Funds of Hedge Funds – Performance, Assessment, Diversification, and Statistical Properties, Elsevier, Oxford, 171-187.

Hall, Brian J. and David E. Weinstein (1996), The Myth of the Patient Japanese: Corporate Myopia and Financial Distress in Japan and the U.S., Working Paper NBER 5818.

Hanka, Gordon (1998), Debt and the Terms of Employment, in: Journal of Financial Economics 48, 245-282.

Harford, Jarrad (1999), Corporate Cash Reserves and Acquisitions, in: Journal of Finance 54, 1969-1997.

Harford, Jarrad and Kai Li (2007) Decoupling CEO Wealth and Firm Performance: The Case of Acquiring CEOs, Journal of Finance 62, 917-949.

Harford, Jarrad, Mansi, Sattar A. and William F. Maxwell (2008), Corporate Governance and Firm Cash Holdings in the US, in: Journal of Financial Economics 87, 535-555.

Harri, Ardian and B. Wade Brorsen (2004), Performance Persistence and the Sources of Returns for Hedge Funds, in: Applied Financial Economics 14, 131-141.

Harris, Milton and Artur Raviv (1988), Corporate Control Contests and Capital Structure, in: Journal of Financial Economics 20, 55-86.

Harris, Milton and Artur Raviv (1991), The Theory of Capital Structure, in: Journal of Finance 46, 297-355.

Harris, Oneil and Charmaine Glegg (2009), Governance Quality and Privately Negotiated Stock Repurchases: Evidence of Agency Conflict, in: Journal of Banking & Finance 33, 317-325.

Harvey, Campbell R. and Akhtar Siddique (2000), Conditional Skewness in Asset Pricing Tests, in: Journal of Finance 55, 1263-1295.

Hege, Ulrich, Lovo, Stefano, Slovin Myron B. and Marie E. Sushka (2009), Equity and Cash in Intercorporate Asset Sales: Theory and Evidence, in: Review of Financial Studies 22, 681-714.

Hellwig, Martin (2001), On the Economics and Politics of Corporate Finance and Control, in: Vives, Xavier (ed.), Corporate Governance: Theoretical and Empirical Perspectives, Cambridge University Press, 95-134.

Henriksson, Roy D. and Robert C. Merton (1981), On Market Timing and Investment Performance. II. Statistical Procedures for Evaluating Forecasting Skills, in: Journal of Business 54, 513-533.

Hess, Dieter, Huang, He and Alexandra Niessen (2008), How do Commodity Futures Respond to Macroeconomic News?, in: Financial Markets and Portfolio Management 22, 127-146.

Hillion, Pierre and Theo Vermaelen (2004), Death Spiral Convertibles, in: Journal of Financial Economics 71, 381-415.

Höchle, Daniel and Markus M. Schmid (2009), Predicting and Explaining IPO Underperformance, Working Paper.

Höchle, Daniel, Schmid, Markus M. and Heinz Zimmermann (2009), A Generalization oft he Calendar Time Portfolio Approach and the Performance of Private Investors, Working Paper.

Hodder, James E. and Jens C. Jackwerth (2007), Incentive Contracts and Hedge Fund Management, in: Journal of Financial & Quantitative Analysis 42, 811-826.

Hoevenaars, Roy P.M.M., Molenaar, Roderick D.J., Schotman, Peter C. and Tom B.M. Steenkamp (2008), Strategic Asset Allocation with Liabilities: Beyond Stocks and Bonds, in: Journal of Economic Dynamics and Control 32, 2939-2970.

Holden, Craig W. and Leonard L. Lundstrum (2009), Costly Trade, Managerial Myopia, and Long-Term Investment, in: Journal of Empirical Finance 16, 126-135.

Holderness, Clifford G. (2003), A Survey of Blockholders and Corporate Control, in: Economic Policy Review, April 2003, Federal Reserve Bank of New York, 51-64.

Holderness, Clifford G. and Dennis P. Sheehan (1985), Raiders or Saviors? The Evidence on Six Controversial Investors, in: Journal of Financial Economics 14, 555-579.

Holmström, Bengt and Jean Tirole (1993), Market Liquidity and Performance Monitoring, in: Journal of Political Economy 101, 678-709.

Holmström, Bengt and Steven N. Kaplan (2001), Corporate Governance and Merger Activity in the United States: Making Sense of the 1980s and 1990s, in: Journal of Economic Perspectives 15, 121-144.

Hood, Matthew and John R. Nofsinger (2007), Hedge Funds in Portfolios of Risk-Averse Investors, in: Journal of Economics and Finance 31, 219-233.

Höpner, Martin (2001), Corporate Governance in Transition: Ten Empirical Findings on Shareholder Value and Industrial Relations in Germany, Working Paper.

Höpner, Martin and Gregory Jackson (2001), An Emerging Market for Corporate Control? The Mannesmann Takeover and German Corporate Governance, Working Paper.

Hsieh, Jim and Ralph A. Walkling (2005), Determinants and Implications of Arbitrage Holdings in Acquisitions, in: Journal of Financial Economics 77, 605-648.

Hu, Henry T.C. and Bernard Black (2007), Hedge Funds, Insiders, and the Decoupling of Economic and Voting Ownership: Empty Voting and Hidden (Morphable) Ownership, in: Journal of Corporate Finance 13, 343-367.

Huang, Jiekun (2009), Dynamic Liquidity Preferences of Mutual Funds, Working Paper.

Hubbard, R. Glenn and Darius Palia (1999), A Reexamination of the Conglomerate Merger Wave in the 1960s: An Internal Capital Markets View, in: Journal of Finance 54, 1131-1152.

Huberman, Gur and Shmuel Kandel (1987), Mean-Variance Spanning, in: Journal of Finance 42, 873-888.

Hund, John, Monk, Donald and Sheri Tice (2008), Uncertainty About Average Profitability and the Diversification Discount, Working Paper.

Hyland, David C. and J. David Diltz (2002), Why Firms Diversify: An Empirical Examination, in: Financial Management 31, 51-81.

Ibbotson, Roger G. and Laurence B. Siegel (1984), Real Estate Returns: A Comparison with Other Investments, in: AREUEA Journal 12, 219-242.

Ilmanen, Antti (1995), Time-Varying Expected Returns in International Bond Markets, in: Journal of Finance 50, 481-506.

IMF (2006), Global Financial Stability Report, April 2006, Washington D.C.

Ineichen, Alexander M. (2003), Absolute Returns: The Risk and Opportunities of Hedge Fund Investing, Wiley, Hoboken.

Iqbal, Javed, Robert Brooks, and Don U.A. Galagedera (2010), Testing Conditional Asset Pricing Models: An Emerging Market Perspective, in: Journal of International Money and Finance, 29, 5, 897-918.

Ivashina, Victoria, Nair, Vinay B., Saunders, Anthony, Massoud, Nadia and Roger Stover (2009), Bank Debt and Corporate Governance, in: Review of Financial Studies 22, 41-77.

Jacobson, Robert and David Aaker (1993), Myopic Management Behavior with Efficient, but Imperfect, Capital Markets: A Comparison of Information Asymmetries in the U.S. and Japan, in: Journal of Accounting and Economics 16, 383–405.

Jagannathan, Murali, Stephens, Clifford P. and Michael S. Weisbach (2000), Financial Flexibility and the Choice Between Dividends and Stock Repurchases, in: Journal of Financial Economics 57, 355-384.

Jagannathan, Ravi, Malakhov, Alexey and Dmitry Novikov (2010), Do Hot Hands Exist Among Hedge Fund Managers? An Empirical Evaluation, in: Journal of Finance 65, 217-255.

Jain, Prem C. (1986), Analyses of the Distribution of Security Market Model Prediction Errors for Daily Returns Data, in: Journal of Accounting Research 21, 76-96.

Jegadeesh, Narasimhan and Jason Karceski 2009, Long-Run Performance Evaluation: Correlation and Heteroscedasticity-Consistent Tests, in: Journal of Empirical Finance 16, 101-110.

Jenkinsson, Tim J. and Alexander Ljungqvist (2001), The Role of Hostile Stakes in German Corporate Governance, in: Journal of Corporate Finance 7, 397-446.

Jensen, Gerald R. and Jeffrey M. Mercer (2003), New Evidence on Optimal Asset Allocation, in: Financial Review 38, 435-454.

Jensen, Gerald R., Robert R. Johnson and Jeffrey M. Mercer (2002), Tactical Asset Allocation and Commodity Futures, in: Journal of Portfolio Management, 28, 100-111.

Jensen, Michael C. (1986), Agency Costs of Free Cash Flow, Corporate Finance, and Takeovers, in: American Economic Review 76, 323-329.

Jensen, Michael C. (1993), The Modern Industrial Revolution, Exit, and the Failure of Internal Control Systems, in: Journal of Finance 48, 831-880.

Jensen, Michael C. (2005), Agency Costs of Overvalued Equity, in: Financial Management 34, 5-19.

Jensen, Michael C. and William H. Meckling (1976), Theory of the Firm: Managerial Behavior, Agency Costs and Ownership Structure, in: Journal of Financial Economics 3, 305-360.

Jin, Li, Merton, Robert C. and Zvi Bodie (2006), Do a Firm's Equity Returns Reflect the Risk of its Pension Plan?, in: Journal of Financial Economics 81, 1-26.

Jiraporn, Pornsit and Kimberly C. Gleason (2007), Capital Structure, Shareholder Rights, and Corporate Governance, in: Journal of Financial Research 30, 21-33.

Jiraporn, Pornsit, Kim, Young Sang, Davidson, Wallace N. and Manohar Singh (2006), Corporate Governance, Shareholder Rights and Firm Diversification: An Empirical Analysis, in: Journal of Banking & Finance 30, 947-963.

Jiraporn, Pornsit, Kim, Young Sang, Wallace N. Davidson (2008), Multiple Directorships and Corporate Diversification, in: Journal of Empirical Finance 15, 418-435.

John, Kose and Eli Ofek (1995), Asset Sales and Increase in Focus, in: Journal of Financial Economics 37, 105-126.

John, Kose and Teresa A. John (2006), Managerial Incentives, Derivatives and Stability, in: Journal of Financial Stability 2, 71-94.

John, Teresa A. (1993), Accounting Measures of Corporate Liquidity, Leverage, and Costs of Financial Distress, in: Financial Management 22, 91-100.

Jung, Kooyul, Kim, Yong-Cheol and René M. Stulz (1996), Timing, Investment Opportunities, Managerial Discretion, and the Security Issue Decision, in: Journal of Financial Economics 42, 159-185.

Jylhä, Petri, Suominen, Matti and Jussi-Pekka Lyytinen (2008), Arbitrage Capital and Currency Trade Returns, Working Paper.

Kan, Raymond and Guofu Zhou (2008), Tests of Mean-Variance Spanning, Working Paper.

Kaplan, Paul D. and James A. Knowles (2004), Kappa: A Generalized Downside Risk-Adjusted Performance Measure, Journal of Performance Measurement 8, 42-54.

Kaplan, Steven N. and Jeremy C. Stein (1993), The Evolution of Buyout Pricing and Financial Structure in the 1980s, in: Quarterly Review of Economics 108, 313-357.

Kaserer, Christoph and Ekkehard Wenger (1998), German Banks and Corporate Governance: A Critical View, Working Paper.

Kassberger, Stefan and Rüdiger Kiesel (2007), A Fully Parametric Approach to Return Modelling and Risk Management for Hedge Funds, in: Financial Markets & Portfolio Management 20, 472-491.

Kat, Harry M. and Faye Menexe (2002), Persistence in Hedge Fund Performance: The True Value of a Track Record, Working Paper.

Kat, Harry M. and Helder P. Palaro (2005), Who Needs Hedge Funds? A Copula-Based Approach to Hedge Fund Return Replication, Working Paper.

Kat, Harry M. and Roel C.A. Oomen (2006), What Every Investor Should Know About Commodities – Part I: Univariate Return Analysis, Working Paper.

Kat, Harry M. and Sa Lu (2002), An Excursion Into The Statistical Properties of Hedge Fund Returns, Working Paper.

Kau, James B., Linck, James S. and Paul H. Rubin (2008), Do Managers Listen to the Market, Working Paper.

Kayhan, Ayla and Sheridan Titman (2007), Firms' Histories and Their Capital Structures, in: Journal of Financial Economics 83, 1-32.

Keating, Con and William F. Shadwick (2002), A Universal Performance Measure, in: Journal of Performance Measurement 6, 59-84.

Kempf, Alexander, Ruenzi, Stefan and Tanja Thiele (2009), Employment Risk, Compensation Incentives and Managerial Risk Taking – Evidence from the Mutual Fund Industry, in: Journal of Financial Economics 92, 92-108.

Khandani, Amir E. and Andrew W. Lo (2007), What Happened to the Quants in August 2007?, Working Paper.

Kim, Oliver and Robert E. Verrecchia (1991), Trading Volume and Price Reactions to Public Announcements, in: Journal of Accounting Research 30, 302-321.

Klein, April and Emanuel Zur (2008), The Implications of Hedge Fund Activism on the Target Firm's Existing Bondholders, Working Paper.

Klein, April and Emanuel Zur (2009), Entrepreneurial Shareholder Activism: Hedge Funds and Other Private Investors, in: Journal of Finance 64, 187-229.

Klock, Mark S., Mansi, Sattar A. and William F. Maxwell (2005), Does Corporate Governance Matter to Bondholders?, in: Journal of Financial & Quantitative Analysis 40, 693-719.

Koijen, Ralph S.J., Nijman, Theo E. and Bas J.M. Werker (2010), When Can Life Cycle Investors Benefit from Time-Varying Bond Risk Premia?, in: Review of Financial Studies 23, 741-780.

Köke, Jens (2004), The Market for Corporate Control in a Bank-Based Economy: A Governance Device?, in: Journal of Corporate Finance 10, 53-80.

Kolasinski, Adam C. and S.P. Kothari (2008), Investment Banking and Analyst Objectivity: Evidence from Analysts Affiliated with Mergers and Acquisitions Advisors, in: Journal of Financial & Quantitative Analysis 43, 817-842.

Kooli, Maher (2006), Funds of Funds and the Diversification Effect, in: Gregoriou, Greg N. (ed.), Funds of Hedge Funds – Performance, Assessment, Diversification, and Statistical Properties, Elsevier, Oxford, 239-250.

Kosowski, Robert, Naik, Narayan Y. and Melvyn Teo (2007), Do Hedge Funds Deliver Alpha? A Bayesian and Bootstrap Analysis, in: Journal of Financial Economics 84, 229-264.

Kothari, S.P. and Jerold B. Warner (2006), Econometrics of Event Studies, in: Eckbo, Espen B. (ed.), Handbook of Empirical Corporate Finance, Elsevier, Amsterdam, 3-36.

Kouwenberg, Roy and William T. Ziemba (2007), Incentives and Risk Taking in Hedge Funds, in: Journal of Banking & Finance 31, 3291-3310.

Kraus, Alan and Robert H. Litzenberger (1976), Skewness Preferences and the Valuation of Risk Assets, in: Journal of Finance 31, 1085-1100.

Krishnan, C.N.V., Petkova, Ralitsa and Peter Ritchken (2009), Correlation Risk, in: Journal of Empirical Finance 16, 353-367.

Kroszner, Randall S. and Philip E. Strahan (2001), Bankers on Boards: Monitoring, Conflicts of Interest, and Lender Liability, in: Journal of Financial Economics 62, 415-452.

Kurth, Andreas (2005), Agency-Probleme und Performance von Initial Public Offerings – Eine empirische Untersuchung von Unternehmen des Neuen Markets, DUV, Wiesbaden.

Kyle, Albert S. (1985), Continuous Auctions and Insider Trading, in: Econometrica 53, 1315-1335.

Kyle, Albert S. and Jean-Luc Vila (1991), Noise Trading and Takeovers, in: RAND Journal of Economics 22, 54-71.

L'habitant, Francois-Serge (2004), Hedge Funds – Quantitative Investments, Wiley, Hoboken.

L'habitant, Francois-Serge (2006), Handbook of Hedge Funds, Wiley Finance, Hoboken.

L'habitant, Francois-Serge and Michelle Learned (2005), Hedge Funds Diversification, in: H. Dichtl, J. M. Kleeberg, C. Schlenger (Hrsg.), Handbuch Hedge Funds, Chancen Risiken und Einsatz in der Asset Allocation, Uhlenbruch-Verlag 2005, 197-211.

La Porta, Rafael, Lopez-de-Silanes, Florencio, Shleifer, Andrei and Robert W. Vishny (1998), Law and Finance, in: Journal of Political Economy 106, 1113-1155.

La Porta, Rafael, Lopez-de-Silanes, Florencio, Shleifer, Andrei and Robert W. Vishny (2000), Agency Problems and Dividend Policies around the World, in: Journal of Finance 55, 1-33.

La Porta, Rafael, Lopez-de-Silanes, Florencio, Shleifer, Andrei and Robert W. Vishny (1997), Legal Determinants of External finance, in: Journal of Finance 52, 1131-1150.

La Porta, Rafael, Lopez-de-Silanes, Florencio, Shleifer, Andrei and Robert Vishny (2002), Investor Protection and Corporate Valuation, in: Journal of Finance 57, 1147-1170.

Lakonishok, Josef, Shleifer, Andrei and Robert W. Vishny (1994), Contrarian Investment, Extrapolation, and Risk, in: Journal of Finance 49, 1541-1578.

Lambrecht, Bart M. and Stewart C. Myers (2007), A Theory of Takeovers and disinvestment, in: Journal of Finance 57, 809-845.

Lang, Larry H.P. and René M. Stulz (1994), Tobin's q, Corporate Diversification, and Firm Performance, in: Journal of Political Economy 102, 1248-1280.

Lang, Larry H.P., Stulz, René M. and Ralph A. Walkling (1991), A Test of the Free Cash Flow Hypothesis – The Case of Bidder Returns, in: Journal of Financial Economics 29, 315-335.

Lang, Larry, Poulsen, Annette and René M. Stulz (1995), Asset Sales, Firm Performance, and the Agency Costs of Managerial Discretion, in: Journal of Financial Economics 37, 3–37.

Larcker, David F. and Thomas Lys (1987), An Empirical Analysis of the Incentives to Engage in Costly Information Acquisitions – The Case of Risk Arbitrage, in: Journal of Financial Economics 18, 111-126.

Le Moigne, Cécile and Patrick Savaria (2006), Relative Importance of Hedge Fund Characteristics, in: Financial Markets and Portfolio Management 20, 419-441.

Leibowitz, Martin L. and Roy D. Hendrikson (1988), Portfolio Optimization Within a Surplus Framework, in: Financial Analysts Journal 44, Mar/Apr, 43-51.

Leland, Hayne E. (1980), Who Should Buy Portfolio Insurance?, in: Journal of Finance, 35, 581-94.

Leland, Hayne E. (2007), Financial Synergies and the Optimal Scope of the Firm: Implications for Mergers, Spinoffs, and Structured Finance, in: Journal of Finance 62, 765-807.

Lengwiler, Yvan (2006), Microfoundations of Financial Economics – An Introduction to General Equilibrium Asset Pricing, Princeton University Press, Princeton.

Lerner, Josh, Antoinette Schoar and Jialan Wang (2008), Secrets of the Academy: The Drivers of University Endowment Success, NBER Working Paper No. 14341.

Lerner, Josh, Schoar, Antoinette and Wan Wongsunwai (2007), Smart Institutions, Foolish Choices: The Limited Partner Performance Puzzle, in: Journal of Finance 62, 731-764.

Levy, Haim and Moshe Levy (2004), Prospect Theory and Mean-Variance Analysis, in: Review of Financial Studies 17, 1015-1041.

Lewellen, Wilbur G. (1971), A Pure Financial Rationale for the Conglomerate Merger, in: Journal of Finance 26, 521-537.

Lewellen, Wilbur, Loderer, Claudio and Ahron Rosenfeld (1985), Merger Decisions and Executive Stock Ownership in Acquiring Firms, in: Journal of Accounting and Economics 7, 209–231.

Li, C. Wei and Ashish Tiwari (2009), Incentive Contracts in Delegated Portfolio Management, in: Review of Financial Studies 22, 4681-4714.

Li, Yuming and Ko Wang (1995), The Predictability of REIT Returns and Market Segmentation, in: Journal of Real Estate Research 10, 471-482.

Liang, Bing (2000), Hedge Fund: The Living and the Dead, in: Journal of Financial & Quantitative Analysis 35, 309-326.

Liang, Bing (2003), The Accuracy of Hedge Fund Returns, in: Journal of Portfolio Management 29, 111-122.

Liu, Jun, Longstaff, Francis A. and Jun Pan (2003), Dynamic Asset Allocation with Event Risk, in: Journal of Finance 58, 231-259.

Longin, Francois and Bruno Solnik (2001), Extreme Correlation of International Equity Markets, in: Journal of Finance 56, 649-676.

Loughran, Tim and Jay R. Ritter (2000), Uniformly Least Powerful Tests of Market Efficiency, in: Journal of Financial Economics 55, 361-389.

Loughran, Tim and Anand M. Vijh (1997), Do Long-Term Shareholders Benefit From Corporate Acquisitions?, in: Journal of Finance 52, 1765-1790.

Loughran, Tim and Jay R. Ritter (1995), The New Issues Puzzle, in: Journal of Finance 50, 23-51.

Macias, Antonio J. (2009), Risk Pricing and Flexibility in Acquisitions: The Economic Impact of Material-Adverse-Change (MACs) Clauses, Working Paper.

MacKay, Peter and Gordon M. Philipps (2005), How Does Industry Affect Firm Financial Structure? in: Review of Financial Studies 18, 1433-1466.

Maksimovic, Vojislav and Gordon Philipps (2008), The Industry Life Cycle, Acquisitions and Investment: Does Firm Organization Matter?, in: Journal of Finance 63, 673-708.

Malkiel, Burton G. (1995), Returns from Investing in Equity Mutual Funds 1971-1991, in: Journal of Finance 50, 549-572.

Malmendier, Ulrike and Geoffrey Tate (2008), Who Makes Acquisitions? CEO Overconfidence and the Market`s Reaction, in: Journal of Finance 89, 20-43.

Mandelker, Gershon N. and S. Ghon Rhee (1984), The Impact of the Degrees of Operating and Financial Leverage on Systematic Risk of Common Stock, in: Journal of Financial & Quantitative Analysis 19, 45-57.

Mann, Alexander (2003), Corporate Governance Systeme – Funktion und Entwicklung am Beispiel von Deutschland und Grossbritannien, Duncker & Humblot, Berlin.

Manne, Henry (1966), Insider Trading and the Stock Market, Free Press, New York.

Mansi, Sattar A. and David M. Reeb (2002), Corporate Diversification: What Gets Discounted? in: Journal of Finance 57, 2167-2183.

Markowitz, Harry (1952), Portfolio Selection, in: Journal of Finance 7, 77-91.

Martynova, Marina V. (2006), The Market for Corporate Control and Corporate Governance Regulation in Europe, Dissertation Tilburg University.

Massa, Massimo, Rehman, Zahid and Theo Vermaelen (2007), Mimicking Repurchases, in: Journal of Financial Economics 84, 624-666.

Masulis, Ronald W., Wang, Cong and Fei Xie (2009), Agency Problems at Dual-Class Companies, in: Journal of Finance 64, 1697-1727.

Mathews, Richmond D. and David T. Robinson (2008), Market structure, Internal Capital Markets, and Boundaries of the Firm, in: Journal of Finance 63, 2703-2736.

Matsusaka, John G. (1993), Takeover Motives during the Conglomerate Merger Wave, in: RAND Journal of Economics 24, 357-379.

Matvos, Gregor and Michael Ostrovsky (2008), Cross-Ownership, Returns, and Voting in Mergers, in: Journal of Financial Economics 89, 391-403.

Maug, Ernst (1998), Large Shareholders as Monitors: Is There a Trade-Off between Liquidity and Control?, in: Journal of Finance 53, 65-98.

Mayers, David (1998), Why Firms Issue Convertible Bonds: The Matching of Financial and Real Investment Options, in: Journal of Financial Economics 47, 83-102.

McConnell, John J. and Chris J. Muscarella (1985), Corporate Capital Expenditure Decisions and the Market Value of the Firm, in: Journal of Financial Economics 14, 399-422.

McConnell, John J. and Henri Servaes (1995), Equity Ownership and the Two Faces of Debt, in: Journal of Financial Economics 39, 131-157.

Meligkotisidou, Loukia and Ioannis D. Vrontos (2008), Detecting Structural Breaks and Identifying Risk Factors in Hedge Fund Returns: A Bayesian Approach, in: Journal of Banking & Finance 32, 2471-2481.

Meoli, Michele, Paleari, Stefano, and Giovanni Urga (2006), When Controlling Shareholders Live Like Kings. The Case of Telecom Italia, Working Paper.

Merton, Robert C. (1981), On Market Timing and Investment Performance. I. An Equilibrium Theory of the Value for Market Forecasts, in: Journal of Business 54, 363-406.

Merton, Robert C. (1993), Optimal Investment Strategies for Endowments, in: Clotfelter, Charles T. and Michael Rothschild (eds.), Studies of Supply and Demand in Higher Education, NBER, 211-242.

Mietzner, Mark and Denis Schweizer (2007), Hedge Funds vs. Private Equity Funds as Shareholder Activists – Differences in Value Creation, Working Paper.

Mietzner, Mark, Schweizer, Denis and Marcel Tyrell (2008), Intra-Industry Effects of Shareholder Activism – Market Reactions to Hedge Fund and Private Equity Investments, Working Paper.

Mikkelson, Wayne H. and Richard S. Ruback (1991), Targeted Repurchases and Common Stock Returns, in: RAND Journal of Economics 22, 544-561.

Mitchell, Mark L. and Erik Stafford (1997), Managerial Decisions and Long-Term Stock-Price Performance, in: Journal of Business 73, 287-329.

Mitchell, Mark L. and J. Harold Mulherin (1996), The Impact of Industry Shocks on Takeover and Restructuring Activity, in: Journal of Financial Economics 41, 193-229.

Mitchell, Mark L. and Todd Pulvino (2001), Characteristics of Risk and Return in Risk Arbitrage, in: Journal of Finance 56, 2135-2175.

Mitchell, Mark L., Pulvino, Todd and Erik Stafford (2002), Limited Arbitrage in Equity Markets, in: Journal of Finance 57, 551-584.

Mitchell, Mark L., Pulvino, Todd and Erik Stafford (2004), Price Pressure around Mergers, in: Journal of Finance 59, 31-63.

Modigliani, Franco and Merton H. Miller (1958), The Cost of Capital, Corporation Finance and the Theory of Investment, in: American Economic Review 48, 261-297.

Modigliani, Franco and Merton H. Miller (1961), Dividend Policy, Growth, and the Valuation of Shares, in: Journal of Business 34, 411-433.

Moeller, Sara B., Schlingemann, Frederik P. and René M. Stulz (2005), Wealth Destruction on a Massive Scale? A Study of Acquiring-Firm Returns in the Recent Merger Wave, in: Journal of Finance 60, 757-782.

Moldenhauer, Benjamin (2007), Insider Ownership, Shareholder Structures and Corporate Governance, Verlag Wissenschaft & Praxis, Sternenfels.

Morck, Randall, Shleifer, Andrei and Robert W. Vishny (1990), Do Managerial Objectives Drive Bad Acquisitions, in: Journal of Finance 45, 31-48.

Morellec, Erwan (2004), Can Managerial Discretion Explain Observed Leverage Ratios?, in: Review of Financial Studies 17,257-294.

Morellec, Erwan and Alexei Zhadanov (2005), The Dynamics of Mergers & Acquisitions, in: Journal of Financial Economics 77, 649-672.

Morellec, Erwan, Nikolov, Boris and Norman Schürhoff (2008), Dynamic Capital Structure under Managerial Entrenchment: Evidence from a Structural Estimation, Working Paper.

Morris, James R. (1976), On Corporate Debt Maturity Strategies, in: Journal of Finance 31, 29-37.

Morton, David P., Popova, Elmira and Ivilina Popova (2006), Efficient Fund of Hedge Funds Construction under Downside Risk Measures, in: Journal of Banking and Finance 30, 503-518.

Myers, Stewart (2003), Financing of Corporations, in: Constantinides, George M., Harris, Milton and René M. Stulz (eds), Handbook of the Economics of Finance, Elsevier, North Holland, XX.

Myers, Stewart C. (1977), Determinants of Corporate Borrowing, in: Journal of Financial Economics 5, 147-175.

Myers, Stewart C. (1983), The Capital Structure Puzzle, in: Journal of Finance 39, 575-592.

Myers, Stewart C. (2000), Outside Equity, in: Journal of Finance 55, 1005-1037.

Myers, Stewart C. and Nicholas S. Majluf (1984), Corporate Financing and Investment Decisions When Firms Have Information that Investors Do Not Have, in: Journal of Financial Economics 13, 187-221.

Naik, Narayan Y., Ramadorai, Tarun and Maria Stromqvist (2007), Capacity Constraints and Hedge Fund Strategy Returns, in: European Financial Management 13, 239-256.

Natividad, Gabriel (2008), The Organizational Efficiency of Internal Capital Markets, Working Paper.

Neftci, Salih N. (1996), An Introduction to the Mathematics of Financial Derivatives, Academic Press, San Francisco.

O'Brien, Thomas J., Schmid Klein, Linda and James I. Hilliard (2007), Capital Structure Swaps and Shareholder Wealth, in: European Financial Management 13, 979-997.

Officer, Micah S. (2004), Collars and Renegotiation in Mergers and Acquisitions, in: Journal of Finance 59, 2719-2743.

Pagano, Marco (1993), The Flotation of Companies on the Stock Markets – A Coordination Failure Model, in: European Economic Review, 37, 1101-1125.

Pagano, Marco and Ernst-Ludwig von Thadden (2004), The European Bond Markets under EMU, in: Oxford Review of Economic Policy 20, 531-554.

Pagano, Marco and P.F. Volpi (2005), Managers, Workers, and Corporate Control, in: Journal of Finance 60, 841-868.

Panageas, Stavros and Mark M. Westerfield (2009), High-Water Marks: High Risk Appetites? Convex Compensation, Long Horizons, and Portfolio Choice, in: Journal of Finance 64, 1-36.

Parrino, Robert and Michael S Weisbach (1999), Measuring Investment Distortions arising from Stockholder-Bondholder Conflicts, in: Journal of Financial Economics 53, 3-42.

Pástor, Lubos (2000), Portfolio Selection and Asset Pricing Models, in: Journal of Finance 55, 179-223.

Pástor, Lubos and Robert F. Stambaugh (2000), Comparing Asset Pricing Models: An Investment Perspective, in: Journal of Financial Economics 56, 335-381.

Pástor, Lubos and Robert F. Stambaugh (2002), Mutual Fund Performance and Seemingly Unrelated Assets, in: Journal of Financial Economics 63, 315-349.

Pástor, Lubos and Robert F. Stambaugh (2003), Liquidity Risk and Expected Stock Returns, in: Journal of Political Economy 111, 642-685.

Patro, Sukesh (2008), The Evolution of Ownership Structure of Corporate Spin-Offs, in: Journal of Corporate Finance 14, 596-613.

Patton, Andrew J. (2009), Are 'Market Neutral' Hedge Funds Really Market Neutral?, in: Review of Financial Studies 22, 2495-2530.

Peltomäki, Jarkko (2007), The Asymmetric Impact of Volatility Risk on Hedge Fund Returns, in: Journal of Applied Finance 17, 88-95.

Pepall, Lynne, Richards, Daniel J. and George Norman (2004), Industrial Organization: Contemporary Theory and Practice, South-Western , Mason, 3rd ed.

Petrella, Giovanni (2005), Are Euro Area Small Cap Stocks an Asset Class? Evidence from Mean-Variance Spanning Tests, in: European Financial Management 11, 229-253.

Peyer, Urs C. and Anil Shivdasani (2001), Leverage and Internal Capital Markets: Evidence from Leverage Recapitalizations, in: Journal of Financial Economics 59, 477-515.

Peyer, Urs C. and Theo Vermaelen (2005), The Many Facets of Privately Negotiated Stock Repurchases, in: Journal of Financial Economics 75, 361-395.

Peyer, Urs C. and Theo Vermaelen (2009), The Nature and Persistence of Buyback Anomalies, in: Review of Financial Studies 22, 1693-1745.

Pintar, Michael (2003), Fixed Income Arbitrage, in: Jaeger, Lars (ed.), The New Generation of Risk Management for Hedge Funds and Private Equity Investments, Euromoney Books, London.

Prezas, Alexandros (2009), Internal Capital Markets, Empire Building and Capital Structure, in: Journal of Economics and Business 61, 173-188.

Proelss, Juliane and Denis Schweizer (2009), Polynomial Goal Programming and the Implicit Higher Moment Preferences of U.S. Institutional Investors in Hedge Funds, Working Paper.

Qiu, Jiaping and Fan Yu (2009), The Market for Corporate Control and the Cost of Debt, in: Journal of Financial Economics 93, 505-524.

Rajan, Raghuram and Luigi Zingales (2003), Banks and Markets: The Changing Character of European Finance, NBER Working Paper 9595.

Rajan, Raghuram, Servaes, Henri and Luigi Zingales (2000), The Cost of Diversity: The Diversification Discount and Inefficient Investment, in: Journal of Finance 55, 35-80.

Ranaldo, Angelo and Laurent Favre (2005), Hedge Fund Performance and Higher-Moment Market Models, in: Journal of Alternative Investments 8, Winter, 37-51.

Renneboog, Luc and Peter G. Szilagyi (2008), Corporate Restructuring and Bondholder Wealth, in: European Financial Management 14, 792-819.

Renneboog, Luc, Simons, Tomas and Mike Wright (2007), Why Do Public Firms Go Private in the UK? The Impact of Private Equity Investors, Incentive Realignment and Undervaluation, in: Journal of Corporate Finance 13, 591-628.

Rhodes-Kropf, Matthew and David T. Robinson (2008), The Market for Mergers and the Boundaries of the Firm, in: Journal of Finance 63, 1169–1211.

Rhodes-Kropf, Matthew and S. Viswanathan (2004), Market Valuation and Merger Waves, in: Journal of Finance 59, 2685-2718.

Riddick, Leigh A. and Toni M. Whited (2009), Corporate Propensity to Save, in: Journal of Finance 64, 1729-1766.

Rieckers, Oliver and Gerald Spindler (2004), Corporate Governance: Legal Aspects, in: Krahnen, Jan P. and Reinhard H. Schmidt (Eds.), The German Financial System, Oxford University Press, New York, 350-385.

Roberts, Michael R. and Amir Sufi (2009), Control Rights and Capital Structure: An Empirical Investigation, in: Journal of Finance 64, 1657-1695.

Roe, Mark J. (1996), Strong Managers, Weak Owners: The Political Roots of American Corporate Finance, Princeton University Press.

Roll, Richard (1986), The Hubris Hypothesis of Corporate Takeovers, in: Journal of Business 59, 197-216.

Rosenthal, Leonard and Colin Young (1990), The Seemingly Anamalous Price Behavior of Royal Dutch/Shell and Unilever N.V./PLC, in: Journal of Financial Economics 26, 123-141.

Ross, Stephen A. (1977), The Determination of Financial Structure: The Incentive-Signalling Approach, in: Bell Journal of Economis 8, 23-40.

Rubinstein, Mark E. (1973), A Mean-Variance Synthesis of Corporate Financial Theory, in: Journal of Finance 28, 167-181.

Ryan, Joe (2006), Examining Market Reaction to Activist Investor Campaigns by Hedge Funds, Working Paper.

Samuelson, Paul A. (1967), Efficient Portfolio Selection for Pareto-Lévy Investments, in: Journal of Financial & Quantitative Analysis 2, 107-122.

Samuelson, Paul A. (1969), Lifetime Portfolio Selection by Dynamic Stochastic Programming, in: Review of Economics and Statistics 51, 239-246.

Santalo, Juan and Manuel Becerra (2008), Competition from Specialized Firms and the Diversification-Performance Linkage, in: Journal of Finance 63, 851-883.

Scharfstein, David S. and Jeremy C. Stein (1990), Herd Behavior and Investment, in: American Economic Review 80, 465-479.

Scharfstein, David S. and Jeremy C. Stein (2000), The Dark Side of Internal Capital Markets: Divisional Rent-Seeking and Inefficient Investment, in: Journal of Finance 55, 2537-2564.

Schauten, Marc B.J., van Dijk, Dick and Jan-Paul van der Waal (2008), Corporate Governance and the Value of Excess Cash Holdings of Large European Firms, Working Paper.

Scherer, Bernd and Li He (2008), The Diversification Benefits of Commodity Futures Indexes: A Mean-Variance Spanning Test, in: Kaiser, Dieter G., Fabozzi, Frank J. and Roland Füss (eds.), Handbook of Commodity Investing, Wiley, 241-265.

Schipper, Katherine and Abbie Smith (1986), A Comparison of Equity Carve-Outs and Seasoned Equity Offerings – Share Price Effects and Corporate Restructuring, in: Journal of Financial Economics 15, 153–186.

Schipper, Katherine and Rex Thompson (1983), Evidence on the Capitalized Value of Merger Activity for Acquiring Firms, in: Journal of Financial Economics 11, 85-119.

Schlingemann, Frederik P., René M. Stulz, and Ralph A. Walkling (2002), Divestitures and the Liquidity of the Market for Corporate Assets, in: Journal of Financial Economics 64, 117–144.

Schmidt, Hartmut, Drukarczyk, Jochen, Honold, Dirk, Schüler, Andreas, Tetens, Gönke and Stefan Prigge (1997) – Corporate Governance in Germany, Nomos Verlag, Baden-Baden.

Schmidt, Reihard H. (2004), Corporate Governance in Germany: An Economic Perspective, in: Krahnen, Jan P. and Reinhard H. Schmidt (Eds.), The German Financial System, Oxford University Press, New York, 386-424.

Schmidt, Reinhard H. and Gerald Spindler (2004), Path Dependence, Corporate Governance and Complementarity, in: Gordon, Jeffrey N. and Mark J. Roe (Eds.), Convergence and Persistence in Corporate Governance Systems, Cambridge University Press, 114-127.

Schmidt, Reinhart and Joachim Schwalbach (2007), Zu Höhe und Dynamik der Vorstandsvergütung in Deutschland, in: Zeitschrift für Betriebswirtschaft 77, 111-122.

Schoar, Antoinette, Wang, Jialan and Josh Lerner (2007), Secrets of the Academy: The Drivers of University Endowment Success, Working Paper.

Scholes, Myron and Joseph Williams (1977), Estimating Betas from Nonsynchronous Data, in: Journal of Financial Economics 5, 309-327.

Schultz, Paul (2003), Pseudo Market Timing and the Long-Run Underperformance of IPOs, in: Journal of Finance 58, 483-518.

Schweizer, Denis (2008), Portfolio Optimization with Alternative Investments, Working Paper.

Schwert, G. William (1996), Markup Pricing in Mergers and Acquisitions, in: Journal of Financial Economics 41, 153-192.

Schwert, G. William (1983), Size and Stock Returns, and other Empirical Regularities, in: Journal of Financial Economics 12, 3-12.

Scott, Robert C. and Philip A. Horvath (1980), On the Direction of Preference for Moments of Higher Order than the Variance, in: Journal of Finance 35, 915-919.

Shahrur, Husayn and Anand Venkateswaran (2009), Industry Prospects and Acquirer Returns in Diversifying Takeovers, in: Journal of Financial Research 32, 23-51.

Shastri, Kuldeep (1990), The Differential Effects of Mergers on Corporate Security Values, in: Research in Finance 8, 175-201.

Shefrin, Herst (2008), A Behavioral Approach to Asset Pricing, Academic Press, Burlington.

Shefrin, Hersh (2005), Behavioral Corporate Finance, McGraw-Hill, New York.

Shenoy, Jaideep (2008), An Examination of the Efficiency, Foreclosure, and Collusion Rationales for Vertical Takeovers, Working Paper.

Shin, Hyun-Han and René M. Stulz (1998), Are Internal Capital markets Efficient? in: Quarterly Journal of Economics 113, 531-552.

Shleifer, Andrei (2000), Inefficient Markets: An Introduction to Behavioral Finance, Oxford University Press, Oxford.

Shleifer, Andrei and Robert W. Vishny (1990), Equilibrium Short Horizons of Investors and Firms, in: American Economic Review 80, 148-153.

Shleifer, Andrei and Robert W. Vishny (1991), Takeovers in the 60's and the 80's: Evidence and Implications, in: Strategic Management Journal 12, 51-59.

Shleifer, Andrei and Robert W. Vishny (1992), Liquidation Values and Debt Capacity: A Market Equilibrium Approach, in: Journal of Finance 47, 1343-1366.

Shleifer, Andrei and Robert W. Vishny (1997a), A Survey of Corporate Governance, in: Journal of Finance 52, 737-781.

Shleifer, Andrei and Robert W. Vishny (1997b), The Limits of Arbitrage, in: Journal of Finance 52, 35-55.

Shleifer, Andrei, and Robert W. Vishny (1986), Large Shareholders and Corporate Control, in: Journal of Political Economy 94, 461-488.

Siegel, Jeremy J. (1994), Stocks for the Long Run: A Guide to Selecting Markets for Long-term Growth, Irwin Professional Publishing, Burr Ridge, Illinois.

Siegmann, Arjen and André Lucas (2002), Explaining Hedge Fund Investment Styles by Loss Aversion, Working Paper.

Signer, Andreas (2003), Generieren Hedge Funds einen Mehrwert, Verlag Paul Haupt, Bern.

Singh, Manohar, Mathur, Ike and Kimberley C. Gleason (2004), Governance and Performance Implications of Diversification Strategies: Evidence from Large U.S. Firms, in: Financial Review 39, 489-526.

Slovin, Myron B., Sushka, Marie E. and John A. Polonchek (2005), Methods of Payment in Asset Sales: Contracting with Equity versus Cash, in: Journal of Finance 60, 2385-2407.

Smith, Clifford W. and Jerold B. Warner (1979), On Financial Contracting – An Analysis of Bond Covenants, in: Journal of Financial Economics 7, 117-161.

Smith, Clifford W. and Ross L. Watts (1992), The Investment Opportunity Set and Corporate Financing, Dividend, and Compensation Policies, in: Journal of Financial Economics 32, 263-292.

Stein, Jeremy C. (1989), Efficient Capital Markets, Inefficient Firms: A Model of Myopic Corporate Behavior, in: Quarterly Journal of Economics 104, 655-669.

Stein, Jeremy C. (1996), Rational Capital Budgeting In An Irrational World, in: Journal of Business 69, 429-455.

Stein, Jeremy C. (1998), Takeover Threats and Managerial Myopia, in: Journal of Political Economy 91, 61–80.

Stiglitz, Joseph E. (1985), Credit Markets and the Control of Capital, in: Journal of Money, Credit and Banking 17, 133-152.

Stoughton, Neal, Wu, Youchang, and Josef Zechner (2008), Intermediated Investment Management, Working Paper.

Stulz, René M. (1988), Managerial Control of Voting Rights – Financing Policies and the Market for Corporate Control, in: Journal of Financial Economics 20, 25-54.

Stulz, René M. (2007), Hedge Funds: Past, Present, and Future, in: Journal of Economic Perspectives 21, 175-194.

Stulz, René M., Walkling, Ralph A. and Moon H. Song (1990), The Distribution of Target Ownership and the Division of Gains in Successful Takeovers, in: Journal of Finance 45, 817-833.

Tetlock, Paul C. (2007), Giving Content to Investor Sentiment: The Role of Media in the Stock Market, in: Journal of Finance 62, 1139-1168.

Thiess, Stefan (2000), Finanzierungsentscheidungen, Informationseffekte und Long-Run Performance am deutschen Kapitalmarkt, DUV, Wiesbaden.

Tirole, Jean (2006), The Theory of Corporate Finance, Princeton University Press, Princeton.

Titman, Sheridan (1984), The Effect of Capital Structure on a Firm's Liquidation Decision, in: Journal of Financial Economics 13, 137-151.

Tobin, James (1958), Liquidity Preference as Behavior towards Risk, in: Review of Economic Studies 25, 65-86.

Treynor, Jack, and Kay Mazuy, (1966), Can mutual funds outguess the market? Harvard Business Review 44, 131-136.

Tuschke, Anja and Gerard Sanders (2003), Antecedents and Consequences of Corporate Governance Reform: The Case of Germany, in: Strategic Management Journal 24, 631-649.

Tversky, Amos and Daniel Kahneman (1991), Loss Aversion in Riskless Choice: A Reference-Dependent Model, in: Quarterly Journal of Economics 106, 1039-1061.

Vasicek, Oldrich (1977), An Equilibrium Characterization of the Term Structure, in: Journal of Financial Economics 5, 177-188.

Vijh, Anand M. (1999), Long-Term Returns from Equity Carve-Outs, in: Journal of Financial Economics 51, 273–308.

Vijh, Anand M. (2002), The Positive Announcement-Period Returns of Equity Carve-Outs: Asymmetric Information or Divestiture Gains?, in: Journal of Business 75, 1, 153 – 190.

Villalonga, Belén (2004a), Diversification Discount or Premium? New Evidence from the Business Information Tracking Series, in: Journal of Finance 59, 479-505.

Villalonga, Belén (2004b), Does Diversification Cause the "Diversification Discount"?, in: Financial Management 33, 5-27.

Viswanathan, S. and Bin Wei (2008), Endogenous Events and Long-Run Returns, in: Review of Financial Studies 21, 855-888.

Vrontos, Spyridon D., Vrontos, Ioannis D. and Daniel Giamouridis (2008), Hedge Fund Pricing and Model Uncertainty, in: Journal of Banking & Finance 32, 741-753.

Vuolteenaho, Tuomo (2001), What Drives Firm-Level Stock Returns?, Working Paper.

Wahal, Sunil and John J. McConnell (2000), Do Institutional Investors Exacerbate Managerial Myopia? in: Journal of Corporate Finance 6, 307-329.

Weber, Anke (2008), An Empirical Analysis of the 2000 Corporate Tax Reform in Germany: Effects on Ownership and Control in Listed Companies, in: International Review of Law and Economics 29, 57-66.

Weber, Peter and Heinz Zimmermann (2010), Hedge Fund Activism and Information Disclosure: The Case of Germany, Working Paper.

Weiss, Lawrence A. and Karen H. Wruck (1998), Information Problems, Conflicts of Interest, and Asset Stripping: Chapter 11`s Failure in the Case of Eastern Airlines, in: Journal of Financial Economics 48, 55-97.

Wenger, Ekkehard and Renate Hecker (1994), Übernahme- und Abfindungsregeln am deutschen Aktienmarkt – Eine kritische Bestandsaufnahme im internationalen Vergleich, in: ifo Studien – Zeitschrift für empirische Wirtschaftsforschung 41, 51-87.

Wermers, Russ (2000), Mutual Fund Performance: An Empirical Decomposition into Stock-Picking Talent, Style, Transactions Costs, and Expenses, in: Journal of Finance 55, 1655-1695.

Williamson, Oliver E. (1970), Corporate Control and Business Behavior, Prentice-Hall, New Jersey.

Winkelmann, Kurt (2004), Improving Portfolio Efficiency, in: Journal of Portfolio Management 30, 23-38.

Woidtke, Tracie (2002), Agents Watching Agents?: Evidence from Pension Fund Ownership and Firm Value, in: Journal of Financial Economics 63, 99-131.

Xiong, James, Idzorek, Thomas, Chen, Peng and Roger D. Ibbotson (2007), Dynamics of Fund of Hedge Funds: Flow, Size, and Performance, Working Paper.

Yamai, Yasuhiro and Toshinao Yoshiba (2005), Value-at-Risk versus Expected Shortfall: A Practical Perspective, in: Journal of Banking & Finance 29, 997-1015.

Zebedee, Allan A., Bentzen, Eric, Hansen, Peter R. and Asger Lunde (2008), The Greenspan Years: An Analysis of the Magnitude and Speed of the Equity Market Response to FOMC Announcements, in: Financial Markets and Portfolio Management 22, 3-20.

Zhang, Lu (2005), The Value Premium, in: Journal of Finance 60, 67-103.

Zingales, Luigi (2000), In Search of New Foundations, in: Journal of Finance 55, 1623-1653.

FSC
www.fsc.org
MIX
Papier | Fördert gute Waldnutzung
FSC® C083411

Kolibri 360 GmbH
Ferdinand-Jühlke-Straße 7
99095 Erfurt, Deutschland
produktsicherheit@kolibri360.de